Suffrage and Beyond

Suffrage and Beyond

International Feminist Perspectives

Edited by Caroline Daley and Melanie Nolan

NEW YORK UNIVERSITY PRESS
Washington Square, New York

This book is dedicated to our mothers,
Alison Watts and Patricia Flett,
with love

Chapter 12 © Nancy F. Cott 1994
Chapter 13 © Ellen Carol DuBois 1994
Balance of material © Auckland University Press 1994

First published in the U.S.A. in 1994 by
NEW YORK UNIVERSITY PRESS
Washington Square
New York, N.Y. 10003

Library of Congress Cataloging–in–Publication Data

Suffrage and beyond : international feminist perspectives /
    edited by Caroline Daley and Melanie Nolan.
        p.   cm.
    Includes bibliographical references and index.
    ISBN 0–8147–1870–1
    ISBN 0–8147–1871–X (pbk.)
    1. Women —Suffrage — History. 2. Women's rights
— History. 3. Women in politics — History. 4. Feminism —
History. I. Daley, Caroline. II. Nolan, Melanie.
JF 848.S83   1994   94–33981
324.6'23 — dc20   CIP

Printed in New Zealand

Contents

Acknowledgements

All of the papers which follow were presented at a three-day conference, 'Suffrage and Beyond', held at Victoria University of Wellington, New Zealand, in August 1993. The conference brought together some of the leading English-writing historians working on suffrage history. We have collected here just sixteen of the fifty-four papers which were presented.

The papers could not have been delivered at the conference or published without the generosity of a large number of people, funds and trusts. Dr Jock Phillips, Chief Historian at the Department of Internal Affairs, thought such a conference would be a good idea and allowed the department's Historical Branch to be its first administrative home. 'Suffrage and Beyond' was New Zealand's largest and best funded history conference to date. We are indebted to the 1993 Suffrage Centennial Trust, Whakatu Wahine, and the Bank of New Zealand. They made the conference financially viable and granted publication subsidies for this book. They supported the travel of Patricia Grimshaw, Nancy Cott, Ellen DuBois, Asunción Lavrin, Karen Offen, Jane Rendall and Carole Pateman. Dame Miriam Dell, Chairperson of the 1993 Suffrage Centennial Trust, and Jill Pierce, the Trust's administrator, were particularly encouraging, as was Theresa Gattung, Chief Manager, Marketing, Bank of New Zealand. With the 1993 Suffrage Centennial Trust and the Bank of New Zealand supporting us, we were able to approach cross-cultural trusts and ask for further assistance to bring historians to New Zealand. We thank the British Council and Francis King for supporting Johanna Alberti, Sandra Holton and Martin Pugh; the New Zealand–United States Educational Foundation and Laurie Cox for a Distinguished Visitor Award to Anne Firor Scott to participate in the conference; the Australia–New Zealand Foundation, Robert Hole and John Arathimos for supporting Ann Curthoys, Jackie Huggins, Marilyn Lake and Susan Magarey; the Japan–New Zealand Foundation and Deidre Kerr who supported Yukiko Matsukawa; and the Swiss Arts Council Pro Helvetica and the Chargé d'Affaires of Switzerland in New Zealand, Peter Graaf, for supporting Margrit Siegenthaler-Reusser.

We are grateful to Kristin Downey, Penny Gapes and Debbie Thornton, History Department, Victoria University of Wellington, and

Barbara Batt, History Department, the University of Auckland, for administrative assistance. Susan Grogan, chairperson of the Victoria department, was supportive and was a member of the original conference committee. Jennifer Ashton, University of Auckland, and James MacLaurin (with the help of a Victoria University research grant) provided valuable research assistance. We are grateful to Diane Atkinson at the London Museum, the Rochester Library, the Auckland Institute and Museum Library, the Australian National Library and the private collections of Karen Offen, Johanna Alberti, Susan Magarey and Asunción Lavrin, for the photographs which are and are not reproduced here. We thank our editor, Elizabeth Caffin, Auckland University Press, the anonymous reader of the manuscript, and Penny Bieder, the copy-editor, for their useful suggestions and comments. We thank David Braddon-Mitchell and Kim Sterelny for their personal support. We are grateful for Email technology which allowed us to keep editing as we moved through New Zealand and Australia over summer. Above all, we thank the authors, whose work was so well received in Wellington, for their patience with our editorial suggestions.

Melanie Nolan and Caroline Daley
May 1994

Contributors

Johanna Alberti was born in Egypt and has lived mostly in England. She teaches mainly for the Open University, Northern Region, England, but also for two other universities in Newcastle and for the Workers' Educational Association. Her publications include *Beyond Suffrage: Feminists in War and Peace, 1914-28* (1989). She is currently working on a biography of Eleanor Rathbone.

Nancy F. Cott has taught US women's history at Yale University since 1975. She chaired the Women's Studies Program there from 1980 to 1987, and is currently Stanley Woodward Professor of History and American Studies. Her major books are *The Bonds of Womanhood: 'Woman's Sphere' in New England, 1780–1835* (1977), *The Grounding of Modern Feminism* (1987), and *A Woman Making History: Mary Ritter Beard Through Her Letters* (1991). Her current research focuses on the history of marriage as public policy in the US. She is also editing a ten-volume series on US women's history for young readers.

Ann Curthoys was born in Sydney in 1945 and educated at the University of Sydney. She completed her doctoral thesis on racism in nineteenth–century New South Wales at Macquarie University. She established and taught the women's studies programme at the Australian National University, 1976–77, and since then has taught at the University of Technology, Sydney, where she is now Professor of Social History. Author of *For and Against Feminism: A Personal Journey into Feminist History and Theory* (1988), she has edited a number of collections and published articles and chapters on many aspects of Australian history. She is currently engaged in two projects, one a history of the Australian 'Freedom Rides' of 1965, the other, a co-authored history of journalism in twentieth-century Australia.

Caroline Daley was born in London, in 1964, and immigrated to New Zealand at the age of eight. She was educated at Victoria University of Wellington, where she wrote a doctoral thesis on the gender relations of a New Zealand community. After a post-doctoral fellowship she took up a lectureship in the History Department at the University of Auckland, where she teaches New Zealand social history and gender relations. She is currently working on a history of gender relations in New Zealand, and in another project is examining the fifty years after New Zealand women were enfranchised. She was on the organising committee of the 'Suffrage and Beyond' conference.

Raewyn Dalziel was born in Lower Hutt, New Zealand, in 1944. After a post-doctoral fellowship spent in London she became a member of History Department at University of Auckland where she is currently an Associate Professor. She has served on University Council, the Council Committee on the Status of Women in the University and the Equal Employment Opportunities Committee. She teaches and publishes on women's history. Her publications include a number of political biographies and she has twice edited special volumes of the *New Zealand Journal of History* on women's history (1989 and 1993).

Ellen Carol DuBois is a Professor of History at University of California, Los Angeles, where she specialises in US women's history. She has been active in the field of women's studies for two decades, publishing extensively on the history of the woman suffrage movement in the US, beginning with her now classic monograph, *Feminism and Suffrage: The Emergence of an Independent Woman's Movement in America, 1848–1869* (1978). She is also the co-editor, with Vicki Ruiz, of *Unequal Sisters: A Multicultural Reader in US Woman's History* (1989). Currently, she is completing a biography of second-generation American suffragist, Harriot Stanton Blatch, *Generation of Power*.

Patricia Grimshaw is a New Zealander by birth and education. She now teaches American history and women's studies at the University of Melbourne, Australia, where she is the Max Crawford Professor of History. She is co-editor of *The Half-Open Door* (1982) and *Australian Women: Feminist Perspectives* (1983), co-author of *Families in Colonial Australia* (1985) and *Creating a Nation* (1994), and author of *Paths of Duty: American Missionary Wives in Nineteenth-Century Hawaii* (1989). Her book *Women's Suffrage in New Zealand* was first published in 1972. It remains the definitive account of the New Zealand suffrage movement and was republished in 1987.

Sandra Stanley Holton is currently an Australian Research Fellow in History at the University of Adelaide. She has published a number of articles on the history of the women's movement and the history of medicine, and is the author of *Feminism and Democracy: Women's Suffrage* *and Reform Politics in Britain, 1900–1918* (1986). At present she is working on a biography of Alice Clark, the historian of women's work.

Marilyn Lake was born in Tasmania in 1949. She was educated at the University of Tasmania and Monash University, Australia. She has taught women's history at Monash, the University of Melbourne and La Trobe University, where she is now a Reader and Director of Women's Studies. Her publications include *Double Time: Women in Victoria – 150 Years* (1985), co-edited with Farley Kelly, *Limits of Hope: Soldiers' Settlement in Victoria 1915-38* (1987) and *Creating a Nation* co-authored with Patricia Grimshaw, Ann McGrath and Marian Quartly (1994). She is currently contracted to write a book on the history of feminism in Australia.

Asunción Lavrin was born in Havana, Cuba, but she has lived most of her life in the US. She was educated at Radcliffe College and Harvard. She has taught in England, Spain, and in several universities in the US. She is currently Professor of History at Howard University, Washington DC. Her doctoral work, on women's religious life in eighteenth-century Mexico, served as a starting point for a career devoted to research in women's history; most of her publications have focused on women, women in the church, ecclesiastical history and twentieth-century feminism in Spanish America. Her recent publications include *Feminism, Women and Social Change in the Southern Cone: 1890–1940* (1984).

Susan Magarey is Director of the Research Centre for Women's Studies at Adelaide University, Australia and editor of the bi-annual journal *Australian Feminist Studies*. Her publications include *Unbridling the Tongues of Women: A Biography of Catherine Helen Spence* (1985), winner of the Walter McRae Russell Award in 1986, *Writing Lives: Feminist Biography & Autobiography* (1993), *Debutante Nation: Feminism Contests the 1890s*, co-edited with Sue Rowley and Susan Sheridan (1993), and *Women in a Restructuring Australia: Work & Welfare*, co-edited with Anne Edwards, forthcoming 1994. She is currently working on a monograph provisionally entitled *The Politics of Passion: Feminism in Australia 1880–1912*.

Yukiko Matsukawa was born in Japan in 1949. After being educated at the graduate school of Ochanomizu University, she became a member of Yamaguchi Women's University, where she is currently an Associate Professor. She teaches and publishes on education and early childhood care. She is a member of the Women's Studies Association of Japan, and her current research focuses on childhood care, education and feminism.

Melanie Nolan was born in Reefton, New Zealand, in 1960 and was educated at the University of Canterbury and the Australian National University. Her doctoral thesis was on the feminisation of white collar labour. She teaches comparative labour and social history at Victoria University of Wellington. She has published a number of articles on the sexual division of labour in Australia and New Zealand and is currently working on a history of the New Zealand state's role in women's economic well-being. She organised the 'Suffrage and Beyond' conference.

Karen Offen is a historian and independent scholar, affiliated with the Institute for Research on Women and Gender, Stanford University, USA. She is secretary-treasurer of the International Federation of Research in Women's History and also serves as president of the Western Association of Women History (USA). She has co-edited two documentaries and most recently, with Ruth Roach Pierson and Jane Rendall, she edited *Writing Women's History: International Perspectives* (1991). Her monograph, *Paul de Cassagnac and the Authoritarian Tradition in Nineteenth-Century France*, appeared in 1991. She is presently completing a book on the woman question in modern France.

Carole Pateman is Professor of Political Science at the University of California, Los Angeles, where she teaches political theory and women's studies and is actively involved in the Centre for the Study of Women and the Centre for Social Theory and Comparative History. In 1991–94 she was President of the International Political Science Association (the first woman to hold the office). She was a Guggenheim Fellow during 1993–94, and presented the Sir Douglas Robb Lectures at the University of Auckland in 1993. Her books include *Participation and Democratic Theory* (1970) and *The Sexual Contract* (1988) and she has published many articles on democratic theory and feminist theory. She is currently writing a book on some aspects of democratic citizenship.

Martin Pugh is Professor of Modern British History at the University of Newcastle-upon-Tyne, UK. He has published widely on electoral reform, politics and the Tories, including *Electoral Reform in War and Peace 1906–1914 (1978), The Making of Modern British Politics 1867–1939 (1982), The Tories and the People 1880–1935* (1985) and *Lloyd George* (1988). Most recently, he has written *Women and the Women's Movement in Britain 1914–1959* (1992), and *State and Society: British Political and Social History 1870–1992* (1994).

Jane Rendall is a Senior Lecturer in the History Department and the Centre for Women's Studies at the University of York, UK. Her research is focused on eighteenth-century women's history, mainly in Britain, and the comparative history of feminisms. Her publications include *The Origins of Modern Feminism: Women in Britain, France and the United States 1780-1860* (1985); *Equal or Different: Women's Politics 1800–1914* (1987); and, co-edited with Susan Mendus, *Sexuality and Subordination: Interdisciplinary Studies in Gender in the Nineteenth Century* (1989). Most recently, with Ruth Roach Pierson and Karen Offen, she co-edited *Writing Women's History: International Perspectives* (1991).

Penelope Schoeffel Meleisea is the International Projects manager of the New Zealand Institute for Social Research and Development. She has worked at the University of the South Pacific, the University of Papua New Guinea and the University of Canterbury, Christchurch. She was National Program Co-ordinator of the Women and Development Network of Australia. Her publications include work on women in development, particularly on gender, status and power, and women's associations in the Pacific Islands.

Kaoru Tachi was born in Japan in 1948. After graduating she became a research fellow of the Institute for Women's Studies, Ochanomizu University, and is currently an Associate Professor there. She has edited and published several books on motherhood, and discourses on women in the workforce and gender in education. Her current research focuses on gender prescriptions in Japanese history, and gender and self-formation.

1

International Feminist Perspectives on Suffrage: An Introduction

MELANIE NOLAN AND CAROLINE DALEY

On 19 September 1893, the adult women of New Zealand won the right to vote. One hundred years later this achievement was celebrated by some, while others used the year to question what suffrage had meant to women's lives.[1] On the whole, historians have been more circumspect than celebratory about the impact of women's suffrage. In August 1993 feminist historians from around the world gathered in New Zealand for the 'Suffrage and Beyond' conference. They came to discuss the achievement of women's suffrage in various countries, and to analyse its impact. The chapters in this book are part of the process of questioning what suffrage has meant for women.

Sixteen of the fifty-four papers presented at the conference are collected here. The internationalism of the conference is reflected in essays about New Zealand, Australia, the Pacific Islands, Japan, South America, the US, Britain, France and Germany. There are obviously many geographical gaps, such as Africa, the Middle East and Eurasia, and they should be borne in mind. However, we hope that the mix of papers from the Old and New Worlds, from east and west, from first- and second-world countries, will be stimulating and will help to break down the ethnocentricism which operates in much suffrage literature. In this regard, we think this relatively international collection makes several very important contributions to the historiography of suffrage and the study of women's citizenship.

First, the comparatively peaceful and quiet suffrage movements in Australasia, which have been underplayed in many suffrage studies, are highlighted here. Several chapters in this book show the 'margins' questioning the history of the 'centre'. Second, consideration of a wider range of suffrage histories leads us to revise the usual or standard account of when and how women's suffrage was achieved. The authors here reassess the gaining of suffrage and what its impact has been. They study the early achievement of women's suffrage in some societies, the relatively late achievement in others, and the post-suffrage era. Chapters on South American, French, Japanese and Pacific Island suffragists remind us that suffrage history should not cease with American women's enfranchisement in 1920, or the achievement of universal suffrage in Britain in 1928. Chapters examining the mid-nineteenth century remind us that the campaign for women's suffrage in Britain and the US began well before the publicity-seeking suffragettes took to the streets. New interpretations of groups of suffragists, as well as individual suffragists, are offered here. Not all are flattering. While the language and representation of these women are examined, so is their racism. Third, many of the authors discuss the internationalism of the suffragists and its importance to their ideas and actions. These were women who strode the world's stage, encouraging and supporting other women in their fight for citizenship rights. Finally, the authors prompt us to consider how suffragists negotiated boundaries in order to achieve women's enfranchisement. The suffragists, and the authors in this book, require us to go beyond the dichotomies that have often contained suffrage histories in the past. The dichotomies between the margins and the centre, between first-wave and post-suffrage studies, between colonial and post-colonial history, and between masculinities and femininities are rejected by many of the authors. They move beyond such dichotomies and offer new approaches to the study of women's suffrage. Most chapters do not slot simply in one theme. Sometimes the authors contradict one another and generate conversations amongst themselves. Our introduction examines some of the relationships and conversations between the papers.

'Marginal' history?
The antipodean women's suffrage movement is well-represented in this book. While the early achievement of women's suffrage in New Zealand and Australia is usually noted in the international literature, these New World societies are often seen as marginal to the suffrage story. Partly because this region did not experience window breaking, mass rallies and hunger strikes, we have been overlooked by suffrage historians who often do not see further than England and the eastern seaboard of the US when they come to develop explanatory models for women's enfranchisement. So what was the Antipodean example?

New Zealand women's relatively early enfranchisement came after a concerted campaign by women and men suffragists. There had been calls for women's franchise since at least 1869, when Mary Muller, using the pseudonym 'Femina', wrote *An Appeal to the Men of New Zealand*, in which she asked New Zealand men to grant women the right to vote. She appealed to men's common sense identifying it as the sense of the common interest. Mrs Muller thought that New Zealand should take the initiative, and grant women the vote before other nations.[2]

Although there were no formal suffrage organisations until Mrs Mary Leavitt of the Women's Christian Temperance Union (WCTU) visited New Zealand in 1885, there had already been attempts in Parliament to introduce women's suffrage. In 1878 Robert Stout introduced a bill to allow women ratepayers to vote and stand for Parliament. In 1879 a further attempt was made, and in 1880 and 1881, Dr James Wallis also tried to pass women's suffrage measures.[3] After the formation of a New Zealand branch of the WCTU in 1885, women began to campaign actively for the vote. The WCTU established a Franchise and Legislation Department, and in 1887 Kate Sheppard was appointed Franchise Superintendent.[4] She co-ordinated suffragists around the country, while also working closely with politicians sympathetic to women's demand for the vote. Suffrage bills were introduced into the Lower House in 1887, 1890, and 1891, but none succeeded. The struggle for the vote intensified, and in 1892 Franchise Leagues were formed. Their members did not, however, support the temperance aims of the WCTU. As well as lobbying politicians, the suffragists began to collect signatures on petitions in support of women's suffrage. In 1891 they collected the signatures of over 10,000 adult women. In 1892 they doubled this effort with a petition of 20,274. Finally, in 1893, they amassed 31,871 signatures, with approximately a quarter of the adult women of New Zealand signing the suffrage petition. Several Maori women are known to have signed the 1892 and 1893 petitions, although at this time Maori women's political energy was mainly directed at achieving voting rights and the right to stand as members of Te Kotahitanga, an inter-tribal Maori parliament.[5]

By 1893 most members of the Lower House did not have strong objections to women being enfranchised.[6] But the passing of the 1893 Electoral Act was not a straightforward matter. Premier Richard Seddon had never been a supporter of women's suffrage, and planned to foil the passage of the bill. Two members of the Upper House took offence at Seddon's antics, and voted for a bill they would otherwise have opposed. And so in a less than propitious way, New Zealand women gained parliamentary support for their enfranchisement. This was not the end of the campaign, however. The Governor had to assent to the bill, and it took Governor Glasgow a week to turn the bill into the Electoral Act. But finally, many years after women had first asked for the vote, they were granted this fundamental right of citizenship in a democracy.

The indigenous Maori women of New Zealand and European – or Pakeha – women received the right to vote at the same time. In most cases they did not, however, vote together. Pakeha women joined Pakeha men at the polling booths and voted for the European Members of Parliament on 28 November 1893. Maori women had to wait until 20 December before they could join Maori men and vote for the four Maori Members of Parliament whose seats had been created in 1867 on the basis of male Maori suffrage. It is estimated that about 4000 Maori women voted in 1893. Maori women and men who fulfilled a £25 freehold property requirement were allowed to vote for the European members, if they so desired. It is not known how many Maori women enrolled on the European roll.[7]

The example of New Zealand's achievement of women's suffrage was lauded by suffragists in other parts of the world. The fact that women in New Zealand took up their voting rights so soon after they were granted – a mere ten weeks after the governor's assent to the franchise bill – and with such vigour – almost 80 per cent of eligible women managed to get onto the electoral roll by voting day, and just over 80 per cent of those turned out to vote – no doubt assisted suffragists elsewhere in their claim that women wanted the right to vote.

While New Zealand touted itself as a world leader in women's rights in 1893, it is often forgotten that women could vote on the Pitcairn Islands in 1838 and Cook Islands women were enfranchised just before New Zealand in 1893. Such facts are usually ignored because of the islands' status.[8] New Zealand claims the accolades because it was the first *self-governing* country to pass legislation providing for universal female suffrage.[9] Record-hunting and trans-Tasman rivalries are one of the more entertaining byways of Antipodean suffrage history. The desire to hold the record for women's suffrage runs deep. A recent historian of Australian female suffrage pointed out that Australia almost inherited New Zealand and its record in 1902: 'In 1893 New Zealand had the status of one of the British colonies of Australasia. If it had decided to federate with the other Australasian colonies, as was first envisaged, Australia would have been able to claim the honour of being the first nation in the world to enfranchise its women'.[10]

Australians are more inclined to suggest that New Zealand's achievement was not quite as good as theirs, since New Zealand women did not achieve the right to stand for Parliament at the same time as they were enfranchised.[11] In 1894 South Australian women won the right to both vote for and become legislators, and their historians, including Susan Magarey in this book, claim this gives Australia the right to be regarded 'on the cutting edge of democracy, ahead of everyone else'. New Zealand women had to wait until 1919 to stand for the Lower House of Parliament, and until 1941 to be eligible to be appointed to the Legislative Council. For its part, New Zealand claims to be ahead of Australia because indigenous Aboriginal women and men in Australia, who had suffrage rights in four states – South Australia, Victoria, New South Wales and Tasmania – were denied federal suffrage under the 1902 Constitution. Aboriginal Australians had to wait until 1962 for the Commonwealth franchise to be officially extended to them. Australia will not celebrate 100 years of universal suffrage until 2062.[12] Moreover, while South Australian women, white and Aboriginal, may have had the franchise and the right to stand for Parliament in 1894, the first South Australian woman was not elected to Parliament until 1959, some 26 years after New Zealand's first woman MP and behind the other state and federal Australian parliaments.

The debate about the early achievement of women's suffrage is particularly intense over the competing claims of South Australia and New Zealand. There are many similarities between them in their suffrage histories. South Australia, of all the Australian colonies, is closest to the New Zealand example, with its non-convict past and early suffrage for both white and indigenous women.[13] The WCTU had a strong presence in both suffrage movements which, in turn, had close links with organised working women. As in New Zealand, an attempt by an opponent of women's suffrage backfired: Richard John Seddon in New Zealand and Ebenezer Ward in South Australia helped rather than hindered suffrage legislation in 1893 and 1894 respectively. And in both New Zealand and South Australia, of the women who enrolled to vote in their first election, more turned out on polling day than their male counterparts.[14]

The relatively early achievement of suffrage in New Zealand and Australia may be a cause for celebration for some, but as several authors in this book suggest, it was not without its problems. In her chapter, Susan Magarey asks why women in South Australia, the first to be enfranchised and have the right to stand for Parliament, did not want to become Members of Parliament. Ann Curthoys explores the late suffrage of Aboriginal people and the reasons why feminists have taken a long time to understand Aboriginal women's struggles in Australia. Clearly, then, there were limits to the region's female suffrage. But by 1908 New

Zealand and Australia, together with a number of Pacific Island nations, shared a regional experience in their early female suffrage.[15] In this they were joined by Scandinavian and mid-western American regions.[16]

The Australasian example allows us to test some of the theories about women's suffrage being advanced in the 'centre'. As the chapters by Raewyn Dalziel and Patricia Grimshaw, among others, suggest, the New World suffragists of the past were engaged in a dialogue with their Old World sisters. Dalziel's focus is on how New Zealand women's suffrage was represented overseas. Grimshaw locates New Zealand's early enfranchisement of women alongside the other places where women won the vote at a relatively early date – the American Mid-West (Wyoming, Utah, Colorado and Idaho), New Zealand, the British colonies of South Australia and Western Australia, the Commonwealth of Australia, and the Australian state of New South Wales. She argues that the idea of women's suffrage was 'in the air' in many places at the time, but that the idea could not become the reality unless certain pre-conditions were met. She suggests that one of these was a colonial farming society with a preponderance of men.

The need to study women's history from an international and comparative perspective comes through clearly in many of the chapters in this book. Australasian historians can enrich their understanding of this region's early enfranchisement of women by comparing the situation here with those elsewhere. As Yukiko Matsukawa and Kaoru Tachi show us, the WCTU strategies of collecting signatures on suffrage petitions and promoting suffrage legislation did not work in Japan. Historians in Australasia need to consider critically the significance of such strategies in this region. Historians at the 'centre' can also test their explanations and refine their analysis of suffrage by contrasting the early sites of suffrage with the countries where the struggle was more protracted. Our explanations have more power if we test our theories on as many cases as possible. In this regard, women's suffrage offers us a rare opportunity. Over the last 100 years, most countries in the world have legislated for female enfranchisement.[17] We may not be able to repeat historical events, but through comparative history we can experiment with our theories, refine them, and improve them.

Reassessing suffrage history

This book reflects the fact that there is a new wave of suffrage historians who are writing exciting new suffrage histories. Suffrage history has been out of favour with historians for many years. Women's suffrage suffered from an association with 'first wave' feminism, with its narrow class and racial base, and its commitment to liberal politics. With white, middle-class, religious organisations like the WCTU at the helm of suffrage campaigns in many countries, suffrage history was seen, until recently, as elite and old-fashioned. It was not part of the new social history which feminist historians in the 1960s and 1970s were engaged in. Those historians who did write about it, did so through the prism of radical, militant and socialist suffragists.[18]

But since the 1980s, historians have been returning to political history, and female suffrage is no longer a neglected topic. In fact, suffrage campaigns and individual suffragists have enjoyed revisionist historians' attention. 'First wave' feminism, which was dismissed and discredited in the heady optimism of the 'secondwave', is now being reassessed. Non-militant suffragists are being recovered, as are their working-class sisters. Women's suffrage is no longer regarded as the sole preserve of the middle class.[19]

It may be that our renewed interest in and sympathy for 'first wave' feminists and feminism is linked to a rise in interest in the *fin de siècle*. As we approach not just the end of the century, but the end of the millennium, it is understandable that we look back at the struggles and achievements of others.[20] Or it may be that our disappointments with 'second wave' feminism has made us more sympathetic to the 'first wave'. The fruits of the 'second wave' have not been as bountiful as feminists had hoped. Perhaps the constant threat of backlash and the rise of the new right has led historians to be more tolerant of the suffragists. For whatever reasons, feminist historians have returned to the study of women's suffrage.

The process of achieving suffrage, the time frame of suffrage, inter-pretations of suffragists, and the impact of women's suffrage, are all reassessed here. Most of the chapters discuss how women's suffrage was achieved, either in an individual country, or in several nations. None of the authors accepts the idea that women were simply granted the right to vote by benevolent men. The 'gift' argument, put forward by various writers in the past, is firmly rejected. Instead, the 'struggle' argument, the idea that women actively fought to achieve suffrage, is strongly defended. Women's agency is to the forefront in these papers. But this is not a celebratory, herstory sense of women's agency. The authors here recognise that there were limits to women's agency. Their work fits into the wider structure and agency debate. This is the debate about whether structures are determinate, how structures are created, and the extent to which individuals or groups exercise agency or create their own history, independent of societal structures. Many women's historians have been rather slow to recognise the dialectical relationship between women's agency and patriarchal structures. They have also been slow to see activity and agency beyond the most radical women. Several of the chapters here concentrate on the 'conditioned' nature of women's agency, or the limits of their suffrage campaigns. This is seen in Ann Curthoy's chapter, where she notes that Aborigines were excluded from the extension of federal suffrage in 1902, and how white Australian feminists have had problems dealing with Aborigines' calls for citizenship. Many of the authors also recognise women's agency where it has previously been ignored. The suffragettes' agency has long been celebrated. What is new now is that the suffragists, and those who opposed women's suffrage, are no longer regarded as passive. Their agency is also considered.[21] Indeed, among the central issues in Carole Pateman's essay are why women opposed their own suffage and why men conceded women's suffrage.

How suffrage was achieved is important. So is when it was achieved. A 'standard model' of women's suffrage, based on British and American history, is dominant in suffrage historiography. It is the model against which much suffrage history is measured. Above all, it sets the time frame and defines the nature of the other movements. Suffrage is associated with, and measured by, the militant and mass movements of the United States and Britain at the turn of the century, leading up to universal suffrage in 1920 and 1928 respectively. Suffrage campaigns which were fought beyond 1928 are regarded as protracted or late, moderate or non-existent, passive or insignificant. Those fought before the turn of the century are often ignored. According to this standard model, 'first wave' feminism had a particular life. By 1920 in the United States and 1928 in Britain, with suffrage won, the 'first wave' feminist movements, single-minded in winning suffrage, had achieved their victories and fragmented.

In this book several authors force us to question the significance of this standard model. It renders the Australasian example unimportant. And as Jane Rendall shows in her chapter, it is also a limited model for studying British history. Rendall takes the British suffragists' struggle back a generation from when it is usually examined and joins a number of historians, including Sandra Stanley Holton in this collection, who suggest that the women's movement before suffrage has been neglected.[22] Rendall questions the dates for both the beginning and the ending of the British suffrage movement.

Other authors consider the post-1928 situation. Karen Offen

explains how the French concept of citizenship meant that women were not enfranchised in France until 1944-45. Matsukawa and Kaoru examine women's suffrage struggles in Japan, a non-Christian country which had suffrage 'bestowed' upon it at the end of the Second World War by the occupying Allied Forces, who were mostly American. Asunción Lavrin examines the Southern Cone nations of Chile, Argentina and Uruguay, as well as Colombia, which achieved female suffrage in 1948, 1947, 1932 and 1954 respectively. Lavrin concentrates upon the tenacity of the opponents of women's suffrage in machismo societies and the problems of getting women to support the suffrage cause. Penelope Schoeffel Meleisea discusses the tardiness of women's enfranchisement in most of Melanesia, Polynesia and Micronesia. Many of these islands were former Australian and New Zealand colonies or trusts. Suffrage for most women of Pacific Island nations did not come until political independence in the last quarter of the twentieth century.

Nowhere did women's suffrage precede male suffrage. As Offen shows, the question of women's suffrage became inextricably intertwined with the broader and highly emotional discussion of overall electoral reform. Women's suffrage was the victim of the French electoral system. Lavrin argues that Southern Cone and Colombian opponents of suffrage were tenacious and took their strength from their desire to retain traditional gender relations. She argues that all the theoretical support for women's suffrage before 1920 was unlikely to have any political resonance in South America until the issue of universal male suffrage was resolved. The catalyst for change was the emergent political populism and the democratisation of the electoral systems in national politics. Matsukawa and Tachi also demonstrate this in the case of Japan. The 1925 Peace-Preservation Act abolished the income qualification for male suffrage. It was a necessary, although not sufficient, pre-condition for female suffrage.

The essays by Offen, Matsukawa and Tachi, Lavrin, and Schoeffel Meleisea explain why it took so long for suffrage to be achieved in France, Japan, the Southern Cone and Colombia, and most of Melanesia, Polynesia and Micronesia. Their notion of what is a late or protracted struggle is defined by the standard model's time scale. Yet the Anglo-American time frame was not the norm. Most countries did not secure female suffrage before the 1940s. At least half the world's population lived in countries without female franchise in 1940.[23] And in many countries where women could vote, suffrage was granted to them on a different basis from men. For example, for a number of years voting was compulsory for men and voluntary for women in Ecuador and Egypt. Only educated women could vote in Jordan in 1955. In Syria, only propertied women were enfranchised in 1949. In South Africa, white women won the vote in 1930 but it is only in 1994 that black women have cast their first ballot. Offen, Matsukawa and Tachi, Lavrin, and Schoeffel Meleisea emphasise the activism of French, Japanese, South American and Pacific women. They set the record straight on those countries which had suffrage campaigns after the United States and British women's suffrage legislation.

According to the time frame set by the standard model, Swiss women had one of the most protracted struggles for suffrage. Women were not able to vote federally in Switzerland until 1971, and it was not until 1991 that women in the Appenzell Interior Rhodes could vote in their canton elections. As Magrit Siegenthaler-Reusser demonstrated at the 'Suffrage and Beyond' conference, the Swiss Alliance for Women's Suffrage was very active and, between 1919 and 1968, 71 votes were held on female suffrage in Swiss cantons.[24] These case studies should make us wary of any claim that a relatively late suffrage date means that suffrage was not the result of a long and vigorous campaign.

Several of the chapters in this book reassess standard interpretations of both individual suffragists and groups of suffragists. First, the position of suffragists as both public and private people, the ways they represented themselves and were represented, the language they used, and the ideologies they advanced are all under scrutiny here. This process of reassessment begins in Patricia Grimshaw's chapter. Grimshaw, influenced by Joan Scott, points out that we need to recognise that suffragists had 'unstable speaking positions'. Their place in the public word of politics was precarious. They attempted to reconcile their private, home life with their desire for citizenship, which meant that they lived a paradox. These women argued for the need to vote in order to preserve the home, yet had to leave the home in order to do so. The arguments they put forward to secure the vote had to vary, depending on the audience they were addressing. Grimshaw argues that we need to embrace such discontinuities in the suffragists' texts and recognise the unstable speaking positions these women held.

Raewyn Dalziel continues this re-evaluation of suffragists in her exploration of how New Zealand suffragists were represented and how they represented themselves, on the international stage. Jane Rendall, in her chapter, is concerned with reassessing British suffragists through an examination of the language they used. It is important that we come to terms with the ways the suffragists were understood and understood themselves. Here Ellen DuBois' essay offers us a useful tool, in the form of the hyphen. DuBois argues that socialist-feminists negotiated, and continue to negotiate the hyphen between socialism and feminism. But just what kind of link is intended when we use a hyphen to link the words 'socialist' and 'feminist' to produce socialist-feminist? DuBois sees socialist-feminist women, like Clara Zetkin, trying to strike a balance with socialist men and with middle-class women's movements. Like Patricia Grimshaw, DuBois is alert to women's unstable speaking positions, and aware of their need to sometimes tell their audience what that audience wants to hear. Nancy Cott, on the other hand, takes at face value Zetkin's assertions that she would have nothing to do with bourgeois women's movements, that she worked in the interests of the working-class rather than the feminist movement. DuBois views this anti-collaborationism as being more rhetoric than reality. Read individually, DuBois' and Cott's chapters have much to offer; read together they raise some interesting points for debate.

A second strand in the reassessments of suffragists to come through strongly in several chapters is the suffragists' racism. This is especially so in the papers by Australian historians Marilyn Lake and Ann Curthoys. Lake argues that white women's citizenship was constituted on explicitly racist grounds. In colonised countries such as New Zealand and Australia, the racism of suffragists is especially contentious. As set out above, Maori women were enfranchised at the same time as Pakeha women in New Zealand while all Aborigines did not gain the federal franchise until 1962 in Australia. It is interesting to note that the Australian constitution of 1901 makes specific mention of New Zealand Maori. Maori men and women living in Australia were allowed to vote, although Aboriginal Australians were not necessarily granted this right.[25] This might be explained as a further lure to entice New Zealand to join the Australian federation, but what explains the fact that Maori men were enfranchised before all Pakeha men were and Maori women were enfranchised in 1893, at the same time as Pakeha women?[26] While the existence of the four separate Maori seats might go part of the way to explain this, Maori who fulfilled a property-owning criteria could enrol in the Pakeha electorates. As a number of Australasian historians have pointed out, Maori proved themselves to their colonial invaders in many ways. Their military prowess in the New Zealand wars of the 1860s was crucial in how the settlers viewed them. Anglo-Saxon attitudes at the time of New Zealand's annexation were also important in the settlers' view of Maori. This was the time of Social Darwinism, and New Zealand officials believed that

Maori were 'superior' natives.[27] The officials also felt protective inclinations for what they regarded as a dying race which had been making 'good' progress towards Europeanisation. They regarded them as more equal to and less different from themselves than Australian colonisers felt towards Aborigines. New Zealand's experience of colonisation was different from Australia's. To these factors we should add the benefits of New Zealand's relatively small geographical size and its lack of a reservations or native reserves system. The net result of these, and no doubt other factors, meant that Maori were able to capture citizenship rights in a way that Aborigines were not.

While for some it is a matter of nationalistic pride that their country was the first to enfranchise women, or the first to let them both vote and stand for Parliament, for many this source of pride is overwhelmed by the low status of their country's indigenous women. This often leads historians to search for a pre-contact golden age, a time when indigenous women's status and role in decision making was relatively high. For example, Schoeffel Meleisea tells us that in pre-Christian Polynesia, rank rather than gender determined status. In New Zealand this assertion is currently being debated.[28] Because some indigenous women were chiefs, priests or war leaders, it may not follow that women in general had significant power. In the West, for example, some women had been heads of state centuries before most women were able to acquire a measure of public power. The issue is what was typical or more prevalent. No doubt we will continue to argue by example, given the inevitably speculative nature of the literature on women's pre-contact and contact history. Moreover, it remains unclear how we could ever measure status and well-being across cultures and centuries. What is clear is that today indigenous women in the Australasian region endure a lower standard of living than their non-native counterparts.

And we are left with a debate over how racist and how progressive the suffragists were. Several of the authors in this book put forward very different interpretations of the suffragists in these regards. Some, like Ellen DuBois, argue that they were progressive, even though they were racist and took a 'moralistic approach to the family and to sexuality'. Others, like Nancy Cott, argue that the suffragists deserving the labels radical and feminist were those demanding sexual and political reforms. Sandra Stanley Holton reminds us of the links between abolitionists – those who opposed slavery – and suffragists. Holton shows us that some suffragists were concerned about racial issues and first took to the public stage under the abolitionist banner. Marilyn Lake, in her chapter, demonstrates the racism of white Australian women in the post-suffrage era and the attempts by some to deal with division between white women and Aboriginal women.

A third strand to the reassessment of suffrage contained in these chapters is a reconsideration of the post-suffrage era. The idea that once suffrage was achieved the organised women's movement disappeared is firmly rejected here. While the post-suffrage women's movement may have fragmented, it did not vanish. The chapters by Marilyn Lake, Johanna Alberti and Martin Pugh reject the idea that once women got the vote nothing more happened. Rather than seeing the achievement of suffrage as the end of organised women's activity, they see it, in Marilyn Lake's words, as 'a new departure point for [women's] agency and mobilisation'. They contextualise the feminist movements of the post-suffrage era by examining the period as much as the politics. The achievement of women's suffrage thus becomes the beginning, rather than the end, of the narrative of women's citizenship. This does not mean, however, that these historians view the immediate post-suffrage period as an unproblematic time in feminist history. All three share the view that in many ways the years after women were enfranchised were confused and confusing.

While voting is a fundamental right of citizens in a democracy, these writers are also interested in women's economic citizenship, and their rights to nationality. In New Zealand, Australia, Britain, Fiji, Nauru, Japan and various other countries, women 'lost' their nationality if they married an 'alien'. Suffrage studies are no longer just concerned with how the vote was won. Nor are they just concerned with middle-class political actors, be they male or female. The chapters in this book indicate that a new type of political history is being embraced by feminists. This is political history informed by social and feminist history. It does not ignore the wider political context of male legislators and laws, but it does not deify them either.

The internationalism of suffragists

Many references are made throughout this book to individual suffragists travelling overseas, taking their suffrage message to other countries.[29] In New Zealand, an organised women's suffrage movement began after the visit of Mrs Mary Leavitt, the travelling envoy of the WCTU. Mrs Leavitt travelled all over the world, spreading the WCTU's gospel, leaving in her wake some eighty-six women's organisations dedicated to achieving women's suffrage.[30] Many New Zealand suffragists, in turn, travelled the Western world, telling women how they had achieved the right to vote and what it meant to them. The internationalism of the suffragists is striking. Raewyn Dalziel demonstrates the international networks and travels of various New Zealand suffragists. Marilyn Lake and Susan Magarey discuss the Australian situation. Sandra Holton looks at the transatlantic travels of some leading British and American suffragists. Yukiko Matsukawa and Kaoru Tachi mention the international connections of Japanese suffragists, who also received a visit from Mrs Leavitt. Asunción Lavrin looks at South American women who travelled and the suffragists who travelled to them.[31]

These chapters clearly demonstrate that some nineteenth- and early twentieth-century suffragists belonged to extensive international networks. They corresponded with like-minded women overseas, and travelled frequently. While the recognition of the international links between suffragists and suffrage organisations is important, a focus on this aspect of suffrage may, inadvertently, lead us back to an undue concentration on middle-class women. We need to be wary of this. Only middle-class and elite women could afford to take long overseas trips. Only they had the time, resources and skills to engage in regular correspondence. The romance of travel should not blind us to the reality of most women's lives.

But this focus on the travel and links between suffragists directs us towards more comparative history. For example, Patricia Grimshaw examines similarities between the early sites of suffrage, Penelope Schoeffel Meleisea compares the suffrage history of Pacific Island women, Asunción Lavrin explores the situation in the Southern Cone nations and Colombia. One of the best known authors of comparative suffrage history, Ellen Carol DuBois, is also represented here.[32] She offers a revisionist overview of suffrage from a socialist-feminist viewpoint, arguing that suffrage movements around the world were noted for their internationalism, and that the women's movement should be conceptualised as an international protest movement. Nancy F. Cott also engages in comparative history: she studies the similarities and differences between the American and German 'first wave' feminist movements during their most radical phases, just after 1900.

When studying suffrage as an international protest movement, Cott reminds us that comparative history is a study of both similarities and differences. It is an important point. Too often the desire to find parallels overwhelms the need to step back and recognise differences. The differences, as well as the similarities, between the suffrage struggles are important in our understanding of this international development. Nowhere is this more clear than in the relationship between colonialism and post-colonialist suffragists. Meleisea Schoeffel, Lavrin and Curthoys all investigate the relevance of suffrage to colonial and post-colonial women political activists and why it was that some indigenous women had greater solidarity with their menfolk than with European women advocating suffragist reforms. Post-colonial women faced a dilemma between supporting international female rights and promoting local indigenous identity.[33]

This raises questions about the limits of the internationalism of suffragists and the imperialism of women's suffrage. Gender politics did not simply transcend national contexts. Matsukawa and Tachi discuss how Japanese women's internationalism was used against them in their suffrage campaign. Members of the Japanese Diet in the years leading up to World War II increasingly portrayed women's suffrage as running counter to Japanese customs. The Japanese women's movement had to contend with the view that it was unseemly and immoral for Japanese women to imitate Western women, including their suffrage rights. As fascism and anti-Western sentiments blossomed, women's suffrage suffered from its Western associations.

The negotiation of suffrage

The final theme to emerge in many of the essays is the need to reassess blatant dichotomies in our histories of suffrage. Gisela Bock has described the process whereby feminist historians' binary vision led them to focus on dichotomies in the 1970s and 1980s.[34] Bock argues that three dualisms recur in feminist history: nature and culture, work and family, and public and private. She suggests that each of these has important implications for gender research, since they are all associated with men (culture, work, public) and women (nature, family, private). Bock points out that feminists have attacked these dualisms. They have criticised them for being Aristotelian legacies and masculinist constructs. Aristotle claimed that sex differences were essential, that it was proper and necessary to draw distinctions between men's and women's work and worlds, and to consider the male world of public and political life as rational, ethical and superior to the female world of private and domestic life. Feminists resisted the value judgements inherent in the Aristotelian bifurcation. They undermined them empirically with studies showing that, rather than being discrete and antagonistic, the two parts of these dualisms were interdependent and interconnected.

Bock goes on to argue that recent feminist historiography, for all of its insights, has merely replaced these traditional dichotomies with three new dichotomies. She argues that feminist historians are now preoccupied with debates about whether to focus on sex or gender, whether equality or difference should be the basis of normative justice, and whether the goal of their research should be autonomy or integration into the 'mainstream'. Bock rightly points out that these new dualisms are reminiscent of the old ones. She advocates moving beyond dichotomies.[35]

A number of the authors in this book have taken up this challenge. Rather than simply updating the dichotomies, they reject such approaches.[36] Most of the chapters, for instance, touch on the public versus private debate, the idea that men were public beings and women were private creatures, but they undermine this dichotomy and upset the stereotypes by showing women as public and political actors in suffrage movements. And in several of the chapters the authors take this further than simply showing women who did not conform. Rather than clinging to ahistorical dichotomies like public versus private, their focus is on how men and women negotiated public space. Neither men nor women are seen as only belonging to one sphere. Now the focus is on the tension as each stakes out a claim to public space.

Much has been written about the 'debate' between equality and difference.[37] Studies such as Carol Bacchi's *Same Difference* suggest these two concepts should be compatible.[38] Several of the authors in this book contribute to the equality versus difference debate. They argue for more sensitive readings of women's language and their political acumen. For instance, Jane Rendall argues that the British suffragists' politics cannot be encompassed simply in the opposition between claims for equality or the representation of difference. Women's suffrage was a response to outmoded views of women's proper place in society. It spoke to anxieties of their own time and culture. For the British suffragists who adopted the individualist language of liberalism, the vote was a means to an end, a way towards education and cultivation. Rendall argues that the early suffragists did not espouse just one idea of democratic practice but were politically sophisticated and used different models of citizenship. She suggests that most women supported both equality and difference arguments, in order to ensure that there was justice in society between the sexes. Susan Magarey makes a similar point in her study.

The debate about equality versus difference is analysed in both Johanna Alberti's and Martin Pugh's chapters. Both accept that in the interwar years in Britain there were splits in the feminist movement, with older feminists arguing for equality, and newer, younger women arguing for difference politics. These women, divided by class and generation, belonged to a range of organisations, some rejecting domesticity, while others used their domestic role as a way to gain political power. Both writers see interwar feminists as engaging in the complex issues of equality and difference. Alberti and Pugh accept that there are no simple or obvious solutions. Alberti sees the awareness and acceptance of difference as one of the strengths of interwar feminism. There are strong echoes of Joan Scott's contention that equality must rest on difference in a 1918 quotation from Eleanor Rathbone, found in Alberti's chapter.[39]

On a slightly different tack, Ann Curthoys argues that the debate between the politics of equality and the politics of difference will never be resolved between defined cultures and genders in a political system. In this she is influenced by Carole Pateman, who, in her chapter, attacks the dichotomy by arguing that its very construction is sexist; equality is based on masculine measures and difference is grounded in patriarchal stereotypes.

The recurring theme, then, is that women's lives and views were complicated and complex. We do not do justice to the suffragists by analysing their lives in terms of dichotomies or simplistic and dualistic debates. While this recognition of the complexities of women's lives is important, many of the essays in this collection move beyond just pointing to the problem. They offer us a new approach to suffrage history, a gendered approach.

Many of the authors in this collection believe that we do not do justice to women's lives if we study them only in homosocial or single-sex groups. While all of the authors focus on women as suffragists, political actors and citizens, some wish to extend this analysis beyond studying just women's relationships with other women. There is a call, first heard from Patricia Grimshaw, to take a gendered approach to suffrage studies.

It is interesting that Grimshaw advocates both a 'woman-centred' approach to suffrage history, and a gendered one. Since the appearance of Caroll Smith-Rosenberg's influential essay, 'The Female World of Love and Ritual', in 1975, historians of women, and feminist historians, have been celebrating a women's culture.[40] At first glance, Grimshaw's desire to retain a woman-centred approach to suffrage history, while also engaging in gender history, seems somewhat contradictory. After all, a woman-centred approach focuses on the ties between women, their shared goals and rituals, while a gendered approach focuses on the relationships between women and men. But as Gisela Bock pointed out in an essay which launched the journal *Gender & History*, gender is about the relationships both *within* groups of women and men, and *between* groups of women and men. Women's history can be gender history. Women's historians are becoming self-conscious about the implications of their work on relationships between groups of women for wider gender analysis.[41]

All of the essays here are gender history and most of them are so self-consciously. Most earn this mantle by studying the relationships within particular groups of women. Some branch out and also look at the relationships between groups of women suffragists and men, be they pro-suffrage or anti-suffrage. Sandra Stanley Holton's essay is a good example of this latter trend. Holton examines the complex relationship between women of the Bright Circle and their male kin, some of whom were active supporters of women's suffrage, and some of whom opposed the extension of the franchise.

Holton and Grimshaw are extending our understanding of suffrage through their gendered approach. As Grimshaw points out, we need to understand the motives of New World men, who passed women's suffrage legislation at a relatively early stage. Too often in feminist suffrage history the focus is on the women activists, and the male legislators, essential for change to take place, are ignored or their role is down-played. But taking a gendered approach to suffrage history should do more than merely add in the role of certain men, be they pro- or anti-women's suffrage. We need to study the ways that the campaign for women's suffrage, and its achievement, affected gender relations.[42]

As Gisela Bock and Joan Scott have pointed out, gender relations are power relations.[43] There are power relations within homosocial groups and between them. Within the women's suffrage movement there were many groups of women, some with more power than others. We need to explore the tensions between these groups. We also need to examine the power relations between groups of women advocating the vote, and those women who opposed the vote. The campaign for the vote saw many women become public, political actors, a role they often retained once suffrage was achieved. We need to explore what this meant for gender relations. How did these women negotiate the gendered boundaries of public life? Did they manage to stake out a place for themselves in a political world previously seen as a masculine domain? Did women lose power by trying to assimilate into men's organisations, as Martin Pugh suggests in this collection, and Estelle Freedman has argued for the American case?[44] Many of the authors in this book who touch on the later twentieth century observe that politics still remains a male territory, with women making up a small proportion of elected members to parliaments.[45] As Carole Pateman argues, women were mobilised in auxiliaries but the rise of the social welfare system occurred at the very time that large areas of men's power in the public realm were consolidated. The welfare state reinforced men's economic power as breadwinners and as heads of households, and hostility to women's participation in the public realm continued. The patriarchal structure of relations and concepts of masculinity and femininity were not threatened, even though masculinities and femininities were continually changing and readjusting.

Several feminist historians have raised concerns about the advent of gender history, and the threat they see it posing to women's history and feminist history.[46] There is a concern that gender history is apolitical. However, given that gender history is the history of power relations within and between gendered groups, this fear seems ungrounded. A gendered approach can allow us to change and broaden the definitions of power and politics, so that they encompass more than high politics and class relations. Domestic politics and the politics of sexual relations must also be studied. As women's history and as feminist history, studies of women's suffrage have remained at the margins of the historical discipline. We have been ghettoised. Perhaps a gendered approach will allow us to renegotiate the gendered boundaries of history.

Conclusion
The wariness of historians at the suffrage conference about celebrating women's suffrage was due to the fact that the fight is far from over. A 1990 United Nation's report on the world's women indicated that in that year only six of the 159 UN member states were headed by women, only 3.5 per cent of the world's cabinet ministers were women, and women held no ministerial positions in 93 countries. Yet in Bhutan, Dominica and Norway women held more than 20 per cent of ministerial positions. In terms of education, women comprised almost two thirds of the world's illiterate population and yet women make up equal numbers of those training in the professions in a number of countries. In the field of paid employment, the report noted that everywhere women were paid less than men, and that few earned over 75 per cent of the male wage rate.[47] Studies show that women in Scandinavia are closer to parity in wages with men than women from Middle Eastern countries.

Just as women's present-day status varies from country to country, so does their suffrage history. This collection allows us to study women's suffrage in a number of nations. It demonstrates the importance of understanding both the particular and the general. We need to understand our own history but we also need to engage in comparative and international studies. Like the suffragists of days gone by, we need to draw on our national and international networks, and listen and learn from one another.

1   For example, in 1993, the annual Hocken Lecture was given by former parliamentarian, Marilyn Waring, on the meaning of suffrage for women's lives. Waring is advocating a quota of 50 per cent of Members of Parliament being women.
2   Mrs Muller's pseudonym is sometimes written as 'Femmina'. A reproduction of 'An Appeal to the Men of New Zealand' can be found in the collection of documents selected by Margaret Lovell-Smith, *The Woman Question: Writings by the Women Who Won the Vote*, New Women's Press, Auckland, 1992, 59-65.
3   For a brief discussion of these early attempts see Patricia Grimshaw, *Women's Suffrage in New Zealand*, 2nd ed., Auckland Univ. Press/Oxford Univ. Press, Auckland, 1987, first published in 1972, 14-20.
4   For a discussion of the history of the New Zealand WCTU, see Raewyn Dalziel, 'New Zealand Women's Christian Temperance Union 1885- ', in Anne Else, ed, *Women Together: A History of Women's Organisations in New Zealand, Nga Ropu Wahine o te Motu*, Historical Branch, Department of Internal Affairs/Daphne Brasell Associates Press, Wellington, 1993, 72-5.
5   By 1897 Maori women gained the right to vote for and to stand as members of Te Kotahitanga. By 1902, when Te Kotahitanga was disbanded, no women had been elected to sit in the parliament. See Tania Rei, *Maori Women and The Vote*, Huia Publishers, Wellington, 1993. For a fuller discussion of the women's involvement in Te Kotahitanga, see Angela Ballara, 'Wahine Rangatira: Maori Women of Rank and their Role in the Women's Kotahitanga Movement of the 1890s', *New Zealand Journal of History (NZJH)*, 27/2, Oct. 1993, 127-39.
6   Raewyn Dalziel contends that 'From the early 1880s a majority of politicians in Parliament supported the principle of the women's vote' in Anne Else, ed, *Women Together*, 56. Jean Garner also argues that 'before 1885, a majority of politicians in both houses had accepted the principle of votes for women', in Jean Garner, 'Sir John Hall and Women's Suffrage', *Historical News*, 67, Oct 1993, 8-11, especially 9.
7   See Tania Rei, *Maori Women and the Vote*, 27, 35-36. The reason we do not know how many Maori women voted for the Maori members in 1893 is that there were no Maori electoral rolls at that time. Nor did Maori voters have the privacy of a secret ballot. Maori were not granted the right to a secret ballot until 1937. See Helena Catt, 'Introduction', in Helena Catt & Elizabeth McLeay, eds, *Women and Politics in New Zealand, Political Science* in conjunction with Victoria University Press, Wellington, 1993, 3.
8   The Cook Islands were a New Zealand protectorate, while the Pitcairns were a British possession. Cook Islands women were granted suffrage three days after New Zealand's Electoral Act but they voted before New Zealand women, on 14 October 1893. See Dick Scott, *Years of the Pooh-bah: a Cook Islands History*, Hodder & Stoughton, Auckland, 1991 and H. L. Shapiro, *The Pitcairn Islanders*, Simon & Schuster, New York, 1968, 142-3. The entire population of 194 Pitcairn Islanders was resettled on Norfolk Island in 1856.
9   Legal Opinion, Ministry of Women's Affairs, Wellington, 1992.
10   Audrey Oldfield, *Woman Suffrage in Australia: A Gift or a Struggle?*, Cambridge Univ. Press, Melbourne, 1992, 21.
11   Betty Serle, *Silk & Calico: Class, Gender & the Vote*, Hale & Iremonger, Sydney, 1988, 11.
12   Pat Stretton & Christine Finnimore, 'Black Fellow Citizens: Aborigines and the Commonwealth Franchise', *Australian Historical Studies*, 25/101, Oct 1993, 521-35. Section 41 of the Commonwealth Constitution was used to disenfranchise 'aboriginal natives of Australia, Asia, Africa and the islands of the Pacific, except New Zealand'. Many commentators erroneously date the extension of Commonwealth suffrage to Aborigines as 1967, the year in which Australians agreed in a referendum to count Aborigines in the census. For a New Zealand view of this, see *Dominion*, 5 January 1994, 12.
13   New South Wales and Van Diemen's Land (Tasmania) were originally penal settlements. Altogether Britain transported 137,000 males and 25,000 females to Australia between 1788 and

1868. No convicts were sent directly to South Australia or New Zealand. See J. B. Hirst, *Convict Society and Its Enemies*, Allen & Unwin, Sydney, 1983.

14   Caroline Daley's commentary on Susan Magarey's paper, 'Suffrage and Beyond' conference, August 1993.

15   See Appendix for the dates of women's suffrage in the colonies and states of Australia.

16   See Appendix for a chronological list of women's suffrage dates.

17   Ibid.

18   See, for example, Jill Liddington, 'Women Cotton Workers and the Suffrage Campaign: The Radical Suffragists in Lancashire, 1893-1914', in Sandra Burman, ed, *Fit Work for Women*, Croom Helm, London, 1979, 98-111; Jill Liddington & Jill Norris, *One Hand Tide Behind Us: The Rise of the Women's Suffrage Movement*, Virago, London, 1978; Andrew Rosen, *Rise Up Women! The Militant Campaign of the Women's Social and Political Union 1903-1914*, Routledge & Kegan Paul, London & Boston, 1974; Midge Mackenzie, *Shoulder to Shoulder: A Documentary*, Knopf, New York, 1975.

19   See, for example, Jill Liddington, *The Life and Times of a Respectable Rebel: Selina Cooper 1864-1946*, Virago, London, 1984 ; June Hannam, *Isabella Ford: A Biography*, Blackwell, Oxford, 1989.

20   For a discussion on *fin de siècle* and women's history see Elaine Showalter, *Sexual Anarchy: Gender and Culture at the Fin de Siècle*, Virago, London, 1992.

21   It is important to make the distinction between the radical, militant suffragettes and the suffragists. Suffragettes chained themselves to railings, fire-bombed post boxes and went on hunger strikes while imprisoned on civil disobedience charges. Suffragists were women who advocated the vote, usually through peaceful and law-abiding means, such as petitions and letters to parliamentarians. Suffragists is the more inclusive term, and is used in this collection as a convenient label for all groups campaigning for women's suffrage.

22   See also Philippa Levine, *Victorian Feminism 1850-1900*, Hutchison, London, 1987. Other papers presented at the conference on this subject included Bettina Bradbury, 'From Civil Death to Separate Property: Changes in the Legal Rights of Married Women in Nineteenth Century New Zealand', unpublished paper presented to 'Suffrage and Beyond' conference, August 1993.

23   See Appendix A for a chronological list of suffrage dates in conjunction with retrospective population estimates in United Nations, *World Population Chart*, Statistical Office of the United Nations, New York, 1990.

24   Magrit D. Siegenthaler-Reusser, 'Switzerland's Specific Way to Women's Suffrage', unpublished paper presented to 'Suffrage and Beyond' conference, August 1993.

25   Oldfield, *Woman Suffrage in Australia*, 65.

26   The 1852 Constitution Act established a voting system based on sex, age and property. Maori and Pakeha men, over the age of 21, with the required property qualification, were entitled to register to vote. In 1867 four new seats in the House of Representatives were created to be held by Maori members. The members were elected on a Maori manhood suffrage. From that time until the election of 1893, Maori males who fulfilled the Pakeha property requirement could vote in both the European election and the Maori election. This dual vote was abolished in 1893. It was not until the 1879 Qualification of Electors Bill that European men who had resided in New Zealand for a year and in an electoral district for six months, were given the vote, regardless of their property-owning status. Even then, some Pakeha males, such as itinerant rural workers, were disenfranchised. For a discussion of New Zealand's electoral system, see Raewyn Dalziel, 'Towards Representative Democracy: 100 Years of the Modern Electoral System', in Atholl Anderson, Judith Binney, David Hamer, Raewyn Dalziel, Erik Olssen, W. H. Oliver and Jock Phillips, *Towards 1990: Seven Leading Historians Examine Significant Aspects of New Zealand History*, GP Books, Wellington, 1989, 49-63.

27   See, for example, Keith Sinclair, 'Why are Race Relations in New Zealand Better Than in South Africa, South Australia or South Dakota?', *NZJH*, 5/2, Oct. 1971, 121-7.

28   Ballara.

29   There are some precedents for this. The internationalism of the suffrage movement has been studied by Richard J. Evans, *The Feminists: Women's Emancipation Movements in Europe, America and Australiasia 1840-1920*, Croom Helm, London & Sydney, 1977. The internationalism of the WCTU has recently been explored by Ian Tyrell, *Woman's World, Woman's Empire: The Women's Christian Temperance Union in International Perspective, 1880-1930*, Univ. of North Carolina Press, Chapel Hill & London, 1991.

30   E. T. James, J. W. James & P. S. Boyer, eds, *Notable American Women, 1607-1950*, vol. 2, Harvard Univ. Press, Cambridge, Mass., 1971, 383-5.

31   Barbara Caine has also written on the internationalism of Australian suffragists and Francesca Miller on the internationalism of women in the Americas. See Barbara Caine, 'Vida Goldstein and the English Militant Campaign', *Women's History Review*, 2/3, 1993, 363-76; Francesca Miller, 'The International Relations of Women of the Americas, 1890-1928', *The Americas*, 43/2, Oct. 1986, 171-82.

32   Ellen Carol DuBois, 'Woman Suffrage and the Left: An International Socialist-Feminist Perspective', *New Left Review*, 186, 1991, 20-45.

33   This is an issue which is beginning to be discussed among Aotearoa/New Zealand Maori. See, for example, Ripeka Evans, 'Mana Whenua, Mana Tangata, Mana Wairua: Maori Feminism', unpublished paper presented to the Winter Lecture Series, Unversity of Auckland, 1993.

34   Gisela Bock, 'Challenging Dichotomies: Perspectives on Women's History', in Karen Offen, Ruth Roach Pierson & Jane Rendall, eds, *Writing Women's History: International Perspectives*, Indiana Univ. Press, Bloomington & Indianapolis, 1991, 1-23. Linda Kerber has also written on the need for women's history to move beyond dichotomies; see Linda Kerber, 'Separate Spheres, Female Worlds, Women's Place: The Rhetoric of Women's History', *Journal of American History (JAH)*, 75, June 1988, 9-39.

35   Karen Offen, Ruth Roach Pierson & Jane Rendall, eds, *Writing Women's History*, xxxv.

36   Feminist labour historians, among others, are also criticising dualistic approaches. See Ava Baron, ed, *Work Engendered: Towards a New History of American Labor*, Cornell Univ. Press, Ithaca & London, 1991, 17-20.

37   See, for example, Joan W. Scott, 'Deconstructing Equality-Versus-Difference: Or, the Uses of Poststructuralist Theory for Feminism', *Feminist Studies*, 14/1, 1988, 33-50.

38   Carol Lee Bacchi, *Same Difference: Feminism and Sexual Difference*, Allen & Unwin, Sydney, 1990.

39   Scott, 'Deconstructing Equality vs. Difference'.

40   Caroll Smith-Rosenberg, 'The Female World of Love and Ritual: Relations Between Women in Nineteenth-Century America', *Signs*, 1/1, Autumn 1975, 1-27.

41   Gisela Bock, 'Women's History and Gender History: Aspects of an International Debate', *Gender & History*, 1/1, Spring 1989, 7-30.

42   For an interesting study on women's suffrage by a historian of masculinity, see David H. J. Morgan, 'Challenges to masculinity: (iii) The suffrage movement', in *Discovering Men*, Routledge, London & New York, 1992, 141-59. In the last ten years there has been a flurry of publishing in the field of men's studies and histories of masculinities. See also Harry Brod, ed, *The Making of Masculinities: The New Men's Studies*, Allen & Unwin, Boston, 1987; Mark C. Carnes & Clyde Griffen, ed, *Meanings for Manhood: Constructions of Masculinity in Victorian America*, Univ. of Chicago Press, Chicago, 1990; Jeff Hearn, *Men in the Public Eye: The construction and deconstruction of public men and public patriarchies*, Routledge, London, 1992; Jock Phillips, *A Man's Country? A History of the Pakeha Male*, Penguin, Auckland, 1987; E. Anthony Rotundo, *American Manhood: Transformations in Masculinity from the Revolution to the Modern Era*, Basic Books, New York, 1993; and Lynne Segal, *Slow Motion: Changing Masculinities, Changing Men*, Rutgers Univ. Press, New Brunswick, 1990.

43   Bock, 'Women's History and Gender History'; Joan W. Scott, 'Gender: A Useful Category of Historical Analysis', *American Historical Review (AHR)*, 91/5, Dec. 1986, 1053-75.

44   Estelle Freedman, 'Separatism as Strategy: Female Institution Building and American Feminism, 1870-1930', *Feminist Studies*, 5/3, Fall 1979, 512-29.

45   See also Janine Haines, *Suffrage to Sufferance: 100 Years of Women in Politics*, Allen & Unwin, St Leonards, 1992; Elizabeth McLeay, 'Women's Parliamentary Representation: A Comparable Perspective', in Catt & McLeay, eds, *Women and Politics in New Zealand*, 40-62.

46   See, for example, Marilyn Lake, 'Women, Gender and History', *Australian Feminist Studies*, 7&8, Summer 1988, 1-9; Judith M. Bennett, 'Feminism and History', *Gender & History*, 1/3, Autumn 1989, 251-72; Joyce E. Canaan & Christine Griffin, 'The New Men's Studies: Part of the Problem or Part of the Solution', in Jeff Hearn & David Morgan, eds, *Men, Masculinities & Social Theory*, Unwin Hyman, London, 1990.

47   *The World's Women: Trends and Statistics, 1970-1990*, United Nations, New York, 1991, 31, 45, 88.

I

New Zealand Women's Suffrage

The New Zealand contingent, including Anna Stout and Dr Alice Burn, at the 1910 London procession to support the Conciliation Bill which would have given British women the vote.
Weekly News, *Auckland Institute and Museum*.

2

Women's Suffrage in New Zealand Revisited: Writing From the Margins

PATRICIA GRIMSHAW

For a group of activists who fought vigorously and ultimately successfully to promote a cause of social equity affecting the civil rights of half the adult population, white western suffragists have had a chequered career at the hands of historians. After the earliest chroniclers, usually participants themselves, recorded the suffragists' exploits, historians for the most part withdrew their attention, except perhaps for the activities of the English suffragettes, and here it was their militancy, not the cause, that was emphasised. Historians tend to measure historical relevance by outcomes: the results of the women's vote appeared curiously insignificant, justifying its omission from mainstream narratives. Women did not vote as a bloc; few women entered national legislatures.

Starting in the 1950s a few female historians began an attempt to recall the suffragists from exile.[1] A contemporary feminist historian has designated these accounts 'descriptive narratives which lauded the march towards enfranchisement in a celebratory fashion'.[2] No sooner had they appeared, it seemed, than practitioners of a new wave of women's history, energised by the women's movement, tried the suffragists and found them wanting. The attitudes of nineteenth- and early-twentieth-century suffragists towards women of other classes and races, and toward gender relationships and family structures in their own circles, quite properly attracted critical scrutiny. Men had fought to widen the ranks of eligibility for voting with arguments which obscured gender. Women fought for the vote as women on behalf of women, which attracted interrogation of their claims to representativeness. Suffragists claimed to fight for the vote for women to improve the lot of humanity, which attracted interrogation of their social vision. And where suffragists were housewives who prioritised their Christian beliefs and were advocates of temperance, historians, who tended to be none of the above, quite reasonably felt distanced from these women's reform agenda.

In a revisionist article, a political scientist recently complained of 'an almost hostile neglect of woman suffrage' in the field of modern feminist scholarship, where historians have turned the focus away from 'high politics' to issues of the politics of the personal.[3] That we should now attempt to bridge that gap is timely, as issues of women's relationship to the state, of women and citizenship, have re-emerged as vitally important. Carole Pateman's innovatory study, *The Sexual Contract*, has alerted us to the ambiguities for women embedded within liberal theory, which posited equality in terms prioritising the rational, autonomous and therefore masculine human being. Women then were obliged to fight for equality in gendered terms, taking their stance on their situations as women, in order to obtain rights that were essentially defined for the opposite sex.[4] Women not only faced this paradox, the American historian Joan Scott suggested in a recent paper, but they *lived* that paradox, day by day and year by year. This new history of suffrage must acknowledge suffragists' unstable speaking positions and embrace the discontinuities in their texts, rather than seek to iron out ambiguities in the interests of a smooth linear narrative.[5] Inspired by new intellectual challenges, and cautioned by postmodern theorists, we can now embark upon a fresh historical consideration of the means by which white women in Western democracies acquired citizenship.

My portion of this task is to look again at the women's suffrage movement in New Zealand. A fruitful way forward, perhaps, is to view this single country's experience in the context of movements in all those locations where women received the vote at a comparably early stage. The male legislatures which extended women the suffrage between the years 1890 and 1902 were those of four states of the American West (Wyoming, Utah, Colorado and Idaho); the British colonies of South Australia and Western Australia, followed by the Commonwealth of Australia and the state of New South Wales; and, of course, New Zealand. These were all small societies, marginal geographically to the political main-springs of the women's movement, and therefore marginal also to the mainstream of historical and feminist scholarship. My essay first attempts a brief sketch of the passage of the vote in these pioneering suffrage locations to suggest some social features which they might hold in common; secondly, it examines historiographical frame-works developed in the later 1960s and 1970s for understanding the separate colonial, state or national campaigns; and thirdly, it suggests directions opened up by recent scholarship for the development of a fresh interpretation of women's suffrage enacted on the margins, and viewed from the margins.

Sites of early suffrage victories

The stories of the achievement of the women's vote in all the early sites are complex, but for brevity's sake can be reduced to some simple chronology. Wyoming entered the Union as a state in 1890, and Utah as a state in 1896, with women's suffrage already enshrined in their state constitutions. As territories, both had enacted women's suffrage when the matter could be dealt with by the territorial legislatures, without a referendum of current voters. Wyoming in 1869 had been a new territory carved out of the so-called Great American Desert, a site of small settlements along trails to the West and the new railway line pushing westwards. The population was very small, with men predominating and lawless behaviour rife. A few women fresh from the East, aware of the controversy surrounding the constitutional amendment for African-American civil rights, saw an opportunity to press for the vote in a fluid political situation, and succeeded in persuading enough legislators to support their case. (The Governor who signed the bill later reported that 'the women were astounded! If a whole troop of angels had come down with flaming swords for their vindication, they would not have been much more astonished than they were when that bill became a law and the women of Wyoming were thus clothed with the habiliments of citizenship.')[6] The national suffrage paper, the *Revolution*, gave the news of this event three lines in an obscure corner. The passage of women's suffrage in the Territory of Utah was not just trivial, it was downright embarrassing: national suffrage leaders appeared to avoid mentioning it at all. For Utah was predominantly a Mormon space, and well-intentioned politicians from outside had been suggesting instituting the women's vote to give Mormon women the chance to vote out polygamy. In retaliation, it appears, Mormon men voted for the suffrage in 1870 to show the world that Mormon women were happy with polygamy. This was not something for feminists to boast about. In their campaign against polygamy, male legislators in Washington removed the women's vote in 1887, this time to reduce the Mormon vote in the territory, in the hopes that the non-Mormon citizens would vote out the offending provision, although polygamy was a church, not a state, matter.[7]

These two early instances of women voting may have seemed oddities in the long march to women's emancipation. Men of both territories, however, validated their earlier decisions when they insisted, against federal opposition, on the inclusion of female suffrage in their new state constitutions in 1890 and 1896 respectively. Women of the territories had also lobbied strongly for this outcome, and the Wyoming women now had women's organisations for this purpose. Colorado and Idaho, amongst many other Mid-Western and Western states where similar attempts were energetically attempted and failed, granted the women's vote after a majority of men approved it in state-wide referenda. After their failure to generate genuine interest in a women's suffrage movement in federal Congress after the Civil War, suffrage leaders such as Susan B. Anthony and Elizabeth Cady Stanton shifted to assisting local suffragists in campaigns to gain constitutional amendments at the state level. Colorado had been admitted to the Union in 1877, Idaho in 1890. In both states women's organisations, especially temperance groups, were active and the political parties included confirmed supporters.

In South Australia and Western Australia the women's vote passed into law by a majority vote in two-house colonial legislatures. These were British colonies, like New Zealand, but with partially independent governments empowered to legislate on a wide range of issues for which regal (or vice-regal) assent was expected to be automatic. Both South Australia's and Western Australia's resources derived mainly from the rural sector, sheep and cattle runs and farming, and (recent in Western Australia) mining. Both, however, had sizeable cities grown up around their main ports, and some developed urban life. Liberalism flourished in South Australia, and women's suffrage had been raised without perhaps much serious hope in Parliament before suffragists, temperance reformers to the fore, pressed the issue to its conclusion in 1894. The Act was promulgated the following year. Temperance reformers undertook the campaign in Western Australia, where the passage of the vote emerged amidst some considerable contestation between radical miners and a more conservative administration over a range of issues. The Premier made a sudden conversion to give party support to the measure, on principle, so he said – because he hoped to offset the radical vote of single men, said others.[8]

The basis for suffrage political rights in the new Commonwealth of Australia, formed by a federation of the six Australian colonies in 1901, was the same as existed already in the separate colonies. Women in South Australia and Western Australia, therefore, automatically received the federal franchise. Aware of the anomalous situation where some, but not all, women in the new nation were full citizens, and under pressure from suffrage organisations in other states, especially Victoria and New South Wales, the new Commonwealth Government conceded the vote to all Australian women in 1902; the same Act, however, excluded Aboriginal women and men, whose acquisition of citizenship rights was a story of the post World War II era. The state legislature of New South Wales, the oldest state, gave white women the vote later the same year.

New Zealand, Australia and her separate states, and those four Western American states in many ways were socially and culturally varied, heirs to differing political traditions and indigenous pressures. There were, however, some common general features worth listing that might have had a bearing on the early achievement of women's suffrage and to which I shall return when I suggest a future research strategy. These were all areas recently occupied by white settlers, based on rural industries, especially farming. Settlers, or their immediate forebears, had displaced an indigenous people, Maori, Aborigines or Native Americans, to take up this land. Men predominated in these populations, and all adult men had the right to vote, for representative legislatures in which political parties were taking modern form. Liberalism was a strong force and there was pressure for greater state intervention in social issues. Predominantly Protestant populations, men and women from Protestant congregations had initiated evangelical associations similarly pressing for state intervention on several reform issues, including temperance.

Marriage rates for women were high in these populations, and birth rates relatively high, but women were entering the workforce, into industries, service occupations and white collar work. Education for women was fast expanding and women were entering the professions, mostly teaching and nursing, but also the more prestigious areas. Some women in these locations had already been granted a range of voting rights at the level of municipal government, on school boards, on liquor licensing boards. Inspired by wider national or international movements, individual women and men advocated the full legislative franchise for women, and women formed small associations to fight for this end. But the most numerous organisation which assumed the vote as its key political goal in each population was the Woman's Christian Temperance Union (WCTU), formed to moderate drinking habits, and oppose male drunkenness, but which also emerged as the principal grassroots suffrage organisation.

Historians on early suffrage victories
During the period from the mid-1960s to 1980 a number of historians addressed the women's suffrage movements in these new societies in ways that have remained crucial to their construction in accepted historical knowledge, doing so within the historiographical contours of one country. These historians were influenced by the fresh perspectives

on the past that emerged from the radicalism of the 1960s and 1970s, especially the Civil Rights movement, the anti-Vietnam war movement, New Left politics and the women's movement. Out of this came the effort to promote women's history as a serious and legitimate concern within the discipline, and eventually as a specialist sub-area that warranted its own learned journals, tertiary appointments and courses. It was a sub-area, however, where practitioners claimed relevance for altering the paradigms for the construction of history as a whole, for redefining the canons of relevance which guided traditional scholarship. Given this ambitious brief and the numbers of historians, especially young female scholars, who were energised by this shift within the discipline, one might have expected intensive concentration on the suffrage movements. This is especially so considering the prominence of such activism in their own past context and the significance for them of civil liberties issues. This did not eventuate. Many of the new scholars of women's history turned to social history, to the study of women of the working class, the poor, the institutionalised, of ethnic or racial minorities. Coming from the left, many looked sceptically at the claims of social reformers to speak for the needs of such people, using frameworks of social control to illustrate the oppressive qualities inherent in such agendas. What was more, social reformers were suspected of quashing radical impulses within oppressed groups, showing the ruling class ways of appeasing anger by making a few ameliorative concessions. These reformers could not properly be eulogised as protagonists for the underprivileged or marginalised.

Such historians of the American movement as Aileen Kraditor, William O'Neill and Andrew Sinclair, for example, brought into question the ideological and social agendas of the national American women's movement. Kraditor viewed the earliest suffragists who were connected to the abolitionist movement as genuinely concerned with issues of social equity and justice. As large numbers of women were swept up into the suffrage movement in the later nineteenth century, however, suffragists promoted the women's vote as a vehicle for social control over undesirable elements in the population, particularly non-Anglo migrants.[9] O'Neill and Sinclair castigated the suffragists for what they perceived as social conservatism, greatly at odds with the demands of women's liberationists of these historians' own contexts. In particular they homed in on the suffragists' defence of the family as a reason for women pursuing the vote, and their justification of a place in public life on the basis of their maternal responsibilities. The very source of women's oppression, the patriarchal family, they pointed out, survived the granting of the vote unchallenged.[10]

Such views of the suffragists were influenced by the conviction that women had really gained very little from political rights, and if the earlier suffragists had been more radical, and more enlightened, women in the twentieth century would have faced a far more satisfactory, and sexually egalitarian, future.

There were at the same time other initiatives in American women's history that eventually shaped alternative interpretations of the suffragists. Scholars such as Nancy Cott, Mary Ryan, Ann Douglas, Barbara Welter and Carroll Smith-Rosenberg, worked through what came to be called a 'woman-centred' analysis.[11] Their scholarship was characterised by very close attention to texts generated by women themselves, to the cultural history of notions of femininity and masculinity in precise historical moments, and by respect for women's capacity to negotiate intelligently their paths within or outside the customary boundaries of their lives. Class issues became less prominent, while issues of gender were prioritised. For the suffragists, Ellen DuBois's path-breaking study of 1978, *Feminism and Suffrage*, offered a sympathetic portrayal of reformers adapting their traditional sources of power and the potentially constraining tendencies within their religious frameworks, to devise a striking argumentative basis for women's civic equality. She posed an entry into understanding women reformers, and suffragists in particular, that offered rather different possibilities from models of social control.[12]

Those historians who examined the first sites of successful women's suffrage campaigns in the later 1960s and the 1970s wrote within the frameworks of social control. Alan P. Grimes in his 1967 study *The Puritan Ethic and Woman Suffrage* noted the phenomenon of the suffrage victories in new societies as a group, when he posed as an enigma that so sophisticated a theoretical concept as women's civil rights, developed within the intellectual circles of London and Manchester, New York and Boston, should have succeeded first in raw, decidedly unsophisticated, male-dominated populations on American and British frontiers of settlement. Turning to the western states, Grimes ascribed the success of suffrage to a so-called 'Puritan revival', the prevalence of a world view 'heavily imbued with a moral commitment to right the wrongs of society and to check by law, where possible, the intrusion of evil'.[13] Because of the very absence of theoretical or political sophistication in these populations, the concept of women's suffrage could blossom, in the expectation that women's political power could be harnessed to eradicate sinfulness through the legislative process: in particular the sinfulness of unruly, profligate, heavy-drinking single men.

Thus women's rights as a radical theory disappeared from view. There were similar tendencies in Australian writing. When Australian women's history had a remarkable flowering from the mid 1970s, many feminist historians were strongly influenced by the New Left, and wrote as protagonists for the dispossessed and the disadvantaged. Two inter- pretations of women's history had marked impact. Anne Summers's *Damned Whores and God's Police* and Miriam Dixson's *The Real Matilda*, both expressed misgivings about the colonial women's movement. Summers's interpretation was shaped within her broader thesis that Australian women, the colonised sex, had historically been controlled by the device of dichotomised models of feminine behaviour: the respected woman who sustained herself in good standing by adhering to rigid standards of propriety; or secondly, the outcast, the deviant, the unacceptable woman who dared to transgress against society's norms. Suffragists stepped willingly into the ranks of 'God's police', by eagerly doing their all to confine other women, in a reforming age, to normative values and beliefs. Dixson, having described Australian women in the 1970s as 'the doormats of the Western world', was disappointed in colonial feminists: she found the nineteenth-century women's movement slight, weak and derivative.[14]

Women's Suffrage in New Zealand, my own study, was published in 1972, although the research was undertaken in the 1960s: it came into print in years more favourable to such topics. I argued that New Zealand had been the site of a small but significant suffrage movement comparable to those of larger Western societies, in an account that focused fairly directly on the campaign itself and the political fortunes of the suffrage within the country's legislature. The temperance reformers, I asserted, were also committed to feminist causes. Within a few years two revisionist interpretations appeared in article form. In the first Raewyn Dalziel attributed the early passage of the women's vote to a particular conjunction of colonial men's need of women's labour and colonial women's satisfaction with their domestic engagements. In a frontier rural economy women found their household skills held at a high premium. When touched by ideas of equal rights, the vote was seen as an extension of their roles as wives and mothers, not as the herald of new possibilities. This restricted vision had 'a strangling effect on the expan- sion of women's role in New Zealand society'.[15] Phillida Bunkle, in the second article, reinforced this latter view. Bunkle argued that the temperance activists of the WCTU laid the foundations for much of the rigid outlook and restrictive legislation that 1970s feminists found most objectionable, particularly in relation to drinking and to sexuality.[16]

Of northern historians Richard Evans alone brought the Australian and New Zealand experience into a broader framework. He surveyed the Australasian women's movements along with the national movements of America and Britain in his study *The Feminists*, in 1977. Sensitive to issues of class, he noted generally that liberal feminists were deficient in identification with working-class women's needs, and he displayed scepticism about the co-existence of temperance and feminism. Overall, he saw the basis for the early success of the women's vote in Australia and New Zealand in the immature state of political parties and political processes.[17]

The 1980s and early 1990s have not been favourable times for historians to develop meta-narratives of past experiences, whether of the centre or the margins of Western historical scholarship. Nuanced studies of particular groups of women have surfaced more frequently, and few historians have faith any longer that the filling in of the pieces will lead to the solution of the giant jigsaw patterns of history. Nevertheless I now move on to suggest some strategies for developing a comparative study of women's suffrage in the Mid-West, in Australia and New Zealand. I do so by no means wishing to discount the challenging insights of those historians who interrogated, sometimes with severity, the feminist credentials of these suffragists. I do so acknowledging the innovatory possibilities offered by historians of suffragists and others elsewhere since the early 1980s.

First, I suggest that elements of the so-called 'woman-centred' analysis retain clarifying potential for understanding the intersection of temperance and feminism in these locations. The 'woman-centred' analysis that inspired a flood of innovatory work in women's history in the United States itself came under sharp scrutiny. Numbers of leading historians now legitimately question whether this approach led to too great a historical concentration on middle-class women rather than the working class, and on white women rather than African-American and women of non-Anglo-American origin.[18] An approach to women's history must first respect the ways women themselves perceived their personal situations; otherwise we assess women through intellectual paradigms inherently unsympathetic to the specificities of women's life experiences. One significant component of these women's subjectivities will be their European origins.

I explore also, however, the implications of an analysis of gender, rather than only of women as a discrete group, for a broader insight into the suffragists' success. In this instance of close interconnectedness of suffragists and male politicians, the nature of the relationship of women to men assessed widely in these societies is crucial. The research plan I offer is driven by the same basic questions as earlier historians: Why did some women in these new white societies campaign actively for the right to vote? And why did enough male politicians decide to support it? But why did other women flock to reinforce the efforts of the female activists? And why did other men, to whom legislators ultimately were answerable, offer sufficient support to embolden the male politicians? What I offer here is a sketch of an interpretative model that might fruitfully be explored across this comparative dimension.

Interpreting women's suffrage on the margins

First, some suggested answers to the question of why suffragists could galvanise women's support: the intersection of evangelical Protestantism, the problem of alcohol and ideas of women's rights, remains crucial for understanding women's assertion of their need for the vote. In all of these communities, members of the Woman's Christian Temperance Union were by far the most numerous among the suffragists, and in a few, this was the sole organisation of suffragists. Only in the large Australian cities did separate suffrage associations exist, but these tended to be a few prominent women banded together without a grassroots membership. Despite some distance from the Woman's Christian Temperance Union, usually derived from greater education and sometimes wealth, these women differed only marginally from their temperance sisters in their formulation of pro-suffrage arguments. Indeed, they were not uncommonly teetotallers themselves, and Protestant Christians. To concentrate on the key issue of temperance and feminism is not, therefore, to overlook such suffragists.

The first point to consider about the WCTU is its American origins, and the diffusion of its agenda back into the Mid-Western states, and out of the United States, southwards to the Australasian colonies. The women's campaign against alcohol, which rapidly turned into a campaign against male drunkenness, in fact began in Ohio in 1873 to 1874 and swept through the Mid-West with amazing rapidity.[19] As women in small towns and large gathered outside saloons singing hymns, or invaded saloons to fall to their knees and pray, the historian of this movement, Jack S. Blocker, claims that it became the largest anyone had seen; extraordinary anger and bitterness surfaced about the maltreatment suffered by women at the hands of men. This was direct action by women, in the style of spontaneous outbursts shown by women in the bread riots of old. National suffrage leaders visited and pleaded with them to get up from their knees and instead fight for the vote; their behaviour amounted to anarchy, to disorder, and was undignified to boot. But it was not the national suffragists who won these activists, but a new organisation, the WCTU, which under a remarkable woman, Frances Willard, captured the anger generated in women by male drunkenness and gave structural understandings for women's legal and economic helplessness in the face of abuse, that broadened a temperance campaign into a women's rights campaign.

Some recent studies have sought to deepen our appreciation of the forces against which the WCTU pitted itself. In *Deliver Us From Evil* Norman H. Clark explored the particularly unlovely face of male drinking in the raw settlements of the Mid-West and the West, the shootings, male fighting, wife battering, child abuse, penury, and ill health that had their origins in drunkenness.[20] Alcohol was, he reminded us, a mood-changing drug, to which perhaps one in ten users was addicted: stripped of its trappings of civilised consumption, the mood changes could have frightening and even fatal outcomes. It was no fantasy of narrow-minded, provincial women that the drug, alcohol, was a threat to their life chances and those of the children of their community. Clark also showed the greed and corruption of the liquor industry as it joined the forces of big business in an age of increasing monopolistic capitalism, and the alignment of a wide range of reformers, unionists and socialists in the Progressive period against its power. Temperance and prohibition were not the goals of arch-conservatives. Frances Willard's biographer, Ruth Bordin, and the historian of the WCTU's international links, Ian Tyrrell, have emphasised the extent to which Willard represented the left–liberal values of the America of her time, as her Christian socialist stance, persuasively introduced to evangelical temperance women, left its mark on the WCTU.[21] Soon the organisation, by far the largest women's group of the late nineteenth century, was in the forefront of campaigns for changes not only in the law relating to marriage, to women's education and professional rights, but on equal pay, labour laws, protective legislation for children, peace and conciliation in place of war. This was the generosity of the platform imported back to small-town, Mid-Western temperance women, and this was the platform exported to the Western world outside of the United States as the WCTU developed its missionary outreach. This was the agenda that WCTU missionaries brought to Australia and New Zealand and to which, for reasons of their own, and in their own way, local women responded.

In an interesting recent article entitled 'Frances Willard and the

Feminism of Fear' Suzanne M. Marilley goes some way to suggest how the feminist genesis of the WCTU's advocacy of the vote could have eluded so many commentators. Whereas the national suffragists recruited women to persuade men that equal rights in America was nonsense if all adult women were excluded, Willard recruited women by arguing that by the vote they would gain 'home protection', by which she meant physical security for themselves and their children. There was a duality in liberation between the 'liberalism of rights' and the 'liberalism of fear', the latter focusing on removing violence and guaranteeing life protection. Mainstream liberals had assumed that men protected women: Willard pointed out that for some women, it was in fact men, even the men closest to them, who constituted the main threat to their security, through their physical and sexual aggression. Frances Willard 'designed and promoted a new and radical vision of the role of women in politics and society that put security, not rights, first', while she counterposed the utility of women's key roles. Thus she devised the strategy of using motherhood 'to mobilise mass numbers of women to undermine male domination'. Willard was able to show women how they could 'fashion meaningful forms of political participation without relinquishing their distinctive identities'.[22] By 1890 the WCTU had 150,000 due-paying members (200,000 if one counted girls and young women below voting age); by contrast the National American Woman Suffrage Association had a mere 13,000. Once drawn into the WCTU, temperance women were exposed slowly but surely to the wider liberalism of rights that Willard also promoted consistently and strongly.

'For God, Home and Humanity' ran the WCTU motto. God proved a powerful force for women in the Mid-West and the Australian colonies to legitimate their movement into a public campaign and their campaign for civil rights. It had to be a God reinterpreted, not the erroneous God that misguided biblical scholars had misinterpreted. This God recognised women as endowed with abilities and intelligence comparable with men, competencies equally needed in home, church and state. And when women's consciences were touched, this God expected from women a dedication equal to men's in righting the wrongs of this world.

The home about which the temperance activists fought was not the home of hallowed Victorian sentiment, but a home which needed to be purged of the anomalies that could exist when men strayed from their faithful paths as honourable husbands and fathers. And so married women's property rights, equal divorce laws, mothers' guardianship rights, women's rights to control sexual access and the frequency of reproduction, women's rights to a say in state regulation of prostitution and the plight of unwed mothers, were all matters temperance reformers could legitimately engage in under the umbrella of 'home protection'. From this reformed home would flow benefits for humanity as a whole – especially for men who, by the women's vote, might be freed from alcohol dependence and its attendant ills, and who would gain women as equals by their side in decision-making at every level. Even warfare would disappear, with nations living in peace when women, nurturant and peace-loving, entered the halls of power. Men in groups – in mining camps, on battle grounds, in Parliament – had a tendency to deteriorate away from women's influence. Women were the sensible, practical, stable sex, and women formed groups to fight for the good of all, not for negative ends.

How, or why, did men support the temperance suffragists? Again, I attempt an outline of some possible answers. The women well knew the male backlash against the vote that their stance could bring. A wily suffragist, the Franchise Superintendent of the state WCTU in Colorado, on the eve of the state referendum for the constitutional amendment urged fellow activists in Denver to a non-partisan stance: the goal right this minute was that men should vote for women's suffrage. She warned campaigners not to talk about purifying politics, or that the woman's vote would eliminate the liquor traffic, or that women would be rightfully eligible to stand for office: 'don't say the least uncomplimentary word about the men, don't antagonise anybody, not even women who say "woman's sphere is in the home" etc.' The suffragists might all believe that women's presence in politics would be a progressive influence, but this was not the time to press this point. 'But let us urge by voice and pen the truth (denied by no sane person) that father and mother, brother and sister, according to Genesis 1:26, have equal rights to record their sentiments at the ballot box.'[23] There was an activist who knew her oats. These were democratic communities, where men might respond to equal rights arguments. The referendum was successful.

But liberal men elsewhere had no trouble denying the concept of equal rights for women. If enough men in these communities supported women's suffrage for the vote to be passed into law, there must have been other influences at work. The answer, I think, lies in an exploration of the intersection of women's rights with the processes by which men in these communities were seeking to establish an identity for themselves in some ways in contra-distinction from men in the metropolitan cultures from which they had separated – yet in some ways, also, in collusion with those men of metropolitan cultures against a non-Anglo-British or Anglo-American world.

To begin with, there was the specific political culture, aspects of which were conducive to women's rights. In his comparative study of temperance and women's suffrage Ross Paulson argues that those places which gave manhood suffrage earliest were also places where men were likely to seek the intervention of the state to protect the interest of those suffering most disadvantage under developing capitalist economies.[24] Control of the liquor trade was among such policies. In these new societies in the 1890s, many men appeared to pride themselves upon their democratic characters, and they often boasted of their support for women's suffrage in these terms: the status-conscious East, or the class-ridden Mother Country, were said to be lagging behind the Mid-West, or the Australasian colonies. These frontier offshoots of the metropolis would show the way. As these men sought a mode of expression of a separate identity, the rights of women of their own group were caught up into a community entity versus the metropolitan culture. Gender divided men and women. But kinship and community also bound them together. For Mid-Westerners, Australasians, *their* women were sturdy pioneers, *their* women were the mothers of the new generation of citizens, *their* women were able and smart. Some frontier men, of course, were horrified at the notion that the women might become politically emancipated instead of continuing to shine their light within the four walls of home, just as some women opposed the vote because they felt that their traditional sources of power took many of them a long way. Sufficient men thought otherwise. Perhaps this goes some way to account for the understated, laconic acceptance with which so many men responded to the suggestion that women should share political power.

Women's suffrage, therefore, was not merely a democratic act in itself. Bringing women into political sharing was also seen as a means of pursuing urban social liberalism, or small-farmer or working-class political goals, in situations where all men could vote, and women's suffrage was fought for all adult women without property qualification. At this period of time there were a number of left-liberal and radical political movements where men were prepared and willing to give some encouragement to women's civil liberties. Before the referendum on the suffrage was held in Colorado, the national suffrage leader, Carrie Chapman Catt, noted that Denver was the best unionised city in the West, women voted in the unions, and there was scarcely an oppositional voice raised there. The Farmers' Alliances also allowed women to speak and vote at meetings, and it was the farming precincts that went solidly for the vote in the referendum.[25] Significantly, the Populist Party, which had links both to the Knights of Labor and to the farmers' organisations, were in power in Colorado in 1893 and in Idaho in 1896 – although in Idaho the Republicans and Democrats also endorsed the women's vote in the referendum.

In Australia and New Zealand the support of pro-feminist liberal men has been noted. Also to be acknowledged fully is the solid support of labour movements, wherever suffragists discounted a property qualification for the vote, and of many men in small farming districts. There were differences in the political cultures of rural and labouring men in the American West and the British colonies, but some parallels can be sustained.

But part of the process of defining identity in these new societies were men aligning themselves with the metropolitan culture in relation to other peoples, other races. The men of these new societies, having recently subjugated (or benefited from others' aggression towards) non-white indigenous peoples, were also keen to sustain white dominance against other possible incursions, of African-Americans, in one case, and of Asians from the populous countries to the north, in the other. Their womenfolk were not only mothers of new citizens, but mothers of the white race which would populate and dominate these new lands. The suffragists themselves might mention indigenous women with some humanitarian concern. But they themselves were not exempt from stressing their right to equal treatment from men on the basis of their common membership of the 'superior' Anglo-American or British race – an improved variety, of course, in the southern hemisphere, or so they believed.

In 1901 a member of the Legislative Council in New South Wales referred dismissively to women voters in the 'three small villages' of New Zealand, South Australia and Western Australia as of 'no practical significance'.[26] We may recoil from such disparagement – but what can historians globally learn from such a comparative study of women's suffrage in these small, white, marginal societies in the American West, Australia and New Zealand? For academics living in these communities, historical events are experienced as both marginal and central at one and the same time; we need not apologise for our engagement. But close attention to the languages of liberalism adopted on white frontiers, to arguments concerning women as architects of and as beneficiaries of state intervention in the social welfare of citizens, and to representations of gender in imperial projects and national identity are also important projects for metropolitan historians. The fortunes of women's suffrage in these marginal communities might be illuminating for historians of more complex societies in revealing more starkly what might otherwise be obscured in the wealth of texts with which they deal. Meanwhile the achievement of women's suffrage in New Zealand may be celebrated as a significant watershed in women's civil rights, explored as the occasion of some challenges to masculine power, acknowledged as a measure of social justice at a time of increasing state intervention, yet interrogated for racial supremacist implications. The full development of such a research endeavour could at the same time pave the way for issues concerning the emergence of New Zealand women's national identity to come to the fore.

1   E.g. Eleanor Flexner, *Century of Struggle*, Harvard Univ. Press, Cambridge, Mass., 1959; Catherine Cleverdon, *The Woman Suffrage Movement in Canada*, Univ. of Toronto Press, Toronto, 1950.

2   Carol Bacchi, '"First Wave" Feminism in Canada: The Ideas of the English-Canadian Suffragists, 1877-1918', *Women's Studies International Forum*, 5/6, 1982, 575-83.

3   Eileen Lorenzi McDonagh, 'The Significance of the Nineteenth Amendment: A New Look at Civil Rights, Social Welfare, and Woman Suffrage Alignments in the Progressive Era', *Women and Politics*, 10/2, 1990, 59-94, 60.

4   Carole Pateman, *The Sexual Contract*, Polity Press, Oxford, 1988; see also her *The Disorder of Women: Democracy, Feminism and Political Theory*, Polity Press, Oxford, 1989; and Anne Phillips, *Engendering Democracy*, Polity Press, Oxford, 1991.

5   Joan Scott, Paper presented to the Ninth Berkshire Conference on the History of Women, Vassar College, Poughkeepsie, NY, 11-13 June 1993.

6   Carrie Chapman Catt & Nettie Rogers Shuler, *Woman Suffrage and Politics: The Inner Story of the Suffrage Movement*, New York, 1923, 79.

7   See ibid., also Susan B. Anthony and Ida Husted Harper, eds, *History of Woman Suffrage*, vol. 4, 1883-1900, Ayer Co., Salem, NH, 1903; The National American Woman Suffrage Association, *Victory: How Women Won It: A Centennial Symposium 1840-1940*, H. W. Wilson, New York, 1940.

8   See Audrey Oldfield, *Woman Suffrage in Australia: A Gift or a Struggle?*, Dianne Scott, 'Woman Suffrage: The Movement in Australia', *Royal Australian Historical Society Journal*, 53/4, 1967, 299-322; Peter Biskup, 'The Westralian Feminist Movement', *University Studies in Western Australian History*, 3/3, 1959, 71-84.

9   Aileen Kraditor, *The Ideas of the Woman Suffrage Movement, 1890-1920*, Columbia Univ. Press, New York, 1965.

10   William O'Neill, *The Woman Movement: Feminism in the United States and England*, Allen & Unwin, London, 1969; William O'Neill, *Everyone Was Brave; A History of Feminism in America*, Quadrangle Books, Chicago, 1971; Andrew Sinclair, *The Better Half: The Emancipation of the American Woman*, Harper & Row, New York, 1965.

11   Nancy Cott, *Bonds of Womanhood: 'Woman's Sphere' in New England, 1780-1835*, Yale Univ. Press, New Haven, 1977; Mary Ryan, *Cradle of the Middle Class: The Family in Oneida County 1790-1865*, Cambridge Univ. Press, Cambridge, 1981; Ann Douglas, *The Feminization of American Culture*, Knopf, New York, 1977; Barbara Welter, ed, *Dimity Convictions: The American Woman in the Nineteenth Century*, Ohio Univ. Press, Columbus, 1975; Carroll Smith-Rosenberg, *Disorderly Conduct: Visions of Gender in Victorian America*, Oxford Univ. Press, New York, 1985.

12   Ellen DuBois, *Feminism and Suffrage: The Emergence of an Independent Women's Movement in America, 1848-1869*, Cornell Univ. Press, Ithaca, NY, 1978.

13   Alan P. Grimes, *The Puritan Ethic and Woman Suffrage*, Oxford Univ. Press, New York, 1967.

14   Anne Summers, *Damned Whores and God's Police: The Colonisation of Women in Australia*, Penguin, Ringwood, Vic., 1975; Miriam Dixson, *The Real Matilda: Woman and Identity in Australia 1788 to the Present*, Penguin, Ringwood, Vic., 1976. See Patricia Grimshaw, 'Writing the History of Australian Women' in K. Offen, R. Pierson, & J. Rendall, eds, *Writing Women's History: International Perspectives*, Macmillan, London, 1991.

15   Raewyn Dalziel, 'The Colonial Helpmeet: Women's Role and the Vote in Nineteenth-Century New Zealand', *NZJH*, 11/2, Oct. 1977, 112-23.

16   Patricia Grimshaw, *Women's Suffrage in New Zealand*, Auckland Univ. Press, Auckland, 1972; Phillida Bunkle, 'The Origins of the Women's Movement in New Zealand: The Women's Christian Temperance Union 1885-1895', in Phillida Bunkle & Beryl Hughes, eds, *Women in New Zealand Society*, Allen & Unwin, Sydney, 1980, 52-76. For my own further examination of the women's movement since 1972 see: 'Bessie Harrison Lee and the Fight for Voluntary Motherhood' in Marilyn Lake & Farley Kelly, eds, *Double Time*, Penguin, Ringwood, Vict. 1985; '"Only the Chains Have Changed"', in Verity Burgmann & Jenny Lee, eds, *Staining the Wattle: A People's History of Australia Since 1788*, McPhee-Gribble/Penguin, Melbourne, 1988; 'Tasman Sisters: Lives of "The Second Sex"', in Keith Sinclair, ed, *Tasman Relations*, Auckland Univ. Press, Auckland, 1988; 'In Pursuit of True Anglican Womanhood in Victoria, 1880-1914', *Women's History Review*, 2/3, July 1993, 331-48; '"Comrades and Equals of Men"? *Tocsin* and "the Woman Question"', in Susan Margarey, Sue Rowley & Susan Sheridan, eds, *Debutante Nation: Feminism Contests in the 1890s*, Allen & Unwin, Sydney, 1993; and Chapters 5, 6 and 8 in Patricia Grimshaw, Marilyn Lake, Ann McGrath, & Marian Quartly, *Creating a Nation*, McPhee-Gribble/Penguin, Melbourne, 1994.

17   Richard Evans, *The Feminists*.

18   Ruth Milkman, 'Women's History and the Sears Case', *Feminist Studies*, 12/2, Summer 1986, 375-400; 'Women's History Goes on Trial', *Signs*, 11/4, Summer 1986, 751-79; see also Nancy Hewitt, 'Beyond the Search for Sisterhood: American Women's History in the 1980s', *Social History*, 10, Oct. 1985, 299-345.

19   Jack S. Blocker, Jnr, 'Separate Paths: Suffragists and the Women's Temperance Crusade', *Signs*, 10/3, Spring 1985, 460-76; also his *'Give to the Winds Thy Fears': The Women's Temperance Crusade 1873-1874*, Greenwood Press, 1985.

20   Norman H. Clark, *Deliver Us From Evil: An Interpretation of American Prohibition*, Norton, NY, 1976.

21   Ruth Bordin, *Frances Willard: A Biography*, Univ. of North Carolina Press, Chapel Hill, 1986; see also her *Woman and Temperance: The Quest for Power and Liberty, 1873-1900*, Temple Univ. Press, Philadelphia, 1981; Ian Tyrrell, *Woman's World, Woman's Empire*.

22   Suzanne M. Marilley, 'Frances Willard and the Feminism of Fear', *Feminist Studies*, 19/1, Spring 1993, 123-46, 129.

23   Suzanne M. Marilley, 'Why the Vote? Woman Suffrage and the Politics of Development in the U.S. 1820-1893', unpublished Ph.D thesis, Harvard Univ., 1985, 387-8.

24   Ross Paulson, *Women's Suffrage and Prohibition: a Comparative Study of Equality and Social Control*, Scott, Forseman, Glenview Ill., 1973.

25   See Catt & Shuler, *Woman Suffrage and Politics*. For an important and useful discussion of gender analysis and politics, see Joan Scott, 'Gender: A Useful Category of Historical Analysis' in her *Gender and the Politics of History*, Columbia Univ. Press, New York, 1988.

26   Cit. Raewyn Dalziel, Review of Oldfield, *Woman Suffrage in Australia*, NZJH, 27/ 2, 1993, 233.

3

Presenting the Enfranchisement of New Zealand Women Abroad

RAEWYN DALZIEL

The enfranchisement of New Zealand women in 1893 was an event of international significance. In all countries with an active suffrage movement a spotlight was focused on New Zealand women in a way that had not happened before and has not happened since. This spotlight was also a searchlight. Suffragists and anti-suffragists abroad eagerly queried how the vote had been won and what changes it had produced. The New Zealand example, it was hoped, would reveal hitherto inaccessible truths about women's suffrage.

This chapter will look first at those people who recounted and interpreted the New Zealand suffrage story to an off-shore audience, mainly in England and America. It will examine the development of a narrative explanation of the process of enfranchisement and the incorporation of New Zealand's women's voting experience and political activity into the suffrage debate. It will be argued that the impact of the New Zealand victory was made problematic by competing versions of the event and its aftermath, and by the role of New Zealand as a colony shaping its political and national identity. The presentation of the suffrage raised issues of women's agency, their nature, and role, involving a politicisation of gender that left New Zealand women's citizenship and political status in an ambiguous position.[1]

Telling the New Zealand suffrage story
Although Wyoming and Utah had enfranchised women at the state level before 1893, their experience did not enter the suffrage debate to anything like the same extent as New Zealand from 1893 and, a year later, South Australia. Whereas the New Zealand campaign had borrowed arguments and strategies from writers and movements overseas, the situation was now reversed with an analysis of the New Zealand victory becoming part of the international debate. With New Zealand as a witness to the results of women's suffrage, the arguments became less abstract, the effects of

women's suffrage no longer hypothetical.

Overseas audiences learned about New Zealand women's suffrage from many sources. Suffragists and anti-suffragists, politicians, political theorists, social reformers and journalists talked and wrote about the event. Some of these people were New Zealanders or knew the country well; some had made brief visits and others had no personal knowledge of the country or of its people. The first reports were received by telegraph, largely gleaned from the local press. Within a very short time these accounts were supplemented by lengthier articles published in the daily and weekly press, in suffrage periodicals, such as, in America, the *Woman's Journal* and, in Britain, the *Englishwoman's Review*, and more widely read journals such as the *Nineteenth Century*.

Almost simultaneously New Zealand suffragists and politicians travelled abroad and gave press interviews, spoke at suffrage rallies and published their views in a variety of ways. Sir John Hall, for instance, paid to have 1200 copies of a fourteen-page speech he had delivered in Parliament in 1890 printed in London by the Women's Printing Society. These were presented to the Central Committee of the National Society for Women's Suffrage (CNSWS) for distribution.[2] Kate Sheppard and Sir George Grey visited Great Britain in 1894 and a parade of New Zealanders followed them over the next twenty years. Maud and William Pember Reeves lived in London from 1896, the Premier Richard Seddon visited in 1897 and 1902, the Colonial Treasurer, Joseph Ward, in 1895 and several times in the early 1900s when he was Prime Minister; suffragists Edith Searle Grossmann and Anna Stout spent some years in London and Ellen Ballance, Kate McCosh Clark, and Sarah Cohen visited more briefly. The former politician, Hugh Lusk, settled in the United States; George Fowlds and Frederick Frankland visited; and some of the travellers to London passed through. The travellers also came to New Zealand – Samuel Clemens, Jessie Ackermann, Henry Demarest Lloyd, Sidney and Beatrice Webb, André Siegfried, Philip and Ethel Snowden, Margaret Hodge and Harriet Newcomb, among others.

As the leader of the New Zealand suffrage movement, Kate Sheppard attracted considerable attention on her visit to Great Britain in 1894–5. The British suffrage movement greeted her warmly. She spoke to a large meeting of combined London suffrage and temperance societies on 9 June 1894, a meeting of over 500 people organised by the Central Committee of the National Society for Women's Suffrage the following month, to a number of local suffrage societies and at the Third Biennial Convention of the World's Women's Christian Temperance Union in June 1895. The

Women's Signal, journal of the British Women's Temperance Association, published an article she had written on women's suffrage and the *Echo* carried a long interview with her in August 1894. Other newspapers reported her visit and speeches on women's suffrage. Sheppard visited Isabella Somerset and Frances Willard of the WWCTU at Somerset's cottage in Reigate and had meetings with British suffragists Millicent Fawcett, Ursula Bright, Eva McLaren, Mary Priestman and Helen Blackburn. She returned to England in 1903 and again in 1908, on the latter occasion travelling through the United States and meeting leaders of the American movement. On these trips she re-established contact with the British and European movements and spoke at several small suffrage gatherings, but health and personal problems prevented more extensive involvement. A paper she prepared for the quinquennial meeting of the International Council of Women, held at Berlin in 1904, was later published, along with several 'testimonials' from leading New Zealand men, by the International Women's Suffrage Alliance as *Woman Suffrage in New Zealand*.[3]

The other major New Zealand suffragist to contribute to the debate in Britain was Anna Stout. Stout arrived in London in April 1909 and stayed for over three years. Away from New Zealand, where her husband was Chief Justice and where she had fallen out with southern leaders of the suffrage movement, Stout's interest in suffrage rekindled.[4] She came to the attention of the British suffrage movement when *The Times* published her defence of New Zealand's suffrage in November 1909. This letter was reprinted as a leaflet by the Women's Printing Society and was often quoted in suffrage literature. She was interviewed by Adela Pankhurst for *Votes for Women*, the journal of the Women's Social and Political Union (WSPU), and joined several WSPU demonstrations and rallies. She wrote a leaflet for the Conservative and Unionist Women's Franchise Association and articles for *Votes for Women* and the *Englishwoman*. In 1912 she engaged in a controversy in *The Times* with Lord Glasgow, a leading anti-suffragist who had had the misfortune to be Governor of New Zealand when women's suffrage was enacted.

New Zealand politicians passing through Britain after 1893 made widely reported speeches on women's suffrage, some of which were reprinted in suffrage pamphlets. William Pember Reeves discussed the suffrage in two books on New Zealand published in London. Other books were published by overseas visitors to New Zealand. Very often these visitors were attracted by the social and economic legislation of the Liberal Government and included commentaries on women's suffrage in their accounts of the country. Samuel Clemens, for instance, reproduced facts and figures on women's voting to show that women were genuinely interested in politics.[5] At least one American, Professor Frank Parsons, Director of the Department of History in the Bureau of Economic Research in Washington, produced a book on the country without ever seeing it. His *Story of New Zealand*, was published in The Equity Series in 1904. Parsons was an enthusiastic promoter of New Zealand as an example of evolutionary progress concluding: 'The Island Commonwealth has shown the way to the solution of the great problems of wealth diffusion and equalization of opportunity. A new civilization has come. A new age has dawned. New Zealand is the birth place of the 20th Century.'[6]

New Zealand women's suffrage thus became an integral part of the literature on New Zealand and on women's suffrage. It was discussed in books, journals, and newspapers. Suffrage pamphlets and leaflets, such as the Equal Suffrage and the Political Equality Series published by the National American Woman Suffrage Association (NAWSA) in the 1890s and early 1900s, frequently focused on New Zealand. Most published accounts of the suffrage movement included a comment on New Zealand, even if it were only inclusion in a list of countries where women could vote.

Activist Antipodean women gained a sense of significance through their international links in temperance, suffrage and peace movements in the 1890s and early twentieth century but the telling of the suffrage story was not simply a desire on the part of New Zealand to parade on a wider stage, the province showing the way to the metropolis. When the suffrage legislation passed, congratulations flooded in from other suffrage movements and New Zealand suffragists were urged to share their experience with the rest of the world. The *Woman's Journal*, the periodical of the NAWSA, shared the view, widely held in American reform circles, that New Zealand was an 'enterprising and progressive community' which had become an 'object of interest all over the civilised world'. The editor, Henry Blackwell, sent congratulations to 'our fortunate sisters of the Antipodes. . . the first to vote for what might be called a real Parliament in a practically independent State'.[7] In 1895 Mary Priestman told Kate Sheppard that there was 'scarcely anything that does more good to women's suffrage in England than seeing those who speak from personal experience'.[8] Carrie Chapman Catt, delivering her annual address to the convention of the NAWSA in 1902, referred to New Zealand and Australia as 'great democracies where self-government would be carried on with such enthusiasm, fervour and wisdom, that they would give lessons in methods and principles to all the rest of the world'.[9] At the end of 1906, when urging New Zealand to join the International Woman Suffrage Alliance (IWSA), Catt stressed that 'since New Zealand has the suffrage it is important that all the world should know about it'.[10] Alice Zimmern's *Women's Suffrage in Many Lands*, published in 1908, claimed that 'In Europe and America we may watch the struggles and aspirations after freedom, but we must turn to the Antipodes to see the achievement . . . .'[11] and in opening the 1908 conference of the IWSA, Aletta Jacobs expressed her appreciation of

> our Australian and New Zealand sisters, who have not hesitated to come from the antipodes and this only to help the women of the less favoured countries to attain the same position in the State, which they themselves already occupy. The action of these delegates shows a generous feeling of solidarity, – and by the manner in which the women of their country use the ballot, they facilitate, more than they can imagine, the work of their sisters in the old world.[12]

The first resolution of the conference recorded the pride of delegates in 'the wise and beneficent use of the ballot by the women of New Zealand for the past fifteen years and by the women of Australia for the last six years, whose noble record largely assists the cause of woman suffrage in all other nations'.[13]

A gift or a struggle?

The initial interest was in the process of enfranchisement. In the years before World War I this process became the subject of a contested narrative, affecting its position in New Zealand history and historiography for the next sixty years. Despite a seven-year concerted campaign and some of the most numerously signed petitions in New Zealand history, the narrative that became dominant went like this. The majority of women in New Zealand had not wanted the vote; there had been no franchise campaign worthy of the name; in some towns prohibitionists had got up an agitation; but in the end the suffrage was the result of a parliamentary process which ultimately saw a couple of anti-suffragists cross the floor in a party manoeuvre and women found that they were able to go to the polls in the 1893 general election. As can be clearly seen, this version of events queried women's political awareness, denied their agency and made them passive recipients of political rights. It was a version that undermined the capacity of the New Zealand victory to vitalise campaigns in other countries, making it contingent on a particular set of political circumstances rather than on a hard-won recognition of fundamental rights.

This narrative emerged very early in the post-suffrage phase and was widely spread overseas. In February 1894 the *Nineteenth Century* published an article by an Auckland doctor, Robert Bakewell, in which he claimed there was 'absolutely no wish for the franchise amongst the immense majority of women, even up to a few weeks before the passing of the Act'. A few 'wild women . . . mainly fanatical Prohibitionists' constituted the women's associations which had small meetings in the main towns. Doing his own research, Bakewell could not find 'one woman in favour of granting the franchise', and yet, surprisingly to him, 'thousands signed the petition in favour of it'.[14] Millicent Fawcett was quick to respond with an article in the March issue of the *Contemporary Review*. She exposed several inconsistencies in Bakewell's argument but did not question his account of the campaign. Perhaps she felt it was beneath contempt for she had already, at a large suffrage gathering the previous November, referred to the thousands of women registering to vote in New Zealand, 'thus contradicting those who assert that "women do not want the Franchise"'.[15]

When the suffrage supporters arrived in London in 1894 they reported the activities of the suffrage movement. Grey for instance praised the Aucklander Amey Daldy, 'the President of the women's organizations' for her work towards the vote.[16] Hall told the *Westminster Gazette* the women's vote was won 'by persistently keeping the subject before Parliament and the country . . . . We have been very fortunate . . . in those who for the last fifteen years have advocated and prepared the public for the Parliamentary enfranchisement of women'. Hall was in fact thinking of the parliamentary supporters of the franchise but he went on to speak of the women who had kept 'the subject at all times before the public, not in a hysterical, but in a sensible and level-headed manner'.[17] Kate Sheppard made a point of describing the suffrage campaign, telling a CNSWS audience that women had worked since 1886 'in unison and with method', forcing a wide social and political discussion of the suffrage.[18] This produced a *Pall Mall Gazette* headline, 'An Awful Suggestion from New Zealand', with a mocking story, warning British politicians of the consequences if British women adopted the same tactics.[19]

The next few years saw the women's campaign fade from the narrative. In 1895 the *Westminster Review* published a claim that 'Voluntarily, without agitation on the part of the great majority of unfranchised women, the right was granted to them by the men'.[20] Hugh Lusk, a former member of the House of Representatives who left the country in 1890 for the United States where he made a career out of writing on New Zealand progressivism, claimed in 1897 that women's suffrage 'was not the result of female agitation, either through the press or on the platform. There were no "Women's Rights" Leagues organised; nor was any public attempt made to denounce the selfishness of men, or to magnify the virtues and intellectual powers of women.' Lusk explained the suffrage as a series of gradual steps towards the incorporation of women in the body politic, first through education and licensing boards and local bodies. 'In this way public opinion in New Zealand advanced step by step, uninfluenced by declamation, or arguments based upon theories which must, in their very nature, be open to question, but moulded gradually by the results of experience, and feeling its way by practical methods to a practical result.'[21] Lusk's version drew veracity from his support of women's suffrage: his writings on New Zealand received extensive coverage in the *Woman's Journal* and were reprinted by the NAWSA.

The most influential writer on the subject however was William Pember Reeves. Reeves was widely read, highly intelligent and opinionated. He had been a journalist in the 1880s, entered Parliament in 1887 and was a cabinet minister in the Liberal Government from 1891 to 1896. Reeves supported women's suffrage, although he was well known for his argument that only women who were qualified to enter a university should be enfranchised.[22] Appointed to the Agent-Generalship in 1896, he was based in London for the rest of his life. With his wife, Maud, Reeves moved in circles of left-wing Liberal politicians and the Fabian Society. Both became sought-after speakers on the suffrage circuit. Extracts from Reeves's speeches frequently appeared in British suffrage pamphlets.

Reeves reached his largest audience with his books, *The Long White Cloud*, first published in 1898, and the two-volume *State Experiments in Australia and New Zealand*, published in 1902. Both books were frequently plagiarised by other writers on New Zealand, including writers on suffrage. Reeves, from a position of authority and with credentials validated both by his native country and by the suffrage movement, commented at length on the suffrage. He saw women's enfranchisement as a 'remarkable constitutional change', but one achieved with little opposition or debate.[23] It had scarcely been an issue in the 1890 general election, the electorate was surprised to learn that a majority in the House of Representatives supported it and the Opposition went along in the hope that women's votes would defeat the government.[24] Women's suffrage in the Antipodes was not 'an intellectual uprising by enslaved Women against the ancient and fraudful rule of tyrant Man. . . the main motives behind the movement were ulterior. They may have been very good motives – some of them were; but they were not the motives that swayed John Stuart Mill.'[25] Most women in New Zealand belonged to the class of those who had political power thrust upon them rather than to the class of those who were born to it or who achieved it.[26] The suffrage passed narrowly 'given freely and spontaneously, in the easiest and most unexpected manner in the world, by male politicians, whose leaders for the most part, had been converted to faith in the experiment by reading the English arguments so gallantly but unavailingly used by Mill and others in controversies on the other side of the earth.' 'No franchise leagues', wrote Reeves, 'had fought year after year, no crowded meetings had listened to harangues from eloquent and cultured women with intellects and powers of expression protesting even more effectually than their words against the political subjection of their sex. No New Zealand female orator or leader of women could by the most polite exaggeration be said to have stood in the forefront and borne a leading part in converting public opinion and swaying public feeling.'[27] According to Reeves, New Zealand women were politically unaware and unsure of themselves; apart from occasional involvement in local body and school affairs they 'knew nothing of public life, and public life knew nothing of them'. Reeves thus accepted the crudest polarisation of the public and the private, admitting none of the connections between the 'services' that women performed 'as housewives and mothers' and their role as citizens of the state.[28]

Reeves had a strong influence on other commentators. Henry Demarest Lloyd wrote that women's suffrage had 'come almost without notice and without agitation'.[29] Siegfried, the French socialist who visited New Zealand in 1899, recognised the work of women suffragists, although adopting Reeves's argument that the vote was the result of political expediency rather than of principle or of popular pressure.[30] Parsons borrowed, unacknowledged, some of Reeves's more memorable phrases relating to the granting of the suffrage. Yet other accounts existed to set aside those put forward by Reeves. Kate Sheppard and Millicent Fawcett tried to counter Reeves's testimony. Sheppard described his account as 'utterly false and misleading' and Fawcett asserted

> It is a mistake to represent that women's suffrage was brought about in New Zealand suddenly or, as it were, by accident. The women of New

Zealand did not, as has sometimes been said [and here she quoted from Reeves] wake up on a fine morning in 1893 and find themselves enfranchised. . . . Sustained, self-sacrificing, painstaking and well-organised work for women's suffrage had been going on in the colony for many years.[31]

Jessie Ackermann, the American temperance reformer and suffragist, restored women to the action in her pamphlet *What Women Have Done with the Vote*. William Sidney Smith, son, husband, and brother of suffragists, published a series of articles on the history of suffrage in the *White Ribbon*, journal of the WCTU, in 1901–2. These were reproduced and referred to in overseas journals at the time but achieved none of the authority of Reeves's account. Even when Smith, outraged at Reeves's denigration of the movement, published the articles locally as a book entitled *Outline of the Women's Franchise Movement in New Zealand*, his narrative sank into oblivion. The writing from within the suffrage movement had little impact outside the movement and almost none on the writing of political history until the 1970s.

Later historians have speculated on why Reeves should have presented such a misleading account. Certainly he was no friend of the Women's Christian Temperance Union (WCTU), which spear-headed the campaign, and he was engaged on a diplomatic mission to promote the trade and protect the credit of his country. He may have thought both required an image of compliant womanhood. But gender, class and personal issues also seem to be relevant. Grimshaw and Fry have suggested that Reeves was impressed by the sophistication and intellect of the women he met in the British movement and that New Zealand women suffered in comparison.[32] After some years in London Reeves was exhibiting the condescension of the expatriate and a blindness to the activities and aspirations of women in general and of the mainly middle-class women who had led the campaign in particular. I am inclined to think also that Reeves believed not just in the superiority of British over colonial women but in the superiority of all men over all women. He found it very difficult to come to terms with women's demands for autonomy within his own family and did not get on particularly well with elite women. He would probably have preferred to retain a traditional set of gender relations but intellectually could not support these.

Women's suffrage in New Zealand fractured the solidarity of women as a disenfranchised group. Although New Zealand women were incorporated into the global sisterhood that western suffragists frequently talked about, they were there on privileged terms. In the hope that their success might assist other women to get out of the pit, a dialectic developed in which the New Zealand experience was called on to counter the arguments of the anti-suffragists. This dialectic focused on four main areas: women's use of the vote, the conduct of elections, the influence of the vote on women and gender relations, and the impact on politics and the empire.

Women's use of the vote

The claim that most women did not want the vote and would shun the ballot box was a favoured argument of all anti-suffragists.[33] Politicians often disingenuously claimed that if women demonstrated their desire for the vote they would give way gracefully. The test was never freely offered to women: women could not vote in referenda on the suffrage. New Zealand women provided a shining example of voters. They had six weeks to register before the first post-suffrage general election. Over 78 per cent of the adult women, that is, 109,461, did so. On polling day 90,290, nearly 83 per cent of enrolled women voted. The percentage of women voters was higher than that for men, but as the male roll had not been revised before the election some doubts exist over the real comparison. These statistics were widely publicised in Great Britain and the United States and, when the 1896 and 1899 general elections produced similar patterns, a sustained argument could be mounted that women were keen to influence the outcome of elections.[34] Opponents might argue that women were a minority in New Zealand, and thus the country was protected from the full force of a female vote, but they could not argue that women would not vote.

The conduct of elections

The New Zealand case also provided evidence on the safety of elections conducted under women's franchise. Nineteenth-century elections, although becoming progressively more respectable, were nevertheless associated with disorder at public meetings and polling booths, with drunkenness and bribery.[35] The anti-suffragists claimed that women should not be exposed to such behaviour. Pro-suffragists expressed the conviction that women's involvement would improve the electoral environment. From New Zealand came a unanimous view that electoral behaviour had improved as a result of women's voting. In London in 1894 Grey claimed that 'the conduct of the people at the hustings [during the 1893 general election] was such as had never happened before'; Hugh Lusk repeated reports 'that there has been a marked and increasing improvement in the proceedings of all kinds, from the public meetings and platform speeches to the quiet and orderly conduct of the voters on election day'.[36] In 1907 the Prime Minister declared to Carrie Chapman Catt that 'The old evil memories of election day, the ribaldry, the fighting, have been succeeded by a decorous gravity befitting people exercising their highest national privilege' and Kate Sheppard claimed, 'The election day is made a closed holiday by law, public houses are closed, and the general aspect is that of a fete day. . . . '[37] Such statements were quoted frequently as in an Equal Suffrage leaflet published in 1898 in the United States, 'Equal Suffrage Promotes Good Order'.

Those who hastened to reassure doubters that women could vote in safety often drew analogies between voting and women's more usual occupations. The threat of the poll was nullified through feminisation. Seddon, in 1902, stated 'since women have had the franchise, we close the hotels, canvassing is stopped, electors are not interrupted on their way to the poll and the entrance to the poll – all is safeguarded in such a way that a woman can go with the same safety and propriety to vote for a Member of Parliament as though she were going to a place of worship.'[38] Richard Oliver extended the analogy to the secular world: 'I know from my own observation, that it is as easy for a woman to vote at a polling place as to visit a shop in the ordinary way.'[39] Ethel Snowden, who visited New Zealand in 1914, used the same analogy: 'Women go to vote as they go to market.'[40] The franchise extended women's access to public places but in the process these places were metaphorically transformed. Voting became one of the most ordinary of everyday events.

The influence of the vote on gender relations
But if women voted and voted safely what about the impact on gender relations? Did women's franchise create sex antagonism? Did it mean that women neglected their husbands, children and homes? Did women's contractual relationship to the state imperil the pre-existing sexual contract that Carole Pateman has argued was at the root of gender relations?[41] In New Zealand suffrage advocates had argued from time to time that pioneering conditions had led to a more equal sexual partnership than in older European societies. The notion of a more independent and less conventional womanhood was a significant part in the construction of the identity of a settler nation, progressive and distinctive from the old world. The economic and social contributions made by freer women to the settler communities were grounds for claiming the vote; in Maori society women could claim mana and authority through their descent

lines and land ownership.[42] Nevertheless the threat of discord between men and women and the notion that women would unsex themselves by participating in politics had been fundamental objections to the suffrage. The collapse of the separation between the private and the public sphere betokened by women's votes was the hardest fear of all to offset.

Once the test was applied, New Zealand voices reassured the outside world that the vote had not destroyed traditional gender roles. The vote had not 'unsexed women, or made them quarrel with their husbands', Reeves told his readers in *The Long White Cloud*.[43] Seddon explained to a delegation from the Central Society for Women's Suffrage in 1902 that his fear

> that woman would be dragged from the high pedestal on which I had always loved to see her, and by entering politics would be drawn into a vortex and not escape without losing that feminine modesty which every true woman must admire and appreciate has proved unfounded. . . . She has not been in the least unsexed; she stands higher today in my opinion than previously.[44]

Women now had 'a wider sphere of action, and, with experience and opportunities, she is now less inclined – she is certainly not forced – into that narrow limit which. . . has been detrimental to the women of the Empire. She has larger and deeper questions to think over; she has to use her influence in respect thereto'.[45]

His successor as Prime Minister, Joseph Ward, in answer to a series of questions from Catt, stated that 'making a pencil mark on a voting paper once in three years has [not] resulted in any loss of grace or beauty among our women'.[46] Anna Stout developed Mill's argument, stating that women's suffrage had led to a new sense of responsibility among women and made 'true comradeship' between men and women possible.[47] The women's vote in New Zealand, she argued in a WSPU pamphlet, had never been a 'sex vote', and had not aroused 'any bitter sex antagonism'.

> The real power of the women's vote in New Zealand is not in opposition, but in its harmony and co-operation with the men's vote. A house divided against itself cannot stand, but the united and loyal comradeship of men and women has secured for New Zealand reforms in legislation which are making the Dominion a paradise for men as well as women and children.[48]

Nor, it was claimed, had women's suffrage had much effect upon women's domestic responsibilities. 'Essentialist' arguments in favour of women's suffrage had always played a significant part in the New Zealand campaign and the continuing dedication of women to their homes and families was now stressed. Seddon addressed the issue in a convoluted way:

> As to the neglect of duties and ties. I answer that point at once and say that, taking the mothers of our Colony, the children of our Colony – any comparison you like to make – those who, like myself, fear something of that kind, may find, as I did, their fears to be groundless.[49]

G. W. Russell, another politician, claimed 'I have never once met with family dissension as the result of Women's Franchise'. In order to win the votes of women, 'politicians had to look at public matters from her point of view. When they did so, they saw that her ideal was not merely money, but happy homes, and a fair chance in life for her husband, her intended husband and her present or prospective family.'[50]

Early in the twentieth century it was claimed overseas that women's suffrage had led to declining marriage and birth rates in New Zealand. It is true that at the time there was public concern about both these so-called facts. The marriage rate had in fact not declined, but, as in most western countries, the birth rate had. This was not, however, the result of women's suffrage – the birth rate had begun to fall at least fifteen years before women got the vote. To counter claims about the birth rate the suffragists argued that, although falling, it was still high for a Western nation and had shown a slight recovery. They also pointed out that New Zealand women were improving the quality of child life by their successful attempts to reduce infant mortality and by the formation of Plunket Societies dedicated to child and maternal health.[51] In a reaffirmation of women's domestic role, Stout argued that 'as a result of the suffrage, New Zealand women have developed a much higher standard of womanhood and the duties and obligations of motherhood' and in 1910 an article in the Englishwoman's Review proclaimed that 'The women of New Zealand have solved for all time the problem of uniting social and political duties with domestic duties'. [52]

Some women commentators distinguished between women's domestic responsibilities and their personal autonomy. In 1894 Kate Sheppard told an English audience

> Some said 'Women's place is at home'. Others said giving women the vote would double the marriage vote. I said the home vote is always the best influence. Others still said, 'It will bring dissension on families.' But the

time has come when a man must allow his wife the freedom of her individuality; she is a human being with thoughts and aspirations.[53]

Sheppard's statement had explosive potential, later realised in her own life. When she readdressed this issue in 1904 she avoided personal relations, focusing on the conditions of working-class families by which she believed 'the social life of a country can be most accurately estimated. . . '. Her argument that homes had not been neglected was substantiated by her observation that 'nowhere are the working classes possessed of such pretty homes, such healthy, happy children, such comfortable and adequate clothing, and such freedom from care' as in New Zealand.[54]

The impact of women's suffrage on political life

In addition to the impact of voting on women, New Zealand was called as a witness to the influence that women had on political life. Women were not able to enter Parliament until 1919, a source of constant frustration to a number of suffragists who recognised this right as a key to effective action from the early 1890s. Given this, the possible influences were two: did women ensure that the men elected to Parliament were of a higher calibre, as was often argued by pro-suffragists, and did their votes result in better legislation?

Some writers believed that women placed personal integrity above issues in politics. Lusk told his American readers that in 1893 and again in 1896 women favoured candidates whose 'personal character stood high and whose political record was irreproachable'.[55] Anna Stout believed that women would not knowingly vote for men of unprincipled or immoral character and Frankland, in a speech to the WSPU in 1910, claimed 'It is notoriously less easy, even though unhappily still possible, for a bad man to get into Parliament since the more righteous half of humanity was admitted to the Franchise.'[56] Views on the character of politicians sometimes depended on the political affiliation of the commentator. Robert Bakewell was horrified with the result of the first post-suffrage election:

> The men elected are nearly all, with only one or two exceptions, of the most uneducated class in the community, either the lowest bourgeois or mere carpet baggers. They have displaced men of education and experience. Such are the results of the Female Franchise! It is to be hoped that it will be a warning to English Conservatives. We shall probably for some years to come be a dreadful object-lesson to the rest of the British Empire.[57]

More pragmatic politicians stood by the quality of New Zealand's MPs regardless of women's voting power. Seddon's view was that 'if there be the slightest doubt or tinge on the character of a man standing for the New Zealand Parliament, he may just as well save his time and his money. . . . [Women's Suffrage] has not had a *purifying* effect – because I claim that we have ever been pure – but it has a preventive effect'.[58] Ward maintained that 'this Dominion has always had a class of representatives in Parliament of which it has no reason to be ashamed, and which it apparently has no desire to change'.[59]

About women's more general influence on political and social life, apart from some early hostile commentaries, the tone was comfortingly re-assuring. Women's suffrage had not brought a revolution as predicted by its opponents. 'Things have not been turned upside down', said Sheppard. 'The country has not been brought to dire destruction, nor have all wrongs been righted. There has simply been an evolution.'[60] Stout maintained 'Experience has proved that the women's vote does not cause any revolution, though it steadily improves the conditions of life for the women and children, and thus ensures a strong, intelligent and progressive people, who do not shrink at shadows or cringe before imaginary dangers.'[61] New Zealand women saw domestic and political life as intertwined. The vote was their leverage on the political system; they intended to use it to improve the position of women and children, to shift the balance of power within gender relations, if not entirely to reconstruct these relations. So the main claim of New Zealanders, both men and women, for women's suffrage was its impact on social legislation. Sheppard told the *Echo* in London in 1894 that 'Generally, the result of women's suffrage has been to strengthen the movement for social and moral reform.'[62] Within three years Reeves maintained that women's suffrage had 'distinctly affected legislation. Laws have been passed because of it; other laws have been modified; changes have been made to the admin-istration of the public service; changes are being made in public opinion outside the public service.'[63]

The impact on legislation of women's votes remained a refrain of the story. Seddon claimed that the result of women's suffrage 'has been the best laws. . . . In reform – social reform – care of children, care of the aged, attention to the afflicted in the various institutions, in all these things women have a very deep interest.'[64] In an afterthought he appealed to the labour interest with a reminder that New Zealand's labour laws were among the most advanced in the world and had, as a result of women's suffrage, improved the position of working women. In 1907 the

Minister of Education and Public Health wrote that women's suffrage 'has made for the moral welfare of the whole community. Without being revolutionary, their influence has been on the side of progress and clean government.'[65] In 1904 Kate Sheppard prepared a list of legislation which showed 'a perceptible rise in the moral and humanitarian tone of the community' brought about by the 'greater civil liberty enjoyed by women'.[66] This list, ranging from legislation for equality in divorce to an Act to curtail smoking by minors, was cited regularly in the following years, in particular by Maude Royden in her 1912 pamphlet *How Women use the Vote* and Chrystal Macmillan in *Facts versus Fancies on Woman Suffrage* (1914). Although little of the legislation has been subjected to rigorous analysis to test the impact of the women's vote on its passage, the least of the claims, that women reinforced the impulse towards legislation which can be seen not only as reforming but also in some cases as socially restrictive and supportive of existing inequalities, seems indisputable. It should also be noted that a number of reforms advocated early in the century by the National Council of Women to further women's civil rights got a very short shrift from the politicians.

Racism and imperialism

The presentation of women's franchise as a shaping event in the nation's political identity focused almost exclusively on European women. Although Maori women had been enfranchised at the same time as European women and on equal terms with Maori men, this fact was rarely noted in overseas literature where the predominant view of New Zealand was as a British settlement colony. When it was, however, concepts of racial superiority were evident. Millicent Fawcett was openly racist in a speech in 1909 when she observed that all British women had been placed in a position of inferiority 'to that of the Maori women of New Zealand, who have more power in developing and moulding the future of the Empire than we have in England. Why should the Maori women be in a superior position to that held by the women of England?' she asked to applause and shouts of 'hear, hear'.[67] Such views illustrate Antoinette Burton's point that a conflict existed within the British suffrage movement over its 'international feminist vision' and its 'determination to lead the women of the world to freedom', between the belief in a global sisterhood and the belief in British superiority.[68] New Zealand suffragists said little in public about the role of Maori women, although some, such as Annie Schnackenberg, had lived for years among Maori. There was never any doubt among women of the WCTU that Maori women should have the vote and it is notable that Kate Sheppard queried statements that in the United States black women were forced to form separate branches of the Union.[69] In New Zealand Maori women both belonged to Unions with European women and had their own branches.

Fawcett linked her criticism of Maori women's suffrage to the control of imperial policy. Imperialism, racism and gender were related in complex ways. The burden of empire had long been an argument against women's suffrage. Expressed most starkly by Lord Curzon of the National League for Opposing Women's Suffrage, the argument drew on the old physical force theory that voters must ultimately be able to enforce their views in armed combat and on the notion that the responsibility of Empire was too great to be entrusted to women.[70] The physical force argument had never had much power in New Zealand where politicians did not control decisions of war and peace outside its borders. Even the Prime Minister argued in 1907 that 'When the contention, that women should not be entitled to vote because they cannot bear arms, is used by one whose mother could only make his life and citizenship possible by passing through pain and danger greater than the average soldier has to face, it becomes inconsistently ridiculous.'[71] Anti-suffragists such as Goldwin Smith believed that New Zealand as a colony and having 'no war-like neighbours', could run the risk of 'emasculating' its government,[72] but New Zealand could provide evidence of women's support of Empire. Anna Stout consistently addressed this issue by arguing that New Zealand women took a broad view of Empire and were 'quite as patriotic and Imperialistic in their sympathies as are those of the U.K.'. New Zealand's record of contribution to Empire was detailed – support of the South African war, support for compulsory military training, the gift of a battleship to the British navy, the emphasis on child health in the name of Empire, Ward's proposal at the 1911 Imperial Conference for imperial federation and an imperial council.[73] While Stout stressed the jingoism of New Zealand under women's suffrage, a small group within the post-suffrage women's movement publicly criticised New Zealand's involvement in the Boer War and the 1909 Defence Act which imposed compulsory military training. In 1911 Reeves referred to the 'growth of a feminine Imperial spirit' in New Zealand, but, apart from the tiny group of pacifists, New Zealand women do not seem to have been developing a critique of Empire.[74] They argued that they could be equal to men in their advocacy of imperial interests, not that they would bring a different spirit to Empire.

Colonial experiment

Although the New Zealand experience became a useful weapon in the propaganda war waged over women's suffrage there were factors that weakened its impact. New Zealand's enfranchisement of women was categorised as an experiment, to be seen in the context of other experiments made by new world countries. The campaign had been marked by a spirit of positive experimentation from its beginning. Mary Muller, in her 1869 *Appeal to the Men of New Zealand*, had asked why the country should not lead in women's suffrage: 'Why ever pursue the hard-beaten track of ages? Have we not enough cobwebs and mists to cloud our mental gaze, enough fetters to impede our onward progress here, that we must voluntarily shackle ourselves with old world prejudices in the way of Government?' 'This change is coming', she asserted boldly, 'but why is New Zealand only to follow? Why not take the initiative? She has but to inaugurate this new position, all will applaud. . . . It will be the spark to the train now laid in most civilized nations.'[75] In supporting an 1878 bill to enfranchise women ratepayers, William Fox, a former Premier, asked, 'Why should we not try this experiment? We are trying all sorts of experiments. . . let us try this experiment.'[76] And another former Premier, Sir George Grey, told the *Westminster Gazette* of his 'resolve to help England through New Zealand – to lead the way by colonial precedent. That is what the colonies will be doing more and more.'[77]

The sense of an experiment was strong in the overseas reception of women's suffrage. The *South Australian Advertiser*, which had watched New Zealand's Liberal legislation with keen interest, claimed that

> To the sociologist and student of political science, New Zealand is just now the most interesting part of this planet. In that country a series of experiments is being carried out that cannot fail to be highly instructive. Principles and theories are undergoing the test of practical application, which is employed with enterprising fearlessness. . . . Progress is swift enough to take away the breath of people who are accustomed to go slowly and are wedded to stereotyped ideas.[78]

Jessie Ackermann argued that conditions were 'more favourable to innovations in this new and democratic land than in the old world from which the early settlers came. The vastness of possibilities was conducive to experimental legislation. The very setting demanded a new social order and a departure from beaten lines.'[79]

For others the experiment showed the irresponsibility of New

Zealand's Parliament and the peculiarity of its social and political situation. Thus the backbencher, John Bevan, had concluded when suffrage legislation was introduced into the House of Representatives in 1887 that 'this is legislation gone mad. It is expedient, visionary, and without a precedent for its establishment.'[80] *The Times* found it easy to dismiss a colonial experiment

> in the adaptable atmosphere of colonial politics, constitutional changes have not all the significance that they have with us at home. There is room for experiment, which does not necessarily throw any very complicated machinery out of gear. . . . Should the change prove successful the future historians of the 'England of the Southern Hemisphere' will be able to claim the honour for her of having led the way in a great electoral reform. Should it fail, no serious mischief will have been done.[81]

The *Pall Mall Gazette* saw the experiment as rather more dangerous: 'How long', it asked, 'is New Zealand going to treat its constitution as an amusing toy . . . a great colony should have a little sense of responsibility?'[82] On the other hand the *Westminster Gazette*, which agreed that women's suffrage was a 'hazardous experiment', believed that New Zealand was 'in a condition to try experiments'. The country's excess of men 'divests the measure of much that would otherwise be startling' but, the *Gazette* warned, the disproportion 'will not be permanent, and it is difficult to go back on a concession'.[83] An anti-suffrage article in the *Westminster Review* of December 1894 claimed that New Zealand politicians had supported women's suffrage 'from the shallow vanity of men who wish to make a sensation by being the first to inaugurate what they believe to be a coming revolution'. [84]

Not only was the suffrage an experiment, but there were opponents of the vote who argued that it did not set a precedent. The New Zealand case was seen as contingent on circumstances that did not apply in other countries. Americans, apart from the progressives, reformers and socialists who saw New Zealand as the advance guard of the twentieth century, took little notice of what was happening in a small country thousands of miles away. In Britain there was a marked reluctance to follow the lead of a colony. C. W. Radcliffe Cooke, a Conservative anti-suffragist, sternly reminded the House of Commons in 1897, 'Generally speaking, the children follow the example of the parent, not the parents the example of the children. . . . When other civilised nations began to grant the franchise to women, it might be time for the most civilised nation in the world to see whether it would be well to follow their example.'[85] In an anonymous *Case against Woman Suffrage* published in London in 1909 it was argued that New Zealand and Australia were very different from Great Britain. Not only did they not have the responsibilities of Empire (responsibilities that the New Zealand government at the time was only too willing to share) but their populations were small and adult women were in a minority. The former New Zealand politician, John Cathcart Wason, now Liberal MP for Orkney and Shetland, could be relied on to provide lengthy testimony during any suffrage debate as to the petty state of public affairs in New Zealand. Whatever New Zealand suffragists might say, or whatever arguments might be mounted using their example, would never be accepted as a legitimate precedent for Great Britain in the minds of men such as Curzon or even the Colonial Secretary, Harcourt, who could not see the vote as a right and who believed fundamentally in the separation of the spheres.

Conclusion

The enfranchisement of New Zealand women became, in the years after 1893, a reference point for other suffrage campaigns, a case study for investigation, an example to be used. New Zealand women themselves became part of the imagery of the suffrage movement.[86] They were presented as icons of modest, responsible, orderly voters. The *Echo* informed its readers that Kate Sheppard was 'the very opposite of the bogey "advanced women" held up to frighten reformers'. She was described as handsome, well-proportioned and in glowing health, 'a good representative of Colonial woman at her best, strong physically and mentally'.[87] Adela Pankhurst began a profile on Anna Stout in *Votes for Women* by saying that Stout was a complete refutation of the notion that the vote would unsex women, a 'charming lady, on whom the sense of responsible citizenship has conferred an added dignity, and who glows with enthusiasm for political progress'.[88] New Zealand could be presented as an advanced nation, in which women's suffrage had improved electoral behaviour, caused little change in voting patterns (the Liberal government which introduced the suffrage bill remained in power for nineteen years after 1893), produced beneficial legislation, a widening of horizons for women and a better relationship between men and women.

It would be tempting but too simple to see the presentation of New Zealand women's suffrage abroad as selectively contrived to combat the case of the antis. After the initial shock of some social and political conservatives, and apart from the narrative of the campaign, the analyses of women's suffrage in New Zealand have a striking similarity. The vote was a symbol of women's equality and citizenship that had been given substance without creating disorder. In the interpretation of suffrage movements around the world, it is common to see New Zealand as situated at the moral reform end of the continuum. The contemporary presentation of the 1893 victory reinforced this view. However, as commentators at the time noted, justice and natural rights had always played a role in the New Zealand case. Kate Sheppard told an interviewer in London in 1894, 'we asked for the suffrage, not on the grounds that it would help us to advance social and moral reforms, but as an act of justice.'[89] In 1907 the Prime Minister wrote 'The main argument, however, which weighed with us, was that of right, of abstract right. If the foundation of government is the consent of the governed, it appears monstrously unfair that one half of the population should not be represented or have any share in it.'[90] The message about women's suffrage that New Zealand conveyed to the outside world was not only about New Zealand women and New Zealand's political life, but about social and political justice. Not to be heeded has always been the fate of small nations.

1   This paper has benefited from insights gained at the 'Suffrage and Beyond' Conference, in particular from papers presented by Patricia Grimshaw, Marilyn Lake and Jane Rendall. I would like to thank them for the ways they are reconceptualising our view of the suffrage.

2   *Speech on Women's Suffrage delivered in the House of Representatives, New Zealand by Sir John Hall, K.C.M.G, August 5th, 1890*, London, [1894]; *Report of the Executive Committee presented at the Annual General Meeting held in the Westminster Town Hall 6 July 1894*, Society for Women's Suffrage, Central Committee, London, [1894], Fawcett Library (FL), London.

3   For a further discussion of Kate Sheppard, see Judith Devaliant, *Kate Sheppard: A Biography*, Penguin, Auckland, 1992.

4   See Raewyn Dalziel, 'Anna Paterson Stout', in Dorothy Page, introd., *The Suffragists*, Bridget Williams Books, Wellington, 1993, 137-43; Roberta Nicholls, 'The Collapse of the Early National Council of the Women of New Zealand, 1896-1906', *NZJH*, 27/2, 1993, 159-61.

5   Mark Twain, *Mark Twain in Australia and New Zealand*, Ringwood, Vict., 1973, 299. This is a facsimile edition of *Following the Equator*, published in 1897.

6   Frank Parsons, *The Story of New Zealand*, Philadephia, 1904, 715.

7   *Woman's Journal*, xxiv/39, 40, 30 Sept., 7 Oct. 1893, 308, 313.

8   2 Feb. 1895, Kate Sheppard Papers, Canterbury Museum.

9   *President's Annual Address delivered by Mrs Carrie Chapman Catt, before the 34th Convention of the National American Woman's Suffrage Association and the First International Woman-Suffrage Conference held in Washington D.C. Feb. 12-18, 1902*, Schlesinger Library, Micro 947, No. 8930.

10   Catt to Sheppard, 3 Dec. 1906, Sheppard Papers.

11   Alice Zimmern, *Women's Suffrage in Many Lands*, London, [1909], 160; *Demand and Achievement: The International Women's Suffrage Movement*, NUWSS, London, 1912, 17, FL.

12   *Report of the Fourth Conference of the International Women's Suffrage Alliance at Amsterdam, Holland June 15-20 1908*, Amsterdam, 1908, 58.

13   Ibid., 5.

14   R. H. Bakewell, 'New Zealand under Female Franchise', *Nineteenth Century*, XXXV/CCIV, 1894, 268-75.

15   Millicent Garrett Fawcett, 'New Zealand under Female Franchise', *Contemporary Review*, LXV,

March 1894, 433-7; *Meeting in St James Hall... 1893*, 7.
16   *Woman's Signal*, 1/18, 1894, 289-90.
17   *Westminster Gazette*, 13 July 1894.
18   *Twenty-third Annual Report of the Central National Society for Women's Suffrage*, London, 1895, 18, FL.
19   *Pall Mall Gazette*, 12 July 1894.
20   Edward Reeves, 'Why New Zealand Women Get the Franchise', *Westminster Review*, 143/1, 1895, 35.
21   Hugh Lusk, 'Remarkable Success of Women's Enfranchisement in New Zealand', *Forum*, 23, April 1897, 176-7, 179. Also see Lusk's leaflet, *Family Suffrage in New Zealand*, Political Equality Series, NAWSA, New York, [1907] and his book, *Social Welfare in New Zealand*, London, 1913, 106-15.
22   *New Zealand Parliamentary Debates (NZPD)*, 68, 1890, 392.
23   William Pember Reeves, *The Long White Cloud*, London, 1898, 378, 380.
24   Ibid., 378-9; *State Experiments in Australia and New Zealand*, vol 1, London, 1902, 110-11.
25   *State Experiments*, 105.
26   Ibid., 103.
27   Ibid., 112-13.
28   Ibid., 113.
29   *Newest England. Notes of a Democratic Traveller in New Zealand*, New York, 1901, 340.
30   André Siegfried, *Democracy in New Zealand*, 2nd ed., edited by David Hamer, Victoria Univ. Press, Wellington, 1982, first published in 1914, 282-4.
31   *White Ribbon*, Feb. 1903, 6-7; Millicent Fawcett, *Women's Suffrage: A Short History of a Great Movement*, London, [1912], 36.
32   Grimshaw, *Women's Suffrage in New Zealand*, 115; Ruth Fry, *Maud and Amber*, Canterbury Univ. Press, Christchurch, 1992, 26.
33   For anti-suffragism see Constance Rover, *Women's Suffrage and Party Politics in Britain 1866-1914*, Routledge & Kegan Paul, London, 1967; Brian Harrison, *Separate Spheres: The Opposition to Woman Suffrage in Britain*, Croom Helm, London, 1978; Jane Lewis, ed, *Before the Vote was Won: Arguments for and against Women's Suffrage*, Routledge & Kegan Paul, London, 1987. For a different interpretation of anti-suffragism see Manuela Thurner, '"Better Citizens Without the Ballot": American Antisuffrage Women and their Rationale During the Progressive Era', *Journal of Women's History (JWH)*, 5/1, 1993, 33-60.
34   See for instance *Report of the Executive Committee presented at the Annual General Meeting held in the Westminster Town Hall, 6 July 1894*, NSWS, London, 1894, FL; *Reply of the National Officers*, Equal Suffrage Leaflet, *Woman's Journal*, Boston, VII/4, May 1900; Kate Sheppard, *Woman Suffrage in New Zealand*, IWSA, 1907; *The Australian Senate on Women's Suffrage*, NUWSS Leaflet, 1911; *Adult Suffrage in New Zealand*, People's Suffrage Federation Leaflet No.21; Chrystal Macmillan, *Woman Suffrage in Practice*, London, 1913.
35   See Raewyn Dalziel, 'Toward Representative Democracy: 100 Years of the Modern Electoral System', in A. Anderson *et al.*, *Towards 1990*, 56-7.
36   *Englishwoman's Review*, 16 July 1894; Lusk, 'Remarkable Success . . .', 180.
37   Sheppard, *Woman Suffrage in New Zealand*, 7, 15.
38   *The Right Hon. Richard Seddon, M.P., Premier of New Zealand on Women's Suffrage*, CSWS, London, 1902, 4-5, FL.
39   *Women's Suffrage in New Zealand and Australia*, CSWS, London, [1904], FL.
40   Ethel Snowden, 'The Women's Vote in New Zealand', *Ius Suffragii*, 9/8, 1915, 286-7.
41   Carole Pateman, *The Sexual Contract*.
42   See Raewyn Dalziel, 'The Colonial Helpmeet', 112-23; Angela Ballara, 'Wahine Rangatira: Maori Women of Rank and their Role in the Women's Kotahitanga Movement of the 1890s', *NZJH*, 27/2, 1993, 127-39.
43   *The Long White Cloud*, 380.
44   *The Right Hon. Richard Seddon. . .*, 7
45   Ibid.
46   In Sheppard, *Woman Suffrage in New Zealand*, 14-15.
47   Anna Stout, 'What the Franchise has done for the Women and Children of New Zealand, Part II', *English Woman*, VI/17, 1910, 129; on this aspect of Mill's work, see Mary Lyndon Shanley, 'Marital Slavery and Friendship: John Stuart Mill's *The Subjection of Women*' in Mary Lyndon Shanley &

Carole Pateman, *Feminist Interpretations and Political Theory*, Polity Press, Cambridge, 1991, 164-80.

48   Anna Stout, *Woman Suffrage in New Zealand*, WSPU, London, 1911, 5-6.

49   *The Right Hon. Richard Seddon...*, 8.

50   In Sheppard, *Woman Suffrage in New Zealand*, 18.

51   *The Times*, 19 Nov. 1909.

52   Anna Stout, 'What the Franchise has done for the Women and Children of New Zealand, Part I', *English Woman*, VI/16, 1910, 7; Stephen Guyon, 'Woman's Suffrage in New Zealand', *Englishwoman's Review*, XLI/CCLXXXIV, 1910, 13-15.

53   *Woman's Signal*, 14 June 1894.

54   'Effects of Women's Suffrage in New Zealand', 9, Sheppard Papers.

55   Lusk, 181.

56   'What the Franchise has Done. . .', 129; F. W. Frankland, *Woman Suffrage in New Zealand: A Speech delivered in the Queen's Hall, Langham Place, London on October 31st 1910*, WSPU, London, n.p., 1910, FL.

57   Bakewell, 275.

58   *The Right Hon. Richard Seddon...*, 5-6.

59   In Sheppard, *Woman Suffrage in New Zealand*, 16.

60   Ibid., 4.

61   *The Times*, 19 Nov. 1909.

62   *Echo*, 9 Aug. 1894.

63   *The Working of Women's Suffrage in New Zealand and South Australia: Speeches by the Hon. W. P. Reeves, Agent General for New Zealand and Hon. J.A. Cockburn, Agent General for South Australia*, NUWSS, London, 1897, FL.

64   *The Right Hon. Richard Seddon...*, 4, 10-11.

65   In Sheppard, *Woman Suffrage in New Zealand*, 21.

66   'Effects of Women's Suffrage in New Zealand', Sheppard Papers.

67   *Women's Suffrage. Wanted: A Statesman. Address delivered by Mrs Henry Fawcett, LLD, at the Athenaeum Hall, Glasgow, November 22nd 1909*, FL.

68   Antoinette Burton, 'The Feminist Quest for Identity: British Imperial Suffragism and "Global Sisterhood", 1900-1915', *JWH*, 3/2, 1991, 46-81.

69   Helen Hood to Sheppard, 21 Feb. 1905, Kate Bushnell to Sheppard, 24 Feb. 1905, Sheppard Papers.

70   See Harrison, *Separate Spheres*, 75.

71   In Sheppard, *Woman Suffrage in New Zealand*, 15.

72   Goldwin Smith, *Essays on Questions of the Day*, London, 1893, 218-9.

73   *The Times*, 19 Nov 1909; Anna Stout, *Women's Suffrage in New Zealand*, Conservative and Unionist Women's Franchise Association, London, [1911?]; Anna Stout, *Woman Suffrage in New Zealand*, 7.

74   Quoted in J. Malcolm Mitchell, *Colonial Statesman and Votes for Women*, Women's Freedom League, London, 1911.

75   [Mary Muller], *An Appeal to the Men of New Zealand*, Nelson, 1869, 4, 13.

76   *NZPD*, 28, 1878, 347.

77   *Westminster Gazette*, 19 June 1894.

78   Quoted in *Woman's Journal*, xxv/1, 1894, 5.

79   Jessie Ackermann, *What Women have Done with the Vote*, New York, 1913, 7.

80   *NZPD*, 57, 1887, 254.

81   *The Times*, 11 Sept. 1893.

82   *Pall Mall Gazette*, 13 Sept. 1893.

83   *Westminster Gazette*, 15 Sept. 1893.

84   Norwood Young, 'The Truth about Female Suffrage in New Zealand', *Westminster Review*, 142/6, 1894, 668.

85   *Great Britain Parliamentary Debates*, XLV, 3 Feb. 1897, 1186.

86   See Lisa Tickner, *The Spectacle of Women: Imagery of the Suffrage Campaign 1907-14*, Chatto & Windus, London, 1987.

87   *Echo*, 9 Aug. 1894.

88   *Votes for Women*, New Series, III/86, 1909, 66.

89   *Echo*, 9 Aug. 1894.

90   In Sheppard, *Woman Suffrage in New Zealand*, 15.

II

Australia and the Pacific

'Day of Mourning'. Aborigines Conference Day of Mourning outside the Australian Hall Sydney on 26 January 1938 protesting about the Australian 'white' sesquicentennial celebrations which overlooked the Aborigines' plight and lack of citizenship rights.
Man, March 1938. *Australian National Library*.

4

Why Didn't They Want to be Members of Parliament? Suffragists in South Australia[1]

SUSAN MAGAREY

How it happened

On 16 August 1894, the upper house of the South Australian Parliament, the Legislative Council, debated the Constitution Act Amendment bill, legislation to give votes to women. It was the eighth measure proposing to enfranchise women to have been considered in the South Australian legislature since E. C. Stirling introduced a motion in favour of votes for women in 1885.[2]

The August 1894 bill was the first that had not been encumbered with an array of provisions either to restrict women's access to the vote, or to use the question of enfranchising women in a distinct – though related – campaign to increase or diminish democratic citizenship among men. Earlier provisions attached to female suffrage bills proposed that the vote be extended only to women who were single or widows, not to married women whose rights were held to be subsumed in those of their husbands; that the vote be granted only to women over the age of twenty-five; or only to those women who owned enough property to have qualified them, had they been men, to have voted in elections for the Legislative Council (for which a property qualification was required until the 1970s). These last were the product of conservative efforts to shore up the power of property against the threats of the new-born Labor Party and its allies in the small 'l' liberal ministry of Charles Cameron Kingston. A final provision, that the whole question be submitted to a referendum, had defeated a similar bill in the previous year.[3]

The polarisation of parliamentary politics between the conservatives, on one hand, and the liberals and their Labor Party supporters, on the other, was new in South Australia at the beginning of the 1890s. Previously, the political scene had been dominated by personal and factional politics and rapidly changing ministries. But in 1890, the defeat of the nationwide Maritime Strike by the employers with the support of the state, prodded the United Trades and Labour Council (UTLC), the metropolitan unions, working men's clubs and democratic associations into organising for representation in Parliament, possible for working men since the introduction of payment for members in 1887.[4] Their joint committee set up in January 1891 became the administrative centre of the United Labor Party (ULP). By 1895 there were ten ULP candidates in the South Australian Parliament and internal organisation was stable. In 1904 the party's first annual conference created a ULP Council, separating the party from the UTLC. In 1905 the ULP was strong enough to form a coalition government headed by its leader Tom Price.[5]

The conservatives marshalled their forces as a defence against organised labour, creating a pressure group rather than a party. The National Defence League, formed in July 1891 and converted into a branch of the Australian National League (ANL) in 1896, endorsed candidates it favoured, but did not bind them to its programme. Nevertheless its influence dominated the Legislative Council for most of the 1890s, and in 1906 it combined with the Farmers' and Producers' Political Union (FPPU) for joint support and selection of candidates.[6]

However, political opinion in South Australia did not align itself exclusively with the two major organisations. On one hand, conservative discontent with the ANL's extremism spawned a number of liberal and independent groups, prototypes for the FPPU formed in 1903, and A. H. Peake's Independent Country Party. The latter, renamed the Liberal and Democratic Union in 1906, formed one half of the 'Lib–Lab' coalition government of 1905–10.[7] On the other hand, radical discontent with the moderation of the ULP found expression in many small, often short-lived democratic reform groups through which the labour movement explored visions of utopian alternative social orders, programmes and strategies to counter domination and exploitation. The district Democratic Clubs and Associations, the Land Reform Leagues, the Single Tax League, the Society for the Study of Christian Sociology, the Allgemeiner Deutscher Verein, the Working Men's Patriotic Association, the South Australian Fabian Society, the district Sociological Classes, and the Working Women's Trade Union and the larger and longer-lived Women's Christian Temperance Union – all were called collectively 'the Forward Movement' or the 'Reform Movement'.[8] In the early 1890s, they were all working strenuously for a '[d]istinct forward movement, lifting up instead of levelling down society'.[9] In the early 1890s the ANL feared the Forward Movement as much as, if not more than, it feared organised labour.[10]

From 1893 to 1899, the liberal Kingston government came from neither of the major political organisations, though it had strong support from the ULP. The Forward Movement's influence among urban electors undoubtedly contributed to Kingston's unprecedentedly long term in office; his government was one of the most progressive liberal ministries in all of the Australian colonies in the nineteenth century, and his six-year tenure made him the longest-reigning premier in colonial South Australia. Moreover, the Forward Movement's whole-hearted endorsement of the campaign for votes for women, and its readiness to publish speeches made by suffrage-campaigners in its weekly paper, the *Voice*, probably contributed to Kingston's decision to support women's suffrage, once it had been established that what the suffragists wanted was the vote on the same terms as men; he had voted against earlier measures for giving votes only to women with property.[11]

The 1894 bill had none of these property restrictions, nor restrictions based on age or marital status. It had only two clauses: one gave women the right to vote in elections for both houses of Parliament, on the same basis as men; the second excluded women from sitting in Parliament. Moreover, it had been introduced as a government measure. And it had been introduced into the Legislative Council where, following the elections for one-third of the members of that chamber early in 1894, there was – most unusually – a non-conservative majority, including six representatives who were labour representatives or sympathisers.[12]

By August 1894, opposition to the bill was getting desperate. One of its opponents was Ebenezer Ward, South Australia's 'silver-tongue', a man who had been sued for divorce by his first wife in 1866, was to be taken to court by his second wife in 1895 for failing to support her and their nine children adequately, and would arrive in the Legislative Council to oppose the Married Women's Protection Bill in 1896 so drunk that he could not read the statement on the paper in front of him.[13] He had been an enthusiastic opponent of female suffrage.[14] On 16 August 1894, he moved that the second clause of the bill – excluding women from sitting in Parliament – be struck out. It was an attempt to wreck the bill by rendering it unacceptable to the House of Assembly. But it was an attempt that failed. The amendment was carried.[15]

The amendment failed to unsettle support for the bill in the lower house, too. There, the only change made was the inclusion of a provision allowing women to vote by post. After various delays, considerable tension and continued lobbying by the suffragists, it was finally brought to a vote, on the morning of 18 December 1894. It was passed, by 31 votes to 14, the two-thirds majority necessary for a constitutional amendment. The house resounded to cheers, and some sexist sneering: '[i]t's a regular hen convention', shouted one defeated member, waving his arms at the government benches.[16]

There was a logic in this extension of democracy occurring first, in Australia, in the colony of South Australia. For unlike the other colonies, and unlike the imperial 'mother' country, Britain, South Australia had enjoyed not only manhood suffrage but also one man–one vote since self-government in 1856.[17] This meant that, once the property limitations attached to earlier female suffrage measures had been removed, the trade unions, the UTLC, and the ULP gave the 1894 bill their wholehearted support.[18] In the other Australian colonies the labour movement expressed sympathy with the women's aspirations, but refused to give them official support until they had succeeded in their own campaign to abolish plural voting, which allowed men to cast votes in every electoral district in which they owned property.[19] The exception was Western Australia where the formation of the Labor Party did not occur until 1901, *after* the passage of female suffrage legislation by the conservative government of John Forrest in an attempt to strengthen the urban conservative vote against the emergent labour movement of the goldfields.[20]

It was a logic which also had extensions that the South Australian legislators did not shirk. Manhood suffrage in South Australia had, at least in principle, also enfranchised Aboriginal Australian men. The 1894 legislation enfranchising women extended the suffrage to Aboriginal Australian women too. In 1896, Point McLeay, an Aboriginal settlement near the mouth of the Murray River, had its own polling station with more than 100 people on the rolls; 70 per cent of them voted in the election that year.[21] Ironically, perhaps, these electors also voted for the representatives who attended the Federal Convention of 1897. One of several held to draft a constitution for the federation of the separate colonies into the Commonwealth of Australia, this was the convention which resolved, despite protests from the South Australians, that Aboriginal Australians would *not* be counted in the censuses of the Australian population. So began the process by which Aboriginal Australians were excluded not only from the federal franchise, but also from the definition of human beings – until 1962.

South Australia's achievement of female suffrage in 1894 was, however, critical to the national enfranchisement of women in 1902. Lobbied by the suffragists, South Australian delegates to the Federal

Convention of 1897 threatened to forego federation rather than allow South Australian women to be *dis*-enfranchised in the federal arena.[22] Just as the achievement of votes for women in New Zealand in 1893 had given impetus and encouragement to the South Australian suffragists, so the South Australian victory, both at home and in the new Commonwealth, gave heart and hope to suffrage campaigners throughout Australia.[23] For once votes for women had been conceded for elections to the Commonwealth Parliament (1902), then most of the other states abandoned their opposition. Western Australia had passed female suffrage legislation in 1899. Following the Commonwealth Parliament's ruling, women were enfranchised in New South Wales in the same year, in Tasmania in 1903 and in Queensland in 1905. Only in Victoria was there continued concerted opposition, and that, too, finally gave up in 1908.[24] Moreover, the fortuitous South Australian precedent, a precedent that was not followed in the other Australian states until after World War I, in conceding to women the right to sit in Parliament – not merely to *elect*, but also to *become* legislators – when extended to the Commonwealth Constitution, established Australia on the cutting edge of democracy, ahead of everywhere else in the world.[25]

There can be no doubt that settler-Australian women wanted the vote, despite the counter-assertions of the press at the time, and of commentators since, from William Pember Reeves in 1902 to Ian Turner in 1967.[26] The absurd belief that Australian women had the vote 'handed to them on a plate' has died hard. But research carried out by historians of the late-twentieth-century Women's Movement, from Anne Summers in 1975 to Audrey Oldfield in 1992, has demonstrated the strenuous work that Australian women put into the suffrage campaigns – organising meetings, forming societies, writing speeches and delivering them, leading deputations to parliamentarians, securing signatures on petitions, making speeches, as Mary Lee said, at their own firesides.[27] They were not, it is true, subjected to the personal and systematic abuses that suffragettes in Britain encountered. No one in Australia, as far as we know, was driven to chaining herself to the railings of a Parliament building, or flinging herself under anyone's horse to draw attention to her cause. But that does not mean that they were passive recipients of a chivalrous gift.

Further, recent research suggests that far more Australian women wanted the vote than has been accepted by those, like Turner, who depicted the suffragists as exclusively middle class. As 'A Busy Mother' wrote, in a letter to the *Brisbane Courier* in Queensland in 1900: 'It is rather hard that because many of us mothers have not time to fight for the vote, it should be taken for granted that we do not want it.'[28] In South Australia, the ranks of the suffragists included not only such members of the Adelaide establishment as Rosetta Birks, daughter of the property-owning founders of the daily newspaper, the *South Australian Register*, and wife of the owner of a highly successful drapery store, but also Agnes Milne, a shirtmaker who wrote to the press under her own name.[29] There is no evidence from which to provide tables of statistics about the class composition of the suffrage campaign, but the evidence that does remain indicates numerical support that was broader than the narrow ranks of the urban middle class. The support of the UTLC and the Forward Movement for the Woman Suffrage League's demand for votes for women on the same terms as men suggests strongly that the campaign was popular among the working class, as does the WSL's insistence that what it wanted was 'woman suffrage irrespective of property or position'.[30] The petition in favour of women's suffrage, organised largely through the branches of the Women's Christian Temperance Union (WCTU), carried into the South Australian Parliament in August 1894 in a great roll, 400 feet long, bore no fewer than 11,600 names (the total population at the time was approaching 350,000); current research suggests that a great majority of those signatures came from supporters outside Adelaide, South Australia's capital city.[31] Moreover, in the first election in which South Australian women voted, in 1896, the percentage of those women enrolled who went to the polls (66.44 per cent) was marginally higher than the percentage of enrolled men who voted (66.33 per cent).[32] It might have been even higher, had the defeated industrialist conservatives not exerted pressure on the men they employed, letting them know that their jobs would pay the price if their wives were seen casting votes at the poll.[33]

Even if the majority of supporters of the women's suffrage campaign *had* been middle class, that fact would not necessarily render the campaign merely an elite concern of a privileged few. Such an argument relies on assumptions about identity politics which render individuals passive prisoners of a class structure defined by men's relationship to the means of production, and women's relationship to men. It is an argument that denies agency to those individuals, the possibility that they might change, and the capacity to act in ways that do not necessarily match their class ascription. As Kay Daniels and Mary Murnane argued of the Australian women's movement at the turn of the century: 'in pursuing their humanitarian and often moral goals, feminists were frequently thrust into confrontation with a society that revealed itself to be more complex, unyielding and contradictory than [their] progressive philosophy suggested'.[34] In South Australia, the moral concerns of some of the middle-class women in the Social Purity Society (SPS), formed in 1882, moved rapidly into the broader concerns of the Working Women's Trades Union, established in 1890, and the wide-ranging concerns of the Woman Suffrage League, formed in 1888.[35] Economically privileged women, pursuing goals that might have begun as middle-class philanthropy, found themselves confronting 'broader questions about the division of resources and the regulation of the economy'. The pursuit of a moral and humane society – the 'soft' politics of the women's movement – was capable of transformation into the 'hard' politics of foreign policy and welfare, politics that divided the parties.[36]

However, it is not so clear whether women wanted the right to become legislators or not. The Woman Suffrage League adopted a constitution in which the third provision explicitly stated that 'no claim is put forward for the right to sit as representatives', and Mary Lee, acknowledged leader of the suffrage campaign in South Australia, stressed that women did not want the right to be candidates, when speaking in a deputation to Premier Frederick Holder in 1892.[37] But the WCTU Convention, meeting in Adelaide in 1893, passed a resolution which declared the clause debarring women from becoming Members of Parliament 'unnecessary and offensive'.[38] The giant petition carried into the House of Assembly in August 1894, just as the third reading of the female suffrage legislation was about to begin in the Legislative Council, reproduced the first part of the constitution of the Woman Suffrage League; this called for votes for women on the same terms as men, but it left out the constitution's final clause which explicitly rejected the notion that women might want to enter Parliament themselves.[39] Elizabeth Nicholls, president of the Suffrage Division of the South Australian branch of the WCTU during the suffrage campaign, and Australasian president of that body from 1891, was to defend the South Australian women for having accepted more than they had asked for like this:

> I am sorry that any of our New South Wales sisters object to women having the right to sit in Parliament; we did not venture to ask for it yet but are very glad to have it, for while we are not anxious to avail ourselves of the right, we believe we shall be far more successful in securing laws for the good of our people if legislators know that in case they fail us we can enter Parliament and make the laws ourselves. . . . It must eventually come to that, for justice demands completely equal political rights and

opportunities for men and women, and the world will never be properly governed until the right to rule is not decided by sex or class, but by character and ability.[40]

Nevertheless, when Mary Lee and Catherine Spence were invited to stand for election in South Australia in 1896, both of them declined. Over the ensuing fifty-odd years, only fifteen women even contested seats in South Australian elections, and they were not successful. Not until 1959 did a South Australian woman gain a seat in the South Australian legislature.[41]

So we have a paradox. Women were proud of having gained this right, even if they had not sought it. But they were then not able to exercise it successfully for a further half century. Yet this should come as no surprise. After all, as North American feminist historians Nancy Cott and Joan Scott have both noted, in Joan Scott's words, 'The history of feminism is the history of women dealing in paradox, and of the radical impossibility for women of resolving the paradoxes with which they are presented.'[42] I want to explore two paradoxes raised by the question presented to the South Australian suffragists of women becoming legislators. The first is a paradox of establishing equal rights between bodies of different sexes. The second is a paradox of liberal democracy itself, a form of government that aspires to egalitarianism in profoundly unequal economic and social conditions. I will focus discussion of the first on Mary Lee, and discussion of the second on Catherine Spence, both women active in the suffrage campaign in South Australia. This is local history, no doubt, but I hope it is local history that will illuminate issues that are also found in far more global discussions of turn-of-the-century feminism.

Two suffragists: Mary Lee and Catherine Spence

Mary Lee arrived in South Australia on an extremely hot Monday, 15 December 1879, daughter of the Protestant ascendancy in County Monaghan in Ireland, widow of the organist and vicar-choral of Armagh Cathedral, mother of seven, three of whom had survived into adulthood.[43] One son, a lawyer, migrated to Adelaide, but became ill there, so Mary Lee, by then aged fifty-eight, migrated to Adelaide with her nineteen-year-old daughter, to look after him. He died less than a year later. Four years later, having turned from the Anglican church to the social reformist Primitive Methodists, Mary Lee erupted into the public world of South Australian politics.

Her first appearance was but a glimmer of what was to come.

Prompted at least partly by news from Britain of what the Roman Catholic bishop of Adelaide referred to as 'the scourge of child-prostitution, like that exposed by W. T. Stead and Josephine Butler', prominent South Australians formed a Society for the Promotion of Social Purity to lobby government to raise the age of consent for girls from thirteen to sixteen years. The society, usually known as the Social Purity Society (SPS), was initiated and headed by men, but had a 'ladies' auxiliary' – its Women's Committee – which included Mary Lee. These women continued to meet, after the main/men's body of the society had dissolved, following the success of their efforts in 1885, a success which contrasted sharply with the twenty-year campaign that feminist leader Rose Scott had to conduct before she achieved similar legislation in New South Wales.[44] By 1888 they had decided that women needed the vote if they were to achieve any change in the rights and welfare of women and children that concerned them. At the public meeting that constituted the Woman Suffrage League on 21 July 1888, a 'very nervous' Mary Lee spoke third, asserting that the 'women of South Australia were no shrieking sisterhood demanding women's rights. They simply asked for a modicum of power to assist in obtaining what were the rights of women.'

From that point on, though, this tiny plump woman, 'five feet nothing', became the guiding force and principal speaker in the South Australian women's suffrage campaign. Appointed co-secretary of the Woman Suffrage League at its initial meeting, she had assumed all of the duties of the league's secretary by the middle of 1889; as the Adelaide press commented, her pen 'flashed throughout the land'. The duties that she took on included not only the league's correspondence and reports to its meetings, applications for membership and collection of the annual subscriptions of one shilling, but also letters to the press, talks at drawing-room meetings, deputations to parliamentarians, and extensive addresses to such bodies as the Adelaide Sociological Class, the Port Adelaide Democratic Association, the Yatala Labor Party, the Democratic Club, the Gawler Literary and Sociological Society, the Hindmarsh Democratic Association and crowded meetings in the iron and steel towns of Port Augusta and Port Pirie, the last of which brought her an audience of over 500, 'a good proportion of which were women'.[45]

It was Mary Lee who forged the link between the women's suffrage campaign and the labour movement that was to prove so crucial to the successful passage of the women's suffrage legislation. At a public meeting in the Adelaide Town Hall on 11 December 1889, she proposed the formation of female trades unions 'in all branches of industry where the sweating system exists', which resulted in the formation of the Working Women's Trades Union at a meeting on 14 January 1890. It was Mary Lee who went to talk to the UTLC in 1891, after the introduction of yet another bill proposing votes for women, but only propertied women, had been introduced, and persuaded them that the Woman Suffrage League repudiated the bill because it wanted the vote for women on the same terms as men, without any extra property qualifications. After this the UTLC once again swung its support behind the suffragists.

It was Mary Lee who came in for most of the personalised opprobrium and mockery levelled at the suffragists, probably because she was their most prominent advocate, possibly because, after her hesitant first appearance on the stage of public politics, she had become more forthright than most in her opinions of the opponents of female suffrage; she called one parliamentarian 'an idiot', and when the elected members of the United Labor Party voted in favour of the referendum clauses attached to the suffrage bill of 1893, she called them 'a lot of nincompoops'. Anti-suffragists' responses were far less restrained. They countered with the couplet: 'Mary had a temper hot that used to boil and bubble/ and ere the franchise she had got it landed her in trouble'. One Member of Parliament wrote to the *Adelaide Observer* to exclaim: 'Poor Mary Lee! How she does froth and foam and stew and scold. I wonder if she manages her household in the same feverish style.' Another conservative opponent wrote to the *Advertiser* to predict that:

> If Mrs Lee obtains the power she desires and is permitted unrestrained to stir the seething cauldron of class discord I may live to see her knitting, counting while the bleeding heads of the thrifty and learned fall beneath the strokes of the guillotine. Then by brute force, the best intellects removed, she may have scope for political experiments.

On her seventy-fifth birthday in 1896, shortly after the first election in which women had voted – elections which had routed all expectations that women would most often vote conservative by returning the liberal Kingston ministry to power – the premier presented her with a 'handsomely bound and artistically engrossed address' which honoured her 'persistent advocacy and unwearied exertions' as the principal source of the success of the female suffrage campaign, and a purse of fifty sovereigns gathered by public subscription. Kingston was also to appoint her to an honorary public office, as official visitor to South Australia's lunatic asylums as part of a broader policy of appointing well-known women to voluntary public office: Augusta Zadow, and following her Agnes Milne, as Female Inspector of Factories; Catherine Spence, who was already a member of the State Children's Council, to the Destitute Board; Blanche McNamara as Inspector of Schools in the Education Department.

Mary Lee died in 1909; her tombstone is decorated with a small marble scroll engraved with the words 'Late Hon. Sec. Women's Suffrage League of S.A.'.

Equality vs. difference

For Mary Lee, the paradox presented by the campaign for votes for women, and its logical extension, women taking their places in the houses of Parliament, was the paradox of claiming equal rights with men, while simultaneously recognising, and promoting, difference between women and men. Like many proponents of female suffrage, she believed that women and men were intellectual equals: 'mind has no sex', she asserted.[46] But experience has. The experience of the majority of women was the experience of working as wives and mothers, experience that emphasised essential bodily differences between women and men – the experience of motherhood, for women. 'If woman is not intended for thought, action, heroism, why is she entrusted with the training of the race, with the education and bringing up of our children?' she asked, rhetorically.[47]

Mary Lee went on to draw analogies between the necessity for class-based political representation and representation grounded in difference. 'How can men raised above the workers, living on a totally different social plane, hedged about with a *chevaux de frise* [sic] of wealth and privilege fairly represent working men?' she asked. She answered her own question:

> They cannot think for working men because they cannot think as working men. They cannot think as working men because they are not working men. Thus, too, how can men represent women? Men cannot think for women because they cannot think *as* women, and they cannot think *as* women because they are *not* women.

The conceptual factor that for Mary Lee, as for many other suffragists (Rose Scott in New South Wales for one), resolved this paradox was a concept of evolution, derived, at several removes, from Darwin. Evolution required *both* 'Man, the physical and passionate' *and* 'woman, the sensitively moral, the tenderly affectionate, uncalculating, unselfish'. For progress, she declaimed, 'we need women *as* women just as we need man *as* man':

> Is progressive civilisation for man only? Can woman be dispensed with in this progress? If not, how can she be allowed to fall behind? Surely it is due to the race – nay, an absolute necessity to it, that she should keep step with its advance. Masculine and feminine influence must be wedded, co-ordinated, in order to fairly round out the moral and spiritual functions of men and women.

'We must go forward and upward', she cried. 'There is no finality in human progress. . . . Surely the time is ripe – aye, rotten-ripe – for change? Then let it come.'[48]

Clearly, Mary Lee was a mistress of the spoken word who might well have threatened anti-suffragist Ebenezer Ward's claim to rhetorical pre-eminence had she gained a seat in the parliament. Yet, when she was invited to stand for election to Parliament as an endorsed Labor Party candidate in 1896, she declined.

We know far more about Catherine Helen Spence than we can discover about Mary Lee; Spence was a novelist and a journalist, and had written most of an autobiography before she died.[49] Born in Scotland in 1825, she migrated to South Australia with her family in 1839, carrying with her an ambition to 'be a teacher first and a great writer after'. She resuscitated her early ambitions in this new environment, and after a brief stint as a governess, built herself four distinct, though overlapping, careers over the ensuing seventy years. The first was as a novelist; the second as a worker in educational and philanthropic causes, the fore-runners of aspects of state-funded welfare; the third was as a talented journalist; and the fourth was as an acclaimed, and loved, public speaker in the cause of electoral reform. She had found that cause as early as 1861, but it was not until the death of her mother, with whom she had lived all her life, in the late 1880s when Catherine Spence was already in her sixties, that she took to the public platforms of South Australia, and others in Melbourne, Sydney, and – in 1893–4 – across the United States and Britain, to promote it. This cause was not votes for women. Rather, it was the electoral procedure called proportional representation – used, these days, in elections to the Australian Senate, and in Tasmania, and, in variant forms, in a number of European nations. In this cause, which she called 'effective voting', she stood, unsuccessfully, for election to the Federal Convention of 1897, thus becoming Australia's first female political candidate. When she died in 1910, she was mourned as 'the Grand Old Woman of Australia'.

Catherine Spence believed herself to have been accounted a 'weak-kneed sister' by the suffragists. This was not because she had any doubts about the value of democracy. She was no Emma Goldman, declaring the campaign for admission to the processes of democracy to be a waste of time, since nothing good could arrive in the capitalist body politic until the people inspired by anarchism had overthrown the principal oppressors of the people: property, church and state.[50] On the contrary, a convert from the Calvinism of the Established Church of Scotland to the Enlightenment rationalism of the Unitarian church, Catherine Spence was an enthusiastic, if critical, disciple of small 'l' liberal John Stuart Mill, with whom she corresponded a couple of times, and whom she visited in the mid-1860s. In 1880, at the request of the Education Department, she wrote what was the first economics text produced for Australian secondary schools; *The Laws We Live Under* contains an explanation of the necessity for the rule of law and an exposition of the functions of government, both marking her clear commitment to liberal democracy. But around the turn of the century, her liberalism developed in directions which brought her politics close to the collectivism of the Single Tax Leagues and the principles of co-operation rather than competition, both central elements of the Forward Movement.[51] She also believed, as ardently as any suffragist, that she was 'entitled to a vote' and she hoped, she wrote, 'that I might be able to exercise it before I was too feeble to hobble to the poll'. She contributed her very considerable talents and energies to the cause of female suffrage, becoming vice-president of the Woman Suffrage League in 1891, joining several of the league's deputations to members of government, addressing drawing-room meetings and public gatherings, enrolling members in the Woman Suffrage League when she travelled to the rural towns of the colony to promote effective voting, making contact with suffragists in the United States and Britain – Charlotte Perkins Gilman, Susan B. Anthony, Jane Addams, Millicent Garrett Fawcett – during 1893–4, when she travelled around the world, giving lectures on effective voting and equal suffrage. Her stature, and the affection with which she was regarded, made her an important factor in the suffrage campaign. Parliamentarians referred to her as 'a well-known authority on political subjects'. The *Voice* stood solidly behind her. The South Australian *Advertiser* noted that 'she believes that the power to vote is a woman's right as much as that of a man, and she pleads that the right should be conceded'; '[h]er arguments' that paper commented, 'are thoughtful and sober, and her language entirely free from the screeching hysteria that has so often brought ridicule and contempt on the cause of "women's rights"'.[52] Her appearance in the House of Assembly on 17 December 1894 was an occasion for parliamentarians to greet her on her return from overseas, and for her to urge their support for votes for women.[53] Yet at the end of her life she observed, 'For myself, I considered electoral reform on the Hare system [of proportional representation] of more value than the enfranchisement of women, and was not eager for the doubling of the electors in number, especially as the new voters would probably be more ignorant and apathetic than the old.'

Equality vs. patriarchy and capitalism

For Catherine Spence, the paradox presented by the campaign for citizenship for women was a two-fold paradox at the heart of liberal democracy in a capitalist economy and a patriarchal gender order, the paradox of demands for egalitarian and altruistic government amidst profoundly unequal economic interests and the continuing subjection of women in their most intimate as well as their most public relationships.[54]

Two of her six novels, *Clara Morison* (1854) and *Mr Hogarth's Will* (1865), contain passionate depictions of the difficulties for women trying to earn their livelihoods in a gender-segmented labour market. Two other novels, *Gathered In* (1881–2/1977) and *Handfasted* (1984), advanced powerful arguments for change to the laws and customs governing marriage as one of the principal means of keeping women financially dependent and hence subordinate to men. Indeed, *Handfasted* did not achieve publication until 1984 because, in 1880, it was considered to be 'calculated to loosen the marriage tie – it was too socialistic, and consequently dangerous'.[55] If women were to continue to be subjected to the authority of fathers, husbands and brothers, then how could they exercise their votes independently and in their own interests?

Her campaign for 'effective voting' was based on the ideal of a parliament of the most intellectually and morally enlightened members of society, elected on individual merit by electors who combined voluntarily to form multiple electorates based on interests which were intellectual, professional, religious, or moral, rather than being primarily economic and regional. The complicated process of counting the votes in the system of proportional representation, which includes a quota and a single transferable vote, would be educational, she maintained. The system itself was the 'fairest' electoral system that a democracy could devise. (It is also the system that has, in the twentieth century in the Nordic social democracies, proved the most enabling for women to gain seats in the legislature.)[56] Without such reform to the electoral system, how could votes and seats in parliament enable women to achieve a collective voice, as women, in the legislatures of the nation?

Catherine Spence was also a popular and engaging public speaker. Like Mary Lee, she could have acquitted herself extremely well as a member of the legislature. But, again like Mary Lee, when she was asked to stand in the 1896 elections, she too declined.

Why wouldn't they stand for Parliament?

There are a host of reasons for these two suffragists to have refused even to consider becoming Members of Parliament. Two were personal and practical: their relative lack of the means to finance an election campaign, and their age. Mary Lee's last years were blighted by poverty, and the income that Catherine Spence earned from her journalism was generally less than £300 a year.[57] Moreover, in 1896, Catherine Spence was seventy-one, and Mary Lee was seventy-five. Yet this second is not an entirely convincing reason; they were not the only suffragists who could have been nominated, but there is no evidence that either they, or anyone else, considered suggesting younger women in their place. Age did not deter either of them from continuing in the public life of the colony/state. Mary Lee took her responsibilities as official visitor to lunatic asylums very seriously. Catherine Spence went on not only to campaign for election to the 1897 Federal Convention, in which she scored 7,383 votes, coming twenty-second out of thirty-three candidates, but also to continue her campaign for effective voting which lasted until she was on her death bed in 1910.

A third reason for their refusal to consider becoming Members of Parliament was their nineteenth-century faith in *other*, non-parliamentary, means of bringing about change leading to greater social justice. They were far from being alone in this. After all, substantial elements in the labour movement had been seeking social justice by direct industrial action, rather than parliamentary representation, only a few years earlier, and were to do so again in the future. Some labour movement people continued to prefer the establishment of new cooperative settlements – in Paraguay, and on the River Murray – to the gradualist politics of party formation and electoral campaigns for years after 1896.[58] Indeed, it requires an anachronistic, insular and politically limited set of blinkers, derived from late-twentieth-century assumptions about the inevitability of parliamentary politics and the confinement of radical political action to campaigning around the ballot box, to make it anything but entirely reasonable to ask – why do we assume that the suffragists *should* have wanted to become Members of Parliament? For the Forward Movement in South Australia, and therefore for both Mary Lee and Catherine Spence as well, gaining seats in Parliament for politically progressive members was only one of many possible means of instituting more genuine equality between women and men. Catherine Spence was acutely aware of these alternatives: she had visited the co-operative village settlements on the Murray in order to write about them for the press; her papers include a lecture on the anarchist Peter Kropotkin; her future-vision novella, *A Week in the Future* (1889) – which anticipated Charlotte Perkins Gilman's *Herland* by twenty-six years – depicted a new world order based on collectivist co-operation rather than individualist competition, a society in which women were not financially dependent on men, a society which had substituted arbitration for war, even though its system of government was little different from an amalgam of the Westminster and the Washington systems of liberal democracy.[59]

But the principal reason for both Mary Lee and Catherine Spence declining their nominations for election lay in their commitment to forming organisations that would enable women to work, collectively, in the interests of women, and their recognition that such a commitment conflicted with the very different priorities of the newly emerged political parties based on the competing economic interests of labour and capital. Mary Lee explained her refusal of nomination in 1896: she did not want, she said, to be 'bound by pledge or obligation to any party whatever'.[60] Catherine Spence's campaign for 'effective voting', and her commitment to the principle of co-operation rather than competition, cut across the lines dividing the new political parties. Rather than accepting nomination for election to Parliament, she went on to attempt to found a South Australian branch of the National Council of Women; to help establish the Co-operative Clothing Company – in which the workers held shares just as the investors did, all women – and to chair its board of management; and to preside over the meeting that founded the Women's Non-Party Political Association. The development of political parties based on economic class, and the competition between them was anathema to her. 'The feud between capital and labour will become more and more bitter', she told the Adelaide Democratic Club in 1892, 'if by your political machinery you exclude all those large bodies of independent thinkers who might bring moderation into your national Councils.'[61] These suffragists were by no means alone in their efforts to build organisations based on a solidarity among women, gender-solidarity, rather than working with the new political parties. Rose Scott, leader of the struggle for women's suffrage in New South Wales, spent several years after 1902 building a network of branches of the Women's Non-Party Political Association in her state.[62] When Vida Goldstein launched her campaign for election to the Australian Senate in 1903 in Victoria where women could still not vote in the state elections, she split the membership of the Women's Federal Political Association by insisting on standing as a *women's* candidate: the WCTU refused to support her, and a group of Labor women went off to campaign for Labor candidates. Vida Goldstein, a suffragist who *did* want to be a Member of Parliament, never gained a seat.[63] Rose Scott spent the last years of the first decade of the twentieth century mourning her members' defection to the branches of the malestream political parties.[64] As political scientists, Marian Sawer and Marian Simms, have argued, 'In Australia the modern party system, which developed early in response to the electoral success of the Labor Party in the 1890s, effectively tamed the women's vote: party loyalty rather than sex loyalty dictated the political behaviour of women.'[65]

Of the nineteen female candidatures for election to the South Australian Parliament between 1894 and 1959, only six were endorsed by the mainstream political parties. Two others ran as Independent Liberal and Unendorsed Liberal, a third as Anti-Communist Labor. The remaining ten included three who had the support of specifically women's organisations: the Democratic Women's Association formed on a proportional representation platform in 1937 by Jeanne Young, a collaborator with Catherine Spence in her effective voting campaign, and the Women's Non-Party Political Association, which also supported proportional representation. The rest campaigned simply as Independents.[66] For these women, clearly, the machinery of the malestream political parties, coupled with the preferential voting system, operated to exclude women.

Paradoxes

In 1986 historian Carol Bacchi noted the paradox of South Australia's achievement of the right for women to stand for election and the long wait before they were able to do this successfully. Bacchi's explanation of this paradox is couched in similar terms to those in which I have explained the paradox confronting Mary Lee: 'prevailing attitudes. . . towards women and their appropriate roles', and the contradictions between them.[67] Mary Lee resolved the paradoxical claims of equality and difference by adding a third term – 'evolution'. Others since, including Bacchi, have deconstructed the binary opposition between the terms 'equality' and 'difference' showing that claims for equality are not necessarily assertions of sameness, so that recognition of difference does not necessarily prohibit granting of equal rights.[68]

Such an explanation – ignoring for the moment the anachronism and political conservatism that formulated the question in the first place – ignores altogether another paradox, one that is crucial to the explanation that Bacchi seeks. And that is the double-edged paradox enacted and written about by Catherine Spence throughout her life: equality for women will require sweeping re-negotiation of the 'sexual contract' at the heart of liberal democracy; change to the gender segmentation of the labour market; to power relationships within marriage; and to the sexual division of labour within households, if the formal achievement of votes for women, and the rather accidental achievement of the right for women to stand for election, can possibly achieve greater equality for women.[69]

1   I would like to thank Sue Hosking for the help with research for this article, Lyndall Ryan for her encouragement and Jean Blackburn, Pat Grimshaw and Anne Levy for their scepticism.

2   *South Australia Parliamentary Debates (SAPD)*, 22 July 1885, c.319. See also Susan Magarey, *Unbridling the Tongues of Women: A Biography of Catherine Helen Spence*, Hale & Iremonger, Sydney, 1985, chapter 8; Helen Jones, *In Her Own Name: Women in South Australian History*, Wakefield Press, Netley, 1986, chapter 4; Oldfield, *Woman Suffrage in Australia*, chapter 2.

3   Jones, *In Her Own Name*, 83, 86, 96-7, 106-14; Oldfield, *Woman Suffrage in Australia*, 24-5, 30-9.

4   Jones, *In Her Own Name*, 222.

5   G. D. Combe, *Responsible Government in South Australia*, Adelaide Government Printer, Adelaide, 1957, 123; F. S. Wallis, 'History of the South Australian Labor Party, 1882-1900 (summary account of the Minutes of the United Trades and Labour Council)', typescript, South Australian Archives (SAA), 6-12, 13-15, 24, 28-30; T. H. Smeaton, *The People in Politics: A Short History of the Labor Movement in South Australia*, Daily Herald, Adelaide, 1914, 10-11, 25-28; E. L. Batchelor, *The Labor Party and its Progress: A lecture delivered to the Democratic Club, Adelaide, on March 5th 1895*, Adelaide, 1895, 4; J. I. Craig, 'A History of the South Australian Labor Party to 1917', unpublished MA thesis, Univ. of Adelaide, 1940, 40, 57; R. L. Reid, 'The Price-Peake Government and the Formation of Political Parties in South Australia', typescript, n.d., SAA, 6.

6   Craig, 'History of the South Australian Labor Party', 60, 62; H. T. Burgess, ed, *The Cyclopedia of South Australia*, 2 vols, Adelaide Cyclopedia Co, Adelaide, 1907, vol II, 167; *Observer*, 18 Jan. 1896.

7   *Observer*, 30 May, 6 June, 13 June, 20 June, 4 July, 5 Sept. 1896; Reid, 'The Price-Peake Government', 9, 3.

8   *Observer*, 26 July 1890; 1 Aug. 1891; 30 July 1892; 7 Oct. 1893; 14 Oct. 1893; 21 July 1894; *Voice*, 9 Dec. 1892; 15 Sept. 1893; 31 Aug. 1894.

9   *Voice*, 7 April, 7 July, 22 Sept. 1893; *Observer*, 1 Aug. 1891.

10   Reid, 'The Price-Peake Government', 6; Craig, 'History of the South Australian Labor Party', 63; Phyllis G. Peter, 'Militancy and Moderation: A Comparative Study of the Trade Union Movements in New South Wales and South Australia in the 1880s', unpublished BA Honours thesis, Univ. of Adelaide, 1959, 78; ANL program in Burgess, ed, *Cyclopedia of South Australia*, vol II, 167.

11   E. J. Wadham, 'The Political Career of C. C. Kingston, 1881-1900', unpublished MA thesis,

Univ. of Adelaide, 1953; Richard Mitchell, 'State Systems of Conciliation and Arbitration: The Legal Origins of the Australasian Model', in Stuart Macintyre & Richard Mitchell, eds, *Foundations of Arbitration: The Origins and Effects of State Compulsory Arbitration, 1890-1914*, Oxford Univ. Press, Melbourne, 1989, 85-7, 93-6; Jones, *In Her Own Name*, 107; Oldfield, *Woman Suffrage in Australia*, 35-6.

12 Oldfield, *Woman Suffrage in Australia*, 36, 38.

13 J. B. Hirst, 'Ebenezer Ward (1837-1917)', *Australian Dictionary of Biography 1851-1890*, vol VI, Melbourne Univ. Press, Melbourne, 1976, 351-2; W. J. Sowden, 'Our Pioneer Press The Register, The Observer and The Evening Journal: A History', typescript with handwritten corrections, 1926, SAA; *Register*, 28 April 1880; 29 May 1880; 30 April 1880; 1 May 1880; 5-7 May 1880; 11 May 1880; 5 Dec. 1895; Caroline A. Gawler to Editor, *Register*, 16 Dec. 1895; *Adelaide Chronicle*, 7 Oct. 1911; *Express and Telegraph*, 9 Oct. 1917; *SAPD*, 2 Dec. 1896, c.435. Matilda Ann Ward sued for divorce on the grounds of cruelty and adultery; under the law governing divorce in 1866 she could not have charged less. Ward, by contrast, could sue for divorce on the grounds of adultery alone. Faced with his wife's charge, Ward counter-petitioned, and after four years of what he would later describe as 'miseries and penalties of the Divorce Court' (*SAPD*, 22 Oct 1896, c.242), a comment suggesting that the court may have decided that Matilda Ward's petition had been well-founded, his divorce was granted in June 1870, see Magarey, 'Sex vs. Citizenship: Votes for Women in South Australia', *Journal of the Historical Society of South Australia (JHSSA)*, forthcoming 1994.

14 See, for example, *SAPD*, 26 Aug. 1891, c.894; 24 July 1894, cc.631-6; 7 Aug. 1894, cc.790, 794; 14 Aug. 1894, cc.884, 894; 15 Aug. 1894, c.930; 23 Aug. 1894, cc.1079-83.

15 *SAPD*, 16 Aug. 1894, c.963; 22 Aug. 1894, cc.1038-39; Pat Stretton & Kathryn Gargett, *1894: How A Parliament of Men Gave the Vote to Women*, State History Centre, Adelaide, 1993, 4.

16 *Observer*, 22 Dec. 1894; *South Australian Chronicle*, 22 Dec. 1894; Cornelius Proud, 'How Woman's Suffrage was Won in South Australia', *Review of Reviews*, 20 Jan. 1895.

17 Oldfield, *Woman Suffrage in Australia*, 17, 22.

18 Jones, *In Her Own Name*, 96-97; Oldfield, *Woman Suffrage in Australia*, 31-2.

19 Oldfield, *Woman Suffrage in Australia*, 17, 40.

20 Ibid., 55-6.

21 Pat Stretton & Christine Finnimore, 'Black Fellow Citizens: Aborigines and the Commonwealth Franchise', *Australian Historical Studies*, 25/101, Oct. 1993, 522-7.

22 Oldfield, *Woman Suffrage in Australia*, 61-2, 213.

23 For example, *SAPD*, 10 July 1894, c.439; Jones, *In Her Own Name*, 97.

24 Oldfield, *Woman Suffrage in Australia*, chapters 1-8.

25 Ibid., 222-3.

26 William Pember Reeves, *State Experiments in Australia and New Zealand*, 2 vols, Macmillan, Melbourne, 1969, first published in 1902, vol. I, 103-4; Ian Turner, 'Prisoners in Petticoats: A Shocking History of Female Emancipation in Australia', in Julie Rigg, ed, *In Her Own Right*, Nelson, Melbourne, 1969, 20.

27 Anne Summers, *Damned Whores and God's Police*, revised, chapter 11; Beverley Kingston, ed, *The World Moves Slowly: A Documentary History of Australian Women*, Cassell, Camperdown, 1977; Ruth Teale, ed, *Colonial Eve: Sources on Women in Australia 1788-1914*, Oxford Univ. Press, Melbourne, 1978; Judith Allen, 'The "Feminisms" of the Early Women's Movements in Britain, America and Australia, 1850-1920', *Refractory Girl*, 17, 1979; Judith Allen, 'Breaking into the Public Sphere', in Judy Mackinolty & Heather Radi, eds, *In Pursuit of Justice: Australian Women and the Law 1788-1979*, Hale & Iremonger, Sydney, 1979; Kay Daniels & Mary Murnane, comps, *Women in Australia*, Univ. of Queensland Press, St. Lucia, 1990, first published as *Uphill all the Way: A Documentary History of Women in Australia*, 1980; Christine Fernon, 'Women's Suffrage in Victoria', *Refractory Girl*, 22, 1981; Gail Reekie, 'With Ready Hands and New Brooms: The Women who Campaigned for Female Suffrage in Western Australia, 1895-1899', *Hecate*, 7/1, 1981; Carol Bacchi, 'First-wave Feminism: History's Judgement', in Norma Grieve & Patricia Grimshaw, eds, *Australian Women: Feminist Perspectives*, Oxford Univ. Press, Melbourne, 1981; Farley Kelly, 'Mrs Smyth and the Body Politic: Health Reform and Birth Control in Melbourne', Anthea Hyslop, 'Agents and Objects: Women and Social Reform in Melbourne 1900 to 1914', Diane Kirkby, 'Alice Henry and the Women's Trade Union League: Australian Reformer, American Reform', all in Margaret Bevege, Margaret James & Carmel Shute, eds, *Worth Her Salt: Women at Work in Australia*, Hale & Iremonger, Sydney, 1982; Magarey, 'Radical Woman: Catherine Spence', Farley Kelly, 'Feminism and the Family: Brettena Smyth', Brian Matthews, 'Dawn Crusade: Louisa Lawson', all in Eric Fry, ed, *Rebels and Radicals*, Allen & Unwin, Sydney,

1983; Anthea Hyslop, 'Temperate Feminists: Marie Kirk and the WCTU', Grimshaw, 'Bessie Harrison Lee and the Fight for Voluntary Motherhood', Farley Kelly, 'Vida Goldstein: Political Woman', Diane Kirkby, 'Alice Henry: Expatriate Feminist', all in Lake & Kelly, eds, *Double Time: Women in Victoria –150 Years*, Penguin, Ringwood, 1985; Magarey, *Unbridling the Tongues of Women*, chapter 8; Jones, *In Her Own Name*, chapter 4; Lake, 'The Politics of Respectability: Identifying the Masculinist Context', in Magarey, Rowley & Sheridan, eds, *Debutante Nation: Feminism Contests the 1890s*, Allen & Unwin, St Leonards, 1993, first published *American Historical Studies (AHS)222/86*, April 1986; Chris McConville, 'Rough Women, Respectable Men and Social Reform: a Response to Lake's "Masculinism"', *AHS*, 22/88, April, 1987; Allen, '"Mundane" Men: Historians, Masculinity and Masculinism', *AHS*, 22/89, Oct 1987; Betty Searle, *Silk & Calico: Class, Gender & the Vote*; Susan Sheridan, 'Louisa Lawson, Miles Franklin and Feminist Writing, 1888-1901', Allen, '"Our Deeply Degraded Sex" and "The Animal in Man": Rose Scott, Feminism and Sexuality 1890-1925', Jenni Mulraney, '"When Lovely Woman Stoops to Lobby"', Magarey, 'Jane and the Feminist History Group', all in Magarey, ed, *AFS*, 7&8, Summer 1988, special issue on Feminism and History; Grimshaw, 'Only the Chains have Changed', in Verity Burgmann & Jenny Lee, eds, *Staining the Wattle: A People's History of Australia since 1788*; Olive Lawson, ed, *The First Voice of Australian Feminism: Excerpts from Louisa Lawson's The Dawn 1888-1895*, Simon & Schuster, Brookvale, 1990; Pam Young, *Proud to be a Rebel: The Life and Times of Emma Miller*, Univ. of Queensland Press, St Lucia, 1991; Diane Kirkby, *Alice Henry: The Power of Pen and Voice. The Life of an Australian-American Labor Reformer*, Cambridge Univ. Press, Melbourne, 1991; Katie Spearritt, 'New Dawns: First Wave Feminism 1880-1914', in Kay Saunders & Raymond Evans, eds, *Gender Relations in Australia: Domination and Negotiation*, Harcourt Brace Jovanovich, Marrickville, 1992; Oldfield, *Woman Suffrage in Australia*; Jan Roberts, *Maybanke Anderson: Sex, Suffrage & Social Reform*, Hale & Iremonger, Sydney, 1993; Jill Roe, ed, *My Congenials: Miles Franklin & Friends in Letters*, 2 vols, Angus & Robertson, 1993, vol. I, chapter 1; Magarey, 'Sexual Labour', Grimshaw, 'The "Equals and Comrades of Men"'?: *Tocsin* and the "Woman Question"', Susan Sheridan, 'The *Woman's Voice* on Sexuality' all in Magarey, Rowley & Sheridan, eds, *Debutante Nation*; Judith A. Allen, *Rose Scott: Vision and Revision in Feminism*, Oxford Univ. Press, Melbourne, 1994; Grimshaw, Lake, McGrath & Quartly, *Creating A Nation*, chapters 7 and 8. For the reference to women making speeches at their own firesides, see Helen Jones, 'Women's Education in South Australia: Institutional and Social Developments, 1875-1915', unpublished Ph.D thesis, Univ. of Adelaide, 1980, 266.

28 *Brisbane Courier*, 4 Sept. 1900, cit. Oldfield, *Woman Suffrage in Australia*, 183.

29 See Magarey, 'Sex vs. Citizenship', S. Cockburn & S. Edgar, 'Robert Thomas (1781-1860)', *Australian Dictionary of Biography 1851-1890*, Melbourne Univ. Press, Melbourne, vol. VI, 1976; Philippa Fletcher, 'An Adelaide Woman of Interest: Agnes Milne, Inspector of Factories, 1896-1906', *JHSSA*, 1987; Fletcher, 'Agnes Milne', in Heather Radi, ed, *200 Australian Women: A Redress Anthology*, Women's Redress Press Inc., Broadway, 1988; *Voice*, 24 March 1893.

30 Jones, *In Her Own Name*, 96-7; Oldfield, *Woman Suffrage in Australia*, 34-5.

31 Jones, *In Her Own Name*, 101-3; I have the information about the current research on the signatories only verbally, from Helen Jones.

32 Jones, 'Women's Education in South Australia', 279-80.

33 D. H. P., 'Women Here Had First Vote 48 years ago', *Mail*, 22 April 1944, Newspaper cuttings vol. 2, SAA, 257. A note on the clipping gives the author's name as Dorothy H. Paynter.

34 Daniels & Murnane, comps., *Uphill All The Way*, 262.

35 Jones, *In Her Own Name*, 24-8, 85-6.

36 Daniels & Murnane, comps., *Uphill All The Way*, 262-3.

37 Jones, *In Her Own Name*, 86; Oldfield, *Woman Suffrage in Australia*, 38, 41.

38 Cit. Oldfield, *Woman Suffrage in Australia*, 41

39 Ibid., 38.

40 Cit. Oldfield, *Woman Suffrage in Australia*, 180.

41 'Women Who Have Stood Up To Be Counted', authorised by A. K. Becker, Electoral Commissioner of South Australia, in 'Women's Suffrage Centenary 1894-1994: A Special Souvenir Liftout', *Advertiser*, 8 March 1994, 12.

42 Joan Wallach Scott, 'Claims for the Vote in France, 1789-1945' paper delivered to the ninth Berkshire Conference on the History of Women, Vassar College, Poughkeepsie, N.Y., 11-13 June 1993 (I am quoting from my notes of her verbal presentation). See also Nancy F. Cott, 'Feminist Theory and Feminist Movements: the Past Before Us', in Juliet Mitchell & Anne Oakley, eds, *What Is Feminism?*, Basil Blackwell, Oxford, 1986, 49.

43   Unless otherwise specified, this account is taken from Jones, *In Her Own Name*; Helen Jones, 'Mary Lee', in Radi, *200 Australian Women*; Oldfield, *Woman Suffrage in Australia*; Elizabeth Mansutti, *Mary Lee: Let her Name be Honoured*, booklet commemorating the centenary of the achievement of women's suffrage in South Australia, Libraries Board of South Australia, Adelaide, 1994.

44   Allen, *Rose Scott*, 97, 115-17, 185-9, 193; Allen, '"Our Deeply Degraded Sex" and '"The Animal in Man": Scott, Feminism and Sexuality 1890-1925', *AFS*, 7&8, Summer 1988.

45   *Voice*, 21 April 1893; 30 June 1893; 1 June 1894; 15 Sept. 1893; 30 March 1893; 20 April 1893; 4 May 1894; 25 May 1894.

46   *Voice*, 28 April 1893.

47   *Voice*, 21 April 1893.

48   Ibid.

49   Unless otherwise specified, this account is drawn from Magarey, *Unbridling the Tongues of Women*.

50   For example, Emma Goldman, *The Traffic in Women and other Essays on Feminism*, Times Change Press, Albion CA, 1970.

51   She wrote about both: on Henry George and the single tax, C. H. Spence, 'A Californian Political Economist', *Victorian Review*, IV/20, 1881; on co-operation rather than competition, 'The Democratic Ideal', MS. and annotated newspaper clipping, n.d., Mitchell Library (ML), a paper which she said had appeared in the *Register*, and which she also planned to give as a lecture in the US during 1893, see *Observer*, 8 April 1893. She also gave it as a sermon in the Unitarian Christian Church in Adelaide, 'Miss C. H. Spence at the Unitarian Church', *Quiz and the Lantern*, 9 May 1895.

52   *Advertiser*, 17 Mar. 1893

53   Catherine Helen Spence, Diary for 1894, MS. held in private hands, imperfect transcription by Magarey held in the Research Centre for Women's Studies, Univ. of Adelaide. See also Jones, *In Her Own Name*, 105.

54   This analysis is indebted to Carole Pateman, *The Disorder of Women: Democracy, Feminism and Political Theory*, chapter 9.

55   This was the comment of the judge/s of a competition run by the *Sydney Mail*, to which she submitted the MS. in 1880, see C. H. Spence, *An Autobiography*, reproduced by the Libraries Board of South Australia, Australiana Facsimile Editions no. 199, Adelaide, 1975, reprinted from the *Register*, Adelaide, 1910, 63.

56   Anne Phillips, *Engendering Democracy*, 80-90.

57   See Jones, 'Mary Lee', in Radi, ed, *200 Australian Women*; Lucy Spence Morice, 'Auntie Kate', n.d., typescript, SAA, cit., Magarey, *Unbridling the Tongues of Women*, 127. Spence's first major campaign for 'effective voting' had been financed by Joanna and Robert Barr Smith; some later campaigns were probably assisted by subscriptions to the Effective Voting League which she formed in 1895.

58   See, for example, Gavin Souter, *A Peculiar People: William Lane's Australian Utopians in Paraguay*, Univ. of Queensland Press, St Lucia, 1991, first published 1968; L. K. Kerr, 'Communal Settlements in South Australia in the 1890s', unpublished MA thesis, Univ. of Melbourne, 1951.

59   C. H. Spence, 'A Fortnight on the Village Settlements', galley proof, Adelaide, 1896, National Library of Australia and 'Memoirs of a Revolutionist', MS., 1905, Ml. Spence, *A Week in the Future*, with an introduction & notes by Lesley Durrell Ljungdahl, Hale & Iremonger, Sydney, 1987, first published in the *Centennial Magazine*, Sydney, 1888-1889. Ljungdahl's introduction demonstrates how extensively Spence borrowed for this work from British social theorist Jane Hume Clapperton's *Scientific Meliorism and the Evolution of Happiness*, Kegan Paul, Trench & Co., London, 1885.

60   Jones, 'Women's Education in South Australia', 274.

61   Magarey, *Unbridling the Tongues of Women*, 156.

62   Allen, *Rose Scott*, chapter 5.

63   Kelly, 'Vida Goldstein: Political Woman', in Lake & Kelly, eds, *Double Time*; Jennifer Mulraney, 'Vida Goldstein', in Radi, ed, *200 Australian Women*, 85-6.

64   Allen, *Rose Scott*, 196-210.

65   Marian Sawer & Marian Simms, *A Woman's Place: Women and Politics in Australia*, Allen & Unwin, St Leonards, 1993, 17.

66   'Women Who Have Stood Up To Be Counted', *Advertiser*, 8 Mar. 1994.

67   Carol Bacchi, 'The "Woman Question" in South Australia', in Eric Richards, ed, *The Flinders History of South Australia: Social History*, Wakefield Press, Netley, 1986, 403.

68   The crucial work is Joan Wallach Scott, *Gender and the Politics of History*, Columbia Univ. Press, New York, 1988, chapter 8, a re-working of 'Deconstructing Equality vs. Difference: or, The Uses of Post-Structuralist Theory for Feminism', *Feminist Studies*, XIV/1, Spring, 1988. See also Carol Lee

Bacchi, *Same Difference: Feminism and Sexual Difference*, 1990.
69   The concept of the 'sexual contract' comes from Carole Pateman, *The Sexual Contract*. Only days after her victory in the Fremantle by-election, and her first step on a road running directly into the inner Cabinet of the Keating government of the Commonwealth of Australia, former premier of Western Australia, Dr Carmen Lawrence, noted as difficulties that have prohibited women's readiness to stand for election to Parliament: young women's responsibility for the care of children and other dependants, and the masculinism of the branches of the political parties, see *Advertiser*, 19 Mar. 1994.

5

Citizenship, Race, and Gender: Changing Debates over the Rights of Indigenous Peoples and the Rights of Women[1]

ANN CURTHOYS

In this chapter I stage a kind of historical conversation between two narratives, two distinct though not mutually exclusive political movements: the struggle of indigenous peoples for citizenship and self-determination; and feminism, women's struggle for equality and autonomy. In each story there is tension between demands for equality, and full recognition of difference. Debates over ends and means have been occurring in both feminist and indigenous peoples' activist circles for decades, at least since World War II, in a number of comparable societies – including New Zealand, Australia, the United States, and Canada. Without wishing to ignore at all the many differences between these movements and debates, there do seem to be some common themes, in particular the degree to which a subordinated group in a particular society should concentrate on achieving full citizenship rights – legal, political, social, economic – and the degree to which that group desires legal and political recognition of difference, of claims to separate and distinct treatment and consideration. My aim in comparing these debates is to develop a broader perspective which might help us understand both, to look for linkages and influences between them, and to find ways through the sometimes difficult and circular debates around questions of equality and difference.

The narratives that I hope to make talk to each other specifically concern indigenous peoples' and women's political activism in Australia during the crucial period of the late 1960s and the early 1970s, when each movement experienced major upheavals and changes in political character. The two movements are, of course, not mutually exclusive in theory, since indigenous women are potentially involved in and directly affected by both. But for this period the two movements were in fact largely distinct, in both political aims and membership.

Equality vs. difference in current theoretical debates

The tensions between desires for equality as against difference are in many ways variations of continuing arguments since the eighteenth century. One influential line of thinking has followed from the Enlightenment, with its powerful rhetoric that we are all born free and equal. Enlightenment thinking promised equality and freedom for all – the emancipation of slaves, serfs, Jews, and oppressed peoples of all kinds into a wider society where all were citizens irrespective of religion and class. It also promised a vindication of the rights of women, as in Mary Wollstonecraft's famous manifesto.[2]

These ideals remain important in both Western and non-Western liberal theory – in Africa, India, and amongst indigenous peoples within Western settler colonial societies. And yet they have also come under heavy fire in post-structural and post-colonial critiques. From its beginnings, the Enlightenment has been seen by critics as itself possibly repressive, particularly of diversity, of difference. In this century, writers like Lyotard have seen Enlightenment claims to equality and universality as too often a presumption that all humanity is like the European.[3] In Derrida's hands, Enlightenment ideals become a 'white mythology'.[4] For Franz Fanon, writing during the anti-colonialist upsurge in Africa in the 1950s and early 1960s, humanism was the foundation of colonial discourse, or racism, and he bitterly attacked the European's claim to universal values: 'the native laughs in mockery when Western values are mentioned in front of him'.[5] Humanism is thus seen not as the foundation for a critique of colonial power and racism, but as the source of ethnocentric, racist, and colonial thinking.

Somewhat similar critiques are made from a feminist perspective. From its beginnings feminism relied on the Enlightenment ideal of the citizen, supposedly universal, free, and equal; the point was to refine this ideal to include women as well as men. As Mary Wollstonecraft declared: 'Let woman share the rights, and she will emulate the virtues of man.' Now, however, it is less clear whether feminism is indeed a form of humanism, or whether it has instead become its most powerful critic, a key player in the development of postmodernist philosophical critique of the claims to universality made on behalf of a Western conception of human reason.[6] A major strand of feminist theory has lost its earlier belief in the possibility of universality and gender neutrality, now seeing universalism as positing a common humanity while retaining the idea and ideal of the individual as male.[7] The question now arises whether, having concluded that the claim to impartial universal reason can be seen as a universalising of distinctively *male* discursive power, feminists should abandon the Enlightenment commitment to the cause of reason and truth, or whether we, more cautious now, nevertheless remain committed to Enlightenment ideals of equality and justice.

Feminists have been concerned with the specifically political dimension of Enlightenment thought, in particular, the question of liberalism. Carole Pateman has been the most powerful proponent of the argument that liberalism cannot ultimately be made compatible with feminism.[8] In Pateman's view, the social contract of liberal theory was made not by individuals, as is usually supposed, but by brothers, a fraternity, by men who share a bond *as men*. Women are still excluded from the central category of 'the individual', the bedrock of contractarian doctrine. The social contract made by this fraternity therefore guarantees not the rights of the individual but the rule of men over women. Feminist attempts to recast the individual who is at the heart of liberal thinking from male to simply a human being, either male or female, are fundamentally mistaken. Women's freedom cannot be gained by pretending that women and men are the same. Pateman's solutions are for women and men to address sexual difference openly. The achievement of legal equality and freedom becomes then, not the end of feminism, but rather, the precondition for the development of women's autonomy, where women become free as women, rather than as like men. Pateman's critique has proved very influential indeed; many feminists now take it for granted that the individual of liberal thought has to be split apart into its male and female components, and thereby released into sexual differentiation and plural identities.[9]

And so liberal humanism has come under serious question from both post-colonial and feminist perspectives. What can indigenous peoples and women make of philosophical and political traditions which have on the one hand offered ideals of equality and freedom, and on the other provided a basis for ethnocentric and male-centred politics? Where do, that is to say, ideals for equality and freedom now lead us?

If we look at actual political movements, both indigenous peoples' and women's, we can see that their relation to liberal–humanist ideals is very complex indeed, providing both inspiration and obstacle, a source for claiming rights by some and for disregarding the claims of others. Claims for equality, and for recognition of difference, regularly intertwine, yet undermine one another.

The Aboriginal movement in Australia

Aboriginal political protest has a history as old as colonisation itself. British invasion of the lands of Aboriginal peoples was marked by violence, bloodshed, and, in the worst but not infrequent cases, wholesale massacres.[10] Colonisation was at its most intense from 1788, the year British occupation of the eastern part of the continent began, to the 1930s, when the last massacres occurred, in the Northern Territory. One region after another was occupied by British settlers, with the assistance of a mixture of private and public police and military forces. Aboriginal populations were severely reduced not only by the process of settlement itself but also by the effects of previously unknown diseases, from smallpox to influenza and pneumonia.

Colonisation and dispossession were expressed through re-naming, as the various Aboriginal groups were de-identified and given, as Eve Fesl points out, labels such as 'indian', 'native', 'black', and, most enduringly, 'aborigine'.[11] The term 'Aboriginal' is not liked by many of the people it is used to describe, being a colonialist rather than a self-identifying name. It has proved difficult, however, to develop an alternative. In contrast to New Zealand, where Maori people share a common language, there are a very large number of different Aboriginal languages. The name by which Aboriginal people identify themselves varies across the country, from Koori in the south-east to Murri in the north-east, Pallawah in Tasmania, Nyunga in the south-west. While the term 'Aboriginal' is inadequate, it continues, in the absence of a generally accepted alternative, to be used, when referring to the indigenous peoples of the Australian continent generally, by many Aboriginal and non-Aboriginal people alike. Meanwhile, a debate over whether 'Koori' can stand for all Aboriginal people, or only for those in the south-east, continues.

Aboriginal resistance took various forms in the nineteenth century, ranging from active resistance to settlement, to petitioning governments and Queen Victoria for land, boats, and the opportunity to live without interference. In each region, an uneasy accommodation was reached, as Aboriginal people began to work for the newly established pastoralists, farmers, and tradesmen, and to forge a living combining aspects of wage-earning with continuing traditional food-getting, and maintaining a relationship to traditional land and associated cultural life. Colonial governments sometimes established reserves and schools for Aboriginal families, often pressed hard to do so by missionaries and philanthropists concerned by the extreme poverty of Aboriginal groups. In some regions these reserves acted as important sites for Aboriginal communal cohesiveness, in others they forced together people from different and sometimes antagonistic tribal groups.

During the early twentieth century the powers of the white managers of reserves and missions gradually increased, and with them the level of detailed surveillance over Aboriginal people's lives. In New South Wales, the practices of the Aboriginal Welfare Board, and its predecessor, the Aborigines Protection Board, were contradictory, on the one hand seeking forced assimilation with the rest of the society through large-scale removal of children from their parents, and on the other maintaining segregated Aboriginal communities on the outskirts of country towns. In many towns there was a three-way struggle for power over Aboriginal people between Aboriginal communities themselves, the Welfare Board, and the local white power structures, including the local town councils which were especially sensitive to the desires of white townsfolk for the segregation of Aboriginal people.[12]

A pattern of segregation continued well into this century, affecting all Aboriginal–European relationships. As Peter Read puts it, by 1965 'there was scarcely a town in the central west of New South Wales where a local Aborigine could try on clothes, sit down for a meal, get a haircut, go to secondary school, run for office, join a club, drink in the lounge bar or work in a shop'.[13] Such policies not only created a racial divide, but could also be used to divide Aboriginal people from one another. As Ann McGrath has shown, there developed in the assimilationist decades after World War II a notion of 'exemption', whereby special 'identity cards' were issued to some Aboriginal people, conferring on them the same privileges as other citizens, such as the right to drink in a hotel and to obtain welfare assistance, but isolating them from non-exempted Aboriginal people. These certificates were often hated, regarded as 'dog licences' issued under a 'Dog Act' which, as McGrath puts it, 'could be used to tie them up wherever whites wanted them'.[14]

By the twentieth century, key sites of struggle were over education, housing, the keeping of children, citizenship and civil rights, and of course, land. An Aboriginal political movement seeking land and citizenship rights became especially organised in the south-east of the continent in the 1920s and 1930s, reaching a peak in the late 1930s, exemplified in 1938 by Jack Patten and William Ferguson's pamphlet, *Aborigines Claim Citizens' Rights*.[15] After a lull during and immediately after World War II, there was from the middle 1950s a rapid growth in organisations called Aboriginal Advancement Leagues and the like.[16] The new organisations often had mixed Aboriginal and non-Aboriginal membership, and attempted to work for improvements in their region in Aboriginal health, housing, and education. Alongside many local Aboriginal communities themselves, these organisations kept up demands for full citizenship rights, including access to all education and town facilities, and an end to interference in the freedom of movement and place of residence of Aboriginal people.

The growth in organisations demanding full citizenship was occurring around the country, though there were major difficulties in the building of a nationwide pan-Aboriginal movement. Despite these difficulties and strong regional differences, Aboriginal activists frequently sought more involvement of the Commonwealth government in Aboriginal affairs, in the hope that this would guarantee citizenship and civil rights as a matter of national policy.[17] (Under the Australian Constitution, Aboriginal affairs were considered solely a states' matter, so much so that Aboriginal people were not counted as part of the national population census.)[18] As part of this process of developing, almost for the first time, a national perspective on Aboriginal political demands, the first Federal Conference of Aboriginal Organisations was held in Adelaide early in 1958, leading to the establishment of the Federal Council for Aboriginal Advancement. Soon afterwards, the name was changed to explicitly include Torres Strait Islanders (the indigenous people of the islands of the Torres Strait to the north of the continent), the organisation becoming the Federal Council for Advancement of Aborigines and Torres Strait Islanders, or FCAATSI.

From the middle 1960s, the pace of change accelerated. The organisations continued to grow in numbers and strength, and protests against discrimination, segregation, and loss of land strengthened. The political positions of the organisations varied, and from region to region there was considerable difference on the degree to which an Aboriginal rights organisation emphasised land rights and cultural identity, and the degree to which it concentrated on the provision of improved education, housing, and health services. An important event was the 'Freedom Ride' which occurred in Australia in February 1965. Consciously modelled on the Freedom Rides in the US of the same period, but applied to a very different situation, the Australian Freedom Ride took place when a group of 29 students from the University of Sydney, including emerging Aboriginal leader, Charles Perkins, travelled by bus around selected towns in New South Wales, protesting against discrimination towards Aborigines, and demanding full Aboriginal citizenship rights.[19]

The hostility by so many white town-dwellers to the Freedom Ride revealed to a national media audience both the depths of racial discrimination, and the determination to protect it. For Aboriginal activists the Freedom Ride signified a change, the emergence of a political style that was more aggressive, more confrontational, and, perhaps most important of all, more optimistic about the possibility of change. The emphasis was on opposing discrimination, and on achieving real changes in the long run such as employment opportunities, education, health, housing. Most significant, perhaps, was the new political prominence of Charles Perkins, who was publicly seen as a leader of non-Aboriginal people, taking on the confident and confrontational style of student radical politics. (Perkins went on to become the first Aboriginal senior public servant, becoming Chairman of the Aboriginal Development Commission and subsequently Secretary of the Department of Aboriginal Affairs.) Equally significant was the massive media coverage, the poverty and segregation of Aboriginal people becoming a focus for a social crusade on the part of the urban media.

There were many reasons for the upsurge in Aboriginal protest from the late 1950s onwards. In the rural areas, unemployment and segregation were major catalysts. Urban communities had been growing in size since the mid-1950s, and urbanisation brought certain freedoms with it. The experience of urban living led to a new element in Aboriginal politics, with many young Aboriginal activists drawing analogies between their situation and the decolonisation and liberation struggles of oppressed peoples elsewhere. Some were interested for a time in the ideals of Black Power in the US, and many people were well aware of the struggle against racism and apartheid in South Africa. Increasingly, people looked to the struggles of indigenous peoples in New Zealand and North America as a truer parallel and source of inspiration. Indeed there were some family connections between Aboriginal people on the Australian east coast and Maori, which also provided influences, contacts, and ideas.[20] What had been purely local struggles were placed in ever widening contexts.

A major development in this period was the increasingly open demand for land rights, the return of lands seized in the context of the original invasion. In 1963 the Yirrkala people in the Northern Territory sent a bark petition in the Gubapuyngu tongue to the Parliament in Canberra demanding an end to Nabalco's mining of their land at Gove, which was placing increasing pressure on their community. In 1966, in the context of a dispute over wages, the Gurindji walked off Wave Hill station, in the Northern Territory, and demanded their land back, their strike becoming a land claim. In 1968, Aboriginal representatives made a legal claim against a mining company and the government, for granting a mining lease at Gove Peninsula, saying the land belonged to them.[21]

By the late 1960s and early 1970s, Aboriginal people's politics were undergoing a major change, becoming more confrontational, more clearly Aboriginal-led, and increasingly seeking not only equal rights but also a greater recognition of Aboriginal difference by virtue of prior occupation of the continent. A major transformation was occurring, which continues still. During the second half of the 1960s, the campaign to change the Constitution to allow federal jurisdiction in Aboriginal affairs gathered speed, promoted both by FCAATSI and the One People of Australia League (OPAL), finally succeeding through a referendum in 1967. This challenged the powers of the state governments, traditionally tied to discriminatory, interventionist, and racist policies, and provided a catalyst for higher expectations and a more aggressive movement.

Peter Read has drawn attention to the way in which this changing political emphasis was registered in the annual meetings of FCAATSI.[22] During the 1960s, FCAATSI's racially mixed membership sought equal citizenship rights – legal, social, and economic – for Aborigines. In 1962 its demands focused on citizenship, an equal standard of living, equal pay, free and compulsory education for detribalised people, and the retention of existing reserves. In 1966 a further principle was added: 'Aborigines and Islanders should be recognised as distinct cultural groups'. In 1967 additional principles were adopted, including Aboriginal people being allowed to choose their own language, culture, and community. In 1968 an Aboriginal closed session voted for fixed Aboriginal representation on the executive. Clearly, the Aboriginal members of FCAATSI were beginning to shift away from a politics of equal rights to one of self-determination and a separate indigenous identity. In 1970 the issue of Aboriginal control of the leadership and of General Meetings was bitterly contested; in the end, the organisation collapsed, to be replaced by new Aboriginal organisations.

From around 1970 significant involvement by non-Aboriginal people in Aboriginal organisations was in decline. Jo Woolmington describes how this occurred in Armidale in New South Wales, and notes that non-Aboriginal supporters were leaving, or being asked to leave, these organisations all over the country.[23] By 1972, a quite different political situation existed. On Australia Day in that year, the anniversary of European invasion and settlement, the Prime Minister, William McMahon, made a statement about Aboriginal policy which, while it did promise some important changes, specifically ruled out any recognition of land rights. The increasingly radical Aboriginal movement protested by setting up a tent encampment of protest on the lawns outside Parliament House in Canberra. It was a striking protest, saying that Aboriginal people were not part of the political system in their own country, so alienated and distinct that they had to form an embassy, like a foreign power. It lasted almost six months, and like the Freedom Ride before it, attracted massive media attention. The Tent Embassy also symbolised a national Aboriginal movement. It was at this time, or slightly before, that the Aboriginal flag was designed; this flag has since become a unifying emblem for Aboriginal activists, for land rights, self-determination, cultural identity, sovereignty, as well as their continuing demand for equal rights and citizenship.[24]

By 1976, as Peter Read tells us, all the seventy mixed-membership advancement organisations which had flourished a decade earlier were either in Aboriginal hands or defunct. He concludes by saying 'The white people have not returned. . . . Indigenous leadership of indigenous organisations is [now] taken as axiomatic.'[25]

The Australian women's movement

During the same period, Australian feminism experienced a turn to a new and more aggressive form of demand for women's rights, and a re-assertion of women's unity and specificity. There had been women's organisations working for the emancipation of women since the mid-nineteenth century, especially with the formation of the WCTUs in the 1880s and the growing organisation for the vote in the 1890s. After the achievement of women's suffrage at a national level in 1902, women's organisations continued to turn their attention to a wide range of issues. Some women's organisations were closely associated with political parties, across the spectrum from socialist to labour to conservative and anti-socialist, while others maintained a strictly non-party position and form of organisation.[26]

By the 1950s, there was a women's rights organisation for every political perspective and social class. On the non-aligned left, there was the United Associations of Women, founded in 1929 from the amalgamation of four existing organisations; on the far left the communist-led Union of Australian Women, formed in 1950; and on the labour Left, the Labor Women's Organising Committees. For the non-aligned professional middle class there were the Business and Professional Women's Clubs, and for the politically centrist and conservative there were the National Council of Women, the Australian Federation of Women Voters, and a range of other organisations, most notably the Country Women's

Association.[27] These very different women's organisations waged major campaigns for women's rights, including active campaigns for equal pay, against widespread sex discrimination in employment, and seeking representation of women at all levels of government and administration, such as the boards of companies and statutory bodies.[28]

These various existing women's organisations, varied in political perspective as they were, by the late 1960s were generally well-established, respectable in tone, using traditional and polite forms of protest, and setting moderate targets. Young politically active women were more likely to be involved in the contemporary anti-war movement, or attracted to the ideals of the 'counter culture', stressing participation and collective consciousness, sexual expression, and a critique of competitive, rationalist, technology-driven Western civilisation.[29] In the late 1960s, isolated by a generation gap from organised feminism, yet finding themselves to be second-class citizens within the New Left, these young women proceeded to invent a new form of feminism for themselves.[30]

In Australia, the inspiration for this new and growing movement called Women's Liberation came initially from the United States through overseas journals, then from Americans migrating to Australia and Australians returning from visits to the United States. Women's liberation groups emerged in each capital city, formed by and large by young women who had been active in the anti-war movement.[31] A key issue in the new women's movement was the question of the exclusion of men from groups, meetings, and activities generally. While the older organisations had been largely female-managed and run, for the younger women the maintenance of female control was a more difficult issue. These women of the New Left found that the very men in the New Left they were accusing of sexism wanted to run the new women's movement. There were many bitter debates around the years 1970–1 about the exclusion of men. Women, many said, needed a separate space to work out their demands; exclusion of men, said others, was itself sexist, and reactionary. Gradually, the issue died down, as women's control of the movement became clearly established.

Although Women's Liberation had initially arisen from the New Left, it very quickly drew support from way beyond it. The new feminist ideas spread through word of mouth, the media, and the literature produced by the movement itself. The new women's movement had an impact on parliamentary politics with the establishment of the Women's Electoral Lobby in February 1972. Its direct emphasis on attempting to achieve change through pressure on the existing political parties, and its participation in the Federal election campaign of that year, placed feminist demands on the wider political agenda.[32] Despite hostility from sections of the media, from politically organised men, and from some conservative women's groups, the new feminist ideas continued to gain ground fairly steadily.

The women's movement of the early 1970s, like its predecessor, contained internal political divisions. There was a counter-cultural, rather anarchist strand, stressing issues of sexuality, culture, representation, and above all the profundity of the differences between men and women. Yet alongside this quite aggressive confrontationalist style, with its emphasis on the need for a total change in thinking, there was also very strongly within modern Australian feminism a desire for, and a lively optimism about, the achievability and efficacy of profound social change through the actions of government, which was considered potentially benevolent and responsive. As Marian Sawer has argued, the form of liberal theory on which this feminist optimism rested was not so much the American individualist tradition that Carole Pateman addresses, as a corporate 'new liberalism' or social liberalism. This form of liberalism, which sought social reform through the agency of a benevolent state, has underlain the Australian welfare state from early in the century when Australia, like New Zealand, was regarded as a 'social laboratory' for the world.[33]

Feminists picked up and very effectively ran with this social liberal tradition. The women in the Women's Electoral Lobby, especially, continued the emphasis on employment rights and opportunities that had distinguished the older women's organisations, seeking equal opportunity, anti-discrimination, and affirmative action legislation. The demand for increased access to affordable childcare was in part related to that for employment opportunities, the two together forming the basis of the demand for greater independence for women. Childcare services were increasingly sought not just as a necessity for working mothers, but as a right for all women and all children.

The fiercest debates within the new feminism of the early 1970s were over the relationship between gender and class. If women are united as a group in a common oppression, these feminists asked, what can one make of class differences between women? For those with socialist politics particularly, the question was how to combine a class and a gender analysis. In practice, many women did so via trade union politics, pressing women's concerns in particular within a framework of class-based and trade union politics. Feminism, which many trade-unionist and other left men saw as divisive, energised a new wave of female trade union activists, in white collar and professional unions particularly.

Looking back on that crucial period of the late 1960s and early 1970s we can now see that it laid the foundations for considerable successes at both a legislative and social level in transforming the social relations between men and women. Increasingly, but not uniformly, the feminist activists of the period looked beyond demands for formal legal and political equality to argue for the provision – often by the agencies of the state – of the social services and social and industrial policies which would create real sexual equality of opportunity via genuine recognition of gender-based bodily and social difference.

And so we have a paradox. The new feminism, which we so often now refer to as 'second wave feminism', rested very much on a philosophical rejection of liberal ideals. The emphasis was on women's difference from men, and on the desire *not* to encourage women to conform to a rationalist male world. Yet just as this emphasis on difference and women's unity and specificity was flourishing, so did Australian feminists make rapid gains of a fairly classical social–liberal kind, winning, through pressure on the agencies of the state, increased employment rights and social services. The Australian women's movement, though active and successful in gaining certain major social changes, remains to this day internally divided on their value.

Intersexions

So far I have been discussing the women's and the indigenous peoples' movements as if they were entirely distinct. In many ways they were. While Aboriginal politics and women's politics both forged ahead and made significant headway during the late sixties and early seventies, at that time they had little to do with one another. Yet they were operating in a single political climate, and there are striking similarities, as the developments in one case paralleled in time the move in the other. The exclusion of non-Aboriginal people from Aboriginal organisations, and the exclusion of men from the Women's Liberation movement, both came to a head in 1970. The doubts about the adequacy of the ideals of equal legal and social rights became stronger for both movements at around the same time, as did the assertion of the importance of social and cultural difference. In both cases the years of the Labor Government of 1972–5 saw a much higher expectation that reform could be achieved through the actions of government.

These are interesting and revealing parallels and analogies. But there is also the question of the influence of each movement on the other. What happened when the question of the rights and struggles of indigenous peoples intersected and collided with questions of gender and sexual difference?

The influence of feminism on Aboriginal women's politics is difficult to gauge. As Heather Goodall and Jackie Huggins demonstrate in their excellent and pathbreaking essay on Aboriginal women's political struggles, Aboriginal women usually operated in an arena quite separate from that of the women's movement. They were significant figures in the growing Aboriginal movement for land rights, employment, housing, education, and health, with women being especially prominent in campaigns around the last two.[34] Their critiques of Aboriginal men were matters internal to their movement; when non-Aboriginal women attempted to enter some of these debates in the late 1980s, there was profound resentment at their doing so.[35]

The influence of Aboriginal women on the non-Aboriginal women's movement was to become profound by the 1990s, but developed very slowly. In the early 1970s, it was still very limited. There was from the beginning some consideration of the implications for feminism of the differences between women of different ethnic backgrounds – between immigrant and Australian-born women, and between Western and non-Western women.[36] Within this larger framework, there was some recognition of the distinctiveness of Aboriginal issues. These were seen largely in liberal–humanist terms – of disadvantage, discrimination, and equal rights rather than invasion, dispossession, cultural genocide, or special rights. Non-Aboriginal women saw Aboriginal women as having a double oppression to fight, and therefore potential membership of two movements, a women's movement and an Aboriginal movement. At the earliest Women's Liberation Conference in Sydney in 1970, one paper, by a non-Aboriginal woman, entitled 'Aboriginal Women in Sydney', began 'Aboriginal women in Australian society today are doubly handicapped', and this idea remained dominant throughout the 1970s.[37]

The impact of feminism on non-Aboriginal women's understanding of Aboriginal protest and demands was paradoxical. In one sense, feminist ideas *did* help non-Aboriginal women to empathise with Aboriginal women. Feminists saw Aboriginal women as part of the same oppressed group to which they themselves belonged – they were all women, all sisters under the skin, in a common kinship, a common oppression. In another sense, though, this assumption of a common female perspective inhibited non-Aboriginal feminists from understanding Aboriginal demands very much at all. As so many Aboriginal women subsequently pointed out, non-Aboriginal feminists generally assumed that Aboriginal women's feminism would be the same as their own. They thought that the issues they were pursuing – employment rights, abortion rights, childcare – were issues for all women, and saw all women as having a common enemy – patriarchal male power. The result was that while many feminists may have supported Aboriginal demands for equal rights and improved conditions, and perhaps for land rights, few saw these demands as impinging on their own concerns. Aboriginal issues did not change their perception of feminist issues. As Heather Goodall and Jackie Huggins put it: 'In their enthusiasm to be anti-racist, white women simply invited Aboriginal women to join their movement, with little apparent recognition of the full horror of racism in Australia, nor of how it continued to damage Aboriginal men as well as women.'[38]

The stumbling block was indeed the feminist understanding of the power and social situation of Aboriginal men. White feminists found it hard to see their own project as having anything in common with the aspirations of Aboriginal men, and frequently saw them as having power in much the same way as white men were supposed to uniformly have. Most non-Aboriginal feminists were profoundly ignorant of the history, situation, and struggles of Aboriginal people. They were quite unaware of the subtle ways in which those agencies which had power over Aboriginal women, such as the various Protection and Welfare Boards, had attempted to drive wedges between Aboriginal men and women, and therefore had little idea how offensive to many Aboriginal women were their own attempts to do the same.[39]

For Aboriginal women, the anti-male style of the women's movement – especially in its more separatist forms – was generally out of place. Aboriginal families, so victimised historically by a European racist society, even to the point of the systematic removal of Aboriginal children from their parents, were something Aboriginal women generally wanted to defend and protect, not attack in the way that much non-Aboriginal women's feminism so vehemently did. Most Aboriginal and Torres Strait Islander women were therefore exceedingly wary of the non-Aboriginal women's movement, expressing a feeling of greater solidarity with their own men than with European–Australian women proclaiming universal sisterhood.[40]

These conflicts emerged very early indeed in the history of modern feminism, when two Aboriginal women walked out of a women's conference in March 1973 in protest at the exclusion of men. They had, they said, extreme difficulty in separating the oppression of Black women from the oppression of Black men.[41] In a landmark article in 1976, prominent Aboriginal lawyer and activist, Pat O'Shane, referring to the tremendous loss of status suffered by Aboriginal men as a consequence of colonisation, asked white feminists to consider this as a tragedy, and went on to say:

> The problem of racism is one that all women in the women's movement must start to come to terms with. There is no doubt in my mind that racism is expressed by women in the movement. Its roots are many and they go deep. . . . So far as the women's movement is concerned it is necessary for women involved to examine carefully whether or not their aims as white women are necessarily those of black women.[42]

For some years, non-Aboriginal feminists resisted and resented these critiques. Gradually, though, Aboriginal issues began to intrude on the consciousness of the Australian women's movement. Like Western feminists elsewhere, they slowly began to come to terms with the fact that their own project, their own history, had been intertwined with colonisation, orientalism, even racism.[43] As Aboriginal demands came to be better recognised and understood in the society generally, a space began to open up in which more productive exchanges between Aboriginal and non-Aboriginal women could occur. Aboriginal women increasingly began a dialogue with non-Aboriginal feminists, attending conferences, speaking out, writing about issues that concerned them particularly, as women.[44]

Some non-Aboriginal feminists began to take the point concerning Aboriginal men. In a special issue on racism produced by the feminist journal *Girls Own* in 1983, the non-Aboriginal women wrote of the need to support Aboriginal people – children, women *and* men, explaining 'Giving support to Aboriginal women only is demanding our terms.' Yet if dialogue increased, we need to take note of Lydia Miller, who wrote recently in the twenty-year commemorative issue of *Refractory Girl*: 'In 1993 Aboriginal women still feel that non-Aboriginal women do not have sufficient understanding of these issues and that they have little or no sympathy for the legacies of colonialist practices which Aboriginal women still bear.'[45]

Conclusion

And so I return to my original question. What indeed *can* women, or indigenous peoples, make of philosophical and political traditions which offer ideals of equality and freedom yet provide a basis for ethnocentric and male-centred politics? Where do, that is to say, ideals for equality and freedom now lead us?

It would seem that in any political movement that neither the politics of equality nor the politics of difference is alone sufficient. Equality without difference can become a way of collapsing a subordinate group to the dominant standard, male or European. Difference without equality provides no basis for negotiation between different groups of citizens within a common political framework. For these reasons, wherever groups of people distinguished from one another on the basis of history, culture, or gender continue to occupy the same political entity, debates of the kind I have been describing can never be fully resolved.

1   I would like to thank the Australian Research Council for financial support for the larger project of which this is a part; Heather Goodall and John Docker for commenting on early drafts; and the audience at the 'Suffrage and Beyond' conference for their stimulating and unexpected questions.

2   Mary Wollstonecraft, *A Vindication of the Rights of Woman*, C. Poston, ed, W.W. Norton & Co., New York, 1975, first published 1792.

3   Jean-François Lyotard, *The Postmodern Condition: A Report on Knowledge*, trans. G. Bennington & B. Massumi, Univ. of Minnesota Press, Minneapolis, 1984.

4   Jacques Derrida, *Margins of Philosophy*, trans. Alan Bass, Univ. of Chicago Press, Chicago, 1982.

5   Franz Fanon, *The Wretched of the Earth*, Penguin, Harmondsworth, 33; quoted in Robert Young, *White Mythologies: Writing History and the West*, Routledge, London, 1990, 124.

6   Pauline Johnson, 'Feminism and the Enlightenment', *Radical Philosophy*, 63, 1993, 3-12.

7   Genevieve Lloyd, *The Man of Reason: 'Male' and 'Female' in Western Philosophy*, Univ. of Minnesota Press, Minneapolis, 1984.

8   Pateman, *The Sexual Contract*.

9   For a more extended discussion of Pateman's work, see my 'Feminism, Citizenship, and National Identity', *Feminist Review*, 44, 1993, 19-38.

10   For general histories, see: Henry Reynolds, *The Other Side of the Frontier*, Penguin, Ringwood, 1982; Reynolds, *Frontier*, Allen & Unwin, Sydney, 1987; Reynolds, *With the White People*, Penguin, Ringwood, 1990; Reynolds, *The Law of the Land*, Penguin, Ringwood, 1987. For regional histories, see Lyndall Ryan, *The Aboriginal Tasmanians*, Univ. of Queensland Press, St Lucia, 1981; Ann McGrath, '*Born in the Cattle*', Allen & Unwin, Sydney, 1987. For histories stressing gender, see Kay Saunders & Raymond Evans, eds, *Gender Relations in Australia: Domination and Negotiation*, Harcourt, Brace, Jovanovich, Sydney, 1992.

11   Eve Mumewa D. Fesl, *Conned!*, Univ. of Queensland Press, St Lucia, 1993, xiv.

12   Heather Goodall, 'Cryin' Out for Land Rights', in Burgmann & Lee, eds, *Staining the Wattle*, 181-97.

13   Peter Read, *Charles Perkins: A Biography*, Viking, Ringwood, 1990, 97.

14   Ann McGrath, '"Beneath the Skin": Australian Citizenship Rights and Aboriginal Women', in Renate Howe, ed, *Women and the State: Australian Perspectives*, La Trobe Univ. Press, Bundoora, 1993.

15   Jack Patten & William Ferguson, *Aborigines Claim Citizens' Rights*, Sydney, 1938.

16   See the reminiscences of Jack Horner, 'From Sydney to Tingha: Early Days on the Aboriginal Australian Fellowship', *Aboriginal History*, 11/1, 1987, 33-40; Jo Woolmington, 'The "Assimilation" Years in a Country Town', *Aboriginal History*, 15/1-2, 1991, 25-37.

17   Goodall, 'Cryin' Out for Land Rights', 195.

18   A federal referendum held in May 1967 recorded 91 per cent in favour of the federal government having concurrent power with the states in Aboriginal affairs and that Aborigines be counted in the national population census.

19   See Read, *Charles Perkins*, for the most detailed account.

20   Heather Goodall, personal communication, Aug. 1993.

21   The judgment, made in 1970, said that it did not, that there was no basis in law for their claim. Twenty-two years later, in 1992, in what is now known as the Mabo case, this judgment was superseded. See M. A. Stephenson & Suri Ratnapala, eds, *Mabo: A Judicial Revolution: The Aboriginal Land Rights Decision and Its Impact on Australian Law*, Univ. of Queensland Press, St Lucia, 1993.

22   Peter Read, 'Cheeky, Insolent, and Anti-white: the Split in the Federal Council for the Advancement of Aboriginal and Torres Strait Islanders – Easter 1970', *Australian Journal of Politics and History*, 36/1, 1990, 73-83.

23   Woolmington, 'The Assimilation Years'.

24   See Stewart Harris, *This Our Land*, Australian National Univ. Press, Canberra, 1972.

25   Read, 'Cheeky, Insolent, and Anti-white', 80.

26   Marian Sawer & Marian Simms, *A Woman's Place: Women and Politics in Australia*; Simms, 'The Australian Feminist Experience', in Norma Grieve & Grimshaw, eds, *Australian Women: Feminist Perspectives*, 227-39; Grimshaw, Lake, McGrath, Quartly, *Creating a Nation*, chapters 8 & 9, 177-230.

27   Winifred Mitchell, *Fifty Years of Feminist Achievement: A History of the United Associations of Women*, UAW, Sydney, 1980; Julie Ellis, 'The Union of Australian Women 1950-1980', unpublished BA (Hons) thesis, History Department, La Trobe Univ., Melbourne, 1980; Norman MacKenzie, *Women in Australia*, Cheshire, Melbourne, 1962.

28   Sol Encel, Norman MacKenzie & Margaret Tebbutt, *Women and Society: An Australian Study*, Cheshire, Melbourne, 1974, 139-43; Ann Curthoys, 'Equal Pay, a Family Wage, or Both?' in Barbara Caine *et al.*, eds, *Crossing Boundaries: Feminisms and the Critiques of Knowledges*, Allen & Unwin, Sydney, 1988.

29   Ann Curthoys, 'Mobilising Dissent: The Later Stages of Protest', in Greg Pemberton, ed, *Vietnam Remembered*, Weldon, Sydney, 1990.

30   Ann Curthoys, *For and Against Feminism: A Personal Journey into Feminist Theory and History*, Allen & Unwin, Sydney, 1988. See also John Docker, '"Those Halcyon Days": The Moment of the New Left', in Brian Head & James Walter, eds, *Intellectual Movements and Australian Society*, Oxford Univ. Press, Melbourne, 1988.

31   Susan Eade, 'Now We Are Six: A Plea for Women's Liberation', *Refractory Girl*, 13-14, 1986, 3-11; Sylvia Kinder, 'Adelaide Women's Liberation: The First Five Years, 1969-74', in Margaret Bevege *et al.*, eds, *Worth Her Salt: Women at Work in Australia*, 367-78; Jocelyn Clarke & Kate White, *Women in Australian Politics*, Fontana/Collins, Sydney, 1983.

32   H. Glezer & J. Mercer, 'Blueprint for a Lobby: the Birth of WEL as a Social Movement', in Henry Mayer, ed, *Labor to Power: Australia's 1972 Election*, Angus & Robertson, Sydney, 1973.

33   See Sawer, 'Reclaiming Social Liberalism: the Women's Movement and the State', in Renate Howe, ed, *Women and the State: Australian Perspectives*, La Trobe Univ. Press, Bundoora, Victoria, 1993, 1-21.

34   Goodall & Huggins, 'Aboriginal Women are Everywhere: Contemporary Struggles', in Saunders & Evans, eds, *Gender Relations in Australia*; C. D. Rowley, *The Politics of Aboriginal Reform*, Penguin, Ringwood,1986.

35   See Diane Bell & Topsy Naparrula Nelson, 'Speaking About Rape is Everyone's Business', *Women's Studies International Forum*, 12/4, 1989, 403-16; 'Letters to the Editor', *WSIF*, 14/5, 1991, 505-13; Jan Larbalestier, 'The Politics of Representation: Australian Aboriginal Women and Feminism', *Anthropological Forum*, 6/2, 1990, 143-57; Diane Bell, 'Reply to Jan Larbalestier', *AF*, 6/2, 1990, 158-65; Diane Bell, 'Intraracial Rape Revisited: On Forging a Feminist Future Beyond Factions and Frightening Politics', *WSIF*, 14/5, 1991, 385-412; J. Atkinson, 'Violence in Aboriginal Australia: Colonialism and its Impact on Gender', *Refractory Girl*, 36, 1990, 21-6; Jan Pettman, 'Gendered Knowledges: Aboriginal Women and the Politics of Feminism', in Bain Attwood & John Arnold, eds, *Power, Knowledge and Aborigines*, La Trobe Univ. Press, Bundoora, 1992, 120-31.

36   See Jan Pettman, *Living in the Margins: Racism, Sexism and Feminism in Australia*, Allen & Unwin, Sydney, 1992.

37   'Jan', *Aboriginal Women in Sydney*, cyclostyled paper for Women's Liberation Conference, 1971, in author's possession.

38   Goodall & Huggins, 'Aboriginal Women are Everywhere', 401-2.

39   Ibid.

40   See Jan Larbalestier, 'The 1980 Women and Labour Conference: Feminism as Myth: Aboriginal Women and the Feminist Encounter', *Refractory Girl*, 20-1, Oct. 1980, 31-9; Fay Gale, ed, *We Are*

Bosses Ourselves: The Status and Role of Aboriginal Women Today, Australian Institute of Aboriginal Studies, Canberra, 1983; Goodall & Huggins, 'Aboriginal Women are Everywhere'; Roberta Sykes, 'Black Women in Australia: a History', in Jan Mercer, ed, *The Other Half: Women in Australian Society*, Penguin, Ringwood, 1975, 313-22; Jocelyn Scutt, ed, *Different Lives: Reflections on the Women's Movement and Visions of its Future*, Penguin, Ringwood, 1987.

41   *Tribune*, 27 Mar-2 April 1973, 11.

42   Pat O'Shane, 'Is there any Relevance in the Women's Movement for Aboriginal Women?', *Refractory Girl*, 12, 1976, 31-5.

43   Joyce Zonana, 'The Sultan and the Slave: Feminist Orientalism and the Structure of *Jane Eyre*', *Signs*, 18/3, Spring 1993, 592-617. For a recent discussion of these issues, see Larissa Behrendt, 'Aboriginal Women and the White Lies of the Feminist Movement: Implications for Aboriginal Women in Rights Discourse', *Australian Feminist Law Journal*, 1/1, 1993, 27-44.

44   Bronwen Levy, 'Sisterhood in Trouble: The Fourth Women and Labour Conference, Brisbane, 1984', *Hecate*, 10/2, 1984, 105-9.

45   Lydia Miller, 'The Women's Movement and Aboriginal Women', *Refracting Voices: Feminist Perspectives from Refractory Girl*, Refractory Girl Publications, Sydney, 1993.

6

Women and Political Leadership in the Pacific Islands

PENELOPE SCHOEFFEL MELEISEA

The women of Pacific Island nations did not have to struggle for suffrage; political independence for most of the island states was negotiated in the last quarter of the twentieth century when women's suffrage was an established element in modern democracy. In most instances the granting of independence was overseen by the United Nations, and the departing colonial powers established democratic frameworks of representation. In all independent Pacific Island countries all persons over the age of twenty-one are now entitled to vote.[1] Since the 1960s, when most of the Pacific Island colonies began the transition to independence, no country has restricted voting rights solely on the grounds of gender. However, a number of countries have placed other restrictions on voting rights. For example, from 1962 to 1990, Western Samoa restricted the franchise to matai (the titled heads of families), who were mainly, but not exclusively, males. In the Kingdom of Tonga nobles and commoners are separately and unequally represented, and this is also the case in Fiji among native Fijians and Indo-Fijians.

I shall argue that in the Pacific Islands the political issue for women has not been the gaining of the vote, although in some countries women, along with men, had to struggle for independence. Instead, I shall suggest, the issue for women has been, and still is, the reconciliation of old political traditions with new forms of democracy. In the post-colonial order the reaffirmation, reinstatement, or even the reinvention of selected traditional institutions, rules or values have been a means of building regional and national identities. For many Pacific Island peoples the assertion of the uniqueness of their cultures and the revival of pride in the past has also been a powerful antidote to the humiliations of colonialism. It has also been a potent political weapon exercised by the elite members of some Pacific Island countries.[2] Although gender relations in most Pacific societies were transformed by Christian and colonial influences, there are elements in many current cultural revitalisation movements around the

Pacific emphasising both Christian and pre-colonial models of gender relations.³ Many of these adopted or recreated traditions deny that it is legitimate for women to assume new roles in the modern state and political order, although it is acceptable for men to do so. Although all Pacific Island states have modern legal systems, largely based on those of the former colonial power, throughout the region there have been attempts to integrate customary law into these frameworks. In this process barriers have been reimposed upon women in the name of preserving cultural integrity.

Women's status

Many Pacific constitutions proclaim the equality of their citizens but also admit the validity of customary law in various spheres. Thus customary laws or norms that deny men and women equal rights in matters such as the inheritance of land, or custody of children often prevail. Similarly behaviour that may contravene the formal provisions of law (such as wife beating) may be regarded as a man's traditional prerogative under customary law. In some countries customary law underlay legal discrimination against women in relation to the citizenship of foreign husbands. While most countries make it possible for men marrying foreign women to obtain citizenship for their wives and children, in Fiji and Nauru women must often leave the country if they marry foreigners.⁴ In the case of Nauru, this law is because land is inherited through matrilineal succession, probably because it was feared that if foreign men were granted citizenship, they might acquire land through their wives and thus rights to phosphate royalties. In some cases colonial administrations codified customs, causing them to be more rigidly enforced than in the past. This has been the case in Fiji where patrilineal descent has been so systematised that the children of Fijian males by non-Fijian women are regarded as Fijians, with all the rights that such identity entails, while the children of Fijian women by foreign husbands are not counted as Fijians.

In some Pacific Islands the colonial authorities changed the rules of inheritance giving rise to new systems now accepted as being part of 'tradition'. In Micronesia the German administration replaced the matrilineal transmission of land, titles and property of Pohnpei with a patrilineal system which effectively disinherited women. A similar situation occurred in Tonga when missionary-inspired late-nineteenth-century land reforms dispossessed women of land rights. While it may be argued that these reforms gave commoner men more secure rights to land than they had previously enjoyed, they did not extend these rights to women or maintain the pre-existing privileges of chiefly women. Such interventions by the colonial powers were inspired by the cultural attitudes of Europe at the time, which saw women as being properly the economic dependants of men.

The customary status of women and the nature of relations between men and women vary greatly in Pacific cultures. In some traditional societies women's status was very low, as in Papua New Guinea highlands societies, where women were subject to control by their kinsmen or husbands at all times throughout their lives.[5] In others it was high, as in some Polynesian societies, where women of aristocratic birth had great privileges, some being priests or even war leaders.[6]

Today there are major overall disparities between the status of women in Melanesia and Polynesia, a situation highlighted by the differences in the rates of participation in secondary and higher education and wage employment in these cultural sub-regions. On each count the situation for women compared with men is one of increasing parity in Polynesia and considerable inequality in Melanesia.[7] The disparity extends to health status and life expectancy. In Papua New Guinea, for instance, there is a higher death rate and shorter life expectancy for females than males in rural areas in most provinces, contrary to demographic norms. Papua New Guinea has among the world's highest rates of maternal and infant mortality and a recent authoritative study shows that this situation is closely linked to women's low status, heavy workloads and poor nutrition.[8] In contrast, life expectancy for women in Polynesia is higher than males' and maternal and infant mortality rates are very low in comparison to most developing countries. Although the historical record indicated that the status of chiefly women in Polynesia declined in the early colonial period, in more recent times women have made continuous although modest gains in health, education and economic status.

Nineteenth-century missions and gender relations

The most profound modern historical influence on gender relations in Pacific societies has been that of the Christian churches. From the early nineteenth century, when various churches began their work in the Pacific Islands, to the present day, missionaries tried to change social institutions. Both European and Pacific Islander missionaries tended to see their own social institutions as more befitting to a Christian way of life than those of the Island societies whom they wished to convert. In particular, customs associated with marriage and domestic arrangements were targeted for reform. In nineteenth-century Polynesia most missionaries thought women were oppressed, although their status was probably higher in many respects than that of women in Victorian England. For example, John Williams wrote of Samoa:

> [I] prayed that, by the blessing of God upon our labours, the day might speedily arrive when these interesting females should be elevated from this terrible degradation, and, by the benign influence of Christianity, be raised to the dignity of companionship with their husbands, and occupy that status in the social and domestic circle which the females of Tahiti, Rarotonga, and the other islands, have attained since the introduction of the Gospel.[9]

Missionaries were troubled by the absence of stable marriage in many Polynesian societies. They deplored the fact that women were used in transactions between men and lacked the right of choice. In Hawai'i missionaries were shocked by the idleness of chiefly women.[10] In the Marquesas, they were horrified that aristocratic women took male concubines.[11] The churches took their ideal of Christian marriage from Saint Paul, that a man should have the right of command over his wife (one only) but also a duty to care for and protect her in a relationship of mutual fidelity. They wished to strengthen the institution of marriage and to teach Polynesians to accept wifehood as a more honourable estate than it was seen to be in the pre-Christian social order. It was believed that Christian marriage would liberate women because its emphasis was upon ties of affection and individual choice of partner.

The Protestant churches educated men to be ministers and women to be their wives so that the couple could provide a role model of proper Christian marriage and family life to the congregations they were sent to serve. In transforming domestic relations, the churches also encouraged new divisions of household labour based on what were considered proper occupations for the sexes in England. For example, in Samoa cooking was the work of young men but in Christian households women were taught to cook using foreign methods and utensils. Similarly, in Samoa men cut their hair short to signify their conversion to Christianity, while women grew their short hair long and arranged it in the style of European missionary wives.

Later missionary influence in Melanesia
The transformation of domestic life in Polynesia and much of Micronesia

was more or less complete by the turn of the century but in Melanesia evangelical work continues among people following traditional religions to the present time. In Melanesia, as in Polynesia, Christian missionaries were concerned about the absence of connubial domestic life in many Melanesian societies. In such societies men and women lived apart a great deal of the time, with men spending much of their time in the communal men's house, and women in their separate households. Through their evangelical activities the churches tried to substitute new models of family life in place of traditional ones.[12] Although the churches affirmed men's traditional right to be heads of families, they required men to accept new roles and obligations towards their wives and to live together in monogamous, conjugal family units. In some areas of Melanesia Christian influence is relatively recent and in a few areas, it has been resisted altogether. For example, colonial and missionary contact with the million inhabitants of the New Guinea highlands did not commence until the 1930s and few changes were brought to the area until the 1950s. Although the highlands have been widely evangelised in the past fifty years, polygyny is still highly regarded there and Christian family alternatives have not been as widely accepted as they have in coastal areas.

In general Christianity liberated Pacific women from one set of customs, which in some societies oppressed women but in others gave women high status or independence, only to replace them with another set of imported customs. These emphasised a woman's primary value as a mother and wife, her primary place in the private domestic sphere, and excluded her (or reinforced her seclusion) from the public sphere of political and ritual action.

Economic change in the colonial era

There were major differences between cultures in the area of the division of labour between the sexes in pre-colonial societies, and some of those patterns of difference exist to the present day. For instance in Melanesia and many parts of Micronesia, women were primarily responsible for growing and preparing food with varying degrees of assistance from men. But in Western Polynesia, particularly in Tonga and Western Samoa, and in some Micronesian cultures, food production was considered to be primarily a male role. There women's major economic roles were associated with the production of manufactured objects such as mats, ornaments, tapa cloth, coconut oil and other goods for domestic use and for exchange.

The overall trend of economic change in third world countries has been to relegate women to the subsistence sector while removing men into commercial production.[13] In the Pacific this has been particularly true of the Melanesian region, where women play major roles in food production. The cash economy opened new opportunities for men as wage earners and commercial farmers but restricted the participation of women. As men moved into the cash economy the share of women's work in subsistence production increased because men were occupied with cash crops or away working in towns or on plantations.

In Polynesia and some areas of Micronesia the cash economy also undermined women's economic roles. For example, Peterson records that in Pohnpei women's major role in producing valuables – cloth, ornaments, and mats – was replaced by the import of goods in the nineteenth century, which in association with the shift from matrilineal to patrilineal land inheritance, led to a reduction in the status of women. More recently Pohnpein women's economic status has been further reduced as their main traditional crops (taro and corn) have been replaced by imported rice.[14] In Samoa women's economic roles were also undermined by the influx of imported goods, and by the commoditisation of certain goods made by women. For example, coconut oil was traditionally made by women as a medicine and cosmetic, but men came to participate in processing it when it became a trade commodity. When the export of coconuts in the form of copra instead of oil was introduced in about 1870, village producers were eclipsed by the plantation economy.[15] The decline in women's former economic roles enabled them to fill in the time by taking on a range of voluntary, community service roles offered to them by the churches, and after 1921, by the colonial administration. This situation encouraged the growth of new, local-level women's organisations from the 1920s, one which also occurred in many other parts of Polynesia.[16]

Women's organisations

The Christian churches introduced women's organisations to most Pacific societies, in the form of women's church auxiliary groups who convened for religious study, to decorate the village church, to raise funds for the church, and to learn sewing and cooking.[17] Such organisations include the Anglican Mother's Union, the Methodist Women's Fellowships, the SDA Dorcas Society, Catholic Women's leagues, and so on. Such organisations flourished around the Pacific throughout this century.

After World War II the colonial authorities in many Pacific Island territories also encouraged the formation of women's organisations. They established what were termed 'social development' programmes which employed female officers with titles such as 'women's interest assistant', whose job it was to offer instruction to village women's organisations in subjects such as nutrition, cooking, sewing, childcare and public health. The South Pacific Commission set up a regional Community Education Training Centre to train women for positions such as these; and Papua New Guinea established a small national training programme within the Administrative College.

During the late colonial period secular women's organisations developed in Polynesia and Fiji, such as Soqosoqo Vakamarama of Fiji, Lagofonua of Tonga and the Fono Aoao a Tina in Western Samoa. These organisations tended to draw their leadership from among the wives of leading chiefs. They placed particular emphasis on the maintenance of cultural traditions and of women's arts and crafts within those traditions. They aimed to promote women's roles as wives, mothers and home-makers but also to represent women's perspectives to governments exclusively composed of men.

There were also two non-sectarian, internationally linked, non-government organisations (NGO) active in the region: the Young Women's Christian Association (YWCA) and the Pacific South East Asia Union of Women (PASUWE). Their leadership was largely made up of the wives of prominent men, although many of these were also people of exceptional achievements in their own right.

The International Decade for Women
Until the mid-1970s women's organisations in the Pacific sought mainly to promote the representation of women's concerns in relation to the family, the welfare of children and young women, and in some countries, to special issues such as the restriction of liquor licensing. The United Nations International Decade for Women paved the way for a more feminist agenda and for a greater focus on the status of women. Issues such as the education of women, the need for greater numbers of women to take decision-making roles, and concerns for women's rights such as the prevention of violence against women began to receive more attention from women's organisations.[18] During the Decade a number of agencies, but most notably the United Nations Economic and Social Commission for Asia and the Pacific (ESCAP), promoted the establishment of 'national machineries for women' in countries around the region. The term 'national machinery' refers to an interlinked government women's bureau and a national women's NGO through which women's programmes could be promoted and participation in a range of activities could be mobilised.

There have been difficulties in establishing strongly based national councils of women and effective women's bureaux in most Pacific Island states. Unfortunately these innovations have not gained the strong support from village-based women that is necessary to make them politically significant. This has been partially because new urban-based, feminist-oriented women's organisations were sometimes perceived as rivals for the few resources and opportunities available to women by the long established and conservatively oriented church and neo-traditional women's groups. The conservative stance of many church women's groups towards contemporary women's issues was because of their Christian family life orientation. They are ambivalent about national councils of women, fearing that the values and aspirations of church women's groups would be overshadowed and that their historical role, as they saw it, in improving women's status was being insufficiently recognised within secular women's organisations.

Because many women's bureaux were staffed by women trained in social development and home economics approaches, they too found some of the new, more feminist agendas threatening. Many of these women began their careers when home economics was one of the few occupations for women with prospects for advancement in the civil service. They had developed their expertise in helping women to become better home-makers. The more activist pursuit of improvements to women's status and equal opportunity was often not an agenda such women would feel comfortable with.

Establishing effective national councils of women has been particularly problematic in Melanesia (although the National Council of Women [NCW] of Fiji has been one of the more successful in the region). In Solomon Islands and Papua New Guinea, perhaps because of their lack of an influential grass-roots constituency, there has been minimal political or governmental support for national councils of women and government women's bureaux. In contrast Vanuatu has had greater success in gaining government support for its national machinery. The Vanua'aku Party, during its struggle for independence in the 1970s, had a women's wing and throughout its term in office from 1980 to 1991, the Party gave the NCW and government women's unit a role, albeit a very modest one, in the government structure. Generally women's programmes around the region have languished for lack of staff and sufficient operational funds. Governments are usually happy to receive aid for women's projects, but most decline to use their national resources for women's activities. Thus aid-funded programmes for women are rarely sustainable.[19]

Guardians of tradition?

The politics of tradition has attracted considerable discussion among social anthropologists in recent years.[20] Cultural revitalisation movements (referred to widely in Melanesian pidgin as 'kastom') tend to lay particular emphasis on 'traditional' gender roles. For example in Tanna, Vanuatu, where I worked in 1991, there is a strong kastom movement. In some villages people have showed their adherence to kastom by eschewing church membership, assuming traditional forms of dress, and rejecting schooling for children, particularly girls. Those in Tanna who espouse kastom as their primary ideology often seek to maintain what they see as proper gender roles and relations in the name of cultural integrity. For such people kastom asserts the correctness of absolute male dominance, and sometimes includes the rejection of modern ideologies that assert the rights of women and organisations, and opposition to institutions that potentially increase the range of choices available to women. In one kastom-oriented community on Tanna that I visited in 1991 the men all wore shirts and trousers but most women wore grass skirts. Most boys were sent to school but very few girls. Grace Mera Molisa, herself ni-Vanuatu, condemns this oppressive misuse of tradition in her poem 'Custom':[21]

> Custom
> misapplied
> bastardised
> murdered
> a Frankenstein
> corpse
> conveniently
> recalled
> to intimidate women

In the minds of many of those who assert the importance of 'tradition', or who mourn the undermining influences of the outside world on island cultures, women are accorded a special responsibility as keepers of traditional culture. 'Tradition' is the frequently invoked rationale for criticising women who attempt to adopt modern lifestyles and values. While men may freely embrace modern economic activities, education, political institutions, mores and fashions, women must do so with caution, particularly in Melanesia. This theme is strongly emphasised in contemporary Papua New Guinea creative writing. For example in his poem 'Yupela meri i senis hariap pinis' ('Woman, you've changed so fast') Baluwe Umetrifo regretfully compares his rapidly modernising and industrialising home province to a modern young woman, corrupted by change. Other PNG male writers castigate modern women as foolish victims and dupes as the result of their abandonment of customary ways.[22] A similar ambivalence about modernity is expressed by the Solomon Island poet Jully Makini Sipolu in her poem 'Civilised Girl'.[23]

In many Pacific Island societies the past is remembered in terms of the subordination of women, although this picture is contradicted or at least modified for many Pacific societies by historical evidence. In Polynesia there is abundant evidence that in the past women, particularly aristocratic women, enjoyed higher status than they do today.[24] Both oral traditions and historical records make it clear that many Samoan women performed traditional pre-Christian priestly roles, yet the dominant Christian Congregational Church of Samoa refuses to ordain women – although historically related Congregational churches in other parts of the world have long done so.

Less attention has been paid to women's status in the early contact period in Melanesia but it is likely that women had higher status in at least some societies in pre-contact times than they do today. For example, Neumann questions whether women were really as powerless as they are now remembered to have been among the Tolai of Papua New Guinea, citing historical references to women exercising apparent authority in land transactions.[25] The invocation of customary norms in defence of male dominance tends to be selectively focused on male interests. For example, in many Melanesian societies patrilineal succession and inheritance roles are sternly invoked to deny women leadership roles or control of property. Yet in matrilineal societies it is commonplace nowadays for the rules of inheritance to be modified in order to allow men to pass property to their own sons, instead of to their sister's sons as tradition would dictate.[26]

As Ralston points out, Pacific Island women have been presented with representations of the past that claim women played only subordinate, domestic roles in precontact times in order to justify the subordination of women in contemporary society.[27] Knowledge that women had more property rights, authority or autonomy in the past, or that some women were chiefs or priests, is therefore empowering information for Island women, enabling them to question contemporary patriarchal structures.

Women and chieftainship
In Polynesian societies today many people believe it is inconsistent with traditional ways for women to be chiefs or to be involved in politics, despite the many historical and contemporary instances of female chieftainship.

For example, in a case before the Lands and Titles Court of Western Samoa in the 1970s, the judges, comprising Samoan matai considered expert in cultural matters, refused to approve the conferring of a high chiefly title upon the title's most genealogically qualified heir. Their grounds were that this heir was less eligible than other contenders because she was a young female. Yet one of Samoa's most famous chiefs in ancient times, from whom most of Samoa's highest titles originate, was also a woman who took her royal titles when she was very young.

In the pre-Christian order throughout Polynesia, rank was a more important ordering principle than gender, because aristocrats, as descendants of the gods, could not be treated as mere humans, be they male or female. The acceptance of Christian teachings in the nineteenth century diminished the beliefs that supported and justified disparities in rank. The overall effect of Christianity and subsequently of colonial rule was the removal of the major distinctions in rank between aristocrats and the generality of humankind. Chiefs whose persons were sacred, who once had supernatural powers of life and death over their inferiors in rank, became in the religious sense, ordinary mortals.

In Samoa the distinctions between different orders and ranks of chiefs diminished as a result and the emphasis of chieftainship came to be on secular, patriarchal leadership. Modern women's committees are based on an introduced structure which gives the wives of matai authority in the women's sphere which was once only exercised by the sisters and daughters of matai. Until quite recently, few women were themselves matai in the sense of holding village titles, although women of high-ranking families had chiefly status in the sense of being shown respect and deference by those of lesser rank. Western Samoa has many thousands of registered matai. Many are of very minor rank, being only influential in their local villages; others have higher status and are influential throughout districts, while four have paramount status being influential and respected throughout Samoa. Since the 1960s there has been a remarkable increase in the number of female matai and this appears to be related to the success of many Samoan women in attaining higher educational qualifications. Many are rewarded by their 'aiga with matai titles and many of the titles held by women are of high (but not paramount) rank.[28]

In Fiji, although Melanesian gender values generally outweigh the Polynesian cultural influences but chiefly political influence has remained a major force, a woman holds one of Fiji's paramount titles, Rokotui Dreketi. In other Polynesian societies where chiefly systems have been eclipsed by new political structures, chiefs, whether male or female, have considerable mana and moral authority within their lineages and districts – but limited political authority. In Cook Islands, many of the few ariki titles of the southern islands are held by women, although lower-ranking titles with more executive authority are held mainly by men.

Women in politics

Throughout the Pacific the effect of Christian teaching and colonial influence was to emphasise that the proper place for women was in the private, domestic sphere. In those societies where women had religious or political authority, this had been largely lost by the mid twentieth century. Furthermore, nationalism in many parts of the Pacific has taken the form of an emphasis on, or reinvention of, traditions to maintain female subservience. It is not surprising then that women have had little if any political voice throughout the region since most island states became politically independent.

Few Pacific Island countries had strong nationalist movements prior to independence and in most countries the colonial withdrawal was negotiated amiably. In countries where strong nationalist movements did arise and where independence involved some element of struggle, there were also quite strong popular anti-independence or anti-nationalist movements as in Vanuatu and Papua New Guinea. Women have played an important but generally invisible role on both sides, as they continue to do in countries such as New Caledonia and West Papua which are still struggling against colonial rule.

Women were also involved in protest movements during the colonial period, but rarely overtly. An interesting instance in which women came to the front lines of anti-colonial protest was in the Am movement (1925–32) in Western Samoa. The movement began as a moderate resistance to intrusively paternalistic policies by New Zealand authorities; however the severity of New Zealand's reaction soon hardened Samoa's response. The Samoans pursued a policy of non-cooperation with New Zealand to the extent of boycotting schools and hospitals in many districts. When New Zealand began to imprison male Am leaders, their wives, sisters and daughters kept the Am movement alive and active. Among other activities, Samoan women took up the peaceful demonstrations started by the men; wearing purple uniforms the women's Am regularly marched through Apia past the colonial headquarters. On one memorable occasion the women escalated their protest with a traditional women's gesture of contempt termed *sigo*, used towards those who wrongfully usurp power. They hoisted their skirts and in unison bared their bottoms at the

Administrator, who had emerged from his office to tell them to go home.[29]

During the late colonial era in the Pacific region temperance became a political issue for women in several Pacific Island countries, as it had been for women in the West in the previous century. The administrations ruling Pacific Islands under United Nations mandates were obliged by the terms of the mandates to protect native peoples under their control from the evils of alcohol. While prohibition was not very successful in Polynesia and Micronesia, where home brewing became a cottage industry, it was more successful in most of Melanesia where people had less historical familiarity with liquor. However, in the 1960s the denial of the right to drink alcohol came to be seen by Pacific Island males as a symbol of colonial oppression, with the result that laws were changed. The resulting liquor consumption boom in many parts of the Pacific was distressing to women who bore the brunt of the social side effects. Thus in places as different as Truk in Micronesia and East New Britain in Papua New Guinea, women who had never been politically active before organised themselves to try to restrict the sale of liquor, although with only partial success.

The question may be asked for the Pacific that is often asked about Western democracies: if women have the vote, why do they not exercise it more strategically in the collective interest of women? To begin to answer this question for the Pacific Islands we must first consider that most Pacific societies, to the present day, are kin-based societies. Kinship relations determine many aspects of an individual's identity, rights and status, their access to resources such as land and other family property, and even matters such as choice of marriage partner.

In recent years, for example, the people of Western Samoa, by a very narrow majority in a national referendum, opted for universal suffrage. The previous system, under which only matai could vote, restricted women's voice in politics because relatively few of Western Samoan's 10,000 or so matai are women. Yet women's suffrage was never a significant issue in Western Samoa. When Matatumua Maimoana, a woman parliamentarian, introduced a motion before the House for the introduction of universal suffrage in the late 1980s, her argument was not one of women's political rights, but of the integrity of the traditional polity. She argued that the restricted franchise was undermining the chiefly system and thus Samoan culture (fa'asamoa) by encouraging the splitting of titles for electoral purposes. Matatumua and other women who have been in Parliament over the years since 1962 (La'aulu Fetaui, Aiono Fana'afi, Sina Annandale, I'iga Suafole, Faima'ala Taulapapa, and Fiame Naomi) undoubtedly knew that Samoan women, when they got the vote under universal suffrage, would vote as men do, for candidates from their own local polities and kin groups. However women and youth may yet change the face of Samoan politics by being more likely to vote for younger candidates and for female candidates, as long as they feel connected to them at the local or kinship level.[30] Western Samoa – even without universal suffrage – has elected seven women to Parliament since 1962.

There have been few women elected to Parliament in other Pacific Island states. The rare women who succeed in winning elections are usually outstanding individuals who manage to win despite their sex, and they usually make their mark in Parliament once elected. For example, in Papua New Guinea Josephine Abaijah was a founder and leader of the separatist Papua Besena movement, while Nahau Rooney held a ministerial portfolio in a Pangu Party-led coalition in the 1980s.[31] In Fiji, Irene Jai Narayan was not only a long-serving Member of Parliament but was among the leaders of the National Federation Party. Following the coup in 1987, Adi Finau Tabukaucoro was appointed to the interim goverment and held the portfolio for Women's Affairs. She is now an appointee of the Council of Chiefs to the Senate. Taufa Vakatale was one of the few elected women in the history of Fiji politics to achieve ministerial rank; she was Minister for Education prior to the 1994 election.

Kinship to powerful leaders and family-based political groupings appears to have assisted some of the few women to have achieved political careers. In Vanuatu, Hilda Lini, sister to the former Prime Minister of Vanuatu, Walter Lini, was the country's first female parliamentarian.[32] She held the health portfolio in the current government until recently. In Cook Islands, Margaret Story was Speaker for about 13 years under the government led by her brother, Albert Henry. In Tonga, a leading conservative spokesperson for the government in recent years has been 'Eseta Fusitu'a, deputy secretary to the cabinet and wife of the noble Speaker of the House. Of the few women who have made their mark as advocates for women and who have stood for Parliament, none have achieved lasting political careers. For example Fanaura Kingstone, a Cook Islander well known as an advocate for women's concerns in the Pacific region, was a Member of Parliament for one term only, as was Papiloa Foliaki, a leading Tongan Catholic laywoman and NGO leader.

Many more women stand for elections in the region than are elected. In 1984, for example, Nahau Rooney noted that 34 women had stood for Parliament in Papua New Guinea in the nine preceding years of independence, but only three had been elected.[33] So far the record suggests that few Pacific women perceive that women do have collective interests needing political representation, and tend not to support women who stand for election. So far women's movements in most Pacific Island countries have not addressed this issue. An exception is the national lobby group, Women in Politics (WIP), founded in Papua New Guinea in 1986. WIP aims to educate women to vote for women who will work for women's interests. In the last national elections members of WIP assisted a number of women candidates, including going out on the campaign trail with them. In Solomon Islands women have also organised themselves to contest elections in the 1980s for the Honiara municipal council (with some success) and more recently for Western Provincial elections (without success).

Conclusion

There are major differences in the contemporary status of women in the Pacific Islands, broadly shaped by different patterns of gender relations and historical experiences among the people of Melanesia, Polynesia and Micronesia. Yet there are some historical resonances in the experiences of Pacific Islands women and women of New Zealand, the USA and Western Europe over the past century: the 'domesticating' influences of women's programmes and organisations for much of this century; the prominence of family life issues in their agenda; alcohol as an issue which mobilised women to political action; and the use of 'tradition' as a justification for the exclusion of women from the political sphere.

In the Pacific Islands sub-region of Polynesia, and some areas of Micronesia, where women have made the greatest progress towards equality, it has been mainly through the medium of modern education and increased participation in modern economic sectors. Although continuing values of kinship and locality among rural people present obstacles to women taking political leadership roles, the overall direction of social change tends to favour increases in women's status. The increasing sexual equality in educational participation and other positive social indicators (such as low maternal and infant mortality rates and high female life expectancy) in Polynesia and much of Micronesia suggest that in the countries of these sub-regions, women will increase their participation in political leadership. This follows the historical trend of gender relations in New Zealand and other urban-industrial societies, including the newly industrialised societies of Southeast Asia. While small Polynesian and Micronesian Pacific nations are unlikely to follow urban-industrial trends on the same scale as the Pacific rim, these island countries have established strong socio-cultural and economic linkages with New Zealand and the rim nations through emigration which will grow over time.

Such trends are less well established in the Melanesian region where international linkages are weaker, societies are more rural, and where twentieth-century social trends which have benefited women around the world have been less influential. Neo-traditional ideologies are strongly asserted among the political elite, as well as among the rural majority, to justify and defend gender inequality, in particular the exclusion of women from leadership roles. The subordinate position of women in Melanesia is reflected in social indicators more typically associated with the 'Third World' such as low female participation in education, particularly at secondary and post secondary levels and the relatively poor health and life expectancy of women and men. These facts suggest the need for a special focus of international feminist concern and support for the women of Melanesia, a region which is less historically familiar to us than Polynesia, of which New Zealand is a part.

1   In Nauru the voting age is 20 and in all but Fiji, Tonga and Western Samoa, the voting age is 18.

2   Epeli Hau'ofa, 'The New South Pacific Society: Integration and Independence', in Anthony Hooper, et al., eds, Class and Culture in the South Pacific, Univ. of Auckland, Auckland, 1988, 1-16.

3   See, for example, the essays on Hawaii, the Marquesas, Papua New Guinea, and Vanuatu in Margaret Jolly & Martha Macintyre, eds, Family and Gender in the Pacific: Domestic Contradictions and the Colonial Impact, Cambridge Univ. Press, Cambridge, 1989.

4   Mere Pulea, 'The Legal Status of Women in the South Pacific', in Women in Development in the South Pacific: Barriers and Opportunities, Development Studies Centre, Australian National Univ., Canberra, 1985, 33-70.

5   Marilyn Strathern, Women in Between: Female Roles in a Male World: Mount Hagen, New Guinea, Seminar Press, London, 1972.

6   Niel Gunson, 'Sacred Women Chiefs and Female "Headmen" in Polynesian History', Journal of Pacific History (JPH), 22/3, 1987, 139-72.

7   See, for example, Peggy Fairbairn-Dunlop, 'Pule 'Oe! Its up to You: Women's Career Patterns in Western Samoa', and Pani Tawaiyole & Sheldon Weeks, 'Trends in Participation of Females in Formal Education in Papua New Guinea', in Eileen Wormald & Anne Crossley, eds, Women and Education in Papua New Guinea and the South Pacific, Univ. of Papua New Guinea Press, Waigani, 1988, 217-37.

8   Joy E. Gillett, The Health of Women in Papua New Guinea, Papua New Guinea Institute of Medical Research Monograph No. 9, Kristen Press, Madang, 1991.

9   John Williams, Missionary Endeavours, John Snow, London, 1938, 351-2.

10   Grimshaw, 'New England Missionary Wives, Hawaiian women and "the Cult of True Womanhood"', in Jolly & Macintyre, eds, Family and Gender in the Pacific, 28.

11   Nicholas Thomas, 'Domestic Structures and Polyandry in the Marquesas', in Jolly & Macintyre, eds, Family and Gender in the Pacific, 72-5.

12   Diane Langmore, 'The Object Lesson of a Civilised, Christian Home', in Jolly & Macintyre, eds, Family and Gender in the Pacific, 84-94.

13   The trend was first documented in Ester Boserup, Women's Role In Economic Development, Allen & Unwin, London, 1970.

14   Glenn Peterson, 'Ponapean Matrilineages: Production, Exchange and the Ties That Bind', American Ethnologist, 9, 1982

15   See Christina Ward Gailey, Kinship to Kingship: Gender Hierarchies and State Formation in the Tongan Islands, Univ. of Texas Press, Austin, 1987 for an extended discussion of the 'commoditisation'

of women's production in Tonga.

16   Penelope Schoeffel, 'The Origin and Development of Women's Associations in Western Samoa', *Journal of Pacific Studies*, 2, 1979.

17   In Samoa, and possibly elsewhere in Polynesia, there were societies of unmarried or unattached women who lived and worked together in their own house, receiving food from their households.

18   See Dorothy Ayers Counts, ed, *Domestic Violence in Oceania*, a special issue of *Pacific Studies*, 13/3, 1990.

19   Meggit cites a not unusual example from a province of Papua New Guinea where a provincial women's programme received an operating budget of $2000 for the year, while a provincial politician travelling overseas was given $6000 for his pocket money.

20   For recent overviews, see Margaret Jolly, 'Specters of Inauthenticity', *The Contemporary Pacific*, 4/1, 1992, 49-72, and Jocelyn Linnekin, 'On the Theory and Politics of Cultural Construction in the Pacific', *Oceania*, 62/4, 1992, 249-63.

21   From *Black Stone*, Mana Publications, Suva, 1983, 24.

22   See the discussion by Larua Zimmer-Tamakoshi in 'Nationalism and Sexuality in Papua New Guinea', forthcoming in *Pacific Studies*.

23   From *Civilised Girl*, South Pacific Creative Arts Society Suva, Fiji, 1981, 21.

24   Gunson, 'Sacred Women Chiefs and Female "Headmen"'. See also David A. Chappell, 'Shipboard Relations between Pacific Island Women and Euroamerican Men, 1767-1887', *JPH*, 27/2, 1992, 147-8.

25   Klause Neumann, 'Tradition and Identity in Papua New Guinea: Some Observations regarding Tami and Tolai', *Oceania* , 62/4, 1992, 311.

26   See, for example, Tom Otto, 'The Ways of Kastam: Tradition as Category and Practice in a Manus Village'; Robert J. Foster, 'Commoditisation and the Emergence of Kastam as a Cultural Category: A New Ireland Case in Comparative Perspective'; Klaus Neumann, 'Tradition and Identity in Papua New Guinea: Some Observations regarding Tami and Tolai', *Oceania*, 266-7, 288-9.

27   Caroline Ralston, 'The Study of Women in the Pacific', *The Contemporary Pacific*, Spring, 1992, 168.

28   Penelope Schoeffel, 'Daughter of Sina: A Study of Gender, Status and Power in Samoa', unpublished Ph.D Thesis, Australian National Univ., 1981.

29   Personal communication: Masiofo Noe Tamasese, Apia, 1977.

30   Personal communication: Hon. Fiame Naomi Mata'afa, Minister for Education, Western Samoa, Aug 1993.

31   Josephine Abaijah was elected President of the PNG National Council of Women in 1993. Nahau Rooney is now a leader of the Manus Provincial Women's Council.

32   Hilda Lini was the first officer appointed to head the Pacific Women's Resource Bureau at the South Pacific Commission, before taking up a political career in Vanuatu.

33   Cited by Pulea, 'The Legal Status of Women in the South Pacific', 37.

III

Protracted Struggles

Women voting in a mock election, Buenos Aires, Argentina, 1920. Dr Elvira Rawson de Dellepiane, a physician and one of the most devoted Argentine feminists and suffragists, is at the centre (no hat, dark dress).
Private collection, Asunción Lavrin.

7

Citizenship, Culture and Civilisation: The Languages of British Suffragists, 1866–1874[1]

JANE RENDALL

> Woman's Place In Creation
>
> An able lecture on the above subject was delivered, October 15th 1869, at the Provincial Hall, Nelson, by Joseph Giles Esq, M.R.C.S., resident magistrate on the Nelson South West Gold Fields . . . . He commenced by observing: 'There is at the present moment a tide in the affairs of women, and no one knows precisely whither it will lead. The existence of the phenomenon is unquestionable. The tide is rising upon the coasts of the leading civilized countries of the earth, and there is little doubt but it will reach our own shores . . .' . In the course of his observations he said: 'In the barbarous epoch, the disparity of physical strength in men and women controlled all the relations between the sexes, – and the somewhat eccentric logic of society concluded that as woman was the weaker she must have been intended to do all the hard work. Therefore, the Indian hunter, having slain his deer, sent the squaws to carry it home; and the Maori of the present day walks at his ease, smoking his pipe, – or, at the utmost holding one end of a string to the other end of which a pig is attached, – whilst the women stagger, bent almost double, under heavy loads of potatoes and kumaras [sweet potatoes] . . .' . (*Manchester National Society for Women's Suffrage Journal*, 3, 2 May 1870, 24-5.)

The first work on women's suffrage published in New Zealand, the *Appeal to the Men of New Zealand* (1869), by Mary Muller of Nelson, appears to have gone entirely unnoticed by the contemporary British women's suffrage movement. Yet, in 1870, the new journal of the Manchester National Society for Women's Suffrage published an extract from a lecture given in Nelson by a Joseph Giles. Giles identified a 'tide in the affairs of women', sweeping through 'the leading civilized countries'. He contrasted that 'civilization' with a 'barbarous epoch' represented through the laborious drudgery of American Indian and Maori women. This chapter hopes, in examining the early history of the British women's suffrage movement, to throw light on why Manchester suffragists should read with interest the words of a Nelson magistrate.

Liberal politics and women's suffrage in Britain, 1866–74

The first generation of British suffragists is surprisingly unstudied. The massive expansion in the literature of British women's history over the last ten years has produced no detailed work on the first thirty years of the suffrage movement, before 1890. Ann Robson, Andrew Rosen and Barbara Caine have begun to explore the origins of the movement, but, interestingly, all have written from outside the United Kingdom.[2] British women's historians have not looked to the liberal politics of Lydia Becker, Millicent Fawcett, Helen Taylor, and their successors, for their subjects. The reason may lie within British women's history itself. The recent expansion of women's history in Britain had its origins in the radical and socialist politics of the 1960s and 1970s, and remains still surprisingly marginal to the academic mainstream (though I myself write from within the academy). Writing on nineteenth-century women has tended to focus on the social history of the period, on the recovery of women in working-class and radical movements, and on feminist movements which challenged moral and social order. So far, with some exceptions, there has been little dialogue with the mainstream of political history or political theory in Britain.

Existing work on liberal feminism in Britain and the United States has related it to individualist traditions which look back to John Locke, and offer a more or less direct transition to John Stuart Mill, and onwards to forms of modern western social democracy.[3] Criticisms have come from those who have stressed the importance of a strand of political argument which rested on the unique and different qualities women might bring to the political sphere.[4] Both approaches have greatly enhanced our understanding. This chapter does not enter that argument directly, but suggests that recent work on the history of liberalism in nineteenth-century Britain, coming from the perspective of the history of ideas, can offer another context for looking at the relationship between feminism and liberalism. Use of such work may help to explain why Joseph Giles wrote as he did of American Indian and Maori women, and why the *Women's Suffrage Journal* published his words. It can also be related to two contemporary concerns of women's history: the meanings that citizenship may have for women, and the ethnocentricity of white Western feminisms.[5]

The new work, by John Burrow, Stefan Collini, and Donald Winch, has moved away from a stress on the pursuit of individual rights or self-interest as the key to mid-nineteenth-century liberal politics in Britain. Leading liberal intellectuals used the term 'altruism', newly coined in 1853, and the language of duty and obligation, to condemn 'selfishness', 'self-interest', and 'egoism'. The framework in which they worked was that of the development of civil society, the key terms 'civilization', and 'progress'. The republican notion of virtue in public life was replaced by that of 'character', an insistence that legislative or political change was inadequate without changes in the qualities and habits of the individual, and of the nation. Burrow, Collini and Winch have also reminded us of the transformation of the fields of law, history, anthropology and sociology in Britain in the 1860s and 1870s, and of the consequences for the study of politics.[6] These revisions offer a context for exploring the meanings – and there were several – of citizenship for that first generation of British suffragists.

British political life in the 1860s and 1870s was still dominated by an aristocratic elite, though one capable of absorbing new energies and of offering appropriate compromises to the challenges of middle-class radicalism. The sheer nervousness with which British politicians, both Conservatives and Liberals, approached the very notion of manhood suffrage needs to be stressed. In these circles the question was not one of universal male enfranchisement, but rather of the 'fitness' of different classes of men for the vote.[7] Before 1867, very approximately, 20 per cent of adult men were enfranchised, and between the Reform Acts of 1867 and 1918 very roughly around 60 per cent.[8]

The birth of the British women's suffrage movement needs to be placed within the context of that surge of Liberal enthusiasm and reform, countrywide, which preceded the election of Gladstone's Liberal Government in 1868, a government which lasted until 1874. The movement united three different groups: a small group of London women activists, involved with the *English Woman's Journal* and with campaigns for educational and legal reform; John Stuart Mill, his stepdaughter Helen Taylor, and a group of mostly male liberals, academics as well as politicians, including Henry and Millicent Fawcett, around him; and provincial networks of women and men, including some Liberal party politicians, in the major cities of Manchester, Edinburgh, Birmingham and Bristol. It was to be the Manchester group, led, dynamically, by Lydia Becker, which was to take the lead.[9]

The merger of these three groups was not an easy one: there were personal, strategic and ideological conflicts. The differences included those between Mill's group, mostly men with academic and philosophical interests, who saw adherence to the women's movement as 'a badge of advanced liberalism', and the grittier style of a determined and energetic provincial movement with much closer links to the politics of popular liberalism and radicalism.[10] The first London society was founded in 1866, the Manchester society a few months later, with others rapidly following. The first central, national committee was set up by the Manchester group in 1871; Mill and Taylor refused to allow the London society which they dominated to affiliate, and split the London suffragists as a result. John Stuart Mill's part in all this was complicated. His political intervention was sought and greatly desired by feminists in 1866 and 1867, his *Subjection of Women* rapturously received in 1869. His support was immensely important. Yet Barbara Caine has rightly written of his manipulative and egotistic management of the suffrage committee to which he belonged. And any reader of the last years of his correspondence is likely to be shocked at his intolerance of disagreement, his rejection of public campaigning, and his inability to work with any but womanly women.[11]

Here I examine the meanings of citizenship to campaigners for women's suffrage from 1866 – the date of the first petition for women's suffrage to the House of Commons – to 1874, the date of the fall of Gladstone's first Liberal Government. The sources used are mainly the contributions by leading suffragists to major journals, and the journals of the movement itself, the *Englishwoman's Review* and the *Women's Suffrage Journal*, together with a selective sampling of private correspondence. The choice of public medium by the suffrage campaigners was itself a significant statement. They made their major contributions to the leading liberal periodicals of the day. The editor of the *Westminster Review*, John Chapman, described it as 'a consistent, zealous and influential advocate of the doctrines of the advanced liberal party'.[12] The *Fortnightly Review*, published from 1865 and edited by John Morley, was widely recognised as the most influential journal among self-styled progressive thinkers in the 1860s and 1870s. Others included *Macmillan's Magazine*, similarly liberal and edited by a friend of Millicent and Henry Fawcett, and the *Contemporary Review*, whose editor, the Dean of Canterbury, was a consistent supporter of women's suffrage from its beginning.[13]

This choice of medium is not a matter of detail. It is clear that suffragists believed that these were the influential opinion-shaping journals, and mobilised all their resources to publish in them, calling upon a word from John Stuart Mill to powerful editors such as Chapman or Morley to help.[14] Though their circulation was small – that of the *Fortnightly* only 2500 in 1872 – they appealed mainly to a liberal and politically aware intelligentsia. Articles on women's suffrage were reprinted as pamphlets, and extracts were likely to appear in the *Englishwoman's Review* from 1865 and the *Women's Suffrage Journal* from 1870, with their arguments reappearing again in reported public lectures. The *Englishwoman's Review*, begun by Jessie Boucherett, continued the work of the earlier *English Woman's Journal* as a general periodical of the women's movement.[15] The *Women's Suffrage Journal* was a kind of regular report from the campaign front, run from Manchester by Lydia Becker. Here I focus on the articles, the lectures and other works of the women, and one man, who shaped opinion in these years: Kate Amberley, Lydia Becker, Barbara Bodichon, Jessie Boucherett, Frances Power Cobbe, Millicent Fawcett, Richard Pankhurst, Louisa Shore, Helen Taylor, and Julia Wedgwood. Their backgrounds ranged from the aristocratic to the professional middle class.[16]

'Lady householders' and 'self-dependent women': the case for equal treatment

In the debate around and immediately following the Reform Bill of 1867, suffragists put the argument that women should be enfranchised on precisely the same terms as men. There is a case here for seeing suffragist argument within a long individualist tradition, and for a comparison between the arguments for enfranchising working men and those for women's suffrage. The popular liberalism and radicalism of working-class men in the campaigns before 1867, and in the election of 1868, drew heavily upon a language which looked back to the seventeenth century, to a biblical gospel speaking of democracy and equality, and to the struggle of the 'people' against the 'feudalism' of the aristocracy. The vote was constituted as a moral responsibility of the individual, who was in the terms of the seventeenth-century Levellers, an independent individual, with a property in *his* labour. Manhood suffrage was still the suffrage of the 'independent' man.[17] By the 1860s such older radical arguments were being supplemented by the concept of the rational, respectable working man as household head and breadwinner.[18]

Before 1867 the franchise rested on a restrictive property qualification, the £10 household in the towns, the 40s freehold in the counties. After 1867 the granting of household franchise in the towns meant that male ratepayers, owners or lodgers, were enfranchised, in theory if not in practice, given the complex requirements for registration. Either qualification meant that married women, who could own no landed property of their own before 1882, could not possibly qualify. Suffragists argued that as independent householders, spinsters and widows should vote, before 1867 on the grounds of a right rooted in property, and after 1867 as householders and taxpayers. When Helen Taylor first put the case for the enfranchisement of spinsters and widows, she did so, in the

Westminster Review for 1866, with extreme caution. Her arguments were cast first of all in terms of the British Constitution: to which she said, 'nothing can be more entirely foreign than Universal Suffrage, or . . . either Personal or Class Representation'. Her authority was that of Lord Somers speaking in 1703 in the House of Lords, who spoke of the vote as the privilege of preserving one's property, the 'birthright' of an Englishman.[19] In the *Englishwoman's Review* in 1866 an article on the consequences of extending the franchise to female householders dwelt particularly on the role of 'lady householders' who might have a particular part to play in the reform of workhouses, and on female farmers, one-tenth of the farmers in England, whose inability to deliver their vote to their landlord could result in their losing their tenancy. But it also speculated on the likelihood of working-class women, likely to be 'innkeepers, lodging housekeepers, small shopkeepers and washerwomen', possessing the vote.[20]

After John Stuart Mill's attempt to amend the Reform Bill of 1867 to include women was defeated, Lydia Becker led a vigorous campaign to demonstrate that all women who paid rates were nevertheless entitled to be placed on the parliamentary register, on two grounds: firstly, that there was significant evidence that in medieval and early modern England, property had given women the right to exercise the parliamentary vote or to send deputies, and secondly, on the legal technicality that the Act of 1867 by using the term 'man' and not 'male person' had generically included 'woman'. The basis of the campaign became 'no taxation without representation'. Becker mobilised large numbers of potential voters, in the Manchester area and elsewhere, in a series of claims, based on extensive historical research, put forward in the courts which registered voters. Presiding barristers were on the whole unconvinced that 'man' really meant 'woman' in this instance, or that they could accept the precedents offered from the reigns of Henry IV, V, and VI, Queen Elizabeth and James I.[21] A few claims successfully placed women on the electoral register, only to be rejected in a higher court. These events did, however, demonstrate that enfranchising women on the same terms as men after 1867 did not involve simply wealthy and propertied women, and they brought Becker much closer to the language of popular liberalism, and to Liberal party organisation, than her London associates.[22]

The publicity given to potential women voters suggested the qualities of citizenship that were being emphasised. These qualities had much in common with those of the 'independent artisan'. A woman called Lily Maxwell, mistakenly placed on the electoral register in 1867, was given an escort to the poll by Lydia Becker. She was, readers of the *Englishwoman's Review* were told, 'an intelligent person of respectable appearance' who 'keeps a small shop for the sale of crockery ware', who had strong political opinions and 'was delighted to have a chance of expressing them'.[23] Similarly, the nine women who actually managed to cast a vote in Manchester in the election of 1868, are described as ranging 'in social grade from the rank of well-to-do shopkeepers down to that of the very poorest labourer' and as displaying genuine political feeling, intelligence and interest, 'a fair sample', it was suggested, 'of the 10,000 eligible women ratepayers of Manchester'.[24] Women voters were respectable, intelligent and engaged in useful, though not necessarily paid, labour. Barbara Bodichon described likely voters as 'the quiet spinster sitting at home teaching her nephews and nieces, or the hardworking widow woman who is carrying on her late husband's trade, the lodging-housekeeper, or the rich Miss Bountiful of Philanthropic Lodge'.[25] These arguments were immeasurably strengthened when in 1869 women ratepayers were given the municipal vote, and after 1870 could vote and be elected to School Boards. The *Women's Suffrage Journal* constantly dwelt on the contrast between the municipal and the parliamentary vote.[26]

The Manchester National Society for Women's Suffrage appealed in a series of memorials to the Prime Minister, the hero of popular liberalism, William Gladstone himself.[27] In 1874 they called for the removal of the electoral disability of women, anomalous, they said, because 'the principle that women may have political power is coeval with the British constitution', and anomalous because it was at odds with the part women were playing and had always played in local government. Women householders had to pay both local and imperial taxation, yet had no control over imperial expenditure as they did in local matters. Women in purchasing property obtained less for their money than men did: one vote rather than two. Increasing numbers of what were described as 'absolutely self-dependent women', working women affected by male combinations and legislative restrictions, were entitled to representation. This was a construction of the case designed to appeal to Gladstone. The rights claimed were those of property and self-dependence, in accordance with the gradual process of constitutional development. In claiming equality in this kind of language, suffragists located themselves within the tradition of British radicalism.

'To develop her moral and intellectual muscle': the politics of individuality

That location, however, needs close scrutiny. The merest sampling of the private correspondence of the leaders of the suffrage movement makes it very clear that the decision to focus upon the claims of propertied and self-dependent women, by definition single or widowed, was quite simply a strategic and expedient one. To Helen Taylor writing to Barbara Bodichon in 1866, 'no idea is so universally accepted and acceptable in England as that taxation and representation ought to go together'. People would listen to the case for single women and widows of property, though not to 'the much more startling general proposition that sex is not a proper ground for distinction in political rights'.[28] Barbara Bodichon, Millicent Fawcett and Lydia Becker all shared a faith in that proposition.[29] They all believed there was no justification for disenfranchising married women: their correspondence and, if carefully read, their public voices make it clear. They recognised that the independent voter of the radical tradition was indeed a masculine individual, and that tradition failed to offer a basis for a broader enfranchisement.[30]

Lydia Becker perhaps came closer than most to a defence of citizenship resting on humanity alone. While sweeping 1600 women ratepayers off the electoral register, Mr Justice Byles, in the Court of Common Pleas in 1869, had agreed when it was put to him that the political status of women was no better than that of dogs and horses, and had refused to allow that 'woman can be man unless in a zoological treatise, or until she is reduced to the status of fossil remains'. Becker wrote in the *Westminster Review* of the attributes distinguishing 'man' – the generic term – from the beasts: speech, reason, moral responsibility and religious faith. From these – not from sex – came the capacity to exercise political functions.[31] Similarly, when the *Women's Suffrage Journal* wrote of those others excluded from the suffrage – 'criminals, idiots, lunatics and minors' – Becker suggested that qualifications for voting should be rooted in the 'intelligence, rationality, and responsibility' of the voter.[32] When the young radical Richard Pankhurst first published in the *Fortnightly Review*, he wrote 'that each individual receives the right to vote in the character of a human being, possessing intelligence and adequate reasoning power.'[33] In a letter to Richard Pankhurst in 1868, Lydia Becker wrote of her own energetic activities on behalf of ratepaying women as only a partial measure on the route to her own ultimate goal, which was 'the full recognition of the principle that every human soul is an independent kingdom – nay a universe – over which the individual is sole sovereign . . .' and she continued, 'Freedom and equality not only do not prevent self-devotion to the welfare of others, but seem essential to it . . .'.[34] Here an argument for autonomy, with Protestant and enlightened roots, has become a precondition of voluntary 'self-devotion to the welfare of others'. For Becker, as for other suffragists, a claim for political rights rooted simply in property and in the interest of the individual did not come easily.

Becker, Bodichon, Cobbe, Fawcett, and Taylor all shared that antipathy to selfishness and self-interest, that commitment to altruism found in the writings of advanced liberalism which Stefan Collini has explored.[35] To Barbara Bodichon, the strongest argument for giving women votes was the influence that enfranchisement would have in increasing patriotism and a public spirit, 'an unselfish devotedness to the public service', going beyond the narrowness of the private family circle.[36] In her lecture on 'Why Women Require the Franchise' Fawcett, condemning the 'domestic selfishness' of indolent wealthy women, recalled the fate of so many of her countrywomen, desperate for education, locked into brutal marriages, a situation which only legislation could change. Suffrage for women was the only way to cleanse the statute book.[37] For Kate Amberley, writing in the *Fortnightly Review* in 1871, political power was to be demanded not as a right, but as a protection, as a way first in which women might 'assist their less fortunate sisters' and, secondly, as a means to a future in which they might freely develop their own faculties.[38]

These arguments go beyond the British radical tradition, and differ significantly from the demands of working men. They owe much to the writings of John Stuart Mill, though they were not limited by them. In his *Subjection of Women* (1869), as in his *On Liberty* (1859), John Stuart Mill's goal was self-development, the highest cultivation of individual faculties, in all their variety and diversity, a kind of cultivation encouraged both by the right kind of marriage, one very much like his own, and by the freedom of the citizen. Only the citizen could experience the invigorating effect of freedom on the character to the full. Mill was also clear that such pleasures were unlikely to be for all; the uneducated and the mediocre in his own society would need help, education, and the right kind of institutions. And beyond Western Europe, in those Eastern societies he designated as stationary and despotic, and in even more 'backward' areas, there was no possibility of such cultured self-development.[39] The danger to such a concept of citizenship within his own society came from the growth of democracy, threatening the tyranny of uniformity, the stifling of individuality. In his *Considerations on Representative Government* (1861) Mill offered a number of solutions to this dilemma: educational tests for voters, plural votes for the better educated, and the disqualification of paupers and non-taxpayers. Another solution was the proposal for proportional representation put forward by Thomas Hare, based on a national list of candidates and a quota preference system, as a means of ensuring the representation of minorities, and in particular the election not of local notables or party hacks, but 'men of talent and character,' clearly men like Mill and his friends.[40] Such a system was designed to counteract the 'collective mediocrity' Mill and such friends feared.

Suffragist claims made for the woman citizen in these years were rooted more in a view of 'individuality' which owed much to Millite liberalism, than in the 'possessive individualism' of the male radical tradition. Yet such a concept also carried with it an inescapable and precise location within one's own 'society', 'nation' and 'civilization'. For these women of the liberal elite, though born into differing backgrounds, nevertheless shared a material privilege and a confidence which enabled them to deploy the political culture and vocabulary of that elite in a gendered way. So the concept of 'individuality' could accommodate sexual difference, the construct of 'society' incorporated women as both the agents and the subjects of social science, and gendered histories of both the British 'nation' and of 'civilization' itself were invoked.

The language of individuality was widely used. Millicent Fawcett, writing in the aftermath of the Paris Commune, wrote that no country was so safe from revolution as one in which its citizens enjoyed perfect freedom, and for her: 'Freedom is nothing but power to exercise the faculties, and how can the faculties be exercised if they are not cultured?'[41] Education and cultivation were to these liberals the key to citizenship. To Julia Wedgwood, describing the narrowness and lack of opportunity of the life of the middle-class woman, female suffrage was to be claimed not as a right, and not as an end in itself alone, but rather as a means: 'We seek to be numbered among citizens quite as much from our need of being awakened to higher duties as from a demand for extended rights. We desire it more for what it would make us than for what it would give us.'[42] Louisa Shore wrote of the angelic image of Victorian women that she 'longed to take off these golden chains, open the hothouse doors, and turn the ethereal prisoner into free fresh air, to develop her moral and intellectual muscle'.[43] And it was the higher responsibilities of citizenship which were to provide this form of muscular character training.

If citizenship was to foster individuality and the development of character, not all members of a society would be ready for such a concept. Many suffragists initially shared Mill's distrust of democracy, and, influenced by him, noted the ways in which he proposed to limit its effects. Helen Taylor actively supported an educational qualification, plural voting, and Thomas Hare's scheme for proportional representation.[44] Millicent Fawcett published two articles on Hare's complex scheme in *Macmillan's Magazine*.[45] Other suffragists joined in this enthusiasm. Barbara Bodichon cited Hare, with Mill and Herbert Spencer, as her authorities for enfranchisement.[46] To Jessie Boucherett, proportional representation provided the ideal solution to disputes that might arise between husband and wife (since each could vote for different candidates without direct conflict), and a means of campaigning for the votes for married women.[47] However, by the early 1870s such schemes hardly seemed a practical possibility. The future lay with the argument of Frances Power Cobbe that the enfranchisement of the limited group of women envisaged might restore 'the just balance in favour of an educated constituency against the weight of the illiterate male voters now entrusted with the suffrage'.[48] There is much more in the language of the early suffrage movement to indicate that what was claimed as citizenship was regarded less as a right, an expression of interest, than as a duty, a responsibility, a trust. In an article in the *Englishwoman's Review*, 'Are Duties and Rights the Same?' the author noted the impression of egotism given by the pursuit of individual rights, even though 'it seemed easy and natural that men should demand their rights. History has accustomed us to it.'

The history that was the record of one class after another asserting its rights – the nobles through Magna Carta, Protestants through the bill of rights, the middle classes through the reform bills, and the working classes through trades unions – might seem easy and natural, yet for women to assert 'rights' had a self-seeking, assertive quality about it. The author looked in a different direction, though one already familiar to both working-class politicians and some women activists: to Italy and to Joseph Mazzini's *Duties of Man* (1858; first English translation 1862) for a work that set duty to others, to one's own society and to humanity, and to a world of future social harmony and the reconciliation of classes, against the pursuit of rights.[49] Mazzini's appeal was clearly echoed elsewhere in the suffrage movement. Kate Amberley concluded her article in the *Fortnightly Review* by quoting extensively from the *Duties of Man* on the role of women and their duty to humanity.[50] The *Women's Suffrage Journal* printed in November 1870, as 'Mazzini on the Franchise for Women', some extracts from a letter from Mazzini to an English woman, in which he urged that the cause, which was also that of the moral education of society, was a religious one, never to be narrowed down to 'what is called a right or an interest': 'let duty be your ground, both in protecting your unhappy sisters and in urging your political claims'.[51]

'The Citizenship of Women, Socially Considered'

If rights were conceived in relationship to a duty or a responsibility to others, it is worth turning to the important suggestions made by Denise Riley, on the significance of the emergence of the 'social' as the ground for women's and suffragist activity.[52] This notion of a civil society, of which women were a part as they had not been a part of the political order, has to be seen as related to two major themes of nineteenth-century thought: its claims to scientific method, and its historicism.[53] The belief in the methods of natural science as the only reliable guide to human knowledge of the world, and therefore to human behaviour, was a pervasive one within this liberal culture. Such a belief underlay the new science of society, the project of discovering the laws that governed social development. Leading suffragist writers did not on the whole see the duties of woman in terms of philanthropy, woman's mission, or sentimental self-sacrifice. In fact, they carefully disassociated themselves from such ideas. They looked instead for a framework of social responsibility which rested on an informed, scientific base, and for the kind of social science debated at the National Association for the Promotion of Social Science, where the women's meeting was reported as a 'Ladies' Parliament' debating questions of education, training and employment. There reform and science came together.[54]

Julia Wedgwood, writing of women who might mistakenly encourage pauperism out of an overly feminised and sentimentally Christian compassion, spoke of a woman's perception of political economy as belonging 'to a secular male world, with which she has nothing to do'. Citizenship should bring a sense of responsibility to replace the easy pleasures of charity, an involvement in the national life, and an understanding of laws of political economy which might end through 'beneficent discipline' the 'rot of pauperism'. With such understanding, women's social sympathies might eventually achieve much in the areas of education and pauperism.[55] Millicent Fawcett, who in these years was not only beginning her suffrage work, but also educating herself as a popular writer on political economy, wrote in liberal journals on the consequences of pauperism, on the importance of working-class payment for education, and on the encouragement of self-help and independence among the poor.[56] The social responsibility of the woman citizen might still rest on strongly individualist assumptions; and in this suffragists were largely at one with popular and Gladstonian liberalism.

But the duty of women as potential voters was not only to take a general responsibility in social legislation, but also to help in the creation of a different kind of marriage, one which again owed much to Mill's ideal. Louisa Shore's article, 'The Citizenship of Women, Socially Considered', takes as its final focus the new kind of marriage that might be expected by 'a truthful free woman, the equal, sympathetic and en-nobling partner of man'.[57] Julia Wedgwood, in her article 'Female Suffrage in its Influence on Married Life', wrote of marriage as 'that sudden generation of power, that sudden enlargement of view which takes place when two human spirits come into moral contact'. She argued that was what marriage should be in all classes of life.[58] Suffragists strongly identified with a social responsibility to make such a form of marriage possible. To those disinclined to claim their rights, the appeal was to their sense of obligation to such sisters – as in that by Millicent Fawcett at Bristol in a lecture in 1871: 'If you don't want rights because you have so many privileges, remember the fate of those among your country-women who are associated with men base enough to avail themselves of the power which the law places so unreservedly in their hands.'[59]

The suffrage movement, from its origins, assaulted what it regarded as outmoded and 'barbaric' laws, and new and unjust legis-lation of all kinds which affected women. There was a close relationship, and a considerable overlap among the activists, between the Manchester suffrage movement and the campaign for married women's property legislation. Suffrage writers were entirely united on this, an issue which most clearly indicated the absence of any female voice in the legis-lature, and the partiality and self-interest of existing legislation.[60] The *Women's Suffrage Journal* and the *Englishwoman's Review* printed long lists of cases of the murder, assault, and beating of wives, often with very little punishment of husbands.[61] The leniency of courts against husbands was constantly attacked, in stories headed 'Killing a Woman versus Street Robbery', 'Censured but not Punished' or 'How Men Protect Women'.[62] The *Journal* printed stories of wives denuded of all their property, and of young children taken from their mothers to be brought up against their mothers' wills as Protestant or Catholic, or Christian in the case of a Muslim mother.[63] They campaigned against legislation proposed in 1871 which would allow a man to marry his deceased wife's sister, and against the failure of attempts to make husbands support their separated wives. And they supported the struggle of 'a band of noble women' against the infamous Contagious Diseases Acts.[64]

History, nationality and civilisation

In July 1871 an editorial of the *Women's Suffrage Journal* – one among many – called for a change in the political condition of women, in the light of the hardships endured by so many, directly traceable to the operation of harsh laws of marriage, and the absence of any effective security for women in the law. In the same issue, under the heading 'Less than Justice for Women', are two accounts, taken from local papers, of wives beaten and starved by their husbands. At the end of these accounts is a paragraph, printed without comment:

> Sir John Lubbock, in his work on the *Origin of Civilization and the Primitive Condition of Man* remarks: 'The position of women in Australia seems indeed to be wretched in the extreme. They are treated with the utmost brutality, beaten and speared in the limbs on the most trivial provocation.'[65]

To explain why Lydia Becker should have added this paragraph, by an archaeologist of prehistory, to an account of wife-beating in London and Dudley, I return to the second major theme of nineteenth-century thought indicated above: the historicism of approaches to the study of society. Citizenship is a question not only of rights and duties but also of identity. Suffragists sought to define that identity through histories which incorporated sexual difference, and which could be distinguished from that history which was a mere history of men, and male-defined classes, demanding their rights.

There is much in the rhetoric and the language of early suffragists to justify an analysis of their identity as a national one, as Britons, as English women, and as Scotch women. Patriotism and public spirit were frequently invoked. So too might be a particular and gendered version of English history. The working-class radicals' appeal to Anglo-Saxon democracy could be paralleled by the notion of early Anglo-Saxon and even early Germanic societies as ones particularly favourable to women. Hints contained in the works of the Roman historian Tacitus on the freedom of women of the ancient Britons, who participated in public councils with Boadicea, and on the participation of women in the councils of early German tribes, could be developed.[66] Frances Power Cobbe could write in 1868 that 'our Teuton race from the days of Tacitus, has borne women whose moral nature has been in more than equipoise with their passions; and who have both deserved and obtained a freedom and a respect unknown to their sisters of the south'.[67] An article on Anglo-Saxon women in the *Women's Suffrage Journal* suggested that they inherited and controlled their own property, took their place in battle and even in public councils: 'The influence of women has been nowhere more effectual, more fully recognised, or more enduring than among the Anglo-Saxons, and nowhere was it more legitimate or more happy'.[68] In the debates over the granting of the municipal franchise to women, much was made of women's part in local government as an essential part of the constitution since the Anglo-Saxons, when they had held ancient rights and offices in parishes and municipalities, as churchwardens, waywardens, overseers of the poor.[69] There is an element here of a 'golden age' of the past, with the loss of the parliamentary vote for women seen as a kind of accidental and temporary deviation from the true principles of the constitution, rooted in local self-government and lost at some point in the seventeenth century.[70]

However, I want to suggest that there was also another somewhat contradictory but ultimately more powerful historical language available to the suffragists of the late 1860s and 1870s, and that is the language of the history of civil society, of civilisation itself, a history in which women had not a marginal or antiquarian but a central role. It is this history which explains why the *Women's Suffrage Journal* might juxtapose Lubbock on Australian Aboriginal people to accounts of wife-beating in Britain, and why – to return to my starting point – Joseph Giles in Nelson might contrast his 'tide in the affairs of women' with the labour of American Indian and Maori women. The theme that united virtually all writing on the suffrage in these years is a consciousness of progress, of participating in a progressive movement of civilisation, to be differentiated from those other parts of the world still dominated by a 'savage' brutality, and by despotic governments. In part, such expressions drew upon the familiar figures of speech of European writing over the past two or three centuries: the very frequent references in suffragist writing to the closed world of the harem and the despotic governments of the East are orientalist commonplaces. But the themes of progress drawn upon were more than mere figures of speech: they were a part of that particular preoccupation with socio-cultural evolution which characterised the third quarter of the nineteenth century.[71] The history of that evolution employed what was called a comparative approach. Crudely, it drew on both the distant European past, and on a variety of evidence around non-European cultures of the present, to create a ladder of socio-cultural development, in which the civilised societies of Western Europe represented the highest point.

Such an approach was already present in Mill's *Subjection of Women*, in which he described the conditions of marriage and the legal disabilities of women as the last survivals of a feudal past.

All the writers considered here shared that perspective. Louisa Shore began her 'Citizenship of Women, Socially Considered' with such a history of woman, who 'in the early ages of the human race' 'literally a slave', was now simply in an age 'still ordered on barbarian principles' in subjection.[72] Kate Amberley wrote in the *Fortnightly Review* of the progress of civilisation, that gradually the heroic and military virtues of the past had given way to more amiable ones, to which women could aspire as well as men.[73] And Millicent Fawcett in a powerful speech at Birmingham in 1872 said in a phrase which is a kind of commonplace, repeated everywhere in histories of civil societies since the Enlightenment: 'The history of civilization is the history also of a steady, progressive improvement in the condition of women'. She too drew a contrast with women 'of savage races', with 'little better lives than beasts of burden', with 'semi-civilizations of the East' valuing women principally as inmates of the harem. The extension of the suffrage would be a part of that 'steady, progressive improvement', for, she asked her audience rhetorically, was that history simply to stop in 1872? Was there not room for further improvement, in a society in which a man might hold his wife on a fire until she burned to death, and the jury recommend him to mercy, as in a recent case at Preston?[74]

One source of such a view of progress lay in a liberal theology. Frances Power Cobbe, for instance, was politically closer to the Conservative than to the Liberal party, but allied herself very clearly with a progressive theology. In the wake of the questioning of the literal truth of the Christian Bible, new possibilities were opening up, of a Deity whose intentions were for a progressively developing universe, whose social prescriptions were adapted to particular stages of society, and who might support women's suffrage in the nineteenth, if not in the first, century. To Frances Power Cobbe the history of civilisation was also the history of the development of a new kind of religious faith, and a new kind of marriage, to be rooted in a religion of individual development, of moral sense and social affections.[75]

But liberal theology was also paralleled by the new developments in what we would term anthropology, although disciplinary boundaries were by no means so clearcut in the 1860s and 1870s. The years in which the claim for the suffrage were being formulated were also the years in which

Henry Maine wrote *Ancient Law* (1861), and *Lectures on the Early History of Institutions* (1875), John McLennan his *Primitive Marriage* (1865), John Lubbock *The Origin of Civilization and the Primitive Condition of Man* (1870), and E. B. Tylor his *Researches into the Early History of Mankind and the Development of Civilization* (1865) and *Primitive Culture* (1871). Marriage and the history of the human family were major concerns of these writers, who wrote and reviewed in the same journals as Millicent Fawcett and Lydia Becker, though their political commitments were varied. Nevertheless their arguments were taken up and actively discussed within liberal circles; they shared assumptions of progressive development, and the view that civilisation brought with it increasing personal freedom and independence for women from the promiscuous, polyandrous, or patriarchal families of the different pasts they were separately constructing.[76]

A knowledge of the general themes, if not the detailed subject matter, of the work of these writers was inescapable. In the third edition of her *Brief Summary of the Laws of England*, of 1869, Barbara Bodichon, for instance, added a note, drawn from Henry Maine's *Ancient Law*, on the Roman law of marriage and on how the 'patria potestas', the power of the patriarch, had gradually been eroded in the shift towards a more individualistic society. She used it to demonstrate how anomalous was the survival of patriarchal power in Britain.[77] Maine argued that the patriarchal family, typical of early Indo-European societies, was gradually being superseded by the emergence of the individual of the modern world, a shift famously characterised as that 'from status to contract', one which he admitted had still to be completed for women in modern Europe.[78] In 1872, he delivered a series of lectures on the history of the legal status of women, and agreed to a personal request from the Manchester women's movement to reprint an essay drawn from the lectures.[79]

The evidence of writers such as Lubbock and Maine reinforced a sense of historic location in a transitional and progressive period, one which looked towards new forms of gender relations in which the enfranchisement of women was a means. Louisa Shore put it straightforwardly: 'The truth is, social circumstances in all civilized communities and notably in this, have outgrown the old theory of women's proper place in the world.'[80]

At the same time, material from other cultures provided an ethnocentric, metaphorical representation of the otherness, the difference, the 'savagery' and the 'barbarism', of the forms taken by masculine power and domination in mid-Victorian Britain. So to Becker, in the *Westminster Review* in 1871, 'The franchise is needed as a protection for women from the uncontrolled dominion of the savage passions of men', passions most frequent in 'the less cultivated classes of society'.[81] To Fawcett it was the quality of self-restraint which marked out the civilised human being from the savage.[82] With the outbreak of the Franco-Prussian War in 1871, the *Women's Suffrage Journal* was to write of the failure of the forces of civilisation to subdue the 'savage instinct in men', inflicting 'a doom of fire, famine and slaughter'. The new influence which might rescue the world from that brute force could only be 'the enfranchisement of that co-ordinate half of the human race which is comparatively free from the savage instinct of destruction'.[83] The *Women's Suffrage Journal* was to give much space over the following year to the cause of peace in Europe.

This analysis of the languages of suffragists has suggested that a more complex perspective than in the opposition between claims for equality or the representation of difference is needed. It can be misleading, as it is for the early years of the British movement, to see arguments put simply in terms of one kind of liberal political language; the case for enfranchisement did call upon the Lockean tradition, but also upon the ideal of individuality, the science of society, and the history of civilisation. Suffragism was integrally linked to a critique of the patriarchal quality of English common law, and to a passionate condemnation of the effects of that law. It was also limited, less by questions of property or marital status, than by a nervousness, shared with male liberals, about democracy. And it was limited by the ethnocentricity of its conscious and declared assumptions of the progressive direction of its civilisation, assumptions at the very heart of mid-Victorian liberal culture in Britain.

Finally, it is possible to reflect a little on the relationship between that culture, and those who watched and read of these suffrage campaigns from Nelson, New Zealand, Joseph Giles and Mary Muller. A little more has been learnt of Giles. He was one of only two friends and supporters of Mary Muller in Nelson, who remembered him as showing 'great interest' in her *Appeal to the Men of New Zealand* (1869). Both Muller and Giles were correspondents of John Stuart Mill, and followed the British women's suffrage cause closely.[84] In 1873 Giles sent Helen Taylor a copy of a ten-verse poem he wrote on Mill's death, 'In Memoriam John Stuart Mill', which had occupied a full page of the *Nelson Examiner* of 4 July 1873.[85] The influence of Mill, and more broadly of that mid-Victorian liberal culture of which he was a part, extended far beyond the British suffrage movement. In Muller's *Appeal* there are clear echoes of the languages of female citizenship traced above. She wrote from Nelson not only of the claims of women householders, but of women as 'educated thinking beings, very different from the females of the dark ages', though their minds might require 'hardening by the principles of reasoning'. She wrote of the married woman educating her children for 'the social sphere to which her heart clings', and of 'deference to the sex' as 'the best test of real civilization'. It is in this context that she asked rhetorically of New Zealand, 'was there ever a finer field for educating the people in the art of government?', and called for New Zealand to 'set the spark to the train now laid in most civilized nations'.[86]

1   I should like to thank the Nuffield Foundation for support during the research and writing for this essay. I am very grateful to Patricia Grimshaw, Catherine Hall, Sandra Holton, Jane Lewis, Keith McClelland, Susan Mendus, Adam Middleton, and Marian Sawer, and to the editors of this volume, for their comments.

2   Ann P. Robson, 'The Founding of the National Society for Women's Suffrage 1866-1867', *Canadian Journal of History*, 8, 1973, 1-22; Barbara Caine, 'John Stuart Mill and the English Women's Movement', *Historical Studies (HS)*, 18, 1978, 52-67, and also 'Feminism, Suffrage and the Nineteenth Century English Women's Movement', *Women's Studies International Forum*, 5, 1982, 537-50; Andrew Rosen, 'Emily Davies and the Women's Movement 1862-7', *Journal of British Studies*, 19, 1979, 101-21. Sandra Holton's fine essay, 'From Anti-Slavery to Suffrage Militancy' in this volume continues this tradition. The older work of Constance Rover, *Women's Suffrage and Party Politics in Britain 1866-1914*, Routledge & Kegan Paul, London, 1967, offers a useful introduction. David Rubinstein, *A Different World for Women: The Life of Millicent Garrett Fawcett*, Harvester Wheatsheaf, Hemel Hempstead, 1991, is a valuable biographical study. Leah Leneman, *A Guid Cause: The Women's Movement in Scotland*, Aberdeen Univ. Press, Aberdeen, 1991, Ch. 1 discusses the early movement in Scotland.

3   Among older works of history and feminist theory, see Evans, *The Feminists* and Zillah Eisenstein, *The Radical Future of Liberal Feminism*, Northeastern Univ. Press, Boston, 1981. Most recent discussion has focused around the important arguments of Carole Pateman, *The Sexual Contract* and *The Disorder of Women: Democracy, Feminism and Political Theory*.

4   See in particular Karen Offen, 'Defining Feminism', *Signs*, 14/1, 1988, 119-56, and the comments and responses by Ellen DuBois, Nancy Cott & Karen Offen in *Signs*, 15/1, 1989, 195-209. For Britain, see Jane Rendall, ed, *Equal or Different: Women's Politics 1800-1914*, Basil Blackwell, Oxford, 1987; Susan Kingsley Kent, *Sex and Suffrage in Britain, 1866-1914*, Princeton Univ. Press, Princeton, 1987; Dina M. Copelman, 'Liberal Ideology, Sexual Difference, and the Lives of Women: Recent Works in British History', *Journal of Modern History*, 62, 1990, 315-45; Philippa Levine, *Feminist Lives in Victorian England: Private Roles and Public Commitment*, Basil Blackwell, Oxford, 1990, Ch. 6; and Barbara Caine, *Victorian Feminists*, Oxford Univ. Press, Oxford, 1992, Ch. 2.

5   On citizenship, see Anne Phillips, *Engendering Democracy*; Ann Curthoys, 'Feminism, Citizenship, and National Identity', *Feminist Review*, 44, 1993, 19-38. On the ethnocentricities of Western feminist historians, see Vron Ware, *Beyond the Pale: White Women, Racism and History*, Verso, London, 1992; Catherine Hall, *White, Male and Middle Class: Explorations in Feminism and History*, Polity Press, Oxford, 1992.

6   Stefan Collini, *Public Moralists: Political Thought and Intellectual Life in Britain*, Clarendon Press, OUP, Oxford, 1991; John W. Burrow, *Whigs and Liberals: Continuity and Change in English Political Thought*, Clarendon Press, OUP, 1988; Stefan Collini, Donald Winch & John W. Burrow, *That Noble Science of Politics: A Study in Nineteenth-century Intellectual History*, Cambridge Univ. Press, Cambridge, 1993, especially Chs. VI-VII; see also Richard Bellamy, *Liberalism and Modern Society: An Historical Argument*, Polity Press, Oxford, 1992, Ch. 1 'Britain: Liberalism Defined', and John Morley, *Recollections*, 2 vols, Macmillan & Co, London 1917, Vol. I, Ch. II.

In this essay I use the term 'liberal' to describe the broad and self-styled 'progressive' culture discussed in the above works, and 'Liberal' to indicate association with the Liberal Party.

7   F. B. Smith, *The Making of the Second Reform Bill*, Cambridge Univ. Press, Cambridge, 1966, Ch.

2; Christopher Harvie, *The Lights of Liberalism: University Liberals and the Challenge of Democracy 1860-1886*, Allen Lane, London, 1976, Ch. 6; H. L. Beales notes the 'sheer obscurantism which surrounded this essential change' in 'A Centenary Tribute to an Appeal for Modernization', in Crick, ed, *Essays on Reform, 1967: A Centenary Tribute*, Oxford Univ. Press, Oxford, 1967, 7.

8   N. Blewett, 'The Franchise in the United Kingdom, 1885-1918', *Past and Present*, 32, 1965, 27-56; H. C. G. Matthew, R. I. McKibbin, J. Kay, 'The Franchise Factor in the Rise of the Labour Party', *English Historical Review*, 91, 1976, 723-52.

9   In addition to the articles by Barbara Caine, Ann Robson & Andrew Rosen cited in note 4 above, see on the *English Woman's Journal*, Rendall, '"A Moral Engine?"': Feminism, Liberalism, and the *English Woman's Journal*', in Rendall, ed, *Equal or Different*, and on the important links between London and provincial anti-slavery networks and the suffrage movement, Clare Midgley, *Women against Slavery: The British Campaigns, 1780-1870*, Routledge, London, 1992, 172-7.

10   John Stuart Mill to Parker Pillsbury, 4 July [1867], in Francis Mineka & Dwight N. Lindley, eds, *The Later Letters of John Stuart Mill, 1849-73*, *The Collected Works of John Stuart Mill*, vols. XIV-XVII, Univ. of Toronto Press, Toronto, 1972, vol. XVI, 1289.

11   Caine, 'John Stuart Mill and the Women's Movement'; see, for instance, the series of Mill's letters to George Croom Robertson from May 1871 to Dec 1872 on the management of the London National Society for Women's Suffrage, in Mineka & Lindley, eds, *Later Letters*, vol. XVII; for Mill's parliamentary role, see Bruce L. Kinzer, Ann P. Robson & John M. Robson, eds, *A Moralist In and Out of Parliament: John Stuart Mill at Westminster, 1865-8*, Univ. of Toronto Press, Toronto, 1992, Ch. 4.

12   Walter E. Houghton et al., eds, *The Wellesley Index to Victorian Periodicals, 1824-1900*, 5 vols, Univ. of Toronto Press, Toronto, 1969-89, Vol. III, 546-53. The best discussion of the character of these periodicals is in the introductory discussion of each in the *Wellesley Index*; see also Collini, *Public Moralists*, 52-7.

13   Millicent Fawcett, *What I Remember*, T. Fisher Unwin, London, 1924, 86; the *Women's Suffrage Journal (WSJ)* 12, 1 Feb. 1871, 17, noted the difficulty of getting the subject discussed in leading periodicals, and the assistance of the Dean of Canterbury in publishing Lydia Becker's 'Female Suffrage', *Contemporary Review (CR)* 4, March 1867, 307-16; see also six letters from Emily Davies to Becker, 17 Jan. - 4 Feb. 1867, Manchester Central Library, Manchester (MCL). The first article on women's suffrage in the *Fortnightly Review (FR)* was Richard Pankhurst's 'The Right of Women to Vote Under the Reform Act, 1867', FR, 10 o.s., 4 n.s., Sept. 1868, 250-4.

14   See, for instance, Barbara Bodichon to Helen Taylor, 'Tuesday' [1866?] Mill-Taylor Papers, vol XII, ff. 118-20, British Library of Political and Economic Sciences (BLPES); Jessie Boucherett to Helen Taylor, 10 Nov. 1866, Mill-Taylor Papers, vol XII, BLPES. Becker, Cobbe & Bodichon also contributed letters and items on the women's movement to other national newspapers, especially the *Daily News, Examiner*, and *Spectator*. For Cobbe's more extensive journalistic career, see the *Life of Frances Power Cobbe as Told by Herself*, with additions by the author and introduction by Blanche Atkinson, Swan Sonnenschein, London, 1905, Ch. XVI.

15   On the *English Woman's Journal*, see Rendall, '"A Moral Engine"'; on the *Englishwoman's Review*, see Janet Horowitz Murray & Myra Stark, 'The *Englishwoman's Review*, An Introduction', in *The Englishwoman's Review of Social and Industrial Questions (EWR)*, vol. I, 1866-7, reprint Garland Publishing, New York & London, 1980, v-xxxi.

16   See, for all except Shore, Taylor & Wedgwood, Olive Banks, *The Biographical Dictionary of British Feminists. vol. I, 1800-1930*, Harvester Press, Brighton, 1985. On Shore, see Louisa Shore, *Poems. With a Memoir by her sister Arabella Shore. And an Appreciation by Frederic Harrison*, John Lane, London, 1897; Barbara Timms Gates, ed, *Journal of Emily Shore*, Univ. Press of Virginia, Charlottesville, 1991, Introduction. On Taylor, see Ann P. Robson, 'Mill's Second Prize in the Lottery of Life' in M. Laine, ed, *A Cultivated Mind: Essays on J. S. Mill, Presented to John M. Robson*, Univ. of Toronto Press, Toronto, 1991. For Frances Julia Wedgwood, see *Who Was Who*, vol. I, 1897-1915, 6th ed, A & C. Black, London, 1988, and the *Wellesley Index*, vol. V, 820-1.

17   Eugenio Biagini, *Liberty, Retrenchment, and Reform: Popular Liberalism in the Age of Gladstone*, Cambridge Univ. Press, Cambridge, 1992, 272-5 and 286-8.

18   Keith McClelland, 'Rational and Respectable Men: Gender, the Working Class and Citizenship', forthcoming in Laura Frader & Sonya Rose, ed, *Gender and Labour in Modern Europe*, Univ. of Chicago Press, Chicago, 1994.

19   Helen Taylor, 'The ladies' petition', *Westminster Review (WR)*, 87 o.s., 31 n.s., January 1867, 63-79, reprinted in Jane Lewis, ed, *Before the Vote Was Won: Arguments for and against Women's Suffrage 1864-1896*, Routledge & Kegan Paul, New York & London, 1987, as 'The claims of Englishwomen to

the suffrage constitutionally considered', the title under which it was reprinted as a pamphlet, London, 1867. See John Stuart Mill to John Chapman, 21 Nov. 1866, *Later Letters*, vol. XVIII, 1216.

20   [Jessie Boucherett?] 'Some Probable Consequences of Extending the Franchise to Female Householders', *EWR*, 1, Oct. 1866, 26-34.

21   On these campaigns, see the *First Annual Report of the Executive Committee of the Manchester National Society for Women's Suffrage, presented at the Annual General Meeting, October 30th, 1868*, Alexander Ireland & Co, Manchester, 1868. M50/1/9/1-2, MCL contains Lydia Becker's extensive collection of newspaper cuttings, from all over Britain, covering the proceedings in the registration courts. The legal arguments cited were based on Thomas Chisholm Anstey's *Notes upon 'The Representation of the People Act, 1867'...With Appendices...*, William Ridgway, London, 1867, 74-104, and *On Some Supposed Constitutional Restraints upon the Parliamentary Franchise*, Social Science Association, London, 1867, 18-27, 48.

22   The relationship between the women's suffrage movement, provincial Liberal Party organisations, and working-class movements for electoral reform still needs more research. Lydia Becker called, unsuccessfully, on the Northern Reform Union to accept the suffragist policy in 1868, but in 1874 persuaded the Electoral Reform Union to adopt it. See Biagini, *Liberty, Retrenchment and Reform*, 306-9; report from *Examiner and Times*, 12 Feb. 1868, and other cuttings for the meeting, M50/1/9/1, MCL; *WSJ*, 58, 1 Dec. 1874, 158-9, 165-7.

23   'Lily Maxwell', *EWR*, 6, Jan. 1868, 359-69.

24   *Second Annual Report of the Executive Committee of the Manchester National Society for Women's Suffrage. Presented at the Annual General Meeting, December 15th, 1869*, Alexander Ireland & Co, Manchester, 1869.

25   Barbara Bodichon, 'A Conversation on the Enfranchisement of Female Freeholders and Householders', *EWR*, 14, April 1873, 107.

26   For instance, *WSJ*, 29, 1 July 1872, 93 and 55, 1 Sept. 1874, 121-2.

27   For the movement's high and unfounded expectations of support from Gladstone, see Ann P. Robson, 'A Birds' Eye View of Gladstone', in Bruce L. Kinzer, ed, *The Gladstonian Turn of Mind: Essays presented to J. B. Conacher*, Univ. of Toronto Press, Toronto, 1985.

28   Draft letter of Helen Taylor to Barbara Bodichon, 9 May 1866, Mill-Taylor Collection, vol XIII, ff. 107-110, BLPES.

29   See Emily Davies to Helen Taylor, 6 Aug. 1866, Mill-Taylor Collection, vol XIII f. 183, BLPES, quoted in Robson, 'The Founding of the National Society for Women's Suffrage', 11; and, among many references, Millicent Fawcett, 'The Electoral Disabilities of Women', *FR*, 13 o.s., 7 n.s., May 1870, 627. There was to be a further split in the movement in 1874 over Becker's decision to support, with regret and on tactical grounds, Forsyth's bill, with a clause explicitly excluding married women; Helen Blackburn, *Women's Record. A Record of the Women's Suffrage Movement in the British Isles...*, reprint, Source Book Press, New York, 1970, first published 1902, 134-9, and *WSJ*, 50, 1 April 1874, 53-5, and 54, 1 Aug. 1874, 105-6. Becker's later conservatism awaits further research, but is clearly indicated in Sandra Holton's 'From Anti-Slavery to Suffrage Militancy' in this volume.

30   In this context it is worth noting that even a limited women's suffrage was not achieved in Britain until manhood suffrage had replaced the old 1867-1918 franchise regime, rooted in property and service qualifications throughout this long period, in 1918. See Matthews, McKibbin & Kay, 'The Franchise Factor'.

31   Becker, 'The Political Disabilities of Women', *WR*, 97 o.s., 41 n.s., Jan. 1872, 50-70.

32   *NSJ*, 15, 1 May 1871, 42.

33   Richard Pankhurst, 'The Right of Women to Vote under the Reform Act, 1867', *FR*, 10 o.s.,4 n.s., Sept. 1868, 250-4.

34   Lydia Becker to Richard Pankhurst, 24 May 1868, Lydia Becker's letter-book, Mar.-Oct. 1868, f. 161, M50/1/3, MCL.

35   Collini, *Public Moralists*, Ch. 2.

36   Barbara Bodichon, *Reasons For and Against the Enfranchisement of Women*, Spottiswood & Co, London, 1869, 5-6, first given as a lecture at the Social Science Association in Manchester, and published as *Reasons for the Enfranchisement of Women*, J. Bale, London, 1866. See Sheila R. Herstein, *A Mid-Victorian Feminist, Barbara Leigh Smith Bodichon*, Yale Univ. Press, New Haven, 159-60.

37   'Why Women Require the Franchise. A Lecture Delivered in the Colston Hall, Bristol, in March 1871', reprinted in Henry Fawcett & Millicent Fawcett, *Essays and Lectures on Social and Political Subjects*, Macmillan, London, 1872.

38   Kate Amberley, 'The Claims of Women', *FR*, 15 o.s., 9 n.s., Jan. 1871, 95-110.

39   On Mill, see Susan Mendus, 'The Marriage of True Minds: the Ideal of Marriage in the Philosophy of John Stuart Mill', in Mendus & Rendall, eds, *Sexuality and Subordination: Interdisciplinary Studies of Gender in the Nineteenth Century*, Routledge, London, 1989; Collini, *Public Moralists*, Ch. 4; John M. Robson, *The Improvement of Mankind: the Social and Political Thought of John Stuart Mill*, Univ. of Toronto Press, Toronto, 1968; Dennis Thompson, *John Stuart Mill and Representative Government*, Princeton Univ. Press, Princeton, NJ, 1976; Bernard Semmel, *John Stuart Mill and the Pursuit of Virtue*, Yale Univ. Press, New York & London, 1984; William Thomas, *Mill*, Oxford Univ. Press, Oxford, 1985; John Gibbins, 'J. S. Mill, Liberalism, and Progress', in Richard Bellamy, ed, *Victorian Liberalism. Nineteenth-century Political Thought and Practice*, Routledge, London & New York, 1990.

40   See Thomas Hare, *The Election of Representatives, Parliamentary and Municipal. A Treatise*, 3rd ed, Longman, Green, London, 1865, first published in 1859; Smith, *Making of the Second Reform Bill*, 212-3.

41   Millicent Fawcett, 'The Education of Women. A lecture delivered at Newcastle, November 13th, 1871', in *Essays and Lectures*, 224ff.

42   Julia Wedgwood, 'Female Suffrage in its Influence on Married Life', *CR*, 20, Aug. 1872, 370, and 'Female Suffrage, Considered Chiefly with Regard to its Indirect Results', in Josephine Butler, ed, *Woman's Work and Woman's Culture*, Macmillan, London, 1869, 255.

43   Louisa Shore, 'The Emancipation of Women', *WR*, 102 o.s., 46 n.s., July 1874, reprinted as *The Citizenship of Women, Socially Considered*, Savill, Edwards & Co, London n.d., and reprinted in Jane Lewis, ed, *Before the Vote*, 218.

44 · Helen Taylor, 'Personal Representation', *WR*, 84 o.s., 28 n.s., Oct. 1865, 305-20; 'The Ladies' Petition', *WR*, 87 o.s., 31 n.s., Jan. 1867, 67n (this note is omitted from the reprinted version in Lewis, ed, *Before the Vote*).

45   Millicent Fawcett, 'Proportional Representation', *Macmillan's Magazine* (MM), 22, Sept 1870, 376-82; and 'A short explanation of Mr Hare's scheme of representation', MM, 23, April 1871, 816-26. Both are reprinted in *Essays and Lectures*.

46   Barbara Bodichon,'Authorities & Precedents for Giving the Suffrage to Qualified Women' *EWR*, 2, Jan. 1867, 64-72.

47   Jessie Boucherett to Helen Taylor, 4 June [1867], Mill-Taylor Collection, vol XII, ff. 162-5, BLPES; [Jessie Boucherett?], 'Debate on the Enfranchisement of Women', *EWR*, 4, 1867, 207.

48   Frances Power Cobbe, *Why Women Desire the Franchise*, National Society for Women's Suffrage, London, n.d., 1.

49   'Are Duties and Rights the Same?', *EWR*, 27, July 1875, 301-6. The first translation of *The Duties of Man*, Chapman & Hall, London, 1862, was by Emilie Venturi, who took an active part in the women's movement, especially the campaigns for reform of the law affecting married women's property, and the repeal of the Contagious Diseases Acts. For Mazzini's popularity, see Biagini, *Liberty, Retrenchment and Reform*, 46-50, and Margot C. Finn, *After Chartism. Class and Nation in English Politics, 1848-74*, Cambridge Univ. Press, Cambridge, 1993, 159-72.

50   Kate Amberley, 'The Claims of Women', *FR*, 15 o.s., 9 n.s., Jan 1871, 110; she quotes from Venturi's translation of the *Duties of Man*, Ch. VI.

51   'Mazzini on the Franchise for Women', *WSJ*, 9, 1 Nov 1871, 95.

52   Denise Riley, *'Am I That Name?' Feminism and the Category of Women in History*, Macmillan, Basingstoke, 1988, Ch. 3; see also Jane Lewis, *Women and Social Action in Victorian and Edwardian England*, Edward Elgar, Aldershot, 1991, 6-16.

53   Stefan Collini, 'Political Theory and the "Science of Society" in Victorian Britain', *Historical Journal*, 23/1, 1980, 203-31.

54   See Kathleen McCrone, 'The National Association for the Promotion of Social Science and the Advancement of Victorian Women', *Atlantis*, 8/1, Fall 1982, 44-66; Lawrence Goldman, 'The Social Science Association, 1857-1886: a Context for Mid-Victorian Liberalism', *English Historical Review*, 101, 1986, 95-134, and 'A Peculiarity of the English? The Social Science Association and the Absence of Sociology in Nineteenth-Century Britain', *Past and Present*, 114, Feb 1987, 133-171; Eileen Janes Yeo, 'Social Motherhood and the Sexual Communion of Labour in British Social Science, 1850-1950', *Women's History Review*, 1/1, 1992, 63-88.

55   Wedgwood, 'Female Suffrage in its Influence on Married Life', 365-6; 'Female Suffrage, Considered Chiefly with Regard to its Indirect Results', 278-89.

56   Her essays on 'Free Education in its Economic Aspects', 'National Debts and National Prosperity' are reprinted in *Essays and Lectures*; see also her *Political Economy for Beginners*, Macmillan, London, 1870, and *Tales in Political Economy*, Macmillan, London, 1874.

57   Reprinted in Lewis, ed, *Before the Vote*, 210.

58   *CR*, 20, Aug. 1872, 368.

59   *Essays and Lectures*, 270.

60   On the relationship between the suffrage campaign and the reform of the laws relating to marriage, see Mary Lyndon Shanley, *Feminism, Marriage and the Law in Victorian England, 1850-1895*, I. B.Tauris & Co Ltd, London, 1989.

61   *WSJ*, 18, 1 Aug. 1871, 86-7, and 20, 1 Oct. 1871, 107.

62   *WSJ*, 23, 1 Jan. 1872, 12-13, and 52, 1 June 1874, 82.

63   *WSJ*, 23, 1 Jan. 1872, 12; 17, 1 July 1871, 73-4; 24, 1 Feb. 1872, 17.

64   *WSJ*, 19, 1 Jan. 1871, 72; and see Shanley, *Feminism, Marriage and the Law*, Ch. 3 for a thorough discussion of these issues.

65   *WSJ*, 17, 1 July 1871, 76: the reference is to Sir John Lubbock, *The Origin of Civilisation and the Primitive Condition of Man: Mental and Social Condition of Savages*, Longmans Green & Co., London, 1870, 73-4. Lubbock's source is Edward J. Eyre, *Journal of Expeditions of Discovery into Central Australia . . . including an account of the manners and customs of the Aborigines, and the state of their relations with Europeans*, 2 vols, London, 1845, vol. II, 321.

66   Biagini, *Liberty, Retrenchment and Reform*, 54-6; for discussion of the gendered version of myths of Anglo-Saxon democracy, see my unpublished paper 'Tacitus Engendered: "Gothic Feminism" and British History'.

67   Frances Power Cobbe, 'Criminals, Idiots, Women and Minors. Is the Classification Sound?', *Fraser's Magazine*, 78, Dec. 1868, 791.

68   *WSJ*, 18, 1 Aug. 1871, 90.

69   *WSJ*, 33, 1 Nov. 1872, 141.

70   *WSJ*, 25, 1 Mar. 1872, 30, and 33, 1 Nov. 1872, 142; Biagini, *Liberty, Retrenchment and Reform*, 319-28.

71   See George Stocking, *Victorian Anthropology*, Free Press, New York, 1987; Peter Bowler, *The Invention of Progress: The Victorians and the Past*, Basil Blackwell, Oxford, 1989, Part I; John W. Burrow, *Evolution and Society: A Study in Victorian Social Theory*, Cambridge Univ. Press, Cambridge, 1966.

72   Shore, 'Citizenship of Women', in Lewis, ed, *Before the Vote*, 184.

73   Kate Amberley, 'The Claims of Women', *FR*, 15 o.s., 9 n.s., Jan. 1871, 106-7.

74   *Mrs Fawcett on Women's Suffrage. Speech delivered in the Town Hall, Birmingham, December 6th, 1872. George Dixon, Esq. M.P., in the Chair (Reprinted from the Birmingham Morning News)*, Birmingham, 1872, 5-6.

75   Frances Power Cobbe, *Dawning Lights: An Inquiry Concerning the Secular Results of the New Reformation*, Edward T. Whitfield, London, 1868, 125-9.

76   See Stocking, *Victorian Anthropology*, Ch. 6. Stocking suggests a different interpretation, which I follow here, from that of Elizabeth Fee, 'The Sexual Politics of Victorian Social Anthropology', in Mary S. Hartman & Lois Banner, eds, *Clio's Consciousness Raised*, Harper & Row, New York, 1974.

77   Barbara Bodichon, *A Brief Summary in Plain Language, of the Most Important Laws of England Concerning Women, Together with a Few Observations Therein*, 3rd edition, revised, with additions, Trubner, London, 1869, first published in 1854, 24-5.

78   On Henry Maine, see George Feaver, *From Status to Contract: A Biography of Sir Henry Maine 1822-1888*, Longmans, London, 1969, Ch. 5, and Collini, Winch & Burrow, *That Noble Science of Politics*, Ch. VII.

79   *The Early History of the Property of Married Women, as Collected from Roman and Hindoo Law*, reprinted in Henry Maine, *Lectures on the Early History of Institutions*, Murray, London, 1875, Ch. 11, first published in 1873, cited in Feaver, *From Status to Contract*, 136-58, and 302. For other evidence of interest in Maine among active suffrage campaigners, see Richard Pankhurst, 'The Right of Women to Vote under the Reform Act, 1867', *FR*, 10 o.s., 4 n.s., Sept. 1868, 250; Frances Power Cobbe, *Life of Frances Power Cobbe*, 478-9.

80   Shore, 'Citizenship of Women, Socially Considered', in Lewis, ed, *Before the Vote*, 201.

81   Lydia Becker, 'The Political Disabilities of Women', *WR*, 97 o.s., 41 n.s., Jan. 1872, reprinted in Lewis, ed, *Before the Vote*, 137.

82   'Free Education in its Economic Aspects. Letter to *The Times*, Dec. 1870', *Essays and Lectures*, 59.

83   *WSJ*, 12, 1 Feb. 1871, 11.

84   See Mary Muller to Kate Sheppard, 18 Aug. 1898, Sheppard Papers, Canterbury Museum Archives (CMA); John Stuart Mill to Mary Muller, 25 Jan. 1870, (copy) Sheppard MSS, CMA;

Joseph Giles to Helen Taylor, 18 July 1873, Mill-Taylor Collection, vol VIII, ff. 36-7. I am grateful to Jo-Anne Smith of Canterbury Museum for copies of these items.

85   Two copies of the poem were sent to Helen Taylor, one by Joseph Giles, and one by his brother, F. Giles, from Stourbridge, England. See F. Giles to Helen Taylor, 8 May 1874, and Joseph Giles to Helen Taylor, 18 July 1873, Mill-Taylor Collection, vol VIII, ff. 34-42, BLPES. It is of course possible that F. Giles may also have sent a copy of his brother's lecture to the *Women's Suffrage Journal* in 1870.

86   Grimshaw, *Women's Suffrage in New Zealand*, 12-15; 'Femmina' [Mary Muller], *Appeal to the Women of New Zealand*, first published 1869, reprinted in Margaret Lovell-Smith, ed, *The Woman Question: Writings by the Women who Won the Vote*, New Women's Press, Auckland, 1993, 56-65. I am grateful to Patricia Grimshaw for a copy of the latter.

8

Women, Citizenship and Suffrage with a French Twist, 1789–1993[1]

KAREN OFFEN

French women obtained the vote less than fifty years ago, in 1944–45. As the French political scientist Janine Mossuz-Lavau recently remarked 'France is one of the last countries in Europe to have accorded women the right to vote and to run for office (*éligibilité*), just before Italy, Belgium, Greece, Cyprus, Switzerland, and Liechtenstein.'[2] The American historian of French suffragism, Steven C. Hause, framed the French case in even broader world comparative terms, again underscoring the astonishing backwardness of a nation whose leaders portrayed it as the vanguard of civilisation: 'By the 1930s, while the French Senate stood intransigent, women were voting in Palestine, parts of China, and several Latin American republics. Women voted in Estonia, Azerbaijan, Trans-Jordan and Kenya but not in the land of Jeanne d'Arc and the Declaration of the Rights of Man. . .'.[3] After World War I, suffragist advocate Cécile Brunschvicg posed the issue in terms of national honour: 'It is humiliating to think that we are Frenchwomen, daughters of the land of the Revolution, and that in the year of grace 1919 we are still reduced to demanding the "rights of woman"', and in 1923 the social Catholic Georges Goyau pointed to the good done by women voting in New Zealand as one more compelling reason why women should exercise the vote in France.[4]

How can this be? Paradoxically, the issue of votes for women (not to mention their eligibility for office) was articulated earlier in France than in virtually any other nation in the world – in 1789, at the outset of the mighty French Revolution. Moreover, in 1848 France became the first major nation in Europe to institute universal *manhood* suffrage without property qualifications, that is, for male individuals. Following enactment of Napoleon's Civil Code of 1804, a law code whose provisions (including those that subordinated women in marriage) were imitated throughout Europe, France became the site of perhaps the most radical and thoroughgoing critique of women's subordination in all Europe; by the 1890s, French women's rights activists had launched the term '*féminisme*' throughout the world. Thus, this long delay in according the vote to women seems startling, a dissonant historical fact that cries out for explanation.

I will explore this issue by responding briefly to three questions. First, when and how was the issue of woman suffrage framed in France? Second, what was required to achieve it? Third, why did it take so long to realise it? In exploring these questions, I will examine successively the periods 1789–1848, 1848–1910, and 1910–1945. Finally, I will pose a fourth question: what difference did woman suffrage make, once enacted? In this last section, I will draw on recent French and Anglo-American scholarship to assess the extent to which French laws and regulations affecting women's adverse legal, economic, and sociopolitical situation changed in the wake of woman suffrage, concluding with a consideration of what remains to be accomplished.

When and how was the issue of woman suffrage framed in France? (1789–1848)

The issue of woman suffrage was initially framed as a fundamental aspect of the debate over citizenship during the early months of the French Revolution. The immediate issue was to decide who would be eligible to vote for representatives to the Estates-General from each of the three estates (nobility, clergy, third estate). Women's petitions and tracts from this period insisted not only that propertied women of the third estate vote, but that women be represented by women in the National Assembly and, further, that women have their own separate and parallel assembly.[5] One of the most important male supporters of political rights for women was the Marquis de Condorcet, who since 1787 had advocated women's *droit de cité* (civic right).[6]

The 'limits of citizenship' for women during the Revolution (to use Olwen Hufton's compelling formulation) were quickly mapped in terms of the public/private (or domestic) distinction (forum/foyer) and in terms of 'public utility'.[7] First, political (or civic) rights were *disengaged* from civil or property rights, even as single adult women were granted full property rights, including the right of equal inheritance with their brothers. The Constitution of 1791 effectively dismissed women from political life, and Talleyrand framed his programme for national education accordingly, insisting on the necessity of women remaining in domestic roles for the common good.[8] Then, despite the continuing claims of a number of women to take part in revolutionary politics, and a flurry of organising of women's clubs, petitioning, speaking, publishing, and even bearing arms, the victors in the debate were the Jacobins of the Convention who (in the heat of war and economic crisis) closed down women's political clubs, sent republican women back to their homes, and guillotined women who, like Olympe de Gouges (who proclaimed the Rights of Women), they believed had stepped out of their 'proper' place.[9]

Some fifty years later, during the revolutionary era of 1848–49, the provisional government established universal manhood suffrage, increasing the electorate by a factor of 40! The rationale provided by the provisional government in 1848 did nothing to veil the deliberate exclusion of the women: 'The electoral law we have made is the broadest that any people on the earth has ever made to convoke the people to exercise *the supreme right of man, his own sovereignty*. We have only respected the exclusions that exist in all other nations.'[10] A few days later a small group of Parisian women, calling themselves the Committee for Women's Rights, demanded publicly why women had been 'forgotten' and prepared a petition to the Provisional Government, headed by the Mayor of Paris, who promptly deferred the issue to the not-as-yet elected National Assembly.[11] The deliberate exclusion of women thus exposed a contradiction at the very heart of the movement for a democratic republic, starkly revealing that the concept 'citizen' was gendered to the core.

The appeal for woman suffrage was pursued in the press and in the clubs by women's rights advocates such as Eugénie Niboyet, Jeanne Deroin, and Victor Considérant in Paris and by Pauline Roland, who attempted to register to vote in the municipality of Boussac. Jeanne Deroin (who in 1849 ran for office, the first Frenchwoman to do so), argued for 'complete and true equality', and invoked the principle (so dear to the hearts of Anglo-American rebels) of no taxation without representation.[12] Notwithstanding their appeals, the National Assembly established only universal *manhood* suffrage in 1848, a radical step in itself, while Considérant's subsequent proposal to extend the municipal vote to single adult women was laughed off the floor.

The new all-male electorate promptly demonstrated its appreciation for enfranchisement by electing Louis-Napoléon Bonaparte president, returning an anti-republican assembly, and subsequently endorsing both the coup d'état of 1851 and the re-establishment of the Empire by overwhelming majorities. This performance led many republicans of an otherwise progressive turn of mind to doubt the wisdom of democracy, of extending the vote to all men, much less compounding the problem by including all women as well. As the German chancellor, Otto von Bismarck, astutely observed during these years, male democracy, still overwhelmingly rural and peasant, might operate as a 'conservative' as much as a 'progressive' force.

This entire discussion of the gender of citizenship, and thus of democracy in France, was itself framed by a larger set of cultural issues, which seem peculiarly French.[13] These are the coupled problems of 'gynaecocracy', or what I call the problem of women and political authority, which as an issue in public discussion dates at least from the late sixteenth century, when women – and heirs through the female line – were legally excluded from the succession to the French throne, and the corresponding complex and insistently repeated public attestations of women's power and influence in French culture. In reappropriating the wisdom of the ancients, especially those of Roman law, early French political theorists insisted on identifying 'virility' with public authority in all its forms, including the monarchy, and associating it as well with their discussion of republics, in which it was believed that women's power would be sharply restricted. These discussions, including the demonisation of 'political' women in French history, notably the queens Catherine de Médicis and Marie-Antoinette, reverberated in historical memory, strongly colouring the subsequent debate about woman suffrage. Such arguments resurfaced again as the French Second Republic embarked on its experiment in mass, male democracy. The point I want to underscore here is that in what one might call 'high political culture' in France, the controversy over women in political life was not a new controversy; it had already been explicit and deeply divisive for several centuries.[14] Debates about democracy and citizenship gave new form, content, and meaning to a well-entrenched older dispute about women and political authority, framed in terms of the mischief women would and could make in affairs of state.

What was required to achieve woman suffrage in France? (1848–1910)

The demand for woman suffrage arose again in the later 1860s, framed as an issue of political rights (*droits politiques*). This time, the French debate resonated with the contemporaneous debates in Britain – following introduction of the Second Reform Bill in March 1865 – and the United States – following the conclusion of the Civil War and the ensuing campaign for a constitutional amendment to enfranchise black men and all women; the state of Wyoming granted women the vote in 1869. In England, single women ratepayers won the municipal vote, though not the national parliamentary suffrage, in 1869.

This phase of the French campaign for woman suffrage was

spearheaded by Julie-Victoire Daubié, who revived the case for single adult women's suffrage, first in her book-length study *La Femme pauvre* , then in *L'Emancipation de la femme en dix livraisons* (1871).[15] Daubié's crusade was accompanied by an extended debate on the issue of women's political rights within the Paris Law School, capped by Prof. Duverger's decisive conclusion against giving the vote to women on the grounds that previous instances of women meddling in French political life had proved pernicious![16] No one suggested that French women were not capable of exercising the suffrage; instead, opponents implied that it was simply inopportune, inappropriate, or alternatively, dangerous.

The political context changed abruptly, however, following the sudden defeat of French armies by Germany in late 1870, the collapse of the Second Empire, the occupation of Paris, the Commune, and the founding of the Third Republic. With the election of a new National Assembly in 1871, in which republicans were barely represented, ambivalence about the practice of universal suffrage by men continued to cloud further discussion of the woman suffrage issue; such ambivalence would plague advocates of women's vote throughout the French Third Republic.

In the mid-1870s freedom of the press and association, opened up briefly during the late Second Empire, were again sharply curtailed. Seriously compounding the political situation was the severe polarisation of partisan political life between anticlerical republicans and monarchist Catholics. The former hesitated to champion woman suffrage for fear that women would support the monarchist Catholic factions that opposed the republic. Even after 1880, when the republicans attained control of all branches of the new government, no major republican faction knew for certain just how women's votes might affect its fragile hold on power; both republicans and monarchists continued to insist on the significance of women's influence. The republicans established state secondary schools for girls to contest Catholic hegemony over women's education. With the notable exception of Hubertine Auclert, who did spearhead a woman suffrage campaign from 1878 until her death in 1914, republican advocates of women's rights thought it best to postpone the suffrage question until the new and fragile republic was more firmly established. Auclert, however, challenged French republicans to realise political equality for women as individuals, arguing that a republic in which women – including married women – were not considered full citizens was no 'true' republic; she continued her campaign by founding a periodical provocatively entitled *La Citoyenne*.[17] Such criticism was not welcome among republicans, for it confronted them squarely on the inclusiveness of the very principles to which they subscribed. But the various republican factions, including the radicals, resisted the implications of Auclert's charges. Before 1900 only the socialists, who were very far from holding power and had little to lose, were willing to risk endorsing the principle of the female vote.[18]

What was required to institute votes for women in Third Republic France? Literally, nothing more than a change of wording in a regime of textual law. The French electoral law of 1848 (and its 1884 amended version, law of 5 April) read: '*Tous les français*'. This was equivocal, since in civil and penal law, the masculine form '*tous les français*' was deemed to encompass women. The British earlier, and before them the Americans in New Jersey (1807), had clarified the situation by stipulating 'men', in line with the electoral laws of other states. In 1860s England, John Stuart Mill proposed effecting the change by amending the term 'men' to read 'persons', which would include women.[19] Could the same tactic be applied in France?

The elasticity of '*tous les français*' was tested several times in court by small groups of women and their male supporters. In 1885, two women, Louise Barbarousse and Marie Richard Picot, attempted to register to vote under the new electoral law of 1884; the Paris Municipal Council denied their request and their appeal was heard by a justice of the peace (*juge du paix*). Two male lawyers, Jules Allix and Léon Giraud, represented their case, pleading on the high ground of 'imprescriptable rights' of the individual as well as national prestige that women should vote in France:

> It is necessary to the glory of the French laws that they leave a place to woman in this sphere of public power, and it will be to the honour of the declaration of the rights of man to acknowledge also the rights of woman . . . . Does not *tous les Français* encompass every individual of the French nationality, without exception of sex?[20]

The judge handed down his denial of the appeal, framed in terms of legal–historical precedent that dodged the issue of principle. Even issues of grammatical gender were freighted with contextual precedent. Judge Carré made the point that precedent from the Revolution was that voting citizens were males only; indeed the Constitutions of June 1793 and August 1795 had expressly spelled out this point.[21] He noted further that the most recent laws stipulate that 'in order to be an elector, one must be a citizen' and that 'the citizen is the Frenchman who has full political and civil rights', therefore since women have neither, and are therefore not citizens, they cannot be electors. In concluding, however, the judge abandoned his air of juridical neutrality:

> Whereas, finally, if women *repudiating their privileges and inspiring themselves with certain modern theories*, believe the hour has come to break the bonds of tutelage with which tradition, law, and custom have surrounded them, they must bring their claim before the Legislative power, and not before the Courts of Law.[22]

An intriguing aspect of the subsequent French suffrage campaign was the mobilisation of historic precedent on the side of women's citizenship and women's suffrage, and the way in which it was done. An important contribution to this effort was Léon Giraud's study on the comparative status of women with respect to public and political rights, which won a prize from the Paris Law Faculty in 1891. Giraud shared the prize with a widely translated treatise by Moïse Ostrogorski, who had argued that the question of determining who would vote was a political question, above all else.[23] With such scholarship at hand, feminists such as Eliska Vincent again attempted to register to vote, while Hubertine Auclert reminded her readers – and their legislators – of women's participation in political life during the *ancien régime*.[24] These advocates of woman suffrage insisted, on the basis of incontrovertible evidence, that women had repeatedly voted in earlier periods of French history, when votes were tied to fiefs or landed property, not to individuals. The Rennes judge, Raoul de la Grasserie, argued for woman suffrage in the *Revue politique et parlementaire* (1894) in terms reminiscent of those used over a century earlier by Condorcet: 'Half humankind is not represented in the various parliamentary assemblies; the laws are made without her and often against her.' Her sex places her outside the class structure: 'the worker, the most illiterate peasant have that choice [to choose their representatives], and the most intelligent, most experienced women cannot . . . . She cannot even choose among those of the opposite sex who will be her masters.'[25] The judge went on to advocate, in principle, that women be permitted to run for office as well – but not right away. But it must come. It would inevitably come. Woman suffrage was, in his eyes, a question of social justice.

In fact, the 1890s witnessed a tremendous outburst of public debate over the woman question, and Hubertine Auclert's term *féminisme* became common currency to describe the burgeoning movement for women's emancipation.[26] Despite the visibility of the issues – reform of women's situation in the Civil Code, including married women's property rights; demands for women's right to work and equal pay; issues surrounding maternity and sexuality – few of the numerous civil and economic reforms advocated by and for women were realised. Male legislators seemed more absorbed in protecting – and controlling – women than in emancipating them, in spite of the valiant efforts by Julie-Victoire Daubié, Hubertine Auclert, and their allies to place the suffrage question before the lawmakers. It was only after 1900 that woman suffrage arrived on the agenda of the Chamber of Deputies.

When, in 1900, the reformer and newspaperwoman Marguerite Durand convened an international congress on women's rights in Paris, the suffrage question occupied a prominent place. By this time many members of the new generation of women's movement leaders had come around to the position long asserted by Auclert; they now agreed that the main reason why substantive and sensible reforms in the laws governing women's situation were not forthcoming was because women had no political power. As René Viviani, deputy and future prime minister of France, declared to the assembled delegates at the women's rights congress: 'In the name of my relatively long political and parliamentary experience, let me tell you that the legislators make the laws for those who make the legislators.'[27] There was no getting around it – women must have the vote in order to realise the feminist programme.

Two woman suffrage bills were introduced into the Chamber of Deputies during the first decade of the twentieth century. The first, in 1901, sought municipal and legislative suffrage for unmarried women, including divorced women and widows; it was referred to committee and quietly buried there. The second, introduced in 1906, sought to confer the vote on all adult women in both municipal and departmental, but not national parliamentary, elections. By this time, however, the question of woman suffrage had become inextricably intertwined with the broader – and highly emotional – discussion on overall electoral reform through proportional representation, brought on by an evergrowing concern for the future of parliamentary democracy in France.

Thus it was in the early twentieth century that French women of all political persuasions, from Catholic to socialist, began to organise their forces to pressure the legislature for woman suffrage. In contrast to the campaign in Britain, French women did not engage in dramatic public demonstrations or deliberate acts of violence against property; in 1908, only two small incidents – including the breaking of ballot-containing urns at one election site by Hubertine Auclert – took place and these were almost immediately disavowed.

In 1909, Jeanne-E. Schmahl, Cécile Brunschvicg, and Marguerite de WittSchlumberger organised the *Union Française pour le Suffrage des Femmes* (UFSF), which they affiliated with the International Woman Suffrage Alliance, to spearhead the French drive for woman suffrage. Disavowing the militant tactics of the English suffragettes across the Channel, virtually all French woman suffrage advocates (except for the integral suffragist Madeleine Pelletier) insisted that French women could – and must – obtain the vote and eligibility to run for office by 'ladylike' means. They were willing to see such measures granted by gradual steps, beginning with the municipal vote, while the political education of women proceeded apace. They were consequently pleased when later in 1909 a parliamentary committee headed by woman suffrage sympathiser and Radical party deputy, Ferdinand Buisson, reported out a suffrage proposal that would give the vote to all women, single or married, at the municipal level.[28] This measure, similar to one enacted in England in the 1860s, would have amended the wording of the 1884 municipal elections law, '*tous les français . . .*' by adding the words '*des deux sexes*'. An alternative proposal was to add '*sans distinction de sexe*' or '*hommes et femmes*' (1923). The remedy was easy – but the resistance remained stiff.

Why did it take so long to achieve woman suffrage in Republican France? (1910–1945)

What happened between 1910 and 1914 prefigured what would happen for the ensuing thirty years. High hopes and energetic promotion of votes for women were invariably followed by delays, compromises, complications, resistances, hostility, and repeated expressions of overt hostility. Women's suffrage advocates scurried to find the right formula for representing the cause: would it be philosophical (the appeal to the principle of rights), expedient (the vote as a means to further reforms benefiting women and children), or commercial (the vote as a reward for services rendered to the nation)?

Despite the restricted nature of the 1909 Buisson committee proposal and the political pressure applied by the women's groups, the legislature refused to act on it pending a decision on the proposed change in the national electoral laws to proportional representation which finally passed in mid-1913. Legislators proved themselves more interested in enacting laws to protect maternity and early infancy. Even so, in 1913 French feminists had reason to be optimistic, and at that point they played the citizen–mother card, the card of sexual difference and relationality, of local and national 'social housekeeping' for all it was worth; in the process, French feminism had become thoroughly nationalised and French maternity 'protected'. The trade-off, in my reading of the evidence, may have been compromises that we today would consider unacceptable on issues of reproductive freedom. Would this be the price of citizenship for French women?[29]

In mid-June 1914, the project of law based on the Buisson report was finally presented to the Chamber of Deputies; in early July French suffragists staged a massive rally on behalf of the proposal at the Condorcet monument in Paris. This was their first – and last – major public demonstration. The timing was terrible; seven days later France was at war. The woman suffrage bill was among the first casualties.

Following the war, increasing evidence suggested that women wanted the vote and were prepared to work hard for it. Others dissented, as was the case of the editor of Le Matin, who was quoted in New York saying:

> . . . woman suffrage will not come in France in the immediate future be-cause the women do not want it. There is no demand for the vote by Frenchwomen. The women will be a power in French political life, but they will prefer to exercise it through their husbands and in their social life, rather than through the coarse medium of the ballot box.[30]

In May 1919 the Chamber of Deputies held its first debate on the women's suffrage question, and finally overrode the proposal for municipal suffrage to grant the vote to 'tous les citoyens français sans distinction de sexe' by a 344–97 margin.[31] Echoing suffrage advocates, demographer and pronatalist advocate Jacques Bertillon insisted that the women's vote would be necessary to refocus candidates' platforms on family protection issues, and on the campaign against alcoholism and debauchery; he was particularly impressed with the importance of women's vote in other countries for resolving the problem of (male) alcoholism.[32]

Throughout the interwar period, however, woman suffrage remained stalemated in the French legislature, hostage to a recalcitrant Senate. Proposed measures juggled various formulae for the level of suffrage to be allowed to women (municipal, departmental, legislative), age qualifications (21, 25, 30), and eligibility for office and public service. Three times more (1925, 1932, and 1935) the Chamber of Deputies cast large majority votes in favor of woman suffrage proposals, but each time the Senate blocked enactment of the proposed measure.[33]

The opposition of republican radical senators continued to express itself as a deep fear that enfranchised women would vote for the Catholic/ right-wing ticket and thereby undermine the secular republic. Meanwhile, Catholic laymen and women had come to appreciate the possibility that Catholic interests might in fact benefit if women were given the vote and that women's sphere might not be irreparably breached by the casting of ballots. In later 1919 the Catholic Church hierarchy had lifted its opposition to woman suffrage.[34] Catholic suffragist organisations such as the *Union Nationale pour le Vote des Femmes* (UNVF), founded as a section of *Action Sociale de la Femme*, and independent from 1925 on, sprang into existence. The UNVF platform – like those of the other secular pro-suffrage organisations – represented the vote as a means to reform, focusing on measures to enhance the conditions of maternity for women and to safeguard the family.[35] Thus in the 1920s and 1930s anticlerical woman suffrage advocates could be found pursuing an alliance with Catholic advocates of the proposed alternative 'familial vote' in order to assure that, if such a measure were passed, married women would be able to cast their own ballots, instead of finding 'their' votes delegated to their husbands.[36]

Even the new wave of secular suffrage agitation fostered by Louise Weiss from 1934 on, however, failed to budge the French Senate as the Third Republic entered its final years of crisis.[37] Nor did the appointment of three women under-secretaries in the Popular Front ministry of Léon Blum mean that the government was prepared to make a stand on the women's vote.[38] The ultimate irony of the French campaign was that woman suffrage was finally achieved in April 1944 – not by the magnanimity of the legislators of the parliamentary republic but by decree of General Charles de Gaulle. The political enfranchisement of women was accorded as a 'paternal gift' of the Liberation and the new provisional government.[39]

How do historians account for this amazing delay in the granting of woman suffrage in France? There seems to be general agreement that the immediate cause was the intransigent resistance of the Radicals in the Senate; both Hause and Kenney, and Paul Smith, agree on this point.[40] Hause argues persuasively that the opposition of the younger radical senators was based not solely on fears of clericalism but on their own underlying social conservatism. Smith posits that woman suffrage was the victim of the French electoral reform movement, rather than its beneficiary; the 'political controversies of the time', he argues, did not serve the suffrage cause.[41] The number one political controversy was that over separation of Church and State, which had evidently left a deep scar in the memories of most Radical senators during their formative years.

Analysing the issue from the perspective of the organised suffrage movement, which Hause and Kenney characterised as 'large, organized, and active', Klejman and Rochefort conclude that no strategy paid off; the movement tried everything short of physical violence. In numerous other countries, women were accorded the vote without lifting a finger to obtain it. Klejman and Rochefort see it as highly ironic that in the end, Frenchwomen were enfranchised in order to 'preserve' republican institutions against the Communist 'threat'.[42]

How can we account for the 'social conservatism', for the 'fear' exhibited by the Radical republican senators? One issue that has not been given the play it perhaps deserves is the issue of numbers itself. The opponents of women's suffrage from 1918 on constantly referred to the fact that, due to war casualties, there were some 2 million more adult women than men (12–13 million compared with 10 million) aged 21 and up.[43] There was an almost nightmarish concern expressed that women voting would outnumber, and therefore outvote, male voters (though admittedly, a mere doubling of the electorate was not in the same category of nightmares as expanding it by a factor of 40, as in 1848). Male senators clearly feared a potential 'gender gap', although they did not call it that, if women came to the polls en masse. Hence, the constant dickering with differential age cut-offs for the women's vote – 25, 30 – and with their status – notably the exclusion of married women – that would minimise the impact of a prospective female voting bloc.

A second issue concerns the content of the promised social housekeeping in which women might participate if they did vote in full force. Under the cover of improving the situation of women and children, lay two severe social problems that were being addressed by women world wide. One was alcoholism, the other was legalised prostitution. These two issues appear increasingly on the agendas of pro-suffrage women and their male supporters after 1918.[44] Indeed, women dabbling in politics might exercise a pernicious influence – on the habits of many male electors. The bars and cabarets might even have to close on election day! Women voters in the Protestant countries had succeeded in enforcing temperance controls, and in France this was a well-articulated concern, though in the final analysis, a futile one.[45]

A third issue concerns the projected reactionary content of the women's vote, and this concerned issues that went beyond the explicit concern with Catholicism, especially after Hindenburg was elected as president in Germany, and Hitler came to power – both riding on, some alleged, the women's vote.[46] But perspectives expressed by Catholic writers in the mid-1920s boded ill for wholehearted women's emancipation, even in France. In her 'Essay on Feminism', Anne de Nantes characterised the vote as only a 'superficial aspect' of a far broader problem and as an expedient in a world already in disarray; if women got the vote they must use it to combat 'the forces of evil' and to defend Catholic liberties. She challenged concepts of 'emancipation' and 'liberty', of 'equality' and 'individualism' as false dogma, propagated by international freemasonry.[47] The Jesuit Albert Bessières, equally a foe of 'atheist materialism', suggested that perhaps Catholic women (inspired by the example of Joan of Arc) could save France a second time if they rose to do their duty. Equality of the sexes and women's independence from the family were anathema, in his view, to Catholic teachings.[48] Such presentations of Catholic teaching on the woman question, coupled with the establishment of a series of women's organisations, including the progressive-minded *Union féminine civique et sociale*, expressly organised to train Catholic women for citizenship, did nothing to reassure the Radical senators who opposed giving votes to women who might put the Church's programme ahead of the welfare of the secular republic.[49]

What difference did woman suffrage make in France? (1945–1993)

René Viviani certainly made an essential point when, in 1900, he stressed that lawmakers make the laws for those who elect them. Paul Valéry put it even more bluntly in 1934, when he fingered the concern of the men in place that women's vote would disrupt their cosy system, and that personal interests were being put before principles; André Tardieu raised the stakes by calling for full women's suffrage as a central point in his programme for constitutional reform.[50] What, then, happened once women got the vote in France?

The story is most interesting, but all too little known. It intersects directly with the long-standing concern about population deficit. From August 1946 on, a full-scale system of state-supported maternity allowances was set in place, payable in cash to the mothers themselves. The very important benefit of free maternity care, prenatal, delivery and post-partum, was included in the social security medical benefits package. Birth premiums were established for each child born; in addition, prenatal allowances payable to the woman to cover her expenses during pregnancy were added, with the explicit intention of discouraging abortion.

All these measures addressed the combined demands of pronatalists and feminists during the previous thirty years.[51]

The subsequent changes in French women's legal and political situation, especially as wives and mothers, were just as significant. In 1946 a clause giving women equal rights in law was incorporated into the Constitution of the Fourth Republic; it was reconfirmed in 1958 by the Fifth Republic. Twenty years later the real action began, especially in the wake of the 'revolution' of 1968, which spelled the end of the Gaullist régime and the birth of the women's liberation movement (MLF). Between 1965 and 1975 most of the long sought reforms, especially in the severely constrained legal status of married women, were granted through state action. These included the complete empowerment of married women with regard to property and personal decisions, rights over children, and, for all women, the legalisation of contraception and abortion. In the 1980s the French state even undertook sponsorship of programmes for family planning. 'Between 1965 and 1985', as the American political scientist Dorothy McBride Stetson stressed in her recent book, *Women's Rights in France*, 'every policy affecting women, from reproduction to retirement, was rewritten' in ways that favoured women. Stetson's French counterpart, Mariette Sineau, put it even more forcefully when she exclaimed that 'a real "decolonization" of the woman' had finally taken place.[52]

What accounts for such a vast and sudden change? It seems that political scientists – and the major political parties on both left and right – had discovered that women, particularly unmarried women, constituted the swinging voters in elections.[53] Furthermore, in the 1970s, the women's vote began to move to the left.[54] Although the French did not then speak of a gender gap as such, the presidencies of Georges Pompidou, Valéry Giscard d'Estaing, and François Mitterrand all acknowledged that women's concerns were public policy issues and attempted to court their votes. By 1981, when the Socialists came to power, the major changes in women's legal position – on issues including reproduction, family, education, work, and sexuality – had already been accomplished. State-authorised contraception was envisioned as a deterrent to abortion, but abortion was also legalised within certain limits. Moreover, in response to populationist concerns, France had already initiated a fully fledged family policy and budget in 1946, which was subsequently revised in the 1970s to create a more positive overall environment for family formation. In the 1980s Yvette Roudy, as Minister of Women's Rights under Mitterrand, supplemented these earlier measures by focusing on equal opportunity employment measures to benefit women. The 'Medals for Motherhood' inaugurated in the 1920s were still in place, but state support for motherhood as well as women's full civil and political rights appeared to have entered the laws and customs of the French nation.

Woman suffrage, so long a sticking point, can now be seen as a significant turning point in French history, both for women and for men. It symbolises a major readjustment in the balance of power between the sexes. What is particularly striking today is that the campaigns being waged by the latest wave of feminist activism no longer take place on the terrain of legal and economic discrimination, but on the newer fields of politics, knowledge, and even language itself.[55]

With reference to politics, it remains the case that even in today's Fifth Republic, the world of French politics (*le pouvoir*) and state authority itself remains what Michelle Perrot has called a 'masculine sanctuary'.[56] In 1972 Gisèle Charzat published a book, on the heels of the 1970 *Etats-Généraux de la femme*, with the title, *Are Frenchwomen Citizens?* In 1981, Colette Piat challenged 'The Republic of Misogynists'. The interviews with politically active women in Laure Adler's new book, *Les Femmes politiques*, underscore the point, as does the accompanying observation that even today women constitute only six per cent of France's current parliamentary representation.[57] Although the barrier of the prime ministership was briefly broken in 1991 by Edith Cresson, the 'glass ceiling' remains in place. What the French call *la classe politique* remains a male bastion – or is it, perhaps, a Bastille?

This Bastille is not a prison but a citadel of power; storming it requires concerted action. To kick off the campaign in 1992, three French feminists published a book-manifesto, *Au pouvoir, citoyennes: liberté, égalité, parité*.[58] The feminist group, *Choisir*, convened an international congress at the UNESCO headquarters in Paris early in June 1993 to consider the theme: 'Democracy for women: a power to be shared'. In the course of this gathering, women's poor representation in parliaments and women's difficulties in acceding to high office were debated by female political leaders from around the world. Those in attendance acclaimed the principle of equitable representation, of *parity* between the sexes in governance, as a *fundamental right*.[59] Their campaign continues today.

With reference to knowledge (and language), a great deal could be said. I will confine myself to one point only – a point about the politics of historical knowledge concerning the very history of French women's suffrage. The British-based historian Siân Reynolds argues that mainstream historians of France (could we call them '*la classe historique*'?) have proved reluctant to acknowledge the significance of women's suffrage and the ensuing revolution in women's status as they have written their histories of twentieth-century France. She notes both the absence of discussion of women's exclusion and of women's obtaining the vote in books on the history of the French republics and contemporary discussion of France's republican tradition. '[The year 1945] has thus acquired the paradoxical status of a "fact" significant for women but not for men' – 'a non-date for the Republic'. She complains that even feminist historians had tended to pass over its importance. She proposes that 'the republic was imperfect and in a very profound sense invalid when it was created and sustained without women' and that this finding should be analysed.[60]

In fact, it is remarkable that the campaign for French women's suffrage has attracted greater scholarly discussion in Anglo–American scholarship on France than it has among the French, where for so many years political history itself was out of fashion. Women's historians in France have themselves only recently re-engaged such issues, focusing on the currently fashionable concept of '*pouvoir*', or power.[61] I would submit, alternatively, that what really need to be re-examined are issues focusing concretely on the gendering of authority in France over many centuries.

In conclusion, I want to underscore the point that in France women's suffrage is but a long chapter in a saga of cultural and political struggle over gender definition, over roles and responsibilities in state-building, over the wielding of sociopolitical authority, that can be documented for at least two centuries before the French Jacobins, in their world-historical encounter with democracy, consigned women to domesticity in the name of public interest and claimed public authority for themselves. Attainment of the vote clearly opened up possibilities for women within the framework of French republican democracy. But it has also opened up the even more important possibility of asking vital questions, with historical content – gender-centred questions – about the development and meanings, both explicit and implicit, of law, politics, government, and about the premises and practices of citizen democracy, motherhood for the nation, and the construction of historical memory itself. The call for gender parity in French political life will test the elasticity and good faith of political leaders who continue to proclaim themselves republican and to assert a unique historical role for their country as a champion of universalised principles of liberty, equality, and justice throughout the world.

1   This paper is a vastly expanded version of my encyclopedia article, 'Women: Movement for Political Rights', in Patrick H. Hutton, ed, *Historical Dictionary of the Third French Republic, 1870-1940*, Greenwood Press, Westport, Conn., 1986, vol 2, 1077-9. All translations are mine, unless otherwise indicated.

2   Janine Mossuz-Lavau, '*Le Vote des femmes: le pouvoir de dire non*', in Michèle Riot-Sarcey, ed, *Femmes, Pouvoirs*, Editions Kimé, Paris, 1993, 59. See also Janine Mossuz-Lavau, 'Women and Politics in France', *French Politics and Society*, 10/1, 1992, 1-8.

3   Steven C. Hause, with Anne R. Kenney, *Women's Suffrage and Social Politics in the French Third Republic*, Princeton Univ. Press, Princeton, NJ, 1984, 254.

4   Cécile Brunschvicg, '*Les Femmes et le suffrage*', *L'Humanité*, 19 May 1919. Geoges Goyau, '*Le Féminisme politique devant la pensée catholique*', in Georges Goyau, *Catholicisme et Politique*, Editions de la Revue des jeunes, Paris, 1923, 230, 232.

5   See especially '*Cahier des doléances et réclamations des femmes, par Madame B...B...*, Pays de Caux, 1789*', reprinted in *Cahiers de doléances des femmes en 1789 et autres textes (CDF)*, EDHIS, Paris, 1981, 1, 47-51; '*Requête des dames l'Assemblée Nationale (1789)*', reprinted in *CDF*, 1, unpaginated. See also Olympe de Gouges, *Les Droits de la femme*, Paris, 1791, as translated by Nupur Chaudhuri in Susan Groag Bell and Karen M. Offen, eds, *Women, the Family, and Freedom: The Debate in Documents, 1750-1950 (WFF)*, Stanford Univ. Press, Stanford, Calif., 1983, vol 1, doct. 26.

6   Marie-Jean-Antoine-Nicolas Caritat, Marquis de Condorcet, '*Sur l'Admission des femmes au droit de cité*', *Journal de la Société de 1789*, 3 July 1790; in English translation, 'Condorcet's Plea for the Citizenship of Women', by John Morley, *Fortnightly Review*, 13, 1 June 1870, 719-24, reprinted in *WFF*, 1, doct. 24.

7   Olwen H. Hufton, *Women and the Limits of Citizenship in the French Revolution*, Univ. of Toronto Press, Toronto, Ont., 1992.

8   Charles-Maurice de Talleyrand-Périgord, *Rapport sur l'instruction publique, fait au nom du Comité de constitution, à l'Assemblée nationale, les 10, 11, et 19 Septembre 1791 [Projet de décrets sur l'instruction publique]*, Paris, 1791, 115-20.

9   Editorial from *La Feuille de Salut public*, as reprinted in *Gazette National, ou le Moniteur universel*, 29 Brumaire, l'an 2e (Mardi, 19 Nov. 1793, vieux style), Réimpression de l'Ancien Moniteur, vol 18 (Paris), 450.

10   Explanation of the provisional government, quoted in Marthe Louis-Lévy, *L'Emancipation politique des femmes; rapport présenté à la première conférence nationale des femmes socialistes (4-5 Juin 1933)*, Librairie populaire, Paris, 1934.

11   An account of this initiative (led by a Mme Bourgeois) and the women's reception at the Hôtel de Ville is given in the brochure, Maïté Albistur and Daniel Armogathe, eds, *Les Femmes électeurs et éligibles*, Paris, 1848; partially reprinted in *Le Grief des femmes*, Editions hier et demain, Paris, 1, 280-1. This incident was reported in the article, '*Les Femmes à l'oeuvre*', *La Voix des femmes*, no 6, 26 March 1848.

12   Jeanne Deroin, '*Aux Citoyens français*', *La Voix des femmes*, no 7, 27 March 1848; English translation in *WFF*, 1, doct. 70.

13   Karen Offen, *The Woman Question in Modern France* (forthcoming), chs 1-2 .

14   For further discussion of these points, see Christine Fauré, *Democracy without Women: Feminism and the Rise of Liberal Individualism in France*, Indiana Univ. Press, Bloomington, Ind., 1991, and Sarah Hanley, 'Engendering the State: Family Formation and State Building in Early Modern France', *French Historical Studies*, 16/1, 1989, 4-27.

15   Julie-Victoire Daubié, *La Femme pauvre*, Guillaumin, Paris, 1866, 240-53; see also her *L'Emancipation de la femme en dix livraisons*, E. Thorin, Paris, 1871. The 1870 edition of *La Femme pauvre*, reprinted in 1992 by Côté-femmes, Paris, does not contain the suffrage demands.

16   Alexandre-Jacques-Véron Duverger, *De la Condition politique et civile des femmes. Réponse à quelques critiques de nos lois; modifications admissibles. 1e partie (seule publiée)*, Marescq, Paris, 1872.

17   Hubertine Auclert, *Le Droit politique des femmes, question qui n'est pas traitée au Congrès international des femmes*, Paris, 1878; my thanks to Claire Moses for transmitting a copy of this text. An excellent English-language biography of Auclert has been published by Steven C. Hause, *Hubertine Auclert, the French Suffragette*, Yale Univ. Press, New Haven, Conn., 1987. See also Edith Taïeb, ed, *Hubertine Auclert: La Citoyenne 1848-1914. Articles de 1881 à 1891*, Syros, Paris, 1982.

18   On the reluctance of socialist men to take up the woman suffrage issue in early twentieth-century France, see Charles Sowerwine, *Sisters or Citizens? Women and Socialism in France since 1876*,

Cambridge Univ. Press, Cambridge, England, 1982, esp. chap. 5. The Second International endorsed full woman suffrage at their Stuttgart Congress in 1907.

19   'An Act (2 William IV, c. 45) to Amend the Representation of the People in England and Wales, 7 June 1832', in David C. Douglas, ed, *English Historical Documents*, vol 11, 1783-1832, ed. A. Aspinall & E. Anthony Smith, Oxford Univ. Press, Oxford, 1959, doct 303, articles XIX and XX. See also John Stuart Mill's 1867 speech before the House of Commons, 20 May 1867; reprinted in Bell & Offen, *WFF*, vol 1, doct. 135. Jane Rendall has brought to my attention that in Britain, 'the situation was complicated . . . by the passing of Lord Romilly's Act in 1850, which ruled that the term "men" should include "women" in legislation, unless women were expressly excluded, as they were in the Reform Act of 1832. So part of the basis of Lydia Becker's claim in 1868 was that the 1867 Reform Act, by using "men" and not "male person", had *not* thus excluded women.' (Personal communication, 2 August 1993.) On the elimination of women's vote in New Jersey, see Judith Apter Klinghoffer & Lois Elkis, '"The Petticoat Electors": Women's Suffrage in New Jersey, 1776-1807', *Journal of the Early Republic*, 12/2, 1992, 159-94.

20   The texts from the *Gazette des Tribunaux* are reproduced in English, in 'The Recent Decision upon Municipal Suffrage in France', *Englishwoman's Review*, 16, 14 March 1885, 106.

21   'Recent Decision', 108. For the constitutional texts, see Maurice Duverger, ed, *Constitutions et documents politiques*, 4th ed., Presses universitaires de France, Paris, 1966.

22   'Recent Decision', 109. My emphasis.

23   Léon Giraud, *De la Condition des femmes au point de vue de l'exercise des droits publics et politiques; étude de législation comparée*, F. Pichon, Paris, 1891. See also Moïse Ostrogorski, *La Femme au point de vue du droit public; étude d'histoire et de législation comparée*, A. Rousseau, Paris, 1892; a revised edition was translated into English as *The Rights of Women: A Comparative Study in History and Legislation*, Swan Sonnenschein, London, & Charles Scribner's Sons, New York, 1893.

24   See the series of articles by Eliska Vincent on women and legislation, especially '*L'Electorat des femmes dans l'histoire*', *Revue féministe*, 1/1, 1 Oct. 1895, 20-6. See also Hubertine Auclert, '*Les Femmes ont voté en France*', in her *Vote des femmes*, V. Giard & E. Brière, Paris, 1908, 65ff. Goyau summarises the earlier situation in '*Féminisme politique*', 213-15, basing his observations on the scholarship of Paul Viollet.

25   Raoul de la Grasserie, '*Le Mouvement féministe et les droits de la femme*', *Revue politique et parlementaire*, 1/3, 1894, 448.

26   See Hause, *Hubertine Auclert*, xx, 90-91, and Karen Offen, 'On the French Origin of the Words "Feminism" and "Feminist"', *Feminist Issues*, 8/2, 1988, 45-51.

27   René Viviani, reported in *La Fronde*, 10 Sept. 1900.

28   See the suffrage section report in *Conseil National des Femmes Françaises. Assemblée générale publique*, no. 4, 1907. See also Maria Vérone, *Appel à la justice adressé par le Conseil national des femmes françaises à la Chambre des députés et au Sénat*, CNFF, 1909, and Ferdinand Buisson, *Le Vote des femmes*, H. Dunod & E. Pinat, editeurs, Paris, 1911.

29   These questions are examined in greater detail in Karen Offen, 'Exploring the Sexual Politics of French Nationalism', in Robert Tombs, ed, *Nationhood and Nationalism in France: From Boulangism to the Great War, 1889-1918*, HarperCollins Academic, London, 1991, 195-209. The mother/social housekeeping argument can be identified much earlier, eg., in the texts of the French feminist-socialist Jeanne Deroin, 1848-49.

30   Quoted in William S. Crawford, 'A Changed World for the Women of France (an interview with Stephen Lauzanne, ed. of *Le Matin*)', *New York Times Magazine*, 23 June 1918, 4-5.

31   See Suzanne Grinberg, *Historique du mouvement suffragiste depuis 1848*, H. Goulet, Paris, 1926, esp. Part II, for an extended account of the debates. See also the analysis of Hause & Kenney.

32   Jacques Bertillon, '*Un essai de vote féminin*', *La Femme et l'enfant*, 31, 15 Jan. 1920, 745. See also his '*Vote féminin - vote familial*', ibid., 25, 15 Oct. 1919, 555-6.

33   A detailed discussion of the legislative votes from 1922 to 1935 can be found in Paul Smith, 'Women's Political and Civil Rights in France, 1919-1940', unpublished Ph.D thesis, Oxford Univ., 1991, esp. Chap. 3. My thanks to Anne Cova for alerting me to Smith's dissertation.

34   Papal endorsement is generally attributed to the rather veiled remarks of Benedict XV to the head of the Catholic Women's Union of Italy, '*Sono avventurati*', published in French as '*Allocution sur la mission de la femme dans la société (21 Oct. 1919)*', in *Actes de Benoit XV*, 3 vols., Bonne Presse, Paris, 1924-1934, vol 2, 68-72.

35   The UNVF's emphasis on national problems and on women's group and associational interests is embodied in two publications: Duchesse de La Rochefoucauld, '*Une Enquête relative aux raisons*

qu'invoquent les françaises pour obtenir le droit de suffrage' (Compte rendu, Séances et Travaux de l'Académie des sciences morales et politiques, n.s. (July-Aug. 1929)), 18 pp., and Duchesse de La Rochefoucauld, et al., Problèmes nationaux vus par des Françaises, Sagittaire, Paris, 1934. For an introduction to this organisation, see Anne Cova, 'The French Feminist Movement and the Politics of Motherhood in France, 1890s-1939', unpublished paper presented to the Ninth Berkshire Conference on the History of Women, Vassar College, June 1993.

36 Proposals for the familial vote recurred during the interwar period, including the proposal by Roulleaux-Dugage in 1923. See especially Robert Talmy, Histoire du mouvement familial en France (1896-1939), 2 vols, Union Nationale des Caisses d'Allocations Familiales, Paris, 1962.

37 On the suffrage campaigns of Louise Weiss, see vol 3 of her Mémoires d'une Européenne, Payot, Paris, 1970.

38 Siân Reynolds is re-examining the gender politics of the Popular Front; see her unpublished paper, 'Women and the Popular Front in France in 1936: Mixing with Men? The Case of the Social Services', presented at the Ninth Berkshire Conference on the History of Women, Vassar College, June 1993.

39 The term is Michelle Perrot's, in her introduction to Laurence Klejman & Florence Rochefort, L'Egalité en marche: Le Féminisme sous la Troisième République, Presses de la Fondation Nationale des Sciences Politiques and des femmes, 1989, 19.

40 Hause & Kenney, Women's Suffrage and Social Policies, esp. Chap. 9; Smith, 'Women's Political and Civil Rights', Chap. 3.

41 Quotes from Smith, 'Women's Political and Civil Rights', 108, 72.

42 Quote from Hause & Kenney, Women's Suffrage, 269; Klejman & Rochefort, L'Egalité en marche, chap 8, 342.

43 Among those concerned with numbers was the founder of the Alliance Nationale, Jacques Bertillon. See, among other publications, his editorial, 'Un essai de vote féminin', La Femme et l'enfant, 31, 15 Jan. 1920, 745.

44 Bertillon (art. cited above) insisted on these connections. See also, for example, Suzanne Lacore, 'La Femme et les fleaux sociaux', Revue féministe du Sud-Ouest, 4/10, Oct. 1923, 149-57; the editorials of Maria Vérone in L'Oeuvre, notably 'Les Françaises veulent voter: Pour combattre l'immoralité', (6 Oct. 1926); 'Contre la prostitution réglementée' (22 Dec. 1926); 'Suppression des maisons de tolérance' (28 Feb. 1928), and the speeches reproduced in Union temporaire contre la prostitution réglementée et la traite des femmes: Discours prononcés le 6 février 1931 à la Salle des sociétés savantes (speeches by Justin Godart, Mme M. Legrand-Falco, Marc Sangnier, Mme Maria Vérone, and Paul Gemaehling), Editions de l'Union temporaire, Paris, 1931.

45 In contrast to many dominantly Protestant countries, the French temperance movement never succeeded in recruiting many women, though the suffrage leaders (many of whom were Protestants) signed on. See Patricia E. Prestwich, Drink and the Politics of Social Reform: Anti-alcoholism in France since 1870, SPOSS, Palo Alto, 1988, 148-52, 187-90.

46 Maria Vérone repeatedly insisted that women were not responsible for electing Nazi candidates; see, for example, her editorials, 'La léon des élections', L'Oeuvre, 12 Nov. 1930, and 'Hitler et les femmes', L'Oeuvre, 20 May 1933. In 1932, the Duchess de La Rochefoucauld, president of the Union Nationale pour le Vote des Femmes, pointed out that Hitler's programme included the elimination of women from political life. See Suzanne Desternes, Trente ans d'efforts au service de la cause féminine (Union Nationale pour le Vote des Femmes), offprint, 1959, courtesy of Anne Cova. I am also grateful to Gisèle Garcia for compiling a list of Vérone's editorials, 1926-1936, as part of her 1992 Vassar honours thesis on Vérone.

For a scholarly assessment of women's vote in Germany, which supports Vérone's observations, see Richard J. Evans, 'Feminism and Fascism', in his book Comrades and Sisters: Feminism, Socialism and Pacifism in Europe, 1870-1945, Wheatsheaf Books, Brighton, Sussex, & St. Martin's Press, New York, 1987. But see also Helen L. Boak, '"Our Last Hope"; Women's Votes for Hitler – A Reappraisal', German Studies Review, 12/2, 1989, 289-310, who argues, against Evans and others, that the women's vote did help bring Hitler to power.

47 Anne de Nantes, Essai sur le féminisme, Aubanel fils aîné, Avignon, 1926, 10-12.

48 Albert Bessières, Le Devoir civique de la femme et le suffrage, Spès, Paris, 1926, 5-6, 18.

49 On the UFCS, see Naomi Black, Social Feminism, Cornell Univ. Press, Ithaca, N.Y., 1989, and Susan Pedersen, 'Catholicism, Feminism, and the Politics of the Family during the late Third Republic', in Seth Koven & Sonya Michel, eds, Mothers of a New World: Maternalist Politics and the Origins of Welfare States, Routledge, New York & London, 1993, 246-76.

50   Paul Valéry, 'Avant-propos', problèmes nationaux vus par des françaises, (cit. note 34 above), 11-12; André Tardieu, 'Le Vote des femmes', La Réforme de l'état, E. Flammarion, Paris, 1934, 111-25.

51   For an extended discussion of these issues, see Karen Offen, 'Body Politics: Women, Work and the Politics of Motherhood in France, 1920-1950', in Gisela Bock & Pat Thane, eds, Maternity & Gender Policies: Women and the Rise of the European Welfare States, 1880s-1950s, Routledge, London, 1991, 138-59. See also Jane Jenson, 'The Liberation and New Rights for French Women', in Margaret Higonnet, et al., eds, Behind the Lines: Gender and the Two World Wars, Yale Univ. Press, New Haven, Conn., 272-84.

52   Dorothy McBride Stetson, Women's Rights in France, Greenwood Press, Westport, Conn., 1987; the following remarks are adapted from my review of Stetson's book in Constitutional Commentary, 7/1, 1990, 130-6. See also Mariette Sineau, 'Droit et démocratie', in Françoise Thébaud, ed, Histoire des femmes, vol 5, Plon, Paris, 1992, 481. For further discussion of the reforms, see Odile Dhavernas, Droits des femmes, pouvoir des hommes, Seuil, Paris, 1978, and Janine Mossuz-Lavau, Les Lois de l'amour: les politiques de la sexualité en France de 1950 à nos jours, Payot, Paris, 1991.

53   Mattei Dogan & Jacques Narbonne, Les Françaises face à la politique, Cahiers de la Fondation Nationale des Sciences Politiques, Paris, 12, 1955.

54   Janine Mossuz-Lavau & Mariette Sineau, Enquête sur les femmes et la politique en France, Presses universitaires de France, Paris, 1983; Janine Mossuz-Lavau, 'Le Vote des femmes en France (1944-1984)', in Daniel Gaxie, ed, Explications du vote, Presses de la Fondation Nationale des Sciences Politiques, Paris, 1985, 209-27.

55   Yvonne Knibiehler, 'Féminisme et maternité', remarks presented at a conference on women and creation, Marseille, May 1985. Typescript in my possession.

56   Perrot, 'Introduction' to Klejman & Rochefort, L'Egalité en marche, 19.

57   See Gisèle Charzat, Les Françaises sont-elles des citoyennes, Denoël-Gonthier, Paris, 1972; Colette Piat, La République des misogynes, Plon, Paris, 1981; and especially Laure Adler, Les Femmes politiques, Seuil, Paris, 1993.

58   Françoise Gaspard, Claude Servan-Schreiber & Anne Le Gall, Au Pouvoir citoyennes! Liberté, égalité, parité, Seuil, Paris, 1992.

59   See Christiane Chombeau, 'Pour un principe de parité entre hommes et femmes dans les instances politiques', Le Monde, 6-7 June 1993. Thanks go to Bernard Sinsheimer for bringing press coverage of this conference to my attention.

60   Siân Reynolds, 'Marianne's Citizens? Women, the Republic and Universal Suffrage in France', in Siân Reynolds, ed, Women, State, and Revolution, Univ. of Massachusetts Press, Amherst, 1987, 102-22, quotes: 103, 119.

61   Cécile Dauphin, et al., 'Culture et pouvoir des femmes', Annales: Economies, Sociétés, Civilisations, 2, Mar-April 1986; in English translation as 'Women's Culture and Women's Power: Issues in French Women's History', in Karen Offen, Ruth Roach Pierson & Jane Rendall, eds, Writing Women's History: International Perspectives, 107-33.

9

Women's Suffrage and Gender Politics in Japan[1]

YUKIKO MATSUKAWA AND KAORU TACHI

Japanese women did not achieve the vote until 1945, when the country was under direct Allied – mainly American – control.[2] Subsequently, many Americans believed that Japanese women owed their suffrage to the Allied Occupation and that they had gained the vote without an organised struggle. Certainly Americans told Japanese women this at the time. At a local women's meeting in the late 1940s, for example:

> As was the custom at that period, an American woman officer said the greetings first, pointing out that 'I think you, Japanese women, are very lucky because one morning you woke up to find women's suffrage on the pillow'. Suddenly, one old woman stood up and cried: 'We did not find women's suffrage on the pillow. I can not remind myself of the services of Ichikawa Fusae without tears. She is suffering from a hard life at Hachioji by raising ducks and cultivating potatoes, because she was purged from public service by American Authorities. Let's send a telegram to thank her in the name of this meeting.' This resolution was welcomed by rapturous applause.[3]

In this essay we outline the background and history of the women's suffrage movement in Japan, focusing on what it was the women and men who worked for suffrage hoped to achieve by gaining the vote. Over time, women's and men's attitudes to women's suffrage changed; before the 1920s the emphasis was on suffrage as a fundamental human right and the key to equality. From the 1920s, however, the idea of suffrage as a right was largely left behind, as both the social reform movements and nationalist movement promoted women's suffrage on the basis that women's 'essential' qualities would help the nation, or at least their own cause. We also look at the role played by the idea of 'national interest' in suffrage, and at the treatment of gender, ethnicity and class in the whole suffrage debate in Japan.

Meiji imperialism and the Japanese women's movement

Forced by foreign powers to open the country, Japan exposed itself to massive Western influence in the middle of the nineteenth century after many years of the isolationist policies of the Tokugawa Shogunate military government. In 1868, with the fall of the Shogunate, a new bureaucratic state was established by the the imperial Meiji Restoration. To catch up with the West, the new government promoted industry, seeking to enrich and strengthen the country. It was thought that strong military and economic foundations were necessary for Japan to avoid the fate of colonisation by Western imperialism.

Westernisation in the 1870s, in the form of educational developments, publications and political ideas on representation, was the key to the beginnings of the modern Japanese women's movement. The state's encouragement of Westernisation led it to introduce a nation-wide education system in 1872, offering elementary schooling to girls as well as to boys. Higher education was also significant. In some instances, Western immersion occurred directly. The state funded the study of five girls in the United States in 1871. One of the five students, Tsuda Umeko, returned to found the Women's English School in 1900, the first private institution to offer higher education for women.[4] The first state institution, the Women's Normal School, had been established in 1874.[5] At the same time, Christian girls' schools of various denominations were opened for the purpose of 'uplifting' the position of women.[6] Missionaries were struck by what was described as the 'miserable' position of Japanese women.[7]

The government was keen to adopt modern ideas, and supported democratic reforms. New ideas abounded. John Stuart Mill's *The Subjection of Women* was partly translated into Japanese in 1879. This was followed by a wave of articles appearing in Japanese which tried to promote understanding of women's rights.[8] As the national political system had not yet been well established, political meetings calling for popular liberty and rights were frequently held in various parts of Japan, together with the study of new ideas. Some women were very active in participating in such political meetings and there were a few towns and villages where women were given the right to vote.[9]

Finding it difficult to maintain national order, the government soon attempted to co-opt and stifle these developments, particularly among women, which its Westernisation policy had sanctioned. When the voices of the popular rights movement became vigorous, it promulgated the 1889 Constitution of the Empire of Japan, as a gift from the sovereign. And in the next year, the government constituted the Imperial Diet, consisting of two Houses: a non-elected House of Peers, and an elected House of Representatives. The House of Peers was composed of members of the imperial family, nobles, and other imperial nominees. They were almost all the conservative elite. The House of Representatives, on the other hand, was relatively weak in composition and power. The government attempted to weaken popular protest and, at the same time, to establish a highly centralised political system. Limited suffrage was introduced: in 1888 and 1889, local and national election laws were enacted, giving the vote to males only who had paid a certain level of taxes. Furthermore, in 1890, women, together with soldiers, police, teachers and students, were forbidden by the Public Assembly and Association Law to hold or even to attend political meetings and to take part in political organisations.

Thus, the state stripped women of all political rights. The few women who had voting rights lost them as a result of the establishment of the new national political system. In addition, the idea that a woman's place was in the home was made clear when the aim of women's education was stated in the 1890 Imperial Prescript on Education: 'Good Wives, Wise Mothers'. A good wife was one who was loyal and obedient to her husband's family. Above all, the Civil Code of 1898 placed women in the most slavish status, with no legal rights. It stated that property rights and parental rights should belong solely to the father, the head of the family, and all property should succeed to the eldest son whose duty it was to be master of the family. Furthermore, chastity was required of wives, but not husbands. Women were thus rendered powerless. It was thought abhorrent for women to show any interest in the public sphere as is evident from a popular saying of the time: 'Women may read novels but shouldn't read the newspaper'. Attending political meetings was said to be 'damaging to a woman's essential feminine qualities'. The opinion was often expresssed that women were not sufficiently advanced to be able to make political decisions.

The state found it hard to manage selective Westernisation and the Japanese women's movement was galvanised in response to its attempts to do so. Christian women started the first organised women's liberation movement when, as in New Zealand and Australia, the World Women's Christian Temperance Union's special representative, Mrs Mary Leavitt, visited in 1886. Fifty-six Christian women founded the Tokyo Kyofukai, Tokyo's Women's Christian Temperance Union. In 1893 it became the Japan Women's Christian Temperance Union (WCTU).[10] Its concerns, as a movement for temperance and social purification, were similar to those of the Australasian movements. Sake, a brewed alcoholic beverage made from rice, was traditionally considered holy in Japan, although excessive drinking problems, particularly domestic violence, were frequent. The Christian family was said to be threatened by the state's introduction of government-licensed prostitution and its sanctioning of polygamy: the state did not prosecute men for having more than one lawful wife. The 1872 Anti-Slavery Law, the Prostitution-Liberation Law, and the 1899 Constitution of the Empire of Japan, did not prohibit prostitution, and brothels were licensed and supervised by the government. The WCTU started a movement to abolish government-licensed prostitution and to promote monogamous marriage based on sexual equality and peaceful family life. In 1889, the union started to petition for monogamous marriage, a dangerous act of protest at the time. Yajima Kaji, the first president of WCTU, petitioned the Chamber of Elders (a quasi-legislative body from 1875 until the establishment of the Imperial Diet in 1890) with more than 800 signatures, at the risk of her life, since her behaviour was against the imperial legal system. Yajima had made her reputation as a nonconformist: she had asked her husband for a divorce and pursued a teaching career, which led to her being appointed as principal of Joshi Gakuin, a Christian girls' school. She delivered her petition wearing pure white and pocketing a dagger; she was prepared for hara-kiri – ritualistic suicide by disembowelment – if required. In the event, she was allowed to present her protest and it was simply ignored. In 1890 the WCTU also started the opposition movement against the Public Assembly and Association Law which forcibly excluded women from holding and attending political meetings and from forming political organisations. The Union's protests met with no success and the regulation was taken over by Article 5 of the Public Order and Police Law in 1900. The WCTU then adopted measures familiar to the Antipodes: public protests, petitions and pressure on the state to change its legislation. The Union maintained its campaigns, in particular against licensed prostitution, in the face of sometimes violent opposition from the prostitution industry.[11]

The women's suffrage movement appears on the stage

From the beginning of Westernisation in Japan, the popular rights movement demanded the establishment of a truly democratic system. Popular rights movement activists like Ueki Emori, whose aim was to democratise Japanese society, had been advocating women's suffrage from the early Meiji period (1870s onwards) as a *fundamental human right* and a necessary element of equality between men and women. From the 1880s, women themselves, especially through the popular rights movement, had begun to raise the issue of suffrage as a universal human right. The poet and essayist Yosano Akiko (1878–1942) was one who held that the vote was a basic right of which women should not be deprived. During and after 1905, a group of socialist women petitioned Parliament almost annually to revise Article 5 of the Public Order and Police Law, which prohibited women from political activity. The group included socialist feminist Fukuda Eiko, author of *Sekai Fujin, Women of the World* (1907), and Endo Iwano Kiyoko, who went on to become a member of *Seito* (a feminist literary magazine), as well as women from Heiminsha (Common People's Organisation), a socialist democratic group. Although their campaign for the revision of the repressive law was not a success, the women's concerns were adopted by Hiratsuka Raicho and Ichikawa Fusae among the aims of the women's suffrage movement.

Feminists began organising a broader suffrage movement in the interwar period. Hiratsuka Raicha founded the Shin Fujin Kyokai (the New Women's Association), a 'social' group, in 1919. It sought women's liberation, including women's suffrage. Membership included both socialist and conservative women. The association ran lecture meetings, founded its own journal, and its members were regular attenders at Parliament. The association concentrated on the Diet petition, demanding the revision of the Public Order and Police Law, saying that women were now sufficiently well-educated to read political articles in the newspapers. At almost every session of the Diet, the society pushed some liberal parliamentary members to introduce a bill for their purpose. At last, in March 1922, the Public Order and Police Law was partly revised and it became possible for women to hold and attend political meetings. However, women were still forbidden from joining political organisations. That the movement was very reliant on several key women became obvious in 1921 when Ichikawa Fusae retired, pleading fatigue. Hiratsuka could not keep the association going by herself and it was dissolved at end of 1922.

While the Shin Fujin Kyokai was active in demanding women's suffrage, the WCTU continued its campaign to ensure women's enfranchisement. Suffrage news often appeared in its journal columns and it supported the New Women's Association campaigns. In 1921, led by Gauntlett Tsuneko and Kubushiro Ochimi, the Japanese Women's Suffrage Association was set up inside the WCTU. Several other women's suffrage societies were also set up about that time (such as the Women's Union, the New True Women's Society, the Women's Temperance Society and the Progressive Society) and were united in 1923 in the Women's Suffrage Union. It was never very strong being undermined by religious and political differences.

The WCTU had a significant impact on the women's suffrage movement because it nurtured a number of suffragists in a feminist group and taught them organisational skills, both directly and indirectly. The local branches and its membership grew slowly, which is not surprising, given that Japan is not a Christian country. However, by 1900 there were more than 2000 members, and in 1926, its membership reached a peak, with more than 150 local branches and a total membership of more than 8000.[12] Many of the members were impressed by the idea of equality of the sexes before God.

The women's organisations co-operated with each other for relief work after the Great Earthquake of 1923 and this led to the formation of the Federation of Women's Associations but, like the earlier Women's Suffrage Union, yet another united suffrage organisation did not succeed. The next attempt at forming an umbrella suffrage organisation was more successful. The WCTU, led by Kubushiro Ochimi, took the lead and invited various representatives to meet in Tokyo in 1924 to form a united organisation solely for women's suffrage, to be known as the League for the Realisation of Women's Suffrage. In 1925 it was renamed the Women's Suffrage League. The League started to issue a journal in 1927, took part in a campaign for fair elections, and canvassed energetically across the country for the purpose of offering political education.

The Universal Suffrage Law was enacted in 1925 and encouraged women's suffragists of all persuasions to hope for female suffrage. The Japanese term *fusm* translated directly as 'universal suffrage'. One might expect this to refer to an electoral system where the right to vote or stand for office is acquired at a certain age, irrespective of one's property or income level, sex, race, social standing, level of education, religion or beliefs. However, this so-called 'universal suffrage' excluded women: in effect, it was universal male suffrage. As a protest against this deceptive terminology, the women's suffrage movement coined the word *fusen* with the same pronunciation but different characters, meaning women's suffrage.

The First Annual Convention of the Women's Suffrage Organisations was held in April 1930 to discuss how to strengthen the women's suffrage movement and political education for women. It was sponsored by the League under the auspices of six organisations: the Japan Women's Suffrage Association, All Kansai Federation of Women's Associations, Proletarian Women's League, Young Women's Buddhist Society, the

Japanese branch of the Young Women's Christian Association, and the Society of Female Primary School Teachers of Japan. Fujitsa Taki was chairperson of the convention, which approximately 480 women attended. Two newly composed suffrage songs were sung and taught to the women, stirring the atmosphere. In June 1930, Ichikawa Fusae became the League's president. This was the beginning of her lifelong service as a prominent leader of the women's suffrage movement in Japan.[13]

The Women's Suffrage League had petitioned the Diet almost every year for female suffrage. Finally, in May 1930, a bill granting franchise for women in local government was passed in the House of Representatives. But the bill was left to lie on the table, undiscussed, at the Committee of the non-elective House of Peers. In early 1931 the government itself proposed a bill to permit franchise for women in local government. The bill was passed in the House of Representatives, but it was rejected by the House of Peers by a vote of 184 to 62. Ironically, the women's movement seems to have been encouraged by this rejection. In February 1931, the Second Annual Convention of the Women's Suffrage Organisations was held, attended by some 800 participants.

Indeed, suffrage organisations mushroomed in Japan at this time. The Women's Suffrage League continued to sponsor lecture trips to raise the political concerns of women in various parts of the country. The League's membership reached a peak, forming 11 local branches with a total membership of more than 1500. But just when Japanese women had finally welded themselves into a strong and growing suffrage lobby, wider political events dashed their prospects of legislative success.

'Universal suffrage' and gender, ethnicity and class

Acting in the 'national interest' has been a strong factor in Japanese suffrage history. The national interest has been defined by class, ethnicity and gender considerations. Class and ethnic representatives campaigned at the same time, and not always with women, for legislative reforms. The National Election Law, enacted in 1889, limited the vote to men over 25 and above a certain income, who had Japanese nationality and resided on the Japanese mainland. The property and income requirements meant that the law discriminated, especially on the basis of class. In 1890 at the first election for the House of Representatives, only one per cent of the total population was eligible to vote. So the principal goal of the Japanese men's suffragists was the abolition of these requirements. They also sought the right to field Proletarian Party candidates in the Diet elections. At the same time as the state instituted the Peace-Preservation Law in 1925, it abolished the income requirements for male suffrage in an attempt to appease the proletarian class. Thus class was a major theme of the struggle for universal suffrage in Japan up to the interwar period. Certainly, Japanese male suffragists gave class priority over gender.

Ethnicity was also a major consideration in Japanese suffrage history. After Japan annexed Taiwan in 1895, and Korea in 1910, neither colony was allowed to have its own Diet.[14] Nor did Japan grant residents of Korea or Taiwan the right to vote in Japanese elections. Ironically, the Japanese Cabinet was to decide in April 1945 to give the vote to male residents of Korea and Taiwan who were over 25 and above a certain income. This was in order to secure the loyalty of the Korean and Taiwanese subjects whom Japan had already begun to call up under the 1944 Military Draft Act. However, with Japan's defeat at the hands of the Allies, the law extending suffrage to the colonies was never executed. In any case, long-term residents of Japan of Taiwanese and Korean descent had been theoretically eligible to vote under the 1889 National Election Law, but in fact there were no eligible voters because of the property and income requirements. In effect, therefore, they were also granted the vote in 1925 when the Universal Suffrage Act extended suffrage to all men in Japan over 25. Voting only applied to the House of Representatives, and in the period 1932–1942 only one Korean was elected.

Membership of the House of Peers, on the other hand, was decided by the Emperor; one Korean representative held a seat from 1932, and one Taiwanese representative from 1934. The movement for Korean suffrage was dominated by a faction who wished to participate in the Japanese Imperial Diet. After a leading member of this pro-colonialist faction was assassinated in 1921 by a member of the anti-colonialist faction, the Japanese state was keen to include Korean and Taiwanese residents of Japan in the Universal Suffrage Bill as a pacifying measure. The state also wanted to be able to draft Korean residents for military service, thus strengthening its armed forces: the right to vote brought with it the duty to serve. Thus ethnicity as well as class figured in the Univeral Suffrage Act of 1925. With the passing of this Act, all male citizens of Japan (and long-term residents of Korean or Taiwanese descent) over the age of 25 were entitled to vote, regardless of class or ethnicity.

As for gender, all women were excluded from the so-called Universal Suffrage Act. The discourse of the men who excluded women from suffrage was the same as elsewhere. Tradition was used against women but not men. Baron Fujimura, a member of the House of Peers, declared against women's political participation in 1920. He said he found it offensive for three reasons: first, it was against the laws of nature – women were not designed for political acitivity – second, all the women he could think of who had been politically powerful were evil, and having such women in power would only lead to terrible consequences for the nation – the examples he gave were Hojo Masako, the famous medieval Japanese woman of influence, various legendary Chinese empresses and Queen Elizabeth I of England; third, he argued that allowing women to be politically active would destroy the *ie*, or patriarchal family system, the basic unit of Japanese *kokutai*, or unique national structure.[15]

There were men who supported women's suffrage and believed it to be an inevitable step in the process of history. Matsumoto Kimihei, for example, a member of the assembly, repeatedly raised women's issues for discussion in the House. At the same time, some men, for example Kagawa Toyohiko, argued that women should be given the vote because their 'natural' maternal qualities would lead to a peaceful society and have a purifying effect on politics. In the 1930s, male socialists and members of the Proletarian Party also wanted to be able to vote alongside them as comrades, in order to overturn the capitalist system.

Women who discussed gender and politics had different ideas about what women could and should achieve by gaining the vote and entering the political sphere. Hiratsuka Raicho, the founder of the feminist literary magazine *Seito,* was a notable example of those who believed that women's involvement in politics was necessary because male politicians had failed to solve major social problems. These women also thought that women in politics would be able to address problems that specifically affected women, for example freedom of choice with regard to marriage, protection of the rights of mother and child, and the safeguarding of women's health by routine treatment of husbands for sexually transmitted diseases. Such women felt that it was women's role to transform male-centred society. Ichikawa Fusae held that 'suffrage [was] the key' to an overall strategy for women's social advancement. Suffrage and women's participation in the political sphere were her life-long goals. Many working-class women and socialist feminists, among them Yamakawa Kikue, sought the vote in order to improve the lot of working women and to gain influence over social policy. They wanted to reform aspects of the capitalist system, especially concerning workplace safety, maternity leave and pay equity. The Japan WCTU also focused on how women's suffrage would 'purify' politics and public life.

Despite these arguments, however, the House of Peers twice turned down the Women's Suffrage (Government) Bill, in 1930 and 1931. It gave similar reasons to those offered by Baron Fujimura when it declined to assent to the bills, which had already been passed by the House of Representatives. The House of Peers said women's suffrage was 'against the customs of Japan and would destroy the *kokutai*'. Furthermore, rising anti-American and anti-European sentiments led to comments that it would be unseemly and immoral for Japanese women to imitate Western women.

Why then did the House of Representatives support suffrage? The House of Representatives had 'national interest' reasons for twice passing the Women's Suffrage (Local Government) Bill. Japan was at war with China, and the state was keen to introduce economy measures, especially in reaction to the recent influence of modernism on Japanese consumer culture. They reasoned that if women were allowed to be involved in politics at a local level (cities, towns and villages), they would become more familiar with the political and economic system and thus more effective advocates and practitioners of economic restrictions. From the House of Representatives' point of view, they were not so much admitting women into the public sphere as extending the definitions of the private sphere to embrace the community. They considered this to be the only way to ensure women's co-operation with national policies and the war effort, while preserving the *ie* family system.[16]

Women's suffrage, then, became a victim of competing male views of national interest. The House of Peers agreed with the House of Representatives that women must help protect the nation; however, they believed that women's main 'war duty' was reproduction, and did not consider suffrage a necessary part of this duty. The Association of Mayors of Cities, Towns and Villages also hotly opposed the Women's Suffrage (Local Government) Bill, presumably out of fear that women would invade local politics. As a result of this combined opposition, Japanese women were able to be coerced into working for the war without being granted the vote.

Women's suffrage, furthermore, became associated with not being supportive of the 'national interest', and the cause suffered as a consequence. War increasingly loomed and Japan entered into the 'Age of Fascism' with the military coming to dominate the government after the Manchurian Incident of September 1931 – when the Japanese Guandong army conquered and occupied Manchuria – and the prime minister's assassination in May 1932. The Third Annual Convention of the Women's Suffrage Organisations, held in the same month of 1932, adopted unanimously a resolution opposing fascism. Furthermore, in

February 1933 at their Fourth Annual Convention, the national budget for that year was discussed and the delegates adopted a resolution demanding decreased military spending. Police control over the Convention was stepped up and the women's suffrage bill was never introduced into the Diet thereafter. The Fifth Annual Convention was held in February 1934, and together with the suffrage demand and opposition to increased military expenditure, the Convention adopted, for the first time, a resolution appealing for protective legislation for mothers and children in need. Multiple suicides of mothers and children were rising rapidly at this time, amid increasing unemployment and deepening economic depression. Other resolutions demanded the revision of the Civil Code and protective labour legislation for women workers. The League re-orientated its national policy towards demanding legislation for the welfare of women and children. The Protective Law for Mothers and Children in Need was passed by the Diet in 1937 and the arbitration law for peaceful settlement of domestic disputes was also enacted in 1939. Along with the expansion of the military autocracy, the country was gradually establishing a wartime infrastructure. The holding of an Annual Convention was abandoned after the Seventh Annual Convention was held in 1937. The League was finally dissolved in 1940, after a sixteen-year campaign, and its journal ceased to be published in the following year. League leaders refocused their energies on local politics; in effect the movement for the purification of municipal administration, the problems of public fish markets and new taxes replaced women's suffrage – until 1945.

'National interest' changes meaning

After the military expansion in Asia, Japan entered the Pacific War against the United States in 1941, and people were severely controlled under the military extremists. Forced to sacrifice too much at home and abroad, Japan accepted the Potsdam Declaration and surrendered unconditionally in August 1945. Only ten days after the surrender, Ichikawa Fusae, Kubushiro Ochimi, and others gathered in the ruins, following the air raids, to organise a women's committee for co-operation in solving women's post-war problems. They were concerned with issues such as women's unemployment, prostitution and so on. One month later, this committee resolved to achieve women's suffrage and made a proposition to the government and political parties. On 10 October 1945, women's suffrage was for the first time agreed to unanimously at the new Cabinet meetings.

On the following day, the Occupation authorities, led by General

Douglas MacArthur, issued an order of five items, ensuring women's liberation by granting the vote to women. He pointed out to the new Japanese prime minister the necessity of revising the Constitution. As a result of the supervision by the Occupation authorities, Japanese women gained the right to join political parties in November 1945, the right to vote and stand for Parliament in December 1945, and the right to join in local government in September 1946.

The principle of sexual equality was promulgated in the provisions of the Postwar Constitution of November 1946 and, in December of the same year, the Civil Code was revised. These revisions effectively abolished the old patriarchal character of the family. Thus, at last, Japanese women achieved legal and political equality with men. However, at the same time as the vote was extended to women, it was revoked for long-term Taiwanese and Korean residents of Japan who had had suffrage since 1925. Even today, they and other foreign residents of Japan still do not have the right to vote. The Japanese state's position is that one must have Japanese nationality, not simply long-term residency, in order to vote. There has been a kind of trade-off between gender and ethnicity in Japan's history of suffrage; before 1945 men had the vote regardless of class and ethnicity; and after 1945 Japanese nationals have had the vote regardless of gender. Before 1945 women sought suffrage for themselves as women, but now when we as women consider women's suffrage (or women in politics) we must include an awareness of class and ethnicity as well as gender.

Gendered politics continued in the post-war period. Japanese women's involvement in grassroots and community politics has been strong, particularly in peace, anti-nuclear, environmental, consumer awareness, children's rights and other social movements. Yet, despite the time and energy poured into grassroots political involvement, there have been few women members of parliament. In the political world, only 6.5 per cent of the members of the Diet in July 1992 and 3.2 per cent of the members of the local assembly in December 1991 were women. Clearly, women themselves are not particularly keen to stand for Parliament, probably because they doubt that they can achieve their ideals in such a male-dominated and corrupt system. Because women have taken on issues neglected by male politicians (such as peace and ecological movements), these movements themselves have come to be seen as 'women's work' or 'women's place'. So even among the activists, 'traditional' gender roles remain and the home, the community, and social reform are still seen as women's sphere. This phenomenon could well be a result of Japanese women's adherence to both the idea of 'purification' and the concept of women's 'essential' qualities. As most activists now accept, we must move beyond suffrage to address the remaining gender and ethnic biases in the political world: in the words of Ichikawa Fusae, *'Kenru no ue nemuru na!'* – 'Don't sleep on your rights!'

1   Many thanks are due to Marilyn S. Higgins, Sadayuki Ashie, Jolisa Gracewood, Kim Fuja, Chigusa Kimura-Steven, Reiko Ishida, Takeshi Ishida, Rie Ohashi, the Ichikawa Fusae Memorial Association at the Fusen Kaikan (Women's Suffrage Centre), and the Japan Women's Christian Temperance Union for their kind co-operation with our research. We thank Melanie Nolan for her help in rewriting our conference paper for publication. All Japanese names here follow the Japanese practice of placing the surname first.

2   For a general discussion of Japanese women and politics, see Susan J. Pharr, *Political Women in Japan*, Univ. of California Press, Berkeley, 1981; Pharr, 'The Politics of Women's Rights', in Robert E. Ward & Sakamoto Yoshikazu, eds, *Democratizing Japan: Allied Occupation*, Univ. of Hawaii Press, Honolulu, 1987.

3   Personal memory of Fujita Taki, professor of Tsuda College and suffrage activist, undated (sometime during 1947-50), cit. Fujita Taki, 'Fujin undo hitosujini: Ichikawa san no hitotonari (Devoted to women's movement: A personality of Ichikawa)', In *Ichikawa Fusae iu hito kankokai* (Publication Committee of 'About Ichikawa Fusea'), ed, *Ichikawa Fusae to iu Hito: 100 nin no Kaisou (About Ichikawa Fusae: Recollections of 100 People)*, Shinjyuku Shobe, 1982, 122.

4   Known today as Tsuda College.

5   Known today as Ochanomizu University.

6   Benjamin C. Duke, compiled, *Ten Great Educators of Modern Japan: A Japanese Perspective*, Univ. of Tokyo Press, Tokyo, 1989, 135-6.

7   Kohiyama Rui, *America Fujin Senkyoshi: Rainichi no Haikei to sono Eikyo (American Women's Foreign Mission: Enterprise and Its Encounter with Meiji Japan)*, Univ. of Tokyo Press, Tokyo, 1992, 192. Kirisutokyo Hoiku Hyakunenshi Hensaniinkai (Publication Committee of One Hundred Years of Christian Early Childhood Education and Care), ed, *Nihon Kirisutokya Hoiku Hyakunemshi (One Hundred Years of Christian Early Childhood Education and Care in Japan)*, Kirsutokyo Hoiku Renmu, Tokyo, 1986, 31-2.

8   Wakita Haruko, Hayashi Reiko & Nagahara Kazuko, eds, *Nikon Jyoseish (A History of Japanese Women)*, Yoshikawa Kobunkan, 1987, 196.

9   Ibid.

10   Nihon Kiristokyo Fujin Kyofukai (Japan Women's Christian Temperance Union), *Nihon Kiristokyp Fujin Kyofukai hyakumenshi (One Hundred Years of the J.W.C.T.U.)* Domesu Shuppan, Tokyo, 1986.

11   Ibid., 284, 429, 471-2, 618-9.

12   Ibid., 17-71 and 498.

13   Katsuko Kodama, *Fujin sanseiken undo shoshi (A Short History of the Women's Suffrage Movement)*, Domesu Shuppan, 1981. Ichikawa Fusae, *Ichikawa Fusae jiden: senzenhen (Autobiography of Ichikawa Fusae: The Pre-War Years)*, Shinjuku Shobo, 1974. Ichikawa Fusae, ed, *Nihon fujin mondai shiryo shusei 2: Seiji (Collection of Materials on Women's Issues in Japan, vol. 2: Politics)*, Domesu Shuppan, 1977. Matsuo Takayoshi, *Futsu senkyo seido seiritsushi no kenkyo (History of the Formation of the Universal Suffrage System in Japan)*, Iwaanami Shoten, 1989.

14   Tanaka Hiroshi, 'Nihon shokuminchi shihaika ni okeru kokuseki kankei no keii: Tiawan/Chosen ni kan suru sanseiken to guntai gimu o megutte' ('Issues of Nationality in Japanese Colonies: Suffrage and Military Service in Taiwan and Korea'), in Aichi Kenritsu, *Daigaku Gaikokugogakubu kiyo (The Bulletin of Aichi Prefectural Univ. Foreign Languages Department)*, 9, 1974, 61-96.

15   The *ie* (literally 'family' or 'house') system was the patriarchal family system in place from 1898 to 1947 under the Japanese Imperial Civil Code. It effectively forced women to live subject to their husband, children and parents-in-law. *Kokutai* was the structure and idea of the Japanese Imperial system in which the *ie* was the basic unit of the nation, and the nation itself functioned as one large *ie*.

16   Saji Emiko, 'Hamaguchi naikakuki no fujin kominken mondai' ('Issues of Women's Local Suffrage Under the Hamaguchi Cabinet'), in *Nihonshi Kenkyu (Studies in Japanese History)*, 292, 1986, 1-25.

10

Suffrage in South America: Arguing a Difficult Cause

ASUNCIÓN LAVRIN

The adoption of suffrage by New Zealand in 1893 served as a role model not just for nations but, more importantly, for women and men who regarded suffrage as a desirable and feasible prospect. Between the early 1910s and the late 1940s, feminists in South America rarely failed to cite New Zealand's model as an inspiration in the pursuit of their own ends, although they knew that it could not simply be copied or used by women living under different legal and political systems. The South American women and men who began thinking about suffrage at the turn of the century knew that they had to find an idiosyncratic formula that would work for them.[1] Suffrage had to be demonstrated to be reasonable, just, and potentially beneficial to society before it became acceptable to those who could make it a reality, the all-male political coterie that ruled their nations. The struggle for suffrage was not easy, and it is an important chapter in Latin American history largely ignored by most social and political historians.

Women earned the vote in Uruguay in 1932, in Argentina in 1947, in Chile in 1948, and in Colombia in 1954. Chilean women voted in the municipal elections of 1935; Uruguayans were unable to vote – for political circumstances – until 1938; Argentineans voted in 1951; and Colombians in 1957. In this chapter, I will dwell on the ideas debated in favour of and against suffrage in four countries of South America: Chile, Argentina, Uruguay, known collectively as the Southern Cone nations, and Colombia, in northern South America. In the period under review, the first half of the twentieth century, we move from the first discussions of feminist ideas to the organisation of women's parties and the full participation of women in national politics.

The struggle for suffrage was more than a battle of words. It was a process to develop a set of values that could adapt to the different political circumstances of a variety of countries without altering their social fabric. Traditional cultural values posed a challenge that feminists and suffragists did not wish completely to undermine. In fact, some of these values were incorporated into their agenda to facilitate the success of suffrage. Enfranchisement was not a central issue in the early feminists' agenda, and for good reasons. A tradition of respect for the inherent rights of people to equal treatment under the law, and the right to vote, did not exist at the time of the independence of Spanish American nations from Spain. Throughout the nineteenth century, and even during a good part of the twentieth century, they were ruled by a powerful oligarchy and, in addition, suffered recurrent cycles of *caudillismo* (the rule of a strong man based on charismatic appeal to a sector of society, and the use of power in disregard of the written law). Property, literacy requirements, service in the army, and the adoption of citizenship for immigrants were some of the qualifications required from men to exercise suffrage. Universal male suffrage was adopted in 1912 in Argentina, 1916 in Uruguay, 1920 in Chile and 1936 in Colombia.[2] The lawyers who wrote the post-independence constitutions assumed that women had a nationality but not a citizenship defined by the exercise of political rights.

Under such political circumstances, reform-minded turn-of-the-century men and women sought to redefine the civil rights of women within the Civil Codes, the legislative bodies that delineated people's rights in family and society. The Civil Codes of the four nations under review were written in the mid-nineteenth century, and in an effort to get rid of 'colonial' influences after independence, they followed the worst examples of contemporary French and English family law, attached to key concepts of Roman law. They defined most women (married and minors) as lacking in juridical personality, and under the authority of the male pater familias (head of the family, father or husband), and established double standards of judgement and punishment for men and women in some transgressions of family law. For social reformers, among whom feminists and suffragists must be counted, the recognition of the rights of women as mothers, wives, and wage-earners, female education, and the solution of public health problems affecting women and children, were more pressing than female suffrage.

While sharing a common legal, religious and cultural heritage, Colombia differed enough to stand, for comparative purposes, as the most traditionalist of the four countries under review, while Uruguay was the most open to political change. The Southern Cone nations developed a multi-party, multi-cultural political milieu with a political flexibility and openness to change not found in Colombia. Between 1916 and 1920 the older social and political elements dominating the Southern Cone nations were successfully challenged by populist movements through universal male suffrage. The constitutional systems of the Southern Cone nations were under strain several times, but recovered through compromise formulae in the first half of the century. Ideological battles between the right and the left did not stop the process of urban growth and urban industrialisation and, while many social and economic problems remained unsolved, there were important moves towards the achievement of social change under centralised states. These countries also paid more than lip service to female education by developing fairly strong primary and secondary educational systems. Secondary education gave women access to universities and Normal Schools, the seed bed of future feminist leaders, who emerged from their universities in increasing numbers after the 1890s. Colombia was a country polarised by two political factions – Liberals and Conservatives – which involved the nation in two bloody civil wars (1900–1903 and 1948–57). The Conservative Party dominated its politics and policies for fifty years before 1930. Colombia's agricultural export economy remained unchallenged and unchanged until after World War II, and the influence of the Catholic Church was culturally and socially overwhelming. Women's education left much to be desired. The first Normal School was founded in 1872 and until 1936 these schools were the only centres of higher education available to women. The university finally opened its doors to women in 1936 under the renovating influence of a Liberal Party president.

Given these important differences, one would expect great disparities in the construction of a feminist and a suffrage discourse between the Southern Cone and Colombia. However, men and women of the four nations shared many concepts which were rooted in their socialisation and the perception of their gender roles in society, as will be explained below.[3] Feminism began to be discussed in the Southern Cone nations between 1898 and 1915; in Colombia, it was not broadly debated in the press until the 1930s. In the Southern Cone, feminism showed the influence of nineteenth-century liberalism and socialism. Liberals maintained that legal equality of men and women was a sine qua non to achieve progress comparable to that of Europe. They endorsed reforms in the Civil Codes to give married and minor women an autonomous juridical personality. They also drew some strength from positivism, fashionable in the last decades of the nineteenth century, which although not favouring women's political activities, favoured assigning more productive social roles to women. Positivism did not elicit any legal benefits for Colombian women, but when the Liberal Party returned to power in 1930, it saw fit to introduce basic changes in the Civil Code similar to those adopted in the nations to the south.

Socialism and anarchism reinforced the reform trend in the Southern Cone countries, where they began to circulate around the 1880s, advocating social and gender reforms, although they went much further than liberals in their proposals to re-structure society. Class consciousness was a strong element in social feminism, targeting the growing number of urban industrial workers in all countries. Anarchism rejected participation in the bourgeois political machine, and it began losing workers' allegiance around the early 1920s, leaving socialism as the dominant ideological and political influence of the left. In Colombia, part of the labour force embraced socialism and even communism in the late 1910s, but the left did not develop a foothold in certain industries until the late 1920s, and its role in dealing with women's issues was much less significant than in the Southern Cone. The Catholic church was active in organising confessional unions in the four countries, limiting the impact of leftist influence on organising women.[4]

Winning the suffrage: a brief overview
In this cultural environment, moulded by Roman law and the Christian tradition of Roman Catholicism, and in which tense political battles were often resolved through physical struggle with the army emerging as a dominant power negotiator among civilian politicos, the cultivation of male and female archetypes (the macho and the virgin) by education and social practice affected the way the idea of suffrage was marketed, and received. When the Uruguayan Women's Alliance for Feminine Suffrage (*Alianza Uruguaya de Mujeres para el Sufragio Femenino*), founded in 1919, re-stated its programme in 1929, it placed female legal equality as its number one goal. Female suffrage was ranked fifth on its agenda. Was this an about-face or a question of tactics? The organisation was following the thought of its founder, Paulina Luisi, who in 1919 had stated that 'feminism is one of the phases in the solution of the social problem. Within feminism, suffrage is one of the elements for solving the problem but, by itself it is insufficient to find all answers.'[5] Relativism in dealing with suffrage indicated that this group – like other women's organisations in South America – preferred a plurality of objectives, a 'holistic' approach to gender-specific issues that placed women face to face with the totality of social problems. Suffrage was a tool to include women in the process of social change, but not an end in itself.

Since the history of women's suffrage and feminism in South

America is only partially available in English, a brief survey of the four nations under review is in order here.[6]

Uruguay

In the first half of the century, Uruguay earned a reputation as an experimental democracy unique in the Americas. Beginning in the first decade of this century and led by a social-reform oriented party, the Colorado Party, the country began a far-reaching programme of social legislation to guarantee workers and women a minimum of individual rights. In 1916 a Constitutional Convention reformed the nation's political structure by adopting universal male suffrage and a plural, co-shared presidency (*colegiado*). It failed to adopt female suffrage, postponing its approval until a two-thirds majority of the legislators agreed to it.

At this point Uruguayan feminism began to stretch its political wings with the foundation of the National Council of Women (1916) and the Uruguayan Women's Alliance for Feminine Suffrage (1919). While the Council had a broad feminist agenda, the Alliance had suffrage as its main goal. Uruguayan reforms were based on a philosophy of 'compensatory feminism', which rested on the assumption that true feminism acknowledged gender differences and should aim at protecting women rather than seeking a gender-blind form of equality.[7] Succinctly put, the male sex had a physiological advantage, and women lacked legal compensation for their vulnerability. Women should not assume male social functions in addition to those intrinsically theirs by virtue of their sex. The state should protect women by suppressing any form of female subordination or physical abuse. Compensatory feminism proposed protective legislation to correct the exploitation of women in industrial societies and, at the same time, to guarantee their individual rights within the family and the body politic. Suffrage was among the latter.

Between 1916 and 1929 the National Council of Women and the Uruguayan Alliance for Feminine Suffrage campaigned inconclusively for women's rights, but they received a shot in the arm in 1929 during the celebration of the nation's centennial. That year, the Alliance received the support of feminist ex-president, Baltasar Brum, the Colorado Party, and the Socialist Party. Even the conservatives of the National Party and the Catholic press changed their standing on suffrage in a significant turn of opinion. They realised that to challenge Colorado political and social reforms, they needed women's support. In 1932 the Senate approved suffrage without discussion, as an aspiration requiring no further justification. The Deputies followed suit, and by December of that year Uruguayan women had full political rights. Actual participation in national elections was postponed until 1938 by a coup d'état in 1933 against the plural executive. However, in 1934 a new Constitution reaffirmed women's suffrage and registration for the 1938 elections began immediately.

Chile

In Chile, a suffrage bill was introduced in Congress by a young conservative deputy in 1917, soon after middle-class women began to organise informal associations of a cultural nature. Early in the twentieth century working women developed their own interpretation of feminism, stressing broad social reforms over political rights.[8] Press debates indicated ambivalence and misgivings about women's suffrage, and even the labour press gave only lip service to the cause. In 1920, Chilean men exercised universal male suffrage for the first time in history and elected populist Radical Party candidate, Arturo Alessandri. He was an advocate of women's suffrage, and after his election middle-class women became seriously engaged in feminist and suffrage discussion. Alessandri had trouble implementing his social legislation, confronting an intransigent Congress, and between 1924 and 1925 he stepped down from the presidency and took a brief exile in Europe. However, he was recalled by the military to serve to the end of his term. A new Constitution drafted in 1925 did not change the status of women as non-voters and non-citizens.

Suffragist sympathisers were in disarray between 1925 and 1932. Several women's organisations founded in the early 1920s promoted feminism in general, but were more interested in the reform of the Civil Codes than in suffrage.[9] During this period Chile witnessed the emergence of a military ruler, Carlos Ibáñez, elected without opposition in 1927 but obliged to resign in 1931. After a short experiment with a socialist republic, Chile returned to a democratically elected government in 1932. This gave women a window of opportunity to make a case for suffrage as part of the national reconstruction.[10] Congressional debates on suffrage took place early in March 1934 and shortly thereafter Congress approved a compromise formula, the municipal vote for literate women over 21 years of age. Women voted in the municipal elections of 1935, 1938, 1941, and 1944. In 1941, ailing president Aguirre Cerda sent a message to the Deputies in support of universal female suffrage, with a literacy qualification effective for both sexes. However, after his death that year, a conservative administration failed to act on his recommendation.

In 1945 a new umbrella organisation, the Chilean Federation of

Feminine Institutions (*Federación Chilena de Instituciones Femeninas* or FECHIF) began pushing for full national suffrage, with the support of leading male politicians of all parties, and of president Gabriel González Videla. Post-war pro-suffrage sentiment was based on the wish to extend the concept of democracy to women in Chile as well as in other Latin American countries still lacking it. The Chilean Senate approved a suffrage bill in 1946, but it took two years more of active campaigning, including presidential pressure, before the bill moved through the bureaucratic channels of the Chamber of Deputies. The bill was finally approved on 15 December 1948 and women voted in the 1952 elections.

Argentina

In Argentina, suffrage had the most fertile ground in all South America, although one of the most difficult courses to run. Since 1862 the city of San Juan, in the western province of San Juan, had a municipal law which made no gender distinctions in the definition of voters. Suffrage was used in a very discreet manner by a small number of women.[11] Feminist centres had been active in Buenos Aires and La Plata since 1905, and in 1910 a Feminist League (founded by Uruguayan-born María Abella de Ramírez) espoused women's enfranchisement as part of a basic four-point programme.[12] Universal male suffrage, voted in in 1912 and first exercised in 1916, opened the gates of politics to new social elements: the working people and the lower middle class. By then, Argentinean middle-class women and the Socialist Party had a well-defined programme of women's rights. The former was closer to the tenets of nineteenth-century liberalism, whereas the latter inherited the ideas of August Bebel and Ellen Key. Within the Radical Party, which won the 1916 elections, those considering themselves 'feminists and suffragists' represented liberal middle-class mainstream feminism.

After 1916, female suffrage in Argentina began to be seriously debated in the press and entered political discussion.[13] Several bills for the adoption of municipal suffrage were introduced in Buenos Aires, but none was ever approved.[14] Between 1919 and 1920, female 'parties' and suffrage associations such as *Asociación Pro-Derechos de la Mujer* (Association for Women's Rights), *Partido Feminista Nacional* (National Feminist Party), and *Partido Humanista* (Humanist Party), were founded to promote women's civil and political rights.[15] In 1920 socialist feminists founded *Unión Feminista Nacional* (National Feminist Union), headed by Alicia Moreau, to stir public opinion in favour of female suffrage. Its mouthpiece was *Nuestra Causa*, a magazine which dealt almost exclusively with suffrage issues, and which provided a forum for feminists of all political orientations.

At the instigation of Alicia Moreau, who had visited the International Workers' Congress in Washington DC in 1919, and had become acquainted with Carrie Chapman Catt and the National American Woman Suffrage Association, the Feminist Party held a mock election in Buenos Aires to demonstrate women's discipline and political awareness. They submitted a suffrage bill to the Deputies for the enfranchisement of women over 22 years of age. This was the first of several bills for national suffrage that went unheeded through the 1920s.[16]

After a military coup in 1930 and one more year of military rule, Argentina returned to constitutionality in late 1931. The 1930s was a polarised decade that saw the rise of right-wing organisations, the growing influence of the military, and the weakening of the Radical Party. Nonetheless, the return to an electoral system gave female suffrage a popularity surge capable of bringing two bills to discussion before the Deputies in 1932. Several ad hoc organisations renewed a public opinion campaign. One of them was willing to accept qualifications of age and literacy for voting, and gathered over 10,000 signatures in support of female suffrage.[17]

On 4 August 1932, a parliamentary commission recommended a bill that would grant suffrage to all Argentinean women at age 18, without any qualifications.[18] After intense debate this bill was approved on 17 September 1932, with ample support from the Radical and the Socialist parties, spurred by the intense campaign raised by women themselves. This bill was one of the Radicals' and Socialists' last-ditch efforts to save Argentina from the rising conservatism of the 1930s.

The suffrage bill required the Senate's approval, however, and this body became women's nemesis for another decade and a half. Arguing the need to study the cost of its implementation, the Senate shelved the bill and never resurrected it, despite many efforts by a number of senators throughout the 1930s and early 1940s. Women gathered in newly formed groups but did not have the political strength to break the Senate's resistance. Besieged by a traditionalist backlash and the rise of fascist sympathisers in the nation, the suffrage bill stalled throughout the World War II years, when Argentina was under a conservative, pro-fascist military regime.[19]

Suffrage was revived by the populist regime led by Colonel Juan Domingo Perón, a man who had helped Argentina turn to the right in the 1930s, but who had built a strong personal support among workers as he served the military regime between 1943 and 1945. After a rather complex struggle for power, Perón became president in 1946. At his side was a woman of great political astuteness, who courted labour, and who perceived the value of women's votes in reinforcing her husband's political strength. It was under her influence that Perón and his congressional majority succeeded in enacting female suffrage in 1947. By mid-1949, Eva Perón assembled the Women's Peronist Party (*Partido Peronista Femenino*), a female organisation parallel to the Peronist party to serve Perón's political interests. In exchange for complete allegiance to Perón, Eva demanded from Perón's official party – the Justicialista Party – a quota of female candidates so that a fixed number of women would be elected. This plan gave Argentinean women effective political power for the first time. In the 1951 elections, when 90.3 per cent of registered women voted, they favoured Perón, who won by a landslide with 2,441,558 votes (65 per cent of the total) against 1,177,051 votes for the Radical Party (30.8 per cent).[20]

Colombia

Colombians arrived late at the feminist table. Not until the early 1930s was suffrage discussed in the press and the Deputies' Chambers. The only reforms accomplished in that decade were a loosening of the restriction on women's civil rights and the opening of higher education to women.[21] In fact, in 1936 a constitutional reform which established universal male suffrage expressly denied it to women, giving them the 'right' to take public jobs, even though they were not voting citizens. In the ensuing eight years suffrage was unassertively discussed in women's magazines. Only a few strong-minded women and men maintained an open commitment to suffrage. In 1944, during the second administration of reformist Liberal president Alfonso López Pumarejo, a women's suffrage bill was introduced in Congress, but it stipulated a waiting period to allow Congress to lay the ground rules for female political participation.

Three women's organisations and one magazine carried out a campaign for suffrage between 1944 and 1954.[22] The 1944 evolutionary suffrage formula proposed by the Liberal Party suffered an onslaught of attacks from conservative Liberals and from traditional Conservatives. Although it was approved by the Deputies (under the proviso that no regulation would be undertaken before 1948), the bill was defeated in the Senate in 1945. When a constitutional reform was enacted in February 1945, women were declared citizens, but suffrage was explicitly reserved for men only. The two national parties, Liberals and Conservatives, found enough reasons to stall the passage of any bill granting women their political rights.

Unfortunately, Colombia was involved in a civil war, known as 'the violence' (*la violencia*), between 1948 and 1957, a situation which led many to argue that the political conditions were too dangerous to grant women the vote. The IX Inter-American Conference, which took place in Bogotá in 1948, just before the violence broke out, re-stated its support for women's suffrage.[23] Involved again in yet another constitutional reform in 1954 to find a solution to the political impasse, Colombian legislators stalled over women's suffrage. Paradoxically, pressure came from the executive, at this point in the hands of a mid-twentieth century *caudillo* and military man, General Gustavo Rojas Pinillas. The Constitutional Assembly approved universal female suffrage on 27 August 1954. The irony of this approval was that, at the same time, the Constitutional Assembly recognised the de facto government of General Rojas Pinillas, a situation which barred male and female citizens from voting until 1958. In 1957 women began exercising their political rights by voting in a plebiscite to decide a political peace formula for the nation.[24] In 1958 they voted in the first national elections.

The debate on suffrage: selling a concept
The struggle for suffrage in South America was an uphill one. The tenacity of its opponents cannot be overstated. They effectively stalled the female vote until nearly the middle of the century in most nations. Suffrage opponents derived their strength from deeply rooted concepts of gender relations, effectively translated into a philosophy of politics in the nineteenth century. To understand the suffragist campaign's complex ideology and varied strategies, we must first survey the gendered definition of politics prevalent in South America in the early decades of this century.

Female political activity was regarded as incompatible with the natural functions of women at home, the locus of women's lives. These were patriarchal societies in which custom and the law enshrined the supremacy of men in the public sector and the family. While a rigid dichotomy of gendered public and private space did not exist in those nations, the confines of the home were regarded as the ideal space for women to undertake the expected mission of their lives: the physical and spiritual nurture of husband and children. Traditionalists, conservatives, and suffrage opponents claimed that women could influence society through the actions of the men whom they raised, and the women to whom they bequeathed the same social roles they played.

Politics was a 'virile activity' belonging to the man's domain, and women need not participate in it to be useful to society.[25] Women and politics should never mingle. In 1886 Colombian jurist, José María Samper, stated that women's physical and psychological make-up was unsuitable for politics. To change the role of the sexes would be to undo the work of Providence, to attempt correcting God's own work.[26] Fifty years later, another Colombian politician felt confident enough to state that: 'nature will impose itself over this proposed legislation . . . . Any law running against the fundamental imperatives of the sexes are [sic] unnatural, against nature, and nature should not be forced.'[27]

Before 1910 only well-educated middle-class men and women thought that suffrage was desirable, let alone feasible. Barring exceptional and 'radical' women, women writing in defence of female activities outside the home showed ambivalence about suffrage and politics, preferring to support education and social work as preparatory to political maturity.[28] *Unión y Labor,* a magazine published by a Buenos Aires group of professional women engaged in social work in the 1910s, was not enthusiastic about suffrage. The editorial board was of the opinion that some women wished to go too fast on the vote and had to prepare to exercise the vote 'consciously and effectively'. In 1911, having printed several articles on female suffrage, they reiterated that their intention was not to encourage women on the vote issue, but to inform their readers on the progress achieved by other societies. One of the ablest members of the group, socialist Sara Justo, denounced the concept of women 'aping' men in their political activities, although her party supported the principle of women's suffrage.[29] The hardest task for South American feminists was not to convince men that they were prepared for suffrage, but to convince other women.

The best opportunity to make an early pitch for suffrage could have been the First International Feminine Congress that took place in Buenos Aires in 1910 but only four papers discussed it. They contained, however, the best summary of ideas advanced by others up to then, and provided a set of arguments which, expanded and refined later on, remained the intellectual defence of suffrage for decades to come. Speaking for the women's vote were Peruvian J. María Samamé, and Argentineans Raquel Messina, a socialist, Anna A. de Montalvo, and María Josefa González, of the National League of Freethinking Women.

Samamé thought that the law had gone too far in 'protecting' women and isolating them from civic life. On the eve of a new era in which democracy would be the ruling political ideology, women should not be excluded from political participation. Her understanding of suffrage was correctly feminist, and astute enough to discern that the rising tide of populism and labour activism would loosen the suffrage restrictions for both genders. Raquel Messina, representing the Socialist Feminine Centre, claimed to speak for the 'popular women who work and think', and demanded universal suffrage for *both* sexes, addressing the fact that most men in the country also did not vote. Suffrage was particularly relevant for working women who, deprived of political rights, were reduced to begging men for social reforms. Class and gender were adroitly mixed in her message. María Josefa González challenged women to take the reins of their own political destiny. Women could ill afford to remain indifferent to politics and ignore the fact that only suffrage would give them the power to change the laws that subordinated them. Anna Montalvo's ideas were anchored in nineteenth-century liberal concepts of justice and equity. Women should vote because they worked, paid taxes, and were considered equal to men in the enforcement of penal justice.[30] She also advanced the concept of the social function of maternity, later popular among socialist feminists. If men earned the right to vote by 'paying' the state with military service, women paid with maternity and with the sacrifice of their children to war.[31]

These arguments helped to prepare the ground for a broader acceptance of female suffrage in the next decade. The participation of Latin American women in several inter-American and European conferences strengthened their convictions and encouraged them to enlist followers at home.[32] The suffragist campaigns in Europe and North America caused either admiration or outright rejection in South America, but the catalyst for change was the emergent political populism and the democratisation of the electoral systems in national politics.[33]

Women's publications were the best vehicles to address the issue of suffrage. Among them, *Nuestra Causa*, a socialist magazine published by Argentinean women between 1919 and 1921, stands out. The early arguments laid out by the 1910 First International Feminist Congress, and all further reflections on women's enfranchisement found a welcome niche in its pages. For one of its editors, Alicia Moreau, suffrage was a genderless right belonging to anybody who worked and paid taxes. Suffrage was also a tool for the expression and defence of a person's natural rights. Women would use it to elect those who represented their gender's rights and interests, identified as legislation on education, child care, labour regulation and anti-alcoholism.[34]

The economic reasons for female suffrage were central to suffrage supporters, who were conscious of the usefulness of an argument used by labour leaders to make their way into the politics of power. Reiterating the economic significance of their work would also make working women aware of their potential political clout, and carry the message to any woman who could herself become a worker, or respected other women's work. Women's right to claim suffrage on grounds of their economic contribution to national productivity and the family budget was a principle adopted by jurists and politicians of several political complexions.[35] Colombian Feminine Union (*Unión Femenina de Colombia*) in 1944 reversed the order of the argument on women and labour, claiming that once women were full citizens they would be in a position to press for equal salaries.[36] Regardless of how it was argued, the economic rationale for suffrage remained critical for nations seeking development at any cost, and one to which suffragists often returned. However, in the last resort, suffrage opponents entrenched themselves in the overarching concepts of gender relations, to which we must turn.

Gender roles and suffrage

Suffrage supporters in South America were deeply preoccupied with gender roles and how the vote would affect women's 'femininity', a concept that was inextricably involved in the discussion of any social and political reform involving women.[37] Since suffrage defined the most political of all activities, no discussion of the vote failed to involve the potential threat of gender role subversion. Femininity was understood as the sum of social and biological qualities that were the essence of being a woman. A feminine woman was charming, genteel, delicate, and sensitive. Some of those qualities could be acquired through education, but they were also imprinted as part of the female genetic differentiation from the male. Neither education nor any other social activity should hinder the development of femininity. Lack of femininity ran against nature.[38]

Feminists and anti-feminists, suffragists and anti-suffragists, shared the belief that the preservation of biological differences between the sexes was essential to maintain a balance in their respective contributions to the social order. Women's 'innate' gender qualities were called forth with predictable regularity to serve the general cause of social reforms and validate the presence of women in politics.[39] The acceptance of feminism – and suffrage as its brainchild – hinged on its characterisation as an ideology that reaffirmed the positive contrasts between men and women before accepting the intrinsic equality of both sexes. Argentine Isabel Salthou, discussing feminism and political activism, declared that the latter should be undertaken preferably by single women or by those who had no aptitude for motherhood.[40] Thirteen years later, this opinion was still held as valid by a man writing from the provincial city of San Luis. He lamented the possibility of women engaging in corrupt political struggle and abandoning their noble role in the family. For him, feminists were egotists who enjoyed 'success before the crumbling feminine altar'.[41] As late as 1947 some Argentine Deputies raised anguished cries for the potential loss of peace within the home if suffrage was approved, while a Colombian Minister of Education warned a graduating class at the Normal School of the dangers posed by suffrage to their femininity.[42]

Not only did feminism subvert gender roles it could also lead to behavioural modification. Uruguayan J. Fernando Carbonell regarded suffrage as an activity for those women who 'could not exercise their maternal and wifely functions', and feminists as *marimachos*, a hybrid cross between male and female.[43] As the suffragist campaign gained momentum in the early 1920s even anarchists entered the arena to attack feminist women, accusing them of having abandoned 'the sweet mission of their sex to snatch the whip of oppression, forsaking their gracious feminine personality, and assuming a hybrid masculine behaviour (*hombrunamiento*)'.[44] Others took the matter of masculinisation one step further, suggesting that feminism led to lesbianism. An Argentinean detractor equated feminism with sexual anomaly, calling feminists women who reneged their sex and became caricatures of men. 'When women appear in public claiming for themselves a male occupation they undergo a sexual inversion; this is immoral.'[45]

In the 1930s, under the influence of 'biological' and eugenic jurisprudence, attacks on all feminist activities were not uncommon. Uruguayan Darwin Peluffo Beisso, a determined detractor of feminism and suffrage, exemplified traditionalists and right-wing sympathisers who claimed that the issue was not whether women could exercise political rights, but whether they should. Was it appropriate for society that women engage in activities pertaining 'biologically' to men? He recommended that political activities should be forbidden to women during the fertile period of their lives, because their potential maternity should not be hindered by any distraction. On the other hand, sterile women would have the 'moral duty' of participating in politics to help sustain the collective interests of the nation.[46] Time did not change this suffragist stereotype of ugly, unfulfilled women. In the mid-1940s, Colombian anti-suffragists used a similar type of ridicule and re-stated their belief that men defined women in politics as well as in marriage, by portraying suffragists as *solteronas*, a contemptuous term for older single women.[47]

Feminists countered such attacks on feminism and suffrage by developing a strategy which they believed suited Latin American women and their cultural and social circumstances. To offset the negative charges of masculinisation early feminists shone in the tasks of reconciling personal rights, social justice, and motherhood. They never abjured femininity. Femininity, argued a Colombian feminist in 1945, was not a quality women could dispose of at their will. It was an 'inherent, immutable and intangible' part of the feminine sex.[48] Since motherhood was an affirmation of femininity, the mother who performed other social tasks could not be accused of masculinisation, and epitomised the possibility of change within a traditional role. This was the example Ernestina López had in mind when she addressed the First International Feminine Congress in 1910 and saw in women's new pursuits the triumph 'of their condition of mothers'.[49] *Unión Femenina de Chile* (Chilean Feminine Union) validated women's suffrage stating that 'women, as mothers, will be able to contribute much to social legislation, based on that experience'.[50]

A new social order and old social roles
South American feminists extended femininity, domesticity, and motherhood into politics to reach the desired goal of active participation in public and political life. Women's assumed higher sensitivity towards others' feelings and their acute sense of moral duty were the bases upon which suffragists and feminists built their claim to a place in the sun. Armed with the vote, women would create a new social order, eradicate vice, rectify injustices, and help create a better society, simply because they were women and their gender endowed them with special sensitivities that men lacked. Gender complementarity would balance male inadequacies. Suffrage, for two Colombian feminist leaders, would carry out:

> a protective action, beneficial to all social classes, especially those lacking everything, who so little trouble male legislators. Women will legislate on women as mothers, on children, and on everything men have forgotten in their ancestral egotism.[51] When women have access to the organs of public power, they will remove all stains, errors, and vices so deeply rooted here, discrediting and impairing conscious citizenship.[52]

When the Argentinean magazine *Mujeres de América* began to print its feminist message for suffrage in 1933, it stated that with the vote women would contribute part of their bounty of goodness to the political battle. 'They would soften more than one rough corner and would bring peace to the belligerent spirits [of men] when they lose their self-restraint.'[53] Argentine writer Josefina Marpons, acknowledged women's fears of becoming either masculinised in politics or men's accomplices. She thought women should use their own distinctive voice to state their own truths. 'To be a feminist does not mean to stop being feminine. To participate in public life we do not have to neglect our homes; quite the contrary, we will have new means to protect it . . . . There is no struggle between the sexes.'[54] For their part, male suffrage supporters used similar stereotypical, but nonetheless appealing, gender views. The mission of women, they argued, was to reform society, and suffrage was the key to fulfilling that mission. Armed with their maternal instinct and practice, women would inject moral values into politics, and strengthen society by defending family, motherhood, and childhood.[55]

Susan Kinsley Kent posits that in England the vote challenged the ideology of separate spheres for the sexes.[56] In South America, suffrage supporters challenged men's exclusive control of political rights, but reaffirmed the distinctive character of their sex and, by extending it into politics, created a separate sphere in the public arena. Carving a space in men's territory – even using the tools of femininity – could not be done without some debunking of men's shortcomings. The conciliatory tone used by most feminists–suffragists when speaking of men and to men did not spare explicit accusations of greediness, egotism, and narrowness of mind in some men. Exploiting the lack of abilities in the opposite sex, however, was not a technique often used by South American suffragists, who used a great deal of restraint for the sake of gaining male support.

Women's organisations for suffrage and beyond

While the earliest feminist or feminist sympathisers had some misgivings about the feasibility of suffrage, they knew they had to organise to be heard. The means used by women to organise themselves in pursuit of suffrage reveal how women put into practice their political concepts. Few of the associations founded before the mid-1910s were outright suffrage supporters. However, by the mid-1910s, women's organisations began to proliferate, spurred by the increasing debate on women's rights, of which suffrage was the most controversial. Their purpose was to create a female political culture acceptable also to men, in whose hands rested the power of deciding the future of any legal or political reform. At least five different types of associations were created from 1916 onwards.

– Firstly, pre-suffrage 'parties' founded before suffrage was approved anywhere in the Southern Cone, such as the Argentinean *Partido Feminista Nacional* (National Feminist Party) and the Chilean *Partido Cívico Femenino* (Civic Feminine Party).

– Secondly, associations to promote suffrage as a cause, and integrate women into existing political parties, such as the Argentinean *Asociación Pro-Derechos de la Mujer* (Association for Women's Rights) and the *Unión Femenina de Chile* (Chilean Feminine Union).

– Thirdly, women's parties organised after the suffrage (national or municipal) was granted to elect women. Such were the Uruguayan *Partido Independiente Democrático Femenino* (Feminine Independent Democratic Party), the Argentinean *Partido Peronista Femenino* (Women's Peronist Party) and the Chilean *Partido Nacional de Mujeres* (National Women's Party).

– Fourthly, umbrella organisations that promoted women's strength through the union of smaller organisations. They sought to give women visibility as an interest group, which could press for the passage of social and economic reforms. Such was the Chilean *Movimiento Pro-Emancipación de la Mujer en Chile* (MEMCH or Movement for the Emancipation of Women), organised in 1935.

– Fifthly, inclusive general organisations – appealing to women as individuals to promote women's issues. *Unión Femenina de Colombia* (Colombian Feminine Union), founded in 1944, called for women, of all classes, religious beliefs, and political affiliations, to join its ranks. It supported suffrage, but it also planned to educate women in civic activities and to act as a pressure group.

This variety not only speaks of different political needs, as defined by the founders, but also of the internal conflict caused by the praxis of politics and the rhetoric of gender. Pro-suffrage women faced many questions. Were women's parties feasible? Was it more advisable to join male parties? Was the strength of women as a gender better used as a quantifiable factor through their own non-political organisations? The answers to these questions lie in women's own conceptualisation of the value of separateness as a political tool. South American women's parties – with few exceptions – failed to survive, but women's organisations were effective in attracting women to become involved in civic life.

An example of failure was the *Partido Independiente Democrático Femenino* (Feminine Independent Democratic Party), founded in 1933 by Uruguayan, Sofía Alvarez Rey. She was a typical active feminist and suffragist who saw limitless possibilities for women in public service and envisioned nothing short of a total transformation of the social structure once women began to vote. Having joined other women in the suffrage campaign, she launched her own party. Its platform was written by the membership. It had ten basic points and twenty-three general points of action. The basic points addressed gender-based social issues, such as the reform of the Civil Code, the suppression of regulated prostitution, and the protection of motherhood and childhood. The twenty-three general points addressed national problems. The party wished to remain exclusively female, dissociated from all that was 'infected and degenerate' in politics.[57] Unfortunately, it was unable to raise enough votes to survive beyond the 1938 elections.

The Feminine Independent Democratic Party posed no threat to the established male-dominated parties. The chances of any political success were slim for an organisation that lacked all the traditional mechanisms for propaganda and mobilisation beyond a group of well-educated women, and could not even gather around itself all the professional women in Uruguay. Speaking against the Independent Democratic Feminine Party, socialist Clotilde Luisi explained that women's parties had three flaws. Firstly, they expressed 'anti-social egotism', that is, women's inability to belong to mixed-gender associations. Gender separation in politics was called a negative narcissistic indulgence. Secondly, they were too weak to confront male parties effectively. Thirdly, their programmes were very limited.[58] Zulma Núñez, founder of *América Nueva*, a feminist magazine, criticised women's parties as an 'absurd situation of the battle between the sexes'.[59] Parties organised by women succeeded when they aimed at municipal elections, an arena small enough to campaign and gather votes. For politics at the national level, women's parties had to contend not just with male resistance, but with women's opposition as well.

Other suffragist–feminists chose to form women-only associations. Women seeking to learn more about themselves and politics were reluctant to mingle with men in traditional parties, fearing rejection, ridicule, or alienation. Preparation for suffrage could be carried out within female organisations, although ultimately they would have to become candidates presented by formal parties.[60] The survival of some umbrella or general women's organisations – not seeking votes themselves – hinged on their dissociation from established politics, and the emphasis on their generic gender nature. In Chile, Elena Caffarena, one of the founding mothers of the Movement for the Emancipation of Women in Chile (MEMCH for *Movimiento Pro-Emancipación de la Mujer en Chile*), successfully resisted pressure from the communist members of her umbrella organisation to take a leftist political stance arguing that 'each organisation has its own functions. For class struggle we have unions; for political struggle we have political parties; for women's struggle we have female organisations such as MEMCH.'[61]

The philosophy behind most women's organisations in South America was that gender collegiality was a sine qua non for survival. The integrity, and even the success, of female organisations depended on being anchored in the accepted assumptions of women's role in society, and on having an over-arching ethical purpose. The insistence on assuming an 'apolitical' stand was nominal at best. The image of women totally detached from the sweat and mud of male politics but engaged in an active pursuit of social causes was contradictory but desirable. It did not threaten men or undecided women, and cast politically engaged women in the traditionally acceptable role of moderators for the common good. This image reappeared whenever and wherever it was needed. Olga Salcedo de Medero, a Colombian celebrating the success of female suffrage in Congress in 1954, stated that 'women should not serve any political party; they should serve women'.[62] The characterisation of women as above political corruption offered a solution to the problem of creating a different model of authority for them. It was also in line with the gendered image of women as embodiments of altruism, and paradigms of selflessness and dedication to higher causes, whose votes should be conditional on an acceptance of their objectives as women.

These guidelines did not, however, ensure ultimate success. The Chilean Feminine Party, founded in 1946, was a women's party claiming to be neither left nor right. The 'apolitical' centrist stand followed an ideological line defined nearly twenty years before, while its endorsement of compensatory feminism traced its roots to the 1920s. It also assumed that the spiritual direction of the home 'corresponds by natural right to women. We must revindicate that right before the law.' Women's birthright to assume the control of the hearth was a concept never broached before by other feminists, and which the party proposed to use as a legal argument for redefining women's status in family law.[63]

Hailing the ratification of universal suffrage in December 1949, Chile's president, Gabriel González Videla, expressed his hope that women 'would come to his aid to humanise Chilean politics and endow it with a deeper and more sincere feeling of fraternity, justice and sensibility', sentiments which portrayed a female political image already familiar in the 1930s.[64] The Chilean Feminine Party entered the 1950 municipal and the 1952 national elections. In the latter María de la Cruz was elected senator with the political support of the president himself. The complete history of this party is beyond the scope of this chapter, but suffice it to say it began to weaken and eventually disappeared after María de la Cruz floundered in her politics, and was impeached for misuse of funds and sympathy with Peronist ideas. The ideological mould created for women's votes thus shaped their debut as well as their demise in Chilean national politics.

The Women's Peronist Party was the brain child of Juan Domingo and Eva Perón, especially the latter, in her own campaign to become the self-appointed leader of Argentinean women. After suffrage became a reality in 1947 Eva Perón organised the party pointedly to serve her own and her husband's political goals. By 1952 it had enrolled 500,000 women, supported by a sleek and well-funded structure. Women were coaxed and extolled for their contribution to the motherland, while being effectively manipulated to rise against an 'enemy' that wished to rob them of what was rightfully theirs.

The political power of the Women's Peronist Party was unrivalled. Unlike any other previous women's party, it had a definite political purpose: complete and unconditional support of the president, underlined by class and gender appeal. To Eva Perón's followers, she was a superb example of womanhood in rebellion, taking justice in her hands to punish the enemies of the people. In conveying her message she aptly used femininity symbols of love, sacrifice for husband, family, and the motherland. In exchange for overwhelming electoral support, women benefited from a fixed quota of candidates in the Peronist Party which allowed it to take to Congress the largest number of female elected candidates in the history of twentieth-century Argentina. With a strong direction and an effective use of traditional femininity and motherhood, women could be effectively mobilised in the political arena. The success of the party was, however, unusual, as it was a tool forged out of populist and emotional appeal to serve a specific cause, and lacking an ideological base of its own. Its exceptional nature makes it difficult to compare to any other women's political institution in South America, but it is, nevertheless, an excellent example of the use and manipulation of gender in politics.[65]

Machismo, marianismo and patriarchalism

Suffragists in South America earned their right to vote. If their campaigns were not marked by confrontation, they were no less a struggle against the difficult odds of institutionalised patriarchalism and culturally machista (endorsing the supremacy of male values) societies. To this confrontation they brought a strong conviction of intellectual equality with men and self-confidence in their own ability to assume social obligations beyond the home. In the process they also acquired a clear understanding that citizenship implied participation in the definition of national policies, and that women's alienation from civic life was unacceptable. They learned to recognise suffrage as a powerful tool without which women would remain marginal to society's interests and unable to implement their own. Their idiosyncratic imprint in the history of suffrage was their belief in women's special abilities as a gender, always perceived as positive and beneficial for society.

The struggle for suffrage meant significant personal growth for women who affiliated themselves with feminism and suffragism, and their efforts helped eventually to change other women's and men's attitudes about their gender's social role. While initially women's votes did not change the Latin American political landscape, the proliferation of women's organisations resulting from feminism and the suffrage campaigns marked a transition into public life nothing short of spectacular. The significance of this transition can only be apprehended by a careful study of the emphasis given in the nineteenth century to domesticity as woman's fate, the resistance offered by traditionalists to suffrage and feminism, and the lasting mystique of femininity and motherhood in their cultural milieu. Unquestionably, suffragists shared the delusion that women's intervention could and would alter the nature of politics itself. In this, they were no different from men who offered all sorts of plans for social reform, or sold emotional mirages dressed up in nationalistic garbs. South American suffragists chose a difficult task by assuming the role of ethical, nurturing protectors of home values, preserving the distinctiveness of their sex while claiming justice on equal grounds to men. Thirty-two years after the last nation in South America yielded the vote to its women, the political process in those nations still bears the marks of strong gender roles. Machismo, marianismo, and patriarchalism meet to produce the Mothers of the Plaza de Mayo, the co-madres of El Salvador, the white-clad figure of Nicaraguan president, Violeta Chamorro, running an election as a widow and grandmother.[66] The official denial of feminism by the Cuban revolution, its slow acceptance by the Nicaraguan revolutionary government, and the small number of women elected – not appointed – to the legislatures, speak to the ongoing protracted struggle for the recognition of women's political power in Latin America. Perhaps Paulina Luisi was right when she stated that suffrage was only part of the process.

To a historian's eye, the issue is whether or not the strong gender specificity of South (and Latin) American politics has really become a tool for female empowerment. My opinion is that unless supported by a well-understood feminist base it will remain a double-edged sword.

1 This chapter is partly based on extensive research carried out for my book *Feminism, Women and Social Change in the Southern Cone, 1890–1940*, now in press, which focuses on Chile, Argentina and Uruguay. I have also surveyed in depth two leading women's magazines in Colombia, *Letras y Encajes* (1926–1951) and *Agitación Femenina* (1944–46), as well as surveys of that country's women's history and samples of *El Tiempo*, the leading newspaper in Bogotá. The suffrage campaign in Cuba, Brazil and Mexico has been studied by Anna Macías, *Against All Odds: The Feminist Movement in Mexico to 1940*, Greenwood Press, Westport, Conn., 1982; Lynn K. Stoner, *From the House to the Streets: The Cuban Woman's Movement for Legal Reform, 1898-1940* , Duke Univ. Press, Durham, 1991; June Hahner, *Emancipating the Female Sex: The Struggle for Women's Rights in Brazil, 1850-1940*, Duke Univ. Press, Durham, 1990.

2 For a political history of these countries in the twentieth century, see, Leslie Bethell, ed, *The Cambridge History of Latin America*, vol. 8, Cambridge Univ. Press, New York, 1990. Also useful are David Bushnell, *The Making of Modern Colombia: A Nation In Spite of Itself*, Univ. of California Press, Berkeley, 1993, and David Rock, *Argentina, 1516-1987, From Spanish Colonization to Alfonsón*, Univ. of California Press, Berkeley, 1987.

3 There are no general histories of women in any of the countries of the Southern Cone. A general survey of women's history, with emphasis on political issues in the twentieth century is Francesca Miller, *Latin American Women and the Search for Social Justice*, Univ. Press of New England, Hanover, New Hampshire, 1991. I have finished a chapter on key themes in twentieth-century women's history in Latin America for the forthcoming volume 6 of the *Cambridge History of Latin America*, possible publication date, 1995. The best bibliographical reference available for works published after 1975 is K. Lynn Stoner, *Latinas of the Americas: A Source Book*, Garland Publishing Inc., New York, 1989. See also Asunción Lavrin, 'Women's Studies', in Paula H. Covington, ed, *Latin America and the Caribbean: A Critical Guide to the Research Sources*, Greenwood Press, New York, 1992, 743-54. For partial surveys of twentieth-century women's history, see Silvia Rodríguez Villamil & Graciela Sapriza, *Mujer, estado y política en el Uruguay del siglo XX*, Ediciones de la Banda Oriental, Montevideo, 1984; Patricia Londoño, '*Cinco ensayos sobre la mujer colombiana, 1800-1956*', unpublished thesis, Univ. de Antioquia, Medellín, 1990; Magdala Velázquez Toro, '*La lucha por los derechos de la mujer en Colombia*', unpublished Ph.D thesis, Univ. Nacional de Colombia, Medellín, 1985.

4 See Paul W. Drake, *Socialism and Populism in Chile, 1932-52*, Univ. of Illinois Press, Urbana, 1978; Charles Bergquist, *Labor in Latin America: Comparative Essays on Chile, Argentina, Venezuela, and Colombia*, Stanford Univ. Press, Stanford, 1986; Asunción Lavrin, 'Women, Labor and the Left, Argentina and Chile, 1890-1925,' in Cheryl Johnson-Odim & Margaret Strobel, eds, *Expanding the Boundaries of Women's History*, Univ. of Indiana Press, Bloomington, 1992, 249-77; Iaacov Oved, *El anarquismo y el movimiento obrero en Argentina*, Siglo XXI, Buenos Aires, 1978; Julio Mafud, *La vida obrera en la Argentina*, Editorial Proyección, Buenos Aires, 1976; Elena Gil, *La mujer en el mundo del trabajo*, Ediciones Libera, Buenos Aires, 1970; Sandra M. Deutsch, 'The Catholic Church, Work, and Womanhood in Argentina, 1890-1930', in *Gender and History*, 3/3, 1991, 304-25; Peter De Shazo, *Urban Workers and Labor Unions in Chile, 1902-1927*, Univ. of Wisconsin Press, Madison, 1983; Jorge Balbis, '*La situación de las trabajadoras durante el primer batallismo*', in Balbis *et al*, *El primer batallismo, Cinco enfoques polémicos*, Centro Latinoamericano de Economía Humana and Ediciones de la Banda Oriental, Montevideo, 1985, 105-27.

5 *La mujer uruguaya reclama sus derechos políticos*, Alianza Uruguaya y Consejo Nacional de Mujeres, Montevideo, 1930; *Acción Femenina* (AF), 3/2, 1919, 27-58.

6 There are few in-depth studies of feminism in any of the countries surveyed in this chapter. See, Miller, *Latin American Women*. See also, Edda Gaviola *et al.*, *Queremos votar en las próximas elecciones, Historia del movimiento femenino chileno, 1913-1952*, Centro de Análisis y Difusión de la Condición de la mujer, Santiago, Chile, 1986.

7   Carlos Vaz Ferreira, *Sobre feminismo*, Sociedad Amigos del Libro Rioplatense, Buenos Aires, 1933, passim. Vaz Ferreira, 1872–1959, was a very influential Uruguayan philosopher. His interpretation of feminism was shared by many key politicians, including José Batlle Ordoñez, twice president of his country and head of the Colorado Party. Vaz Ferreira's lecture was printed 18 years after it was delivered at the University of Uruguay in Montevideo. See also Emilio Frugoni, *La mujer ante el derecho*, Editorial Indo-Americana, Montevideo, 1940.

8   A nineteenth-century conservative politician, Abdón Cifuentes, proposed female suffrage in 1865 as an idea for the future. See Lavrin, 'Women, Labor and the Left, Argentina and Chile, 1900-1925', passim.

9   For example, the *Partido Cívico Femenino*, founded in 1922, placed suffrage ninth in the rank of its objectives. See its mouthpiece, *AF*, 2/14, 1923, 14-15.

10   *Unión Femenina de Chile*, a national organisation, was founded in 1931. It consistently supported women's suffrage. *Bando Femenino*, a small group organised in 1926, expanded into a women's party, the *Partido Femenino Nacional* early in 1932. Also organised early in that year was a committee to promote suffrage, *Comité Pro-Derechos de la Mujer*. Although acting independently, these groups gave the concept of women's suffrage a maximum of exposure in the press.

11   *Unión y Labor* (L), 1/12, 1910, 22-3; Aldo A. Cocca, *Ley de sufragio femenino*, 'El Ateneo', Buenos Aires, 1948, 14-17.

12   Luis R. Longhi, *Sufragio femenino*, Imp. Baioceo y Cía., Buenos Aires, 1932, 139; *La Nueva Mujer* (*NM*), La Plata, 1/1, 1910, 1.

13   Alicia Moreau, 'El sufragio femenino', *Revista Socialista Internacional*, 3/4, 1911, 93-4; Mariano Abril, 'El sufragio femenino', *Revista de Derecho, Historia y Letras* (*RDHL*), 45, 1913, 95-9; Nestor Tomás Auza, *Periodismo y feminismo en la Argentina, 1830–1930*, Emecé, Buenos Aires, 1988; María del Carmen Feijóo, 'Las luchas feministas', *Todo es Historia*, 1978, 7-23.

14   Cocca, *Ley de Sufragio Femenino*, 14-17.

15   *Nuestra Causa* (*NC*), 1/5, 1919, 111, 114; 1/12, April 1920, 280; 2/13, May 1920, 22; 2/19, 1920, 152-3; *Mujeres de América* (*MA*), 3/16, 1935, 32-33; Lily Sosa de Newton, *Diccionario biográfico de mujeres argentinas*, Plus Ultra, Buenos Aires, 1986, 191-2.

16   *NC*, 2, 13, May 1920, 20; Argentina, Cámara de Diputados, *Diario de Sesiones* 1925, 2, 8-38; Cocca, *Ley de Sufragio*, 63-71; Mario Bravo, *Derechos políticos de la mujer*, Imprenta 'La Vanguardia', Buenos Aires, 1930.

17   Carmela Horne de Burmeister, *Como se organizó en la Argentina el movimiento femenino en favor de los derechos políticos de la mujer por el Comité Argentino Pro-Voto de la Mujer, hoy Asociación Argentina del Sufragio Femenino*, Imprenta Riera y Cía., Buenos Aires, 1933.

18   Argentina, Cámara de Diputados, *Diario de Sesiones*, 1932, vol. 6, 22-111; Aldo Coca, *Ley de sufragio*, 100-23.

19   de Diputados, *Diario de Sesiones*, 1938, vol. 2, 580-2; 1933, vol 3, 713; *VF*, 2/21, 1935, 16; 5/9, 1937, 4-6; 5/59, 1938, 13-14, 33-34; 10/109-10, 1943, 33; *MA*, 1/1, 1933, 48-49; 1/3, 1933, 41, 59; Moreau de Justo, 'El momento político', *VF*, 5/49, 1937, 4-6; Alicia Moreau de Justo, '10 Razones en favor del sufragio femenino', *VF*, 5/61, 1938, 4-5.

20   Estela dos Santos, *Las mujeres peronistas*, 64. For Eva Perón see, Nicolas Fraser & Marysa Navarro, *Eva Perón*, Norton, New York, 1980, and 'Evita's Charismatic Leadership', in Michael L. Conniff, ed, *Latin American Populism in Comparative Perspective*, Univ. of New Mexico Press, Albuquerque, 1982; Julie M. Taylor, *Eva Perón: The Myths of a Woman*, Univ. of Chicago Press, Chicago, 1979; Carmen Llorca, *Llamadme Evita. Un destino único de mujer*, Editorial Planeta, Madrid, 1980; Eva Perón, *La razón de mi vida*, Ediciones Peuser, Buenos Aires, 1951.

21   Toro, 'La lucha por los derechos de la mujer en Colombia', 157-243.

22   They were: 1. *Unión Femenina de Colombia*, founded in 1944 to promote the improvement of women's status in society; 2. *Alianza Femenina de Colombia*, founded in Bogotá in 1946; 3. The National Feminine Organisation, *Organización Nacional Femenina*, founded in 1954 with headquarters in Bogotá. In the provincial city of Tunja, *Agitación Femenina*, a women's magazine, was published between 1944 and 1946.

23   The nations of the Americas gathered in the Inter-American conferences in Montevideo, 1933, and Lima, 1938, and the 1945 Charter of the United Nations adopted resolutions recognising women's political and civil rights. Colombia, Chile, Argentina and Uruguay were signatories to these treaties.

24   Nearly two million women voted on this occasion. See Toro, '*La lucha*', 242.

25   Carlos Pellegrini, *Estudio sobre el derecho electoral*, Imprenta del Plata, Buenos Aires, 1869, 10-26; Pedro E. Aguilar, *Derecho electoral*, Imprenta y Casa Editora Argos, Buenos Aires, 1893, 95-110;

José Manuel Estrada, *Curso de derecho constitucional*, 3 vols, Librería del Colegio de Cabaut y Cía., Buenos Aires, 1901-02, 2/336; Florentino González, *Lecciones de derecho constitucional*, Imp. Lit. J.A.Berheim, Buenos Aires, 1869, 125-8. Citing John Stuart Mill, González conceded female capacity for political activity, but he would only award it to single or widowed women, barring it for married women.

26   Toro, 'La lucha por los derechos de la mujer', 153.

27   Toro, 'La lucha por los derechos de la mujer', 199, quoting senator Rafael Bernal Jiménez.

28   de Ramírez, a Uruguayan living in La Plata, Buenos Aires, was a 'radical' for her period. Calling herself a 'freethinker', she advocated equal education for both sexes, equal employment opportunities and equal salaries, sharing rights over children, divorce and political rights for women. She founded two magazines, *Nosotras* 1902-4, and *La Nueva Mujer* (NM), 1910-12. She also founded a *Liga Feminista* in 1910. See, de Ramírez, *Ensayos feministas*, 2nd ed., Editorial, '*El Siglo Ilustrado*', Montevideo, 1965.

29   See, Sara Justo, 'La mujer y la política', *UL*, 1/4, 1910, 24-6. For other statements, see, *UL*, 1/12, 1910, 22-3; 2/17, 1910, 8; 3/25,1911, Editorial.

30   The most quoted source among the liberal feminists in South America was John Stuart Mill, *On the Subjection of Women*, first translated into Spanish by Chilean Martina Barros Borgoño in 1873. See, 'La esclavitud de la mujer', *Revista de Santiago*, 2, 1872-73.

31   *Primer Congreso Femenino Internacional. Historia, Actas y Trabajos*, Imp. A. Ceppi, Buenos Aires, 1910, 368-78, 400-13.

32   Paulina Luisi, a Uruguayan suffrage advocate, travelled extensively in Europe after 1913. Argentinean Moreau and Chilean Labarca, travelled in the United States in the 1920s. Carry Chapman Catt toured South America in 1923 and Doris Stevens gathered a substantial number of votes for her married women's citizenship proposals at The Hague among Latin Americans. For further data, see Miller, 'The International Relations of Women of the Americas, 1890-1928', *The Americas*, 43/2, Oct. 1986, 171-82. See also her *Latin American Women and the Search for Social Justice*, 82-4, 94-6. Note that Colombian women were unready to enter into the suffrage debate until much later.

33   '¿Es conveniente en Chile conceder a las mujeres el derecho del sufragio.?', Informal poll published in *Revista Chilena*, 10/31, May 1920, 62-79. For Argentina see, Miguel Font, *La Mujer, Encuesta Feminista Argentina*, n.p., Buenos Aires, 1921. These two journalistic enquiries into suffrage were carried out among chosen intellectuals and politicians of the period. Font's· book contains 64 personalities and institutions. The Chilean poll included 17 opinions. Results showed a mixed feeling about suffrage with no clear majority for those in favour or against, given the qualifications offered by many.

34   Moreau, '*Por que pedimos el derecho al sufragio*', *NC*, 3, 24 June 1921, 272. In Uruguay, socialist Frugoni used the economic argument of women's participation in the labour force to support and defend the proposal to include female suffrage in the new Constitution drafted in 1917. See Frugoni, *Los nuevos fundamentos*, Maximino García, ed, Montevideo, 1919, 57.

35   Juan Carlos Rébora, *La emancipación de la mujer. El aporte de la jurisprudencia*, Librería y Editorial 'La Facultad', Buenos Aires, 1929. This rather conservative jurist conceded that women had already established their right to citizenship as wage earners.

36   'Unión Femenina de Colombia, Objeto', *AF*, 1/1, 1944, 2.

37   The first commentator on feminism in South America, Argentinean Quesada, having visited the US, confessed to be dazzled by the 'marvelous spectacle' of North American women. Their education, their artistic and literary production and the equality that social customs had granted them impressed Quesada deeply. What he most admired, was that the process *had NOT hurt the essential feminine nature of those women*. See, Quesada, *La cuestión femenina*, Imprenta de Pablo E. Coni, e hijos, Buenos Aires, 1899, 12-20, 32-5, emphasis mine. See also, Lavrin, 'Female, Feminine, Feminist: Women's Historical Process in Twentieth-Century Latin America', Occasional Paper, Univ. of Bristol, School of Modern Languages and Department of Hispanic, Portuguese, and Latin American Studies, Fall 1989.

38   There are no in-depth studies on the education of women in the nineteenth century. For writings of the period, see Alfredo Lombardi, 'La mujer y su función social', *El Monitor de la educación común*, 39, Buenos Aires, 1910, 544-50. He stated, 'Do not obstruct women's path to science and progress. . . but for our own sake, let us not forget what is our [respective] place in society. Women [belong] in the family and [should be in] the family for the sake of society and humanity.' While discussing the creation of secondary schools for women in 1912, conservative Uruguayan deputy, Lafinur, deprecated higher education because 'the question of feminism begins with such [educational] stimulants'. See, María Julia Ardao, *La creación de la Sección de Enseñanza Secundaria y Preparatoria para Mujeres en*

1912, Editorial Florensa y Lafón, Montevideo, 1962, 34-5. Female education is discussed by Eugenio M. Hostos, La educación de la mujer, Imprenta Sud-America, Santiago, 1873; Carlos Octavio Bunge, El espíritu de la educación, Taller Tipográfico de la penitenciaría Nacional, Buenos Aires, 1901. All the Ministers of Education in the Southern Cone during the period under review were men. Only Chile appointed one woman, Amanda Labarca, to the Ministry during the mid-1920s.

39   Although we cannot here trace the roots of the value-system sustaining this concept of femininity, it was validated by centuries of Spanish colonial tradition, by the Italian and Spanish immigrants in Uruguay and Argentina, and German Catholics in Chile, and by the power of the church in Colombia. For supporters of a feminism inclusive of maternal roles, see Francisco Gicca, La mujer, Su pasado, su presente y sus reivindicaciones en el porvenir, Imp. Mercantil, Buenos Aires, 1915; Mercedes G. Humano Ortiz, Emancipación de la mujer, Imp. de José Traganti, Buenos Aires, 1918; W. Tello, 'El feminismo argentino', RDHL, 63, 1919, 456-9; Ernesto Nelson, 'Feminismo de ayer, de hoy y de mañana', Nosotros, 15/36, 1920, 441-59; José Bianco, Mi feminismo, Talleres Gráficos Argentinos de L. J. Rosso, Buenos Aires, 1927; Labarca, ¿A dónde va la mujer?, Ediciones Extra, Santiago, 1934.

40   María Isabel Salthou, 'El problema feminista en la República Argentina', Unpublished Ph.D thesis, School of Philosophy and Letters, Univ. of Buenos Aires, 1920. She repeated an argument often maintained by opponents of feminism. Educated women who would know how to vote were a minority. Most women were impressionable, weak, and lacked enough education. While there are many ignorant men who vote, to add to their ranks all ignorant women would cause greater social problems.

41   Felipe S. Velázquez, El proyecto de ley instituyendo el voto cívico femenino, Imp. Casa Celorrio, San Luis, 1933.

42   Estela Dos Santos, Las mujeres peronistas, 18-21; Ofelia Uribe de Acosta, Una voz insurgente, Editorial Guadalupe, Ltda., Bogotá, 1963, 210-11; AF, 1/7, 1945, 3.

43   J. Fernando Carbonell, Feminismo y marimachismo, Publicaciones del 'Centro Natura', Montevideo, 1909. Marimacho was a term used against feminists in Spanish America to deny their femininity and portray them as sexually deviant.

44   La Protesta, Buenos Aires, 9 Sept. 1923.

45   Interview with Luis Reyna in Miguel Font, La mujer, 136-41. See also Julia Casal de Espeche, Misión Social de la mujer argentina, Talleres Gráficos de Olivieri y Domínguez, La Plata, 1922.

46   Darwin Peluffo Beisso, Femineidad y política. Sobre el voto de la mujer, n.p., Montevideo, 1931.

47   See AF, 1/1, 1944, 14-15. A cartoon portrayed the suffragist as a spinster wearing glasses, a shapeless hat, and an umbrella, and resembling a scarecrow.

48   María Emilia Forero, 'El voto femenino', Letras y Encajes, LE, 18, 223, 1945, 72-6.

49   Keynote speech by Dra. Ernestina López, Primer Congreso Femenino Internacional, 35-6.

50   'Por que queremos el voto', Nosotras, 2/29, 1932, 5.

51   Idalia Vassalis, 'Los derechos de la mujer', LE, 10/126, 1937, 2283-4. Years later, the founder of a women's school, and a socially highly placed Colombian matron, Teresita Santamaría de González, reiterated these ideas. She expected women to vote for other women who would legislate on maternity and childhood protection, female education, respect for women's workers in the work-place, etc. See Lucila Arango, 'Con Doña Teresita Santamaría de González', LE, 18/216, 7037-43.

52   'Como piensan nuestras mujeres, El voto femenino', AF, 1/1, 1944, 7. Statement by Atilia Sánchez. For her part, Josefina Calderón de Reyes believed that when women voted 'there will be more purity in suffrage' because women would choose moral and responsible leaders.

53   MA, 1/1, 1933, 15. 'What Chilean women offer when they demand the vote is a broad, maternal, disinterested and generous co-operation. This is not a gesture of party politics or a subversion of order; it is the practical expression of the need to exercise an apostolate of peace and harmony among all social classes, joining in a sincere and disinterested embrace the Chilean family.' Anonymous, 'Opportunity', Nosotras, 2/29, Santiago, 1932, 3.

54   Rosa Scheiner, 'Lo real en la emancipación de la mujer', VF, 2/14, 1934, 20-2; Josefina Marpons. '¡Ciudadanas!', VF, 1/5, 1933, 19, 35.

55   See Bravo, Derechos políticos de la mujer, Imprenta 'La Vanguardia', Buenos Aires, 1930, passim; Rogelio Araya's opinion, as quoted by Leopoldo Bard in his own support of a bill for women's suffrage, in Argentina, Cámara de Diputados, Diario de Sesiones, 1925, vol. 2, 30; Uruguay, Asamblea General, Cámara de Representantes, Diario de Sesiones, 31st Legislature, 1st Period, vol. 381, 131-2.

56   Susan Kinsley Kent, Sex and Suffrage in Britain, 1860–1914, Princeton Univ. Press, Princeton, 1987, 207.

57   Ideas y Acción (IA) is the best source to study the programme and activities of this party. See 1/

1, 1933, 1-2. The newspaper survived for six years.

58   National Archives of the Nation, Montevideo, Luisi's papers, Box 257, folder 8, No. 25.

59   *América Nueva (AM)*, 1/8, 1933, Editorial. Argentinean and Uruguayan socialists claimed that members of the *Partido Independiente Democrático Femenino* were making a laughing stock of themselves, aping 'the grotesque type of the famous Mrs. Pankhurst, the caricaturesque English suffragette. . .'. See, *La Vanguardia*, 31 Dec. 1932, 1.

60   Chilean conservative women belonging to the Acción Patriótica de Mujeres de Chile elected several women in the 1935 municipal elections with the support of the Conservative Party. The conservative association Asociación Nacional de Mujeres elected two women to serve on Santiago's municipal board in 1938. See Gaviola *et al.*, *Queremos votar*, 62-3 and VF, 1/1, 1935, 2.

61   *MN*, 3/27, 1941, 2. The organisation's goals were the 'integral emancipation of women, especially their economic, juridical, biological and political emancipation'. Caffarena was married to a communist and was a leftist herself.

62   *El Tiempo (ET)*, Bogotá, 22 Aug. 1954, 1. María Currea de Ayala, another speaker on the occasion, sustained that given the grave lack of ethics in Colombia, women had the obligation of forming a 'third party, neither centrists, liberal, conservative or communist, but political in the social sense of the word'. Organised in a vast national network, women would have the moral strength to pressure the government to fulfil its promises, and would help sustain a balance in the political arena. See ET, 29 Aug. 1954, 21.

63   Platform of the Partido Femenino Chileno published in Felícitas Klimpel, *La mujer chilena, El aporte femenino al progreso de Chile, 1910–1960*, Editorial Andrés Bello, Santiago, 1962, 128-9. 'The Chilean Feminine Party is formed by independent women, who have chosen not to limit themselves to join parties of the Right or the Left. Its unity springs from a mystical humanitarianism which seeks to carry out a political program based on the interests of women and the motherland.' Declaration by María de la Cruz, head of the party, for *El Mercurio*, Santiago, 2 Feb. 1951, quoted in Klimpel, *La mujer chilena*, 137.

64   Gaviola *et al.*, *Queremos votar*, 77-8. See also *El Mercurio*, Santiago de Chile, 16 Dec. 1949, 37; 17 Dec., 3; 19 Dec., 3. In its lukewarm editorial of 17 December, *El Mercurio* reiterated the idea that women should unite and exercise the spirit of order which was *co-substantial* with their *nature*. That spirit could help them to cure the vices of politics.

65   Fraser & Navarro, *Eva Perón*, 107-9.

66   *Marianismo*, a term coined by anthropologist Evelyn P. Stevens, means the cultivation of the image of women as embodiments of spiritual values best represented by the Virgin Mary, and the use of such qualities to gain power within and outside the family. See Stevens, 'Marianismo, the Other Face of *Machismo* in Latin America', in Ann Pescatello, ed, *Female and Male in Latin America: Essays*, Univ. of Pennsylvania Press, Pittsburgh, 1973, 89-101.

IV

Comparing Suffrages

Banquet, International Council of Women, Berlin, 1904. Eighty-four-year-old
Susan B. Anthony is sitting on the right wing of the table, sixth from the front.
Rush Rhees Library, University of Rochester.

11

From Anti-Slavery to Suffrage Militancy: The Bright Circle, Elizabeth Cady Stanton and the British Women's Movement

SANDRA STANLEY HOLTON

Introduction

A new direction has become apparent in the history of the women's movement in Britain in recent years which, by identifying women's networks based on friendship and kinship relations, offers fresh perspectives in this field.[1] Such an approach serves to shift our attention away from the context of broader political and intellectual movements, and formal organisations and institutions.[2] As a consequence, a new dynamic of women's political activity is being revealed in personal value systems, and in the bonds of family, friendship and community.[3] Equally significant for re-charting the history of the women's movement has been a fresh appreciation of its international dimension.[4] This essay focuses on the network formed by the women of the Bright family circle, and its links with the American women's movement, most especially through the friendships of Elizabeth Cady Stanton among this circle. Private hospitality together with shared values, memories, experience, jokes and reading, and the mutual aid and moral support these fostered, were as important to the functioning of such a network as joint membership of organisations or the more formal set-pieces of public receptions, demonstrations, conferences and conventions.

The charting of the Bright network, together with the fresh perspective on the British movement provided by such an exercise, uncovers several aspects which previously had remained invisible. To begin with, it brings to light an alternative leadership within the nineteenth-century women's movement in Britain among the women of the Bright circle, one which was generally more radical in its approach than that provided by figures such as Emily Davies, Lydia Becker or Millicent Garrett Fawcett.[5] The memoirs of the American suffragists, Elizabeth Cady Stanton and her close friend and colleague, Susan B. Anthony, together with the chronicles of the suffrage movement in the preparation of which they co-operated, are the only readily available sources to show the Bright circle operating as a network both within the British movement, and internationally.[6] Members of this group frequently worked together in a co-ordinated way in the formation of the committees and organisations of the women's movement which occurred in the late 1860s. But it is evident also in the behind-the-scenes manoeuvrings and alliances which formed part of the pressure-group politics in which they were engaged, and the struggles over policy-making within the women's movement itself. Hence a focus on this network in turn clarifies the nature of some of the tensions which on a number of occasions disturbed the nineteenth-century women's movement in Britain. It is a picture which can now be confirmed by examining an extensive collection of correspondence among women of the Bright circle, a collection which has only recently come to light, and which includes also some previously unknown letters between Elizabeth Cady Stanton and Susan B. Anthony and members of this circle.[7]

The transatlantic links of the Bright circle encompassed three generations of women's rights activists. Such a focus, then, serves secondly to review and reassess some of the continuities and ruptures which marked women's political activity, stretching from social and political reform movements in the 1840s and 1850s, through the beginnings of an organised women's movement in the 1860s–90s, to the militancy of the twentieth-century suffrage movement. To begin with, there are the continuities provided in terms of personnel. One of the original members of the Bright circle, Anna Maria Priestman, for example, as a young woman sewed for the great Anti-Corn Law League and Anti-Slavery Bazaars of the 1840s. In the 1860s, 1870s and 1880s she helped establish the first suffrage societies, assisted Josephine Butler's campaigns against the Contagious Diseases Acts, and formed the first Women's Liberal Association. In late old age she hosted meetings of the Women's Social and Political Union (WSPU). Cross-generational friendships among members of this circle also ensured such continuities. Among the first generation, Ursula Bright was an influential example and guide for both Emmeline Pankhurst and Harriot Stanton Blatch (daughter of Elizabeth Cady Stanton), each of whom would go on to establish militant suffrage organisations, in Britain and the United States respectively. Equally, Alice Clark, of the third generation, enjoyed close, formative relationships with her great-aunts, most especially the Priestman sisters, who lived nearby during her childhood, and Priscilla Bright McLaren, with whom she lived for a time while working in Edinburgh.

But such continuities are evident also in the tactics of civil disobedience, and in the emphasis on popular education and agitation which characterised a number of women's organisations formed in the 1890s to which various members of the Bright circle lent their support, and in which a number of leading militant suffragists served their political apprenticeship. Moreover, such tactics provided the form for early militancy in the years 1903–7, an aspect of the activities of the WSPU which has been overshadowed in existing accounts by the more spectacular violence characteristic only of late militancy in the years immediately preceding World War I. A focus on the Bright circle reveals, somewhat unexpectedly then, long-standing Quaker forms of social protest as one of the sources of early militant practices. Another is to be found in the Garrisonian conception of the reformer's role which travelled to Britain from the United States through the anti-slavery campaigns, a conception which eventually found adherents among Quaker and Unitarian women abolitionists there, including members of the Bright circle. This was a conception which saw 'the agitation of public sentiment' as the central role of the reformer, and this role itself as something quite distinct from that of the politician.[8] As such it was one which rejected any compromise on grounds of political pragmatism, and fostered an unbending intransigence in those who held to such an approach. It was this intransigence which was frequently at the heart of disputes between members of this network, and other sections of the suffrage leadership.

The Bright circle and reform movements, 1840–70

Extensive connections of kinship provided the foundation of the Bright circle of women activists, connections further extended by mutual friendships among its members. These relations were often reinforced also by shared membership of reform movements and organisations, and by shared religious affiliation, most especially membership of the Society of Friends. At this time Quakers were required to marry only within the Society, or face disownment. Many marriages were the outcome of a couple's meeting at one of the many large gatherings each year where Quakers from different parts of the country might come together. This was the case with Elizabeth Priestman and John Bright, who met at the annual general meeting of his old school, Ackworth, in 1838. Elizabeth was the eldest daughter of the Priestman family of Newcastle. Her mother was a descendant of the Wilson family, which claimed a number of notable women preachers among earlier generations.[9] Her father was a successful tanner, and a prominent advocate of temperance in the Newcastle region. Elizabeth herself had already gained a reputation for her work on behalf of this cause. The Priestman family was also committed to the abolition of slavery overseas, and to universal suffrage at home.[10]

John Bright was a member of a Rochdale family of cotton spinners, already known in his own locality for his forceful opposition to church rates. This was a long-standing grievance among dissenting sects, which resisted these forced contributions to the established church. John Bright's father, like many other Quakers, had suffered the legal penalty of distraint of goods for his resistance to such impositions. Nonetheless, John Bright's emergence in his own locality as a radical public speaker alarmed some members of his family, who would have preferred that he held to the established quietist practices of the Quakers built upon principles of passive resistance, civil disobedience, and moral suasion. There was a hope that Elizabeth Priestman and her family might save him from the political career, now beckoning him away from the other-worldly life which remained the Quaker ideal.[11] Such an ideal was already being undermined among this younger generation of Quakers by the Evangelical call to good works in this world. Families like the Priestmans might still conceive of their commitment to causes such as anti-slavery and temperance primarily in terms of the 'Inner Light' they believed to reside in each individual, but by this time their efforts were also beginning to take on a more worldly dimension.

The correspondence among the sisters of John Bright and Elizabeth Priestman at the time of their marriage suggests that such a union was also seen as an opportunity to expand the friendship circles of the women of each family. Close attachments were formed among the female siblings of the couple, largely through the exchange of letters, given the considerable distance between their homes. These friendships survived the early death of Elizabeth Priestman Bright less than two years after her marriage. She left behind an infant daughter.[12] This bereavement also appears to have propelled John Bright into a political career. Richard Cobden visited the grieving husband and, so the Bright legend has it, successfully urged on the young orator his duty to use his powers on behalf of the campaign against the Corn Laws by reminding him of the 'thousands of houses in England at this moment where mothers and daughters are dying of hunger'.[13]

In his subsequent political career John Bright received important moral and practical support from his dead wife's family, especially his sister-in-law, Margaret Priestman (subsequently Wheeler, and then Tanner), as well as from his own sisters. And this support was clearly part of a more generalised humanitarian impulse which also informed these women's work for the abolition of slavery, and for temperance. It was an impulse which recognised basic human rights to autonomy and freedom, and which acknowledged too the material base necessary for the realisation of such rights. It was the women of these families who had to organise the soup kitchens on which their workers depended in times of unemployment and want, who provided the private philanthropy which eased the poverty that might follow from the drinking habits of bread-winners, and who sewed endlessly on behalf of fund-raising efforts, both for the Anti-Corn Law League and for the welfare of slaves and the abolition of slavery.[14]

The Bright and Priestman sisters formed fond and long-standing friendships among themselves out of such shared concerns, and provided emotional support and consolation for each other in the several bereavements experienced by each family in the years following the death of Elizabeth Priestman Bright. Most pressingly, perhaps, they shared the care of her baby daughter, Helen, as the bereaved husband embarked on a national career which was to take him to London and a seat in the House of Commons. His sister, Priscilla Bright, and his sister-in-law, Margaret Priestman, became his close political confidantes in these years, a role which was later to be assumed by his first child, Helen.[15] In these years, too, John Bright's sisters and sisters-in-law played an active part in the work of the Anti-Corn Law League. This included fund-raising activities, attendance at public meetings and canvassing support in working-class districts.[16] A younger brother, Jacob Bright, subsequently recalled this work when speaking in support of women's suffrage some decades later, in answer to those, including John Bright, who would deny this basic right: 'They did not say then that women should be confined to their houses (cheers). They got them to work, and they got them to come and sell, and turn merchants in public places.'[17]

The Anti-Corn Law League provided middle-class women in Britain with one of their earliest opportunities for, and experience of, political campaigning. In its support they turned to many of the campaign methods they had first put to use a decade earlier in the abolition movement, for example the collection of petitions and fund-raising through bazaars which they also supplied with hand-made goods for sale. Not surprisingly, therefore, the early 1840s was also a time when women in this circle began to discuss women's rights. Priscilla Bright established something of a political salon in Rochdale, where this question was discussed alongside the other radical causes to which she and her circle of family and friends were committed. Frederick Douglass was a guest at one of these occasions, when 'he would not be convinced' about votes for women, though he subsequently changed his views. Thomas Carlyle left an altogether sardonic account of his attendance at one of these soirées. Here he 'communicated large masses of my views to the Brights and Brightesses, and shook peaceable Brightdom as with a passing earthquake'. Priscilla Bright for her part 'gave vent with all the moral courage I possessed' to rebut his ridiculing of the Quaker humanitarian causes to which she and her circle were committed.[18]

It was at this time, too, that Elizabeth Cady Stanton formed her first friendships with some members of this extended kinship circle. The World Anti-Slavery Convention met in London in 1840, where one of the American delegates was Henry Stanton, whom Elizabeth Cady had just married. Their visit to England was to combine both a wedding tour and anti-slavery campaigning, and one of the families with whom they stayed during their travels was the Priestmans of Newcastle. As the standard histories attest, this visit was also to mark the beginnings of Elizabeth Cady Stanton's subsequent commitment to women's rights, and her momentous friendship with another of the American delegates, Lucretia Mott. Lucretia Mott, alongside a number of other women, had been selected as a delegate by the Garrisonian wing of the American abolition movement, that section which eschewed pragmatic politics, compromise and gradualism in favour of the exertion of 'moral force' in pursuit of the absolute, immediate and uncompensated end to slave-holding.

The encouragement that the Garrisonians gave women abolitionists to speak in public had been one of the issues which had finally precipitated a formal split within the American movement, only shortly before the London convention. The presence of women in the Garrisonian delegation was to prove equally disruptive there. The British organisers insisted that their invitation had been intended only for men. British clerics instructed the convention on the biblical authority for excluding women from such a role. In the event the American women delegates were not allowed to join the main body in the convention proceedings, but had to sit separately from the male delegates in a gallery. In protest at this treatment, William Lloyd Garrison himself refused to participate in the business of the convention.[19] Elizabeth Cady Stanton was among the far more numerous group of women who attended without any official standing, but who were outraged both at the treatment accorded Lucretia Mott and her colleagues, and at the attitudes to women among male abolitionists which the controversy had revealed. These were the circumstances in which her friendship with Lucretia Mott was forged, a friendship which also led to her introduction to the work of Mary Wollstonecraft.[20] The two women were eventually able to meet again in 1848, during a visit by Lucretia Mott to upstate New York for a Quaker annual meeting. Their reunion became the occasion for the Seneca Falls convention on women's rights, and the drafting of the Declaration of Sentiments, the original manifesto of the women's movement in America.

Kathryn Kish Sklar has recently provided a very fine comparative analysis of the impact of this convention on the formation of a women's movement in each country. This argues that its differing outcomes in Britain and America reflected two distinct 'women's political cultures', political cultures which themselves reflected the different political contexts in which women abolitionists had to work, and the varying 'opportunity structures' for political expression available to American and British women.[21] Certainly, the impact of events at the Anti-Slavery Convention was altogether less clear-cut among British women abolitionists, though many who were to become prime movers on women's rights in Britain were present. Elizabeth Cady Stanton herself was particularly struck by the comparative conservatism of British abolitionists, and most especially of the English Quakers, at least in comparison to Hicksite Quakers like Lucretia Mott.[22] John Bright, for example, expressed his disapproval of the adoption of public roles by American women, and never became a reliable supporter of women's rights.[23]

Nonetheless, the convention had established friendships between British and American women abolitionists which were subsequently to form a basis for links between the American and British women's movement, most especially among the Quakers who frequently provided hospitality for the visiting Americans.[24] William Lloyd Garrison and Frederick Douglass, too, formed life-long friendships among this circle, which also provided subsequently some of the earliest converts to the Garrisonian approach to abolition, including Priscilla Bright McLaren and the younger Priestman sisters, Anna Maria and Mary.[25]

This was an approach which refused to acknowledge pragmatism in politics. Instead, it held to a forceful and uncompromising expression of the humanitarian principles on which they based their demand, calling for the immediate and uncompensated end to slave-holding. It was a case, which by extension, also supported the involvement of women in public life, and women's civil rights, despite the notoriety and dissension which it created for the abolition movement. It was an approach which Elizabeth Cady Stanton was also to apply in campaigning for women's rights. Equally, by the time Elizabeth Cady Stanton returned to Britain in the 1880s, the women friends she had made on her first visit were to be found among the most advanced and venerated pioneers of women's rights in Britain.[26]

The period following the abolition of slavery, coinciding as it did with the election of a reforming government in Britain, and more especially with the campaign for a new Reform Bill, saw the rapid emergence of women of the Bright circle into leading roles in the women's movement. By this time the original sisterhood which included Priscilla Bright, Margaret Bright Lucas, Margaret Tanner, Anna Maria Priestman and Mary Priestman had been extended by the marriage of a younger brother, Jacob Bright, to Ursula Mellor, daughter of a wealthy Liverpool merchant. It was enlarged also by the coming into adulthood of daughters and nieces of this circle, notably Agnes McLaren, Priscilla Bright McLaren's step-daughter, and her nieces Lilias and Anne Frances Ashworth (daughters of her sister, Sophia Bright, who had died young), together with Helen Priestman Bright, whom she still regarded almost as her own daughter. Helen Priestman Bright also ensured the extension of this circle into a third generation. In 1866 she married William Stephens Clark, the son of a Quaker shoe-manufacturing family in Somerset which had also played an active part locally in the temperance and abolition movements. Several of her children were to continue the role of this circle in providing leadership for the women's movement well into the twentieth century.

The late 1860s also saw other male relatives of this circle join John Bright in the House of Commons, notably his brother Jacob Bright, and his brother-in-law, Duncan McLaren. In subsequent decades, the sons of Duncan and Priscilla Bright McLaren, Charles and Walter, were to be added to their number. Both married into families with well-established links to the women's movement: Charles married Laura Pochin, whose mother had written one of the earliest women's rights pamphlets, and whose father had chaired one of the first public meetings calling for women's suffrage; Walter married Eva Muller, whose sister Henrietta Muller was also prominent in radical women's rights circles. Both Laura and Eva McLaren became leading figures in the women's movement in the last decades of the nineteenth century.

Priscilla Bright McLaren and Ursula Bright now spent much of each year in London, becoming part of a radical political coterie there. The outlook of these Radical–Liberals drew especially on the ideas of John Stuart Mill, who had also been elected to Parliament in these years. Aubrey House, the home of Clementia and Peter Taylor, another Radical MP, became its focus. It was in the library of Aubrey House that the first petition for women's suffrage was pasted up for Mill to lay before the House of Commons. Several members of the Bright family circle subscribed to the

London committee which had organised this petition, including Lilias Ashworth, Anna Maria Priestman, Ursula Bright, Margaret Tanner, and Margaret Bright Lucas.[27] The goal at this point was to secure an amendment to the forthcoming Reform Bill which would establish the principle of sexual equality in the franchise laws. These political radicals soon found themselves at odds with the more conservative among the leadership of the women's movement, most notably Emily Davies. Very soon they came to replace this leadership, as figures like Emily Davies withdrew to concentrate on other campaigns.[28] Clementia Taylor took over from her as the secretary of the London Society. Ursula and Jacob Bright came to the fore in the leadership of the influential Manchester Society, while Priscilla Bright McLaren was a key figure in the formation of an Edinburgh Society, and the Priestman sisters in Bristol, the Ashworth sisters in Bath, and Helen Priestman Bright Clark in Somerset helped establish the Bristol and West of England Society.

These Radical–Liberal women among the Bright circle shared an extensive outlook on women's rights. They lent their support also, for example, to the movement for improved schooling and access to higher education for their sex, and for women's access to training for the professions. Among their number Agnes McLaren, after several years of suffrage speaking and organising, turned her attention in the early 1870s to the campaign to establish medical training for women at Edinburgh University. She herself was among the earliest women students there, and subsequently qualified as a doctor, as did Anne Clark, sister-in-law of Helen Priestman Bright Clark. Members of this circle became increasingly preoccupied also, however, with more contentious questions which centred on sexual relations between men and women. The marriage laws had been a source of concern among women's rights advocates since Barbara Leigh Smith established the first committee to work for their reform in the 1850s. With the commencement of a forceful campaign for women's suffrage, however, the issue took on a fresh urgency. According to the doctrine of coverture, the legal personality of women became subsumed after marriage under that of husbands, and with this loss went also their capacity to hold real property. Such property remained the qualification for enfranchisement in Britain, even within the provisions of the new Reform Bill.[29]

Conservative advocates of women's suffrage such as Emily Davies sought, for that reason, to exclude married women from the suffrage demand. This was the source of some of the tensions in the late 1860s which led her to withdraw from any active role in suffrage organisations.

With the support of John Stuart Mill, Radical–Liberal suffragists were able to insist on a compromise formulation of the demand which argued in terms of sexual equality. This effectively excluded married women because of the existing law relating to married women's property rights, but such a formulation at least gave no sanction to the doctrine of coverture.[30] It was this situation which encouraged Radical–Liberal suffragists to begin in 1867 a parallel demand for reform of the law relating to married women's property. Members of the Manchester Suffrage Society provided the lead, including Ursula and Jacob Bright, Elizabeth Wolstenholme, who now became secretary of the Married Women's Property Committee, and Lydia Becker, secretary of the Manchester Society, who now became in addition the treasurer of the new committee. In this effort they again had the support of John Stuart Mill, and his step-daughter and amanuensis, Helen Taylor.

But even Mill found the approach of those he now dubbed 'the Bright and Becker set' too confrontational when they became closely associated with a further cause taken up by Radical–Liberal suffragists in 1870, the campaign for the repeal of the Contagious Diseases Acts.[31] This series of three measures passed during the 1860s sought to control the incidence of venereal disease within the defence forces, by bringing under compulsory medical surveillance those women identified by police as prostitutes.[32] Such legislation offended Radical–Liberal opinion because it entailed an assault on the civil liberties of women in garrison towns and naval ports, unequal treatment between men and women (the male clients of prostitutes were not brought under a similar surveillance), and a double standard of morality which condoned illicit male sexual expression while punishing women for exercising a similar freedom, and did so with considerable severity (women who did not comply with the requirements of the acts might face prison sentences with hard labour). Mill himself opposed the legislation. But he objected to any association between the cause of repeal and the demand for women's enfranchisement. His own double standards with regard to 'strong-minded women' are evident in this objection to the new campaign, which he attacked for introducing to the women's movement 'common vulgar motives and tactics'.[33]

Though Josephine Butler provided charismatic leadership for the new campaign, it was provincial Radical–Liberal suffragists who prompted her to take on the role, and members of the Bright circle who undertook much of the day-to-day management of the Ladies' National Association for the Repeal of the Contagious Diseases Acts (LNA). Josephine Butler later recalled her initial consultation with Margaret Tanner and Mary

Priestman: 'So gentle, so Quakerly, yet convinced that we three poor women must raise the country.' In the subsequent campaigns Margaret Tanner and Mary Priestman undertook the financial and secretarial work of the new society, while Anna Maria Priestman, Ursula Bright, Priscilla Bright McLaren, and her sister Margaret Bright Lucas all took an active part in the work of the LNA, and remained close and fervent supporters of Josephine Butler when she directed her attentions to the organisation of an international campaign against the state regulation of prostitution in the 1880s. Younger generations of this circle were also brought into the campaigns.[34]

In these various ways, then, the women of the Bright family circle had emerged as an effective political network in the late 1860s and early 1870s. It was one which had played a significant role in establishing a national suffrage movement by bringing into existence influential provincial societies to act as a counterweight to the more moderate leadership which initially prevailed in the London society. In the early 1870s the Manchester Society, under the leadership of Ursula and Jacob Bright and Lydia Becker, had promoted the formation of a Central Committee of the National Society for Women's Suffrage. Radical–Liberal suffragists, including Clementia Taylor, had already departed from the London Society because of Mill's dominant presence within it, and his opposition to any association with the agitation against the Contagious Diseases Acts. The establishment of the Central Committee, with Jacob Bright as its convenor, allowed the provincial societies a greater voice in the direction of the suffrage campaign nationally. It also gave more effective expression to the Radical–Liberal outlook on women's rights, as well as a base for an alternative leadership for the suffrage movement, and the women's movement more generally. Millicent Garrett Fawcett tried to broker a compromise between the provincial and metropolitan leaderships of the movement, but to no avail. In the event she chose to stay loyal to Mill and the London Society. Under Mill's leadership this attempted to maintain a separate existence from the Central Committee for the next few years, only weakening yet further its own influence on the direction of the movement nationally.[35]

Members of the Bright circle figured largely in an alternative leadership, given their prominence in the provincial suffrage societies, and in a number of other campaigns, notably the Married Women's Property Committee and the Ladies' National Association. They shared a Radical–Liberal outlook on women's subjection which took them beyond a search for formal equality of the sexes. The revelation of the blindness, even hostility, to women's claims among their own male kin and radical friends only served to reinforce the sense of sisterly solidarity which such women felt with the less fortunate of their sex.[36] The unsympathetic views of John Bright himself were one of the greatest burdens which the women of the Bright circle had to carry. This national figure, generally revered for his nobility of soul, and deeply loved by most of his female relations, might privately dismiss women's demand for the vote thus: 'My gardener says that there is nothing he dislikes so much in his poultry yard as a "crowing hen" and men-women are not a pleasant addition to our social arrangements.' Priscilla Bright McLaren's devotion to her brother remained lifelong. But on his death she sadly concluded, in writing to his equally devoted eldest daughter, Helen Priestman Bright Clark: '. . . he could worship what he called charming women, but he could *never* bear women to assert themselves'.[37]

The Bright circle and Elizabeth Cady Stanton's participation in the British women's suffrage movement

When Elizabeth Cady Stanton returned to Britain for a visit in 1882, one of her goals was to renew old friendships, and to secure introductions to all the leading reformers of the day. This was easily achieved through her earlier links with the Priestman family. Letters from other members of the Bright circle were also waiting for her on her arrival. Much visiting followed, and an interview with John Bright himself was soon arranged. Elizabeth Cady Stanton appears to have been in a mellow mood on that occasion, enjoying the courtesy shown her by this leading world statesman, and in her turn forbearing to raise the question of women's suffrage, as his anxious female relatives had advised.[38] Besides this meeting, her diary for her stay indicates a progression from the home of one member of this circle to another over the following year.

Elizabeth Cady Stanton's eldest daughter had married an Englishman during this visit, and was now Harriot Stanton Blatch. When Harriot became pregnant, her mother extended her stay until the birth the following year of a daughter, Nora, named after Ibsen's heroine. When the time came to return to the United States, Elizabeth Cady Stanton wrote to the Priestman sisters, recalling 'those merry chats with peals of laughter' which they had enjoyed together. She also expressed the hope that her British friends would help her daughter find a role within the women's movement in her adopted home. Priscilla Bright McLaren commiserated with her on the parting that was to come, and made her this undertaking: 'We will all promise to love your daughter – I may be far from her, but my heart will hold her as a treasure left to us by you – and having her with us we have not altogether lost you.'[39]

The period of Elizabeth Cady Stanton's first return to Britain had been a critical one, with a new Reform Bill coming before Parliament, and intensifying tensions within the women's movement itself. At her insistent urging, Susan B. Anthony had joined her in Europe in February 1883 to lend what aid she might to the cause. At the heart of the dissension among British suffragists was the question of the position of married women. Lydia Becker had broken with her radical colleagues in the mid-1870s, when she became convinced of the need to exclude married women from the suffrage demand, and to suspend the campaign for married women's property rights, simply on grounds of political pragmatism. Ursula Bright, with other radical suffragists had resisted these developments, and she had helped stage a re-invigorated campaign to reform the married women's property laws.[40] One of the first public events in which Elizabeth Cady Stanton had participated on her return to Britain had been a meeting to celebrate the passage of a new Married Women's Property Act in 1882, which considerably extended women's rights over whatever property they brought to a marriage. Sadly, however, this bill had been so amended during its passage through Parliament as to leave intact the doctrine of coverture. As a consequence, the question of whether or not to exclude married women from the suffrage demand remained a live issue among British suffragists.

Ursula Bright made this celebratory meeting the occasion to state her clear determination to see married women included in the suffrage demand.[41] When it became known that the proposed women's suffrage amendment to the forthcoming Reform Bill explicitly excluded married women, Ursula Bright organised for a move against this to come from the platform at a major suffrage demonstration in London. Elizabeth Cady Stanton was to be present at this demonstration, and Ursula Bright sought her support in this move.[42] When it failed, she sought to organise the emerging opposition to the exclusion of married women from the amendment.

Elizabeth Cady Stanton was then asked to consult with the dissidents at a protest meeting organised by Ursula Bright, and it was at this point that she made a direct intervention in the British suffrage movement.[43] She advised British suffragists to ask for the vote for all women, both married and unmarried, and attempted to mobilise her friendship network among the Bright circle in support of this position. To begin with many even among this advanced circle remained cautious. Priscilla Bright

McLaren, for one, sought to make Elizabeth Cady Stanton more aware of the difficulties confronting the British women's movement in the conservative society in which they lived. But within a few months even she was expressing exasperation with the central leadership. Though she had no time for the 'cat and dog work' which continued between Lydia Becker and Ursula Bright, she now firmly declared that in future: 'I shall go in strong for married women'.[44]

The campaign mounted by the official leadership of the suffrage movement for a women's suffrage amendment to the Reform Bill was by any standards a feeble one. It so frustrated various members of the Bright circle, even those who felt Ursula Bright's stance to be overly confrontational and divisive, that they defied the views of Lydia Becker, and undertook a series of more forceful interventions in the public debate. Instead of secret machinations among parliamentary cliques in the capital, they sought to engage in a large-scale popular campaign throughout the country, and direct confrontations with leading members of the government. Priscilla Bright McLaren was among those who helped organise a series of impressive suffrage demonstrations in the largest provincial cities. For her part, Helen Priestman Bright Clark joined in an attempt to secure a suffragist deputation of leading Liberal women to the prime minister, Gladstone. She also used a major Reform demonstration in Leeds, presided over by John Bright, to face down her father on the question, and to establish the extent of support for women's suffrage among the rank-and-file supporters of the Liberal Party. Susan B. Anthony travelled north to enjoy the spectacle. Anna Maria Priestman meanwhile had formed the first Women's Liberal Association, in Bristol in 1881, at least in part because of her frustration with the weak lead being offered by the suffrage movement itself at this critical time for their cause.[45] But all these efforts proved fruitless, and women were once again left out of the Reform Act which eventually passed in 1884. The suffrage movement was left bitterly divided, and organisational fracture followed in the succeeding five years, reinforced by the splits which occurred in the Liberal Party itself over the question of home rule for Ireland.[46]

Elizabeth Cady Stanton had enjoyed good relations with all sections of the suffrage leadership during her first return visit to Britain, despite these controversies. By the time of her second return in 1886, however, she was far more closely aligned with the dissidents. The official leadership now refused to send a delegation over to America for the first international convention of suffragists. The event had been planned to mark the fortieth anniversary of the Seneca Falls convention, a celebration which Elizabeth Cady Stanton and Susan B. Anthony had been working for since their 1883 stay in Europe. Once again, Elizabeth Cady Stanton looked to her network among the women of the Bright circle for support, and a small delegation of British suffragists was quickly put together by Priscilla Bright McLaren and the Priestman sisters.[47]

By the time of her last visit to Britain in 1890, Elizabeth Cady Stanton was publicly associated with one of the dissident organisations which had come out of the fracturing of the suffrage movement there in the previous few years. This was the Women's Franchise League (WFL), the first suffrage organisation to be formed to promote a demand for women's suffrage which expressly included married women. Harriot Stanton Blatch had been among its founding members, and believed its formation to have been a direct outcome of her mother's intervention in the British movement over this question. Elizabeth Cady Stanton herself had become a corresponding member within the first year of its formation. And by the time of this last visit to Britain, Ursula Bright had moved into its leadership.[48]

Militancy and the continuities of suffrage history

The WFL remained a small and loosely organised body. Its historical significance lies not in its size or scale of influence, however, but in certain continuities within the British movement of which it is evidence. These continuities entailed a looking back to some of the origins of radical suffragism as well as indicating some new directions for the suffrage movement which were to find fullest expression in the early militancy of the twentieth-century women's movement. To begin with, the WFL harked back directly to the Garrisonian legacy. William Lloyd Garrison the younger was one of the main speakers at its inaugural meeting, and emphasised the Garrisonian view of the reformer's role. Such an approach was fully evident in the intransigent stance which the WFL was to take on the question of the inclusion of married women in the demand. During the 1890s it actively, sometimes abrasively, opposed compromise of women's suffrage measures which would, in fact, have enfranchised some married women, while not explicitly including them as a category to be enfranchised. Its most considerable achievement was the part it played in securing the local government vote for all qualified married women under the Local Government Act of 1894. By this measure the application of the doctrine of coverture to the franchise laws ceased to be a real issue, and the way was open for the reunification of the suffrage movement in

1897 under the umbrella organisation, the National Union of Women's Suffrage Societies.[49]

The very forcefulness of the WFL refusal ever to modify its central demand looked forward to the militant stance which the WSPU was to adopt under the leadership of Emmeline Pankhurst. Both Emmeline Pankhurst and Harriot Stanton Blatch served their suffrage leadership apprenticeships on the Executive Committee of the WFL, working alongside Ursula Bright.[50] The strategies each was to adopt in the new organisations they formed subsequently followed the past practices of the WFL, most especially in emphasising the need to secure publicity for their demand, however unfavourable, to encourage popular interest in the issue, and to attempt to build alliances between the middle-class women's movement and working-class women's groups.

For her part, Elizabeth Cady Stanton was brought in touch with new directions in British politics, most particularly, perhaps, through her daughter's membership of the Fabian Society. She wrote to the Priestman sisters recommending Karl Pearson's *Ethics of Free Thought* to them, especially his account of 'matriarchates' and the history of men's relationship to their children, promising: 'we will analyse these sons of Adam . . . in the meantime sharpen up your intellectual tweezers that we may dissect them from the marrow of their bones to the outermost cuticle of their skins, from the grey matter in their brains to the shortest hair on their crowns'.[51]

Other continuities are also evident in the early forms of militant activity in Britain, most especially in tax resistance. This was a tactic which was effectively used by another of the early leaders of the WSPU, Dora Montefiore, who claimed to have learned it from Quaker friends, almost certainly the Priestman sisters.[52] They themselves had attempted to introduce the tactic to the women's movement several decades before, though without success. Similarly, militant demonstrators originally sought arrest and imprisonment by token acts of violence such as tapping policemen on the face, as a means of bringing attention to their demands. Here again is evidence of the Quaker legacy in women's social protest, one based on principles of passive resistance and civil disobedience. It was only gradually that such an approach was supplanted in the activities of the WSPU by more sensational kinds of protest, as Dora Montefiore and other advocates of what was sometimes referred to as 'constitutional militancy' were expelled from its leadership.[53] Even then Anna Maria and Mary Priestman, together with other members of the Bright circle, including Ursula Bright, continued to offer open support for the new, 'militant' style of campaigning.[54] Meanwhile 'constitutional militancy' was kept alive in organisations like the Women's Freedom League, the Tax Resistance League, and the New Constitutional Society, and here again are to be found in evidence those members of the Bright circle, like Alice Clark, Sarah Bancroft Clark, and Kate Thomasson who felt unable to accept the newer, more violent forms of militancy adopted by the WSPU.[55]

Harriot Stanton Blatch also organised a more restrained form of militancy when she returned to the United States to live in the first years of the twentieth century. But the operation of this transatlantic network continued in the US tours she helped organise for leading British militants like Annie Cobden Sanderson and Emmeline Pankhurst.[56] Such evidence, then, suggests that militancy did not, at least initially, entail a complete rupture with earlier phases of the suffrage movement, but that it drew on pre-existing radical currents within that movement, and was able to mobilise to good effect long-established transatlantic networks.

Previously, militancy has generally been read backwards from its endpoint in the extreme violence of arson and bombing of the 1912–14 years, rather than the radical suffragism of the 1890s from which it emerged. It is this focus which has sometimes led earlier historians to seek explanations for militancy in personal or social pathology. It has also led them to pay far less attention to the early years of militancy and the quite different tactics of civil disobedience and moral suasion which were then at its heart.[57] If, on the other hand, attention is directed back to the circles within which Emmeline Pankhurst and Harriot Stanton Blatch served their apprenticeships in the suffrage movement, the origins and nature of militancy appear more complex. From this viewpoint it is possible to recognise its roots in a radical tradition which reached back to the abolition movement, the Anti-Corn Law League, and non-conformist opposition to an established church, a tradition which emphasised civil disobedience, passive resistance, and moral suasion, and which, in Britain at least, drew especially on Quaker experience and long-standing tactics such as tax resistance. The findings presented here suggest also that some modifications are necessary in the current frameworks operating in American suffrage history. Militancy no longer appears purely as a British initiative, imported through the experience of figures like Harriot Stanton Blatch, Alice Paul and Lucy Burns in the British movement. Instead, it emerges as the outcome of a cross-national impulse, one which both Elizabeth Cady Stanton and Harriot Stanton Blatch helped foster in Britain, and one for which Harriot Stanton Blatch established a somewhat different form of expression in the United States.

1 See, for example, Anne Morley & Liz Stanley, *The Life and Death of Emily Wilding Davison*, Women's Press, London, 1988; Johanna Alberti, *Beyond Suffrage: Feminism in War and Peace*, Macmillan, London, 1989; Philippa Levine, *Feminist Lives in Victorian Britain*, Blackwell, Oxford, 1990.

2 See, for example, Andrew Rosen, *Rise Up Women: The Militant Campaign of the Women's Social and Political Union 1903-14*, Routledge & Kegan Paul, London, 1974; Sandra Stanley Holton, *Feminism and Democracy: Women's Suffrage and Reform Politics 1900-18*, Cambridge Univ. Press, New York, 1986.

3 See, for example, the essays in Jane Rendall, ed, *Equal or Different: Women's Politics, 1800-1914*, Blackwell, Oxford, 1987; Sandra Stanley Holton, 'The Suffragist and the "Average Woman"', *Women's History Review (WHR)* 1/1, 1992, 7-24.

4 See, for example, Diane Kirkby, *Alice Henry, the Power of Voice and Pen: the Life of an Australian-American Reformer*, Cambridge Univ. Press, Cambridge, 1991; Ellen DuBois, 'Woman Suffrage and the Left: an International Socialist-Feminist Perspective', *New Left Review*, 186, 1991, 20-45; Jo Vellacott, 'A Place for Pacifism and Transnationalism in Feminist Theory: the Early Work of the Women's International League for Peace and Freedom', *WHR*, 2/1, 1993, 23-56; Barbara Caine, 'Vida Goldstein and the English Militant Campaign', *WHR*, 2/3, 1993, 363-5.

5 This circle has only recently begun to receive recognition in accounts of the nineteenth-century women's movement; see, for example, Patricia Hollis, *Ladies Elect: Women in English Local Government 1865-1914*, Clarendon, Oxford, 1987, 53, 143; Levine, *Feminist Lives*, 5, 17-18, 28, 33, 35, 94. Among earlier historians, Bertha Mason, *The Story of the Women's Suffrage Movement*, Sheratt & Hughes, London, 1912.

6 Elizabeth Cady Stanton, *Eighty Years and More (1815-1897): Reminiscences of Elizabeth Cady Stanton*, repr. Source Book Press, New York, 1970, first published in 1898; Theodore Stanton & Harriot Stanton Blatch, eds, *Elizabeth Cady Stanton as Revealed in her Letters, Diary and Reminiscences*, 2 vols, Harper, New York, 1922; Ida Husted Harper, *The Life and Work of Susan B. Anthony*, 2 vols, reprint, Arno Press, New York, 1969, first published in 1898, which also reproduces parts of the diaries and letters of its subject.

7 My attention was originally drawn to this topic while researching the life of the pioneer women's historian, Alice Clark, among the Millfield Papers which form part of the private Clark family archive (CA), at C. & J. Clark, Street, Somerset, and which contain the correspondence of three generations of women who were part of the Bright circle, including Anna Maria Priestman, Mary Priestman, Margaret Tanner, Priscilla Bright McLaren, Helen Priestman Bright Clark, Esther Clark Clothier, Alice Clark, Hilda Clark, Margaret Clark Gillett and Sarah Bancroft Clark. I am grateful to Richard Clark for permission to draw on this collection of papers for the research presented here, and to Jean Brook, Museum & Archives, C. & J. Clark, for her assistance during this research. Much of the two American suffragists' correspondence has recently become more widely available through the Elizabeth Cady Stanton–Susan B. Anthony microfilm project, now based at Douglass College, State University of New Jersey, Rutgers, and I am grateful to Patricia Holland for providing me with relevant photocopies from this microfilm collection. Copies of those letters found from Elizabeth Cady Stanton and Susan B. Anthony to the Priestman sisters, and to Alice Clark are now held by the microfilm project at Rutgers.

8 Ellen Carol DuBois, *Feminism and Suffrage: The Emergence of an Independent Women's Movement in America 1848-69*, Cornell Univ. Press, Ithaca, 1978, 38.

9 See John Somervell, *Isaac and Rachel Wilson, Quakers of Kendal 1714-1785*, Swarthmore Press, Swarthmore, 1924 for an account of Elizabeth Priestman's mother and grandmother.

10 Keith Robbins, *John Bright*, Routledge & Kegan Paul, London, 1979, 19; Mary Priestman to Anna Maria Priestman, 12 July 1849, Box 14, Millfield Papers, CA.

11 George Macauley Trevelyan, *The Life of John Bright*, Constable, London, 1913, 34-43; John Travis Mills, *John Bright and the Quakers*, 2 vols, Methuen, London, 1935, vol. 1, 383-94.

12 Rachel [Priestman] to Sophia [Bright], 23 Nov. 1841, Box 14; Anna Maria Priestman to Margaret Priestman, 30 May 1844, Box 17, both Millfield Papers, CA; Priscilla Bright McLaren to Mary Martindale, 6 May 1845, cit. Mills, *Bright*, vol. 1, 299-30.

13 Cit. Trevelyan, *Bright*, 43.

14 On shared philanthropic and Anti-Corn Law League interests, see Rachel [Priestman] to Sophia [Bright], 23 Nov. 1841; Mary Priestman to Anna Maria Priestman, 1 Jan. 1842, 28 Nov. 1842, both Box 14; Priscilla Bright to Margaret Priestman, 18 May 1846, 20 Oct. 1846, both Box 44; Anna Maria Priestman's diary of her visit to London for the Anti-Corn Law League Bazaar at Covent

Garden, May 1845, Box 11; on their shared interest in abolition, see, for example, Anna Maria Priestman to Priscilla Bright McLaren, 9 Dec. 1862, Box 17; Anna Maria Priestman to Margaret Tanner, 7 July 1864, Box 17, all Millfield Papers, CA.

15   Mills, *Bright*, vol. 1, 139; Trevelyan, *Bright*, 35; Robbins, *Bright*, 33, 45, 66-7; Charles McLaren, 'Reminiscences of John Bright', Newspaper Cuttings, vol CC 160, Friends House Library, London.

16   The importance of the Anti-Corn Law League as a training for women's rights campaigners is a commonplace in the British literature, see for example H. J. B. Heath, *Margaret Bright Lucas: The Life Story of a 'British Woman'....the Sister of the Rt. Hon. John Bright...*, London, 1890, 14.

17   Cit. 'Women's Suffrage: Public Meeting in Edinburgh 17 Jan. 1870, Queen Street Hall', Edinburgh National Society for Women's Suffrage, Edinburgh, [1870]. For further evidence on women's role in the League, especially in fund-raising see J. B. MacKie, *The Life and Work of Duncan McLaren*, 2 vols, Thomas Nelson & Sons, London & Edinburgh, vol. 1, 244-5.

18   See reminiscences of this salon in Priscilla Bright McLaren to Mrs Mills, n.d. and Thomas Carlyle to Jane Welsh Carlyle, 13 Sept. 1847, both cit. Mills, *Bright*, vol 1, 28-9; also Isabella Petrie Mills for the record of Frederick Douglass's visit and the recollection that 'Slavery, temperance and the need of the vote for women were the subjects most often studied and discussed' on these occasions, cit. Mason, *History*, 26

19   Elizabeth Cady Stanton, Susan B. Anthony & Matilda Joslyn Gage, eds, *History of Woman Suffrage*, vol. 1, repr. Arno Press, New York, 1970, first published 1881, 50-62.

20   Stanton, *Eighty Years*, 82-5; 148-51.

21   Kathryn Kish Sklar, '"Women Who Speak for an Entire Nation": American and British Women Compared at the World Anti-Slavery Convention, London, 1840', *Pacific Historical Review*, 59, 1990, 453-99, esp. 455-6, 498. See also my 'Educating Women into Rebellion: Elizabeth Cady Stanton and the Creation of a Transatlantic Network of Radical Suffragists', *American Historical Review*, 99, 1994 (forthcoming), for a further comparison of the political contexts in which suffragists worked in the two countries, and Clare Midgley, 'Anti-Slavery and Feminism in Nineteenth Century Britain', *Gender and History*, 5/3, 1993, 343-62 for an examination of the British case in particular.

22   Stanton, *Eighty Years*, 79-83.

23   Robbins, *Bright*, 23.

24   Clare Taylor, ed, *British and American Abolitionists: an Episode in Transatlantic Understanding*, Edinburgh Univ. Press, Edinburgh, 1974, brings together a valuable selection of correspondence between abolitionists in the two countries.

25   Mary Priestman to Anna Maria Priestman, 15 Oct. 1846, Box 14, Millfield Papers, CA; C. Duncan Rice, *The Scots Abolitionists*, Louisiana Univ. Press, Baton Rouge, 1981, 48, 178-9, identifies Priscilla Bright McLaren as amongst the British Garrisonians. See also Midgley, 'Anti-Slavery', 347, for the gradual extension of the Garrisonian approach among women abolitionists in Britain.

26   Sklar, 'Women Who Speak', 485-9, 466, discusses the different significance of such 'immediatism' in each country, and examines also the analogies which Lucretia Mott, for example, made between the social position of women and slaves. DuBois, *Feminism*, 33-8 , argues that Elizabeth Cady Stanton was especially important in developing such an approach to reform among women's rights activists in the United States. I also discuss the significance of the Garrisonian approach for the British movement in 'Educating Women into Rebellion'.

27   London National Society for Women's Suffrage, circular of 6 July 1867, which lists the previous year's subscribers, enclosed with letter from Clementia Taylor, 6 July 1867 to an unknown recipient, Box 24, Millfield Papers, CA; Florence M. Gladstone, *Aubrey House, Kensington 1698-1920*, Arthur L. Humphrys, 1922, 44-50.

28   On the early divisions among British suffragists, see A. P. W. Robson, 'The Founding of the National Society for Women's Suffrage', *Canadian Journal of History*, 8, 1973, 1-22; Barbara Caine, 'John Stuart Mill and the English Women's Movement', *Historical Studies*, 18, 1982, 52-67 and 'Feminism, Suffrage and the Nineteenth Century Women's Movement', *Women's Studies International Forum*, 5, 1982, 537-50.

29   Sklar, 'Women Who Speak', 479-83, suggests that the varying qualifications for the franchise in the US and Britain 'channelled women's energies differently', especially in the case of Quaker women, whose male kin had also been disfranchised until 1832 because of their religious nonconformity.

30   I examine the significance of this issue for the Radical-Liberal perspective on women's rights in more detail in 'Educating Women into Rebellion'. Jane Rendall, 'Citizenship, Culture and Civilisation: the Languages of British Suffragists, 1866-1874' in this volume explores the varieties within Liberal thought on citizenship more widely, and see also Eugenio Biagini, *Liberty, Retrenchment and Reform:*

Popular Liberalism in the Age of Gladstone, 1860-80, Cambridge Univ. Press, Cambridge, 1992 and Catherine Hall, *White, Male and Middle-Class,* Polity Press, Oxford, 1992, which each emphasise the importance of notions of independence in radical thought.

31   Cit. Caine, 'John Stuart Mill', 60.

32   Judith Walkowitz, *Prostitution and Victorian Society: Women, Class and the State,* Cambridge Univ. Press, Cambridge, 1980.

33   John Stuart Mill to George Croom Robertson, 20 Oct. 1871, in John Stuart Mill, *Collected Works,* Frances E. Mineka & Dwight N. Lindley, eds, Toronto Univ. Press, Toronto, 1972, vol 17, 1816-7.

34   Josephine Butler cit., Walkowitz, *Prostitution,* 92. See Paul McHugh, *Prostitution and Victorian Social Reform,* Croom Helm, London, 1980, 169-72 for a more detailed account of the role of the Priestman sisters in the LNA.

35   Mill, *Works,* vol. 17, 1818 n. 2.

36   This is not to deny the undoubted limitations placed on such sisterhood by a sense of racial and moral superiority among middle-class women with regard to black and working-class women, see Hall, *White, Male,* 208, and Midgley, 'Anti-Slavery', 354-6 for more extended discussions of this point.

37   John Bright to Thorold Rogers, Priscilla Bright McLaren to Helen Priestman Bright Clark, both cit. Robbins, *Bright,* 214, 233 respectively.

38   Stanton & Blatch, *Stanton,* vol. 2, 197-8.

39   Elizabeth Cady Stanton to 'Widow and Spinsters' [the three Priestman sisters], 30 Oct. [1883], Box 23, Millfield Papers, CA; Priscilla Bright McLaren to Elizabeth Cady Stanton, 10 Nov. 1883, the Elizabeth Cady Stanton Papers, Vassar College Libraries, with my thanks for permission to quote this material.

40   I examine this issue in more depth in 'Free Love and Victorian Feminism: the Divers Matrimonials of Elizabeth Wolstenholme and Ben Elmy', *Victorian Studies,* 1994, (forthcoming).

41   Report of final meeting of the Married Women's Property Committee, *Journal of the Vigilance Association,* 15 Dec. 1882, 110; Mrs Jacob Bright, 'Letter of Mrs Jacob Bright...', n.d. [circa 1883], M50/2/20/2, Manchester Public Library Archive.

42   Ursula Bright to Elizabeth Cady Stanton, 7 July [1883], 'Elizabeth Cady Stanton Correspondence', a bound volume of typescript copies of her correspondence (henceforth ECSC), Douglass Library, the State Univ. of New Jersey, Rutgers. My thanks to the Douglass Library for permission to quote from this source, and to Keith Jones for background information on the collection.

43   Harper, *Anthony,* vol. 2, 567-8. Anthony herself was against any such intervention.

44   Stanton & Blatch, *Stanton,* vol. 2, 208-9; Priscilla Bright McLaren to Elizabeth Cady Stanton, 17 July 1883, ECSC; Priscilla Bright McLaren to Helen Priestman Bright Clark, 19 Jan. 1884, Box 36, Millfield Papers, CA. These events are discussed in more detail in my 'Educating Women'.

45   Anna Maria Priestman to Priscilla Bright McLaren, 28 Nov. 1883, Box 17; Alice Scatcherd to Anna Maria Priestman, 27 Oct. 1883, Box 22; Priscilla Bright McLaren to Helen Priestman Bright Clark, 9 Oct. 1883, Box 36, all CA; Helen Priestman Bright Clark, Millicent Garrett Fawcett, Priscilla Bright McLaren and I. M. S. Tod to William Ewart Gladstone, March 1884, M50/2/1/37, Manchester Public Library Archive.

46   I discuss these splits in more detail in 'Educating Women'.

47   Stanton, *Eighty Years,* 408; Elizabeth Cady Stanton to the Priestman sisters, 21, 26 Feb. 1888, Box 23, Millfield Papers, CA.

48   I discuss the Women's Franchise League more fully in 'Educating Women'.

49   For the optimistic reception which greeted this advance see Alice Clark to Esther Clark, 27 Nov. 1893, which also records that their aunt, Ursula Bright, had resisted the compromise which had brought this concession from the government. Sylvia Pankhurst, *The Suffragette Movement,* reprint, Virago, London, 1977, first published 1931, 116-8, also emphasises the significance of the achievement, but gives the credit for it to Ursula Bright.

50   Harriot Stanton Blatch & Alma Lutz, *Challenging Years: The Memoirs of Harriot Stanton Blatch,* G. P. Putnam's Sons, New York, 1940, 73.

51   Stanton to Miss Anna [Maria Priestman], 8 Sept. [1890], Box 23, Millfield Papers, CA.

52   Dora Montefiore, letter to the Editor, *Women's Signal,* 17 June 1897, 383. At this time she was working closely with Anna Maria Priestman in the Union of Practical Suffragists, which this Quaker veteran of the women's movement had formed as a ginger group within the Women's Liberal Federation

in an attempt to bring it to a firmer commitment to women's suffrage, see report of its first annual meeting, *Women's Signal*, 27 May 1897, 331.

53   Dora Montefiore, *From a Victorian to a Modern*, Archer, London, 1927, 72-84.

54   Anna Maria Priestman and Ursula Bright were among those who provided 'Special Messages from Notable Women' at a major WSPU rally in 1910, see *Votes for Women*, 17 June 1910, while Eva McLaren lauded 'the zeal and enthusiasm' of the militants at a Women's Liberal Federation annual meeting, *Votes for Women*, 14 May 1909. See also Florence E. Haig to Anna Maria Priestman, 24 Dec. n.d, Box 24; Alice Clark to the Priestman sisters, 18 July 1911, Box 75; Lilias Ashworth Hallett to Alice Clark, 26 Feb. 1907, Box 76, all Millfield Papers, CA.

55   Alice Clark was among those who resisted paying their taxes, for example, see *Daily News*, 1 March 1907, cutting, Box 76, Millfield Papers, CA. Margaret Kineton Parkes, 'The Tax Resistance Movement in Great Britain', n.p, n.d, tells the story of the Tax-Resistance League, but in general these organisations have received little attention.

56   Blatch & Lutz, *Challenging Years*, 99-100, 113-15.

57   See the very influential account in George Dangerfield, *The Strange Death of Liberal England*, Capricorn, New York, 1935 and compare with Stanley & Morley, *Emily Wilding Davison*; Sandra Stanley Holton, '"In Sorrowful Wrath": Suffrage Militancy and the Romantic Feminism of Emmeline Pankhurst', in Harold L. Smith, ed, *British Feminism in the Twentieth Century*, Edward Elgar, Aldershot, 1990, 7-24.

12

Early-Twentieth-Century Feminism in Political Context: A Comparative Look at Germany and the United States

NANCY F. COTT

Anyone investigating feminism at the turn of the twentieth century cannot fail to recognise that she or he is looking at an international movement, one in which ideas and tactics migrated from place to place as individuals in different countries travelled, looked for helpful models, and set up networks of reform. Modern women's movements in industrialised nations have shared many contours, although each has its own timing, intensities and internal conflicts. I intend to look here at the similarities and differences in the most radical phase of 'first-wave' feminism (the period just after 1900) in two countries, Germany and the United States, in an effort at comparative, if not yet international, history.[1]

In both Germany and the US at that time there were more than one, sometimes intersecting, more often contending movements of women in existence. In response to the economic, political and social transformations of the era, women organised by class, region, religion, ideology and interest as much as they organised as women. In the two nations a similar *range* appeared, including church women eager to protect social order and improve family life, wage-earning women striving for higher pay and better working conditions, socialist women organising for working-class power, some middle-class women most concerned for legal rights, education, and the vote, and others pursuing birth control or the social welfare of mothers and children. But the relative size and strength of these diverse groups (within the range) differed. The most striking contrast lies in the prominence of issues having to do with sex, reproduction, and the maternal body, in Germany. German women's outspokenness on these issues provided a model for the minority of women activists in the US who wanted to translate convictions about sexual emancipation into practice and policies, but who were rowing against the mainstream, where public discussion concerning political voice was the strong flow, and sexual emancipation was a small undercurrent.

The American nation and the German Empire

The US and Germany bear comparison, since they were both capitalist economic giants advancing in technological and industrial leadership. The US population was half as large again as that of the German Empire (about 92 million as compared to 63 million, in 1910), more ethnically and racially diverse but not as rigidly stratified by class and occupation. If economically comparable, the two nations were politically very different. Formally a representative democracy with popular elections for officials at local, state and federal levels, the political system in the US was dominated by two moderately liberal political parties that fielded candidates with only small competition from socialists and other political interest groups. By the late nineteenth century (as a legacy of the Civil War), the two parties' most salient affiliations were regional: the Democrats' stronghold was the South, and to a lesser extent the West, where agrarian interests were primary; the Republicans predominated in the industrialised Northeast, where the bulk of the nation's population resided, and so captured the national government. Manhood suffrage (with no property qualification) was the norm everywhere, but racism made a mockery of this in the South, where states imposed poll taxes and unfairly administered literacy requirements on purpose to deprive most African-Americans of their use of the ballot.

The German Empire was less consistent than the US in opening the door to representative politics through widespread voting. States (like Prussia) and some cities (like Hamburg) set their own requirements for voting for local offices, and several had steep property qualifications. The lower house of the Reichstag (the national parliament) was elected by manhood suffrage. Because of the absolutism of the Kaiser and his chancellor, however, the parliamentary body had comparatively little power over imperial policy. Numerous parties ran candidates for the Reichstag, and these were not regional but class-based parties, separately appealing to and answering the needs of the great landlords, the big industrialists, the liberal bourgeoisie, and blue-collar workers.[2]

German women thus not only lacked the vote, but lived in a country where property qualifications inhibited men's exercise of the franchise and where the authoritarianism of imperial policy could undermine the effectiveness of voting altogether. The paternalistic absolutism of the German government echoed through its system of family law. The Civil

Code (renewed in 1896 and 1900) declared the husband the decision-maker, the owner of his wife's property (though not her earnings), and guardian of the children. At this time in the US, married women in most states could maintain in their own names the property they brought into the marriage and also owned their income earned outside the home; upon the break-up of a marriage, courts usually credited mothers' parental prerogatives over fathers' (especially if young children were involved).[3]

Socialists' agenda for women

The largest number of women organised for the purpose of progressive political change in Germany were working class, gathered under the banner of the women's associations of the Social Democratic party (SPD); whereas the largest number in the US were middle class, gathered into reforming clubs, temperance and social welfare organisations, and suffrage groups. Despite the Reich's prohibition of the Socialist Party from 1878 to 1890, Germany produced the most powerful socialist movement in Europe in the subsequent twenty-five years; the SPD was the largest and fastest-growing party in the Reichstag before the Great War. The German socialist women's movement was characterised by a series of ironies. It gained strength despite absolute bans (passed in the mid-nineteenth century in Prussia, Bavaria and Saxony) on women's membership in political parties or attendance at public political meetings.[4] These prohibitions meant that socialists had to organise women separately from men and ostensibly non-politically, and that kind of woman-oriented organising proved to be very successful. The movement was especially Marxist, not only because the earlier anti-Socialist law scared away the wishy-washy, but also for the ironic reason that the illegality of political participation for women kept them out of the legislative arena where they might be in touch with non-socialist influence toward reformism. Also ironically, when in 1908 the ban on women's political activity in Prussia and elsewhere was lifted, the Socialist women's movement flourished in numbers but not in overall impact. The number of joiners shot up – from about 30,000 in 1908 to near 175,000 in 1914 – but women's autonomy, visibility and influence in the party relatively decreased, as a result of merging with men. After integration in 1908, Socialist women were underrepresented at the top levels of the party and regarded as secondary, shunted into social welfare work rather than sharing equally in policy decision-making.[5]

   Clara Zetkin, to whom the movement owed much of its strength and left orientation, was the principal leader of socialist women not only in Germany but in Europe. Under her prodding, the SPD as early as 1891 supported what it felt bourgeois liberalism ought to have already accomplished, namely the vote and equal civil rights for women, legal equality within marriage, removal of bars against women's admission to universities and professions, and an end to the double standard of sexual morality, as well as industrial regulation and maternity insurance. Despite the feminist character of these goals, historians differ on the question of whether or not the intent of the socialist women's movement in Germany at this time was feminist, that is, consciously opposed to gender hierarchy and aiming to undermine male domination. Zetkin as leader insisted that she was pursuing working-class, not feminist goals – that the vote for all women, for instance, was advocated in the specific interests of the working class. She maintained that working-class women's aims were opposed to the interests of bourgeois women and she was uncompromising on the matter of cross-class collaboration among women, ruthlessly cutting out comrades who built bridges to middle-class women's organisations. (Indeed, she instigated the ban on united front efforts at the International Socialist Women's Conference in 1907.)

Early in her career Zetkin had taken a very equalitarian stance toward women's status, but by the mid-1890s she championed the cohesive working-class family, in which the wife and mother was helpmeet and educator, as the unit most likely to foster the emancipation of the proletariat. This seems to have been a strategic move on her part. The socialist women's movement in Germany, several historians have noted, was very strongly oriented toward the needs and interests of married women, that is, the wives of socialist men, its largest female constituency.[6] Both male leaders' patriarchalism and working-class women's expectations in Germany tempered the potentially sex-neutralising bent of Marxism – its theoretical capacity to regard both men and women equally in their roles as workers – and in practice the German movement idealised the socialist woman's sex-specific role as wife and mother.

The US Socialist Party, which was puny compared to its German relative – claiming about 126,000 members in 1912, of whom 10 to 15 per cent were women – shared most of these attitudes towards sexual roles. Both the large German immigrant constituency and the midwestern, evangelical Christian component of the Socialist Party in the US oriented it toward social purity; its rhetoric tended to sentimentalise woman as the socialist companion and mother or as the sexual victim of capitalism. Also, American socialists tended to eschew any public radicalism about sexual roles because they had to combat the frequent accusation that socialism meant the collectivism of women and the destruction of monogamy.[7]

Social reform and suffrage

In the US, socialist women's activism was dwarfed by the large and growing crowd of middle-class women activists and suffragists, of whom as many as two million belonged to the National American Woman Suffrage Assocation by 1917.[8] Since the 1850s, middle-class women's organis-ations had been voicing the aims for women articulated earliest in Germany by the SPD. The demand for female suffrage emerged early in the US not only because of the tradition of popular sovereignty and the diffusion of the franchise among white men but especially because of the politics of the late 1860s (after the Civil War and the emancipation of the slaves), when the Republican Party decided on a strategy of enfranchising freed black men. The most outspoken and ambitious American women leaders, who had been in favour of woman suffrage for two decades, shared the political world view of Radical Republicans who gave cardinal im-portance to the vote to address the condition of emancipated slaves. The Radical Republicans expansively declaimed that exercising the fran-chise was the basic freedom from which all other freedoms would flow, the basic political right without which all other rights could not be safeguarded. While these men thought the ballot was the key to freedom for ex-slaves, women activists thought it was the key to their own freedom as well. Women activists were inspired to feel that the vote was a natural right – one of the unalienable rights, necessary to protect one's person and property under government – rather than a privilege, as the framers of the constitution had seen it.[9] Thus the politics of race and sectionalism along with the constitutional doctrine of popular sovereignty made the women's movement in the US the first in the Western world to centre on the ballot.

Suffragists in the US took part in a wide-ranging 'woman movement' with educational, charitable, occupational, and other social reform aims in the latter half of the nineteenth century. Women involved in such efforts came increasingly to support the campaign for the ballot, especially after 1905. Seeking social goals – whether unions for wage-earners, or better garbage collection, or the elimination of prostitution, the establishment of temperance, or schools and playgrounds – women came to believe that they would never achieve them without the political clout of the vote. The result was a proliferation of local woman suffrage groups, most of which affiliated with the national federation, the National

American Woman Suffrage Association, established in 1890.

Given the bans on German women's participation in politics at this time and the absence of manhood suffrage, a comparably broad-scale national suffrage association was impossible there. During the nineteenth century, Germany did not see anything near the scale of US women's voluntarist efforts. A pioneering liberal women's association, founded in 1865, was weak and quiet in the 1870s and 1880s in respect for Chancellor Bismarck's militarist authoritarianism. The end of the Bismarck era in 1890 allowed a re-emergence of middle-class liberalism, however. In 1894 a federation of bourgeois women's charitable, civic, patriotic and feminist organisations, the *Bund Deutscher Frauenverein* (BDF), was organised. It originally brought 34 women's associations together; by 1901 it included 137 associations with about 70,000 members.[10] Although woman suffrage agitation proper in Germany was a pale shadow of its vigorous American counterpart, the BDF in 1902, with nearly 100,000 members, declared woman suffrage urgently desirable, while the comparable umbrella group in the US, the General Federation of Women's Clubs, did not endorse the ballot until 1914. The BDF may have been moved in this direction because it was competing with socialist women's organisations for the allegiance of women.[11]

The BDF spurred activism in the late 1890s by challenging the legal position of married women in the Civil Code, and also, quite successfully, by opposing state-regulated prostitution – by agitating around questions of women's sexual dignity, male licence, and state enforcement of the commercialisation and sexual degradation of women's bodies. In Germany, where brothels in major cities were regulated by the police (despite the illegality of prostitution), anti-prostitution campaigners took an approach similar to Josephine Butler's campaign in England, demanding an end to the state's collusion with – indeed, institutionalisation of – the double standard of morality.[12]

In the US, in contrast, where prostitution was (with very minor exception) unregulated, anti-prostitution campaigners saw the state – in the form of prohibitory laws – as a source of remedy. As early as the 1830s in the US, 'moral reform' societies, through which evangelical Protestant women publicised and condemned male patrons of prostitutes, had brought the double standard of sexual morality into the open and attempted to reform prostitutes themselves. Similar local efforts, along with aims to raise the age of consent and to end wife-beating, were forwarded by the Women's Christian Temperance Union in the 1870s and 1880s. Around the turn of the century both men and women, with frequently differing strategies and levels of sympathy for prostitutes, renewed anti-prostitution campaigns in big cities from east to west coast and instigated state and city vice commissions. Many suffragists wished to eliminate prostitution, and led or joined local campaigns, but such efforts did not outpace their other social reform aims nationwide.[13]

The furore over prostitution regulation was a leading edge in Germany at this time, however. It involved various actors: a men's morality association, the Catholic centre party, social vigilance groups analogous to social purity advocates in the US, as well as women of more than one attitude. Out of this fray, a cadre of unmistakably feminist leaders emerged, including Lily Braun, Marie Stritt, Anita Augspurg, Lida Heymann, Minna Cauer, Adele Schreiber and Helene Stöcker. Influenced by international contacts, these women had already founded local feminist groups or publications; they proceeded to infiltrate the BDF and by 1898 had moved it towards more explicit statements of women's emancipation. When the existing structure of the BDF did not give, they founded new organisations, both the Union of Progressive Women's Associations and the first group to work specifically for the ballot, the German Union for Women's Suffrage (*Deutscher Verband für Frauenstimmrecht*). This suffrage union was founded in 1902 in Hamburg, a city which ruled itself like a state and did not prohibit women's political participation as Prussia did. It had been the site of the most dramatic campaigning against regulated prostitution.[14]

The new militants saw the demand for woman suffrage – for universal suffrage, which was their standard – as radical and potentially transformative of the state, which indeed it was. But the women's suffrage movement in Germany faced specific problems stemming from the authoritarian nature of the Reich and the class polarisation of politics. The women who formed the suffrage union did not ally with the SPD (despite the party's endorsement of the vote for women). At first they avoided such alliance because it might have provoked police reprisals in Prussia or Bavaria for their engaging in politics (before 1908). Later, mutual hostility stronger than the common goal of votes for women kept the two groups apart. The SPD did not want or need mainly bourgeois women suffragists who could not embrace the proletarian consciousness and a revolutionary stance.

The suffrage union did seek alliances among the small liberal parties, but the men in these parties became increasingly unreliable as supporters of universal suffrage, especially after 1907 when they moved from an oppositional to a more accommodationist stance toward the government and, alarmed at the popularity of the SPD, accepted new or continuing inequitable qualifications for male voters in several German states. Once women could join these political parties (as they could by 1908), their own political allegiances became differentiated. Rather than flourishing after the legalisation of women's political participation, woman suffrage groups suffered indecision, infighting and fragmentation: their numbers rose, but their success at coalition sank.[15] Some suffragists compromised the goal of universal suffrage and accepted the notion that women's voting rights need only match men's in a given state. If male voters had to be qualified by property ownership, then female voters might as well. Such a position was, of course, much less daringly democratic than the SPD demand for universal suffrage. Analogous views surfaced episodically in the US, where some Southern white suffragists were perfectly content to keep blacks disfranchised while seeking the ballot for themselves. Some Northern suffragists approved of educational qualifications for voting for both men and women.[16] The explicit goal of national suffrage organisations in the US was removing the sex barrier to voting, rather than bringing about universal suffrage.

Sexual reform: a different approach

Another new German association avoided the mire of political alliances, but provoked its own controversies. This unique organisation for sexual reform – the most interesting formation in German feminism – was called the *Bund für Mutterschutz* (League for the Protection of Mothers). It was founded in 1904 by Ruth Bré, who that same year published a book called *The Right of Motherhood*, in which she advocated matriarchal families and envisioned rural communes populated by mother–child dyads, free of marriage and of paternal domination. The following year, the same women who were energising the BDF and the suffrage movement, joined by some male intellectuals (both liberals and socialists), took up this organisation as the vehicle for advocating a new sexual ethics. By 1908 the *Mutterschutz* league had grown to ten affiliated branches in different cities, and was spreading its ideas through frequent public lectures and two serial publications. Its membership was never very large – probably not more than 3500 to 4000 – but its impact went far beyond its own membership.

Amidst high-pitched concern for the German birth rate among spokesmen for the state, the *Bund für Mutterschutz* articulated a new concept of mothers' rights, for reproductive freedom and autonomy for women. It advocated the replacement of conventional morality with a 'new ethics' that opponents called sexual anarchy or free love. Its principal leaders, Adele Schreiber and Helene Stöcker, challenged the patriarchal family for oppressing women and criticised the state for failing to reward mothers' – including unmarried mothers' – work of child-rearing. The group aimed to destroy the concepts of 'legitimacy' or 'illegitimacy' in childbearing. Its new ethics would legalise 'free unions' (that is, informal marriages), equalise the legal rights of husband and wife, make divorce easy, establish sex education in schools, bring state maternity insurance coverage to unmarried mothers, and make birth control legal and available.[17] In directing demands of this sort toward the state, these sexual reformers implicitly acknowledged a role that the imperial bureaucracy had taken on as far back as Bismarck's era. The German empire's pro-natalism (and wish to fend off socialism) made it precocious in state-administered welfare provision for women and children: from the 1880s, German women workers had weeks-long mandatory maternity leave, and received 'confinement money' to replace lost earnings.[18]

Members of the *Bund für Mutterschutz* were greatly influenced by the thinking of Ellen Key, a Swedish writer whose books, *The Century of the Child, Love and Marriage*, and *The Renaissance of Motherhood*, were widely read on both sides of the Atlantic in this period. In an era of sexology dominated by male writers, Key was a female apostle of sexual liberation, romanticising female eroticism and linking it to bodily health and spiritual harmony. She claimed that women's fulfilment was intrinsically bound to the nurturing expressed in maternity – but where Victorians walled off motherliness from heterosexual desire, Key connected the two. She argued that sexual love was sacred and self-sanctioning, and only those marriages enshrining such love were really valid; women should be free to love, and to end marriages which did not bring them sexual satisfaction. In refusing to bow to legal or patriarchal authority and insisting on women's sexual subjectivity, Key was a radical. She championed unwed mothers and advocated state subsidies or 'motherhood endowment' by which the state would recognise maternal labour, for single mothers. A socialist, opposed in principle to the economic dependence of women on men, she contended that marriage was an economic partnership in which the wife/mother earned the ownership of half of her mate's income or assets.[19]

German feminists in the *Bund für Mutterschutz* incorporated Key's radical challenges without assuming (as she did) that motherhood need be all-encompassing. Key derided the Anglo-American feminist emphasis on women's right to work, and scorned emulation of men; she labelled the consequences of mothers' careers outside the home 'socially pernicious, racially wasteful and soul-withering', and in contrast boosted 'motherliness' as the font of unselfish ethics and social co-operation. In the 1890s she even opposed woman suffrage, though she switched to support by 1905. The German leaders Adele Schreiber and Helen Stöcker, while also emphasising women's differences from men, were, in contrast, devoted suffragists. Following the ideas of the American feminist Charlotte Perkins Gilman as well as those of Key, they sought the panoply of economic freedoms for women along with what they called the 'right to motherhood'.[20] Schreiber, for instance, worked avidly to repeal laws that forced women teachers to leave their jobs if they became pregnant.[21] Another leader in *Mutterschutz*, Lily Braun, campaigned to set up employment agencies through which single mothers might find work while raising their children. She also agitated for occupational health regulations, and tried to organise labour unions for domestic workers; she recommended similar associations for actresses, waitresses and prostitutes.

Braun provides an interesting example of an activist who found a home base in the *Mutterschutz* league. An aristocrat by birth and an early advocate of the vote for women, she became a socialist in the mid-1890s but found herself swimming against the tide in the SPD because of her intensely feminist concerns. An astute critic of capitalism, and especially of the degradation of both work and motherhood that women suffered under it, Braun also realised that the abolition of capitalism would not itself remove all of women's oppressions. She had no illusions that the public comradeship of men and women in work or politics would automatically translate into equalitarian private relationships: women would have to wrest their freedoms from men. In her proud view, women were not only different from men but better: more humane, nurturant, co-operative. Therefore full freedom for women, which would enable them to command the broadest scope of endeavours, represented a pre-eminently social goal to her.[22]

The 'new morality' or 'new ethics' of the *Mutterschutz* league, which generated alarm and resistance along with eager support, was the central issue in the German women's movement between 1904 and 1908, affecting the socialist women's groups on the one side and infiltrating the mainstream federation, the BDF, on the other. There were numerous socialists, besides Braun, involved. One of the *Mutterschutz* league's main policy proposals, the expansion and enhancement of paid maternity leave, was also advocated by the SPD. Despite the party's official conservativism on sexual issues (neither the SPD nor the Socialist Party of the US ever endorsed birth control), individual socialists of the pre-war generation were important proponents of the 'new ethics' in Germany (as they were in the US, too). No doubt it was the very class-crossing appeal of *Mutterschutz* ideas that made Clara Zetkin such a fierce opponent of Braun in the SPD. Braun's cultural critique of capitalism, her intentions to investigate and thereby improve the conditions of women's work, her proposals for communal housekeeping and for day care were, in Zetkin's view, reformism of the rankest type, which additionally elevated women's issues beyond (and diverged from) revolutionary struggle.[23]

In the face of the increasingly coercive pro-natalist policies of the imperial government, including harsher enforcement of criminal laws against abortion and proposals for new prohibitions of birth control, the *Mutterschutz* league stood not only for free motherhood but for reproductive freedom, the equal right *not* to bear children. It campaigned for birth control, notably among working-class women, and fought vigorously against proposals for bans on contraceptives.[24] In 1908, the influence of *Mutterschutz* members in the BDF was great enough to bring that federation almost to the point of endorsing the legalisation of abortion. Influenced by *Mutterschutz* advocates, the BDF's own Legal Commission took a position recommending that the clause criminalising abortion in the Civil Code ought to be repealed. By only a narrow margin did the BDF vote down the recommendation.[25]

This near victory was truly Pyrrhic, however. It caused moderates and conservatives in the BDF to rally against the radicals in its ranks, to oust the woman who had been president for a decade, Marie Stritt, who was a *Mutterschutz* member, and replace her with the conservative Gertrud Baumer. With new freedom of association, women's organisations swelled with women from the rightward-leaning upper bourgeoisie who influenced the BDF to let the anti-feminist German evangelical women's league join in while the *Bund für Mutterschutz* was kept out. By 1910 the *Mutterschutz* group was rent by personal battles between Stöcker and Schreiber; like the suffrage movement it spun off warring fragments. Like the liberal parties, the BDF turned rightward during these years; by 1911, the federation viewed the *Mutterschutz* league as a sworn enemy because of its sexual radicalism. But that defining sexual radicalism was fading. In the *Mutterschutz* movement, the members who remained challenged bourgeois morality less and embraced eugenics more, taking a cue from sterilisation laws being passed in the US to limit the reproduction of the 'unfit'. The 'new ethics' through which women tried to claim sexual autonomy, authenticity and adventure was co-opted by a eugenic and *volkisch* mentality that stressed reproduction for the Fatherland.[26]

In the US there was no organisation comparable to the *Bund für Mutterschutz*, and none got anywhere near endorsing the legalisation of abortion nor concertedly took up a 'new morality'. Individuals did, however, often stimulated by European thinkers. There were some distinctly feminist forms to these challenges. A call for 'sex rights on the part of women' was one of the hallmarks of the younger, educated women who first actually called themselves 'Feminists' in the 1910s. The very use of the term feminist was connected with a livelier recognition of female sexuality than women's rights advocates in the US had ever before shown. Young feminists in the years just before World War I abandoned the traditional claim of female moral superiority, which was tied to sexual purity. They criticised the double standard, not from the narrow path trod by their predecessors but from the field of sexual liberation, urging greater frankness about and expression of women's sexual desires.[27] To them, sex outside of marriage had the appeal of outlawry, befitting feminist aims to explode the structure of conventional society: it involved a Nietzschean transvaluation of values, erasing the boundaries between the pure and the 'fallen' woman. The American women who called themselves feminists rather than simply suffragists were nearly a decade behind the Germans in moving in this direction, but like them were frequently inspired by Ellen Key and cited her as an authority. Several of Key's works were translated and published in the US in the early 1910s, having, a male journalist claimed, 'a profounder influence in this field than any other book since John Stuart Mill's *Subjection of Women*'. Rheta Child Dorr remembered that in 1912 Key was regarded as a 'tremendous radical', and 'everybody who used to read Charlotte Perkins Gilman was now reading [her]', although her 'very name was anathema to most suffragists'.[28]

Key's message of female sexual liberation seems to have had a greater impact on American feminist leaders than her apotheosis of motherhood. Among important spokeswomen, birth control agitator Margaret Sanger most wholly adopted Key's ideas. When she founded her law-defying newspaper, the *Woman Rebel*, in the spring of 1914, Sanger located the 'basis of Feminism' less in 'masculine-dominated' concerns (such as employment) than in 'the right to be a mother regardless of church or state'. A few American women took pains to find out about the *Mutterschutz* league itself. New York writer Katherine Anthony went to Europe to find out what was going on, and in 1915 published a book called *Feminism in Germany and Scandinavia*, which highlighted the league's intent to transform 'sex slavery' into 'volitional motherhood'. One of Anthony's friends, the Chicago philanthropist and philosopher Ethel Sturges Dummer, who had also gone to Germany for personal contact with *Mutterschutz* leaders, saw such intents as 'far more fundamental' than the aim for political rights, far more 'radical' because they 'would change not only law but custom, would reverse the attitude of mind towards marriage'. An American newspaperwoman who wrote a series of articles about the *Mutterschutz* group in 1912 could not find a wide-circulation magazine publisher to take it, however, because editors maintained that 'nice' women were not interested in illegitimacy.[29]

The sexual conservatism of the American public in general and of the suffrage movement in particular kept most such moves toward a 'new ethics' private.[30] Unlike the German women who simultaneously embraced the *Mutterschutz* league and campaigned for the vote, mainstream suffrage leaders in the US hastened to disavow any connection between the vote for women and transformation of sexual standards. Carrie Chapman Catt, for instance, who led the National American Woman Suffrage Association to victory, declared in 1914, 'Free love is not and never has been a tenet of suffragists . . . . If suffragists have a common aim along the line of morals it is toward self-control in private life, stricter laws for the control of public vice, and the enforcement of those laws.' She took pains to note that Ellen Key, whom she called 'the great Swedish advocate of free love', had been an *anti*-suffragist.[31]

Conclusion

In both Germany and the United States there were proponents of socialism, of ameliorative social reform, of woman suffrage, and of sexual emancipation, but the relative numerical strength and organisational effectiveness of these advocacies differed. Socialist women's organising never nearly matched that of middle-class women's reform in the US as it did in Germany. Germany's powerful Socialist Party led demands for women's rights as a party measure, while the relative weakness of the Socialist Party of the US meant that American socialist women in many locales worked with bourgeois women in campaigns for the vote (despite the official socialist ban on collaboration).[32] Middle-class women's voluntaristic reform activity, on the other hand, was altogether a larger phenomenon in the US than in Germany. But similar interests in children's and women's welfare – the 'maternalism' that has recently been a focus of interest for historians of the modern welfare state – characterised such efforts in both countries.[33]

Both countries' suffrage movements were largest and most vigorous in the early twentieth century. Women in the two nations must have related differently to the states from which they were seeking change, the Americans seeing their local governments as more beneficent and their national government as more manipulable, than the Germans. In corollary, German suffragists tended to justify their claims as a matter of duty to the state and social welfare, the Americans more individualistically.[34] The German movement was hampered by absolutist government and the lack of manhood suffrage; it was caught in the class struggle manifest in party organisations; its intent to find partisan allies (after 1908) led its members into divided allegiances, so that its factionalism was destructive. When women got the vote in Germany, it was because the revolution of 1918 brought the SPD into power which established universal suffrage as a long-stated party measure.

The suffrage movement in the US, in contrast, was empowered by the nation's half-century-long tradition of manhood suffrage, which supplied a unifying point of departure by differentiating all women from all men. In a basically two-party system the American suffrage movement worked in a non-partisan (or as some liked to say, all-partisan) fashion, not seeking to ally with one party or the other; and its factionalism – especially when the National Woman's Party appeared in the 1910s to contest the domination of the National American Woman Suffrage Association – arose more from difference of tactics than from difference of principle. American women (except those who were prevented by racial discrimination at the polls) gained the vote by constitutional amendment in the wake of gratitude for women's war work, but then only after many decades of campaigning and after a significant proportion had been enfranchised at the state level (especially between 1917 and 1919), thereby changing the outlook of Congressmen and Senators who voted on the constitutional amendment.

In Germany, the willingness of women who were also suffragists and/or socialists to make public and radical demands for sexual emancipation – however briefly that coalition of demands lasted – stands out. The *Bund für Mutterschutz* had no organisational parallel in the US. In both countries, the feminists who held the most promise for the future were those who combined sexual *with* political demands, who did not see these as mutually exclusive, either in fact or strategically. It is not clear, however, that more courage to demand women's reproductive freedom or a less inhibited voice on sex would have changed the progress and consequences of the US suffrage movement one way or the other. (Nor does it seem that more discretion on these issues in Germany would have halted the rightward trend in the BDF or kept the suffrage movement from self-destructing.) If there is a particular and outstanding feature of feminism in the US in this period it is its conjunction with the mass mobilisation of women for the vote without partisan affiliation as such. Each instance of unique formation, then – regarding the body in Germany and the vote in America – matches national political characteristics: in Germany, the state's enforcement of sexual difference and involvement (beginning during the Bismarck era) in body and family issues from prostitution to maternity insurance; in the US, a broadly diffused franchise.

Despite the political and social differences between the two nations, which would seem to dictate different consequences, what was desired by feminists in both places was remarkably the same: in short, recognition of the full scope of humanity in women. Common political strains dogged their efforts to change gender hierarchy. Practical and ideological conflicts of priority between socialism and feminism were similar in both countries, despite the different scale of the two socialist movements. Socialism was undoubtedly more influential in putting women's rights on the agenda in Germany than in the US, however. Although the party systems were very different, suffragists in the two countries had similar problems meshing feminist goals with male partisan priorities. The fragmentation in the German suffrage movement over alliances with the liberal parties after 1908 eerily mimicked the first split in the woman suffrage movement in the US (1869), when suffragists' erstwhile Republican allies supported the ballot for emancipated male slaves but not for women.[35] An intent to define or isolate and follow 'pure feminism' as a way out of political entanglements of class or party (or, in the US, of race) appeared as one (doomed) solution in both the German suffrage situation and in the US.[36]

Both national histories also suggest, ironically if not tragically, that women forced to be 'outsiders' succeed better in organising themselves vigorously and with concerted direction: the exciting German radical movements took place *before* the law of association was changed to enable women's political participation; afterwards socialist women were less effective as a group voice, and bourgeois women activists were both very divided by competing partisanships and sunk by the class conservatism of their larger numbers. In the US the relevant comparison to 1908 is 1920, when the constitutional right to vote went into effect; afterwards, women's groups, ever more diverse, were never so united nor vociferous for a goal as they had been when women were not full citizens.[37]

Neither German feminists nor those in the US had the impact that they should have had. Although their analyses of women's subordination were clearsighted and far-reaching and their strategies for change rational, they made only small dents in gender hierarchy. This comparative look reinforces the perspicacity of historian Mary Ritter Beard's observation, made in the 1930s, that 'the political economy in which feminism has to function is the prime consideration'.[38] Feminism does not have a history discrete from the rest of historical process; it comprises part of the social order it inhabits. One never wants to neglect the internal history of ideas, strategies, tactics, in feminist advocacy itself, but interpreting these in political context has the most to teach us, to enable the present to read the past most usefully.

1   On the internationalism of the women's movement, see Ellen Carol DuBois, this volume. As a historian of the US, I can draw on two decades' study of primary and secondary sources for the American side of this comparison; my knowledge of German developments is admittedly superficial in comparison and relies wholly on secondary sources in English. I am especially indebted to the work of Richard Evans: 'Bourgeois Feminism and Women Socialists in Germany, 1894-1914: Lost Opportunity or Inevitable Conflict', *Women's Studies International Quarterly*, 3/4, 1980, 355-76; *Comrades and Sisters: Feminism, Socialism and Pacifism in Europe*; 'The Concept of Feminism: Notes for Practicing Historians', in Ruth-Ellen B. Joeres & Mary Jo Maynes, eds, *German Women in the Eighteenth and Nineteenth Centuries: A Social and Literary History*, Indiana Univ. Press, Bloomington, 1986, 247-58; *The Feminist Movement in Germany, 1894-1933*, Sage, London & Beverly Hills, 1976; *The Feminists*; 'Theory and Practice in German Social Democracy 1880-1914: Clara Zetkin and the Socialist Theory of Women's Emancipation', *History of Political Thought*, 3/2, 1982, 285-304; and of Amy Hackett: 'Feminism and Liberalism in Wilheline Germany, 1890-1918', in Berenice Carroll, ed, *Liberating Women's History*, Univ. of Illinois Press, Urbana, IL, 1976; 'The German Women's Movement and Suffrage, 1890-1914: A Study of National Feminism', in Robert J. Bezucha, ed, *Modern European Social History*, D.C. Heath, Lexington, MA, 1972, 354-86; 'Helene Stöcker: Left Wing Intellectual and Sex Reformer', in Renate Bridenthal, Anita Grossman & Marion Kaplan, eds, *When Biology Became Destiny: Women in Weimar and Nazi Germany*, Monthly Review Press, New York, 1984; and Jean Quataert, 'Unequal Partners in an Uneasy Alliance: Women and the Working Class in Imperial Germany', in Marilyn Boxer & Jean Quataert, eds, *Socialist Women: European Socialist Feminism in the Nineteenth and Early Twentieth Centuries*, Elsevier, North-Holland, NY, 1978; *Reluctant Feminists in German Social Democracy, 1885-1917*, Princeton Univ. Press, Princeton, NJ, 1979.

2   See Alan Dawley, *Struggles for Justice: Social Responsibility and the Liberal State*, Harvard Univ. Press, Cambridge, MA, 1991, 57-9, 131-3, for a brief comparison between political structures of the US and Germany.

3   See Evans, *Feminist Movement*, 12-14 on the Civil Code; Michell Grossberg, *Governing the Hearth: Law and the Family in Nineteenth-Century America*, UNC Press, Chapel Hill, North Carolina, 1985, on domestic relations law in the US.

4   Evans, *Feminist Movement*, 10-11.

5   See especially Karen Honeycutt, 'Socialism and Feminism in Imperial Germany', *Signs*, 5/1, 1979, 30-41.

6   Early on, Zetkin criticised the nuclear family as a site of bondage for women and envisioned its erosion as increasing industrialisation brought women economic independence. See ibid. and Evans, 'Theory and Practice'.

7   See Mari Jo Buhle, *Women and American Socialism*, Univ. of Illinois Press, Urbana, 1981. For numbers in the Socialist Party, see Arthur Link & William A. Link, *The Twentieth Century: An American History*, Harlan Davidson, Arlington Heights, IL, 1983, 34. Cf. Evans, *The Feminists*, 187 n. 76.

8   Kraditor, *The Ideas of the Woman Suffrage Movement 1890-1920*, 5.

9   See Eric Foner, *Reconstruction, 1863-1877*, Harper & Row, New York, 1988, 228-80; Ellen DuBois, 'Outgrowing the Compact of the Fathers: Equal Rights, Woman Suffrage, and the United States Constitution, 1820-1878', *Journal of American History (JAH)*, 74/3, 1987, 836-62. Within the German suffrage movement from the 1890s to 1908 there was a range of opinion whether the vote was the 'foundation' of or 'capstone' to women's advances; the radicals (like American suffragists) took the former position. See Hackett, 'The German Women's Movement and Suffrage,' 367-70.

10   Evans, *Feminist Movement*, 37.

11   On BDF and suffrage, see Hackett, 'The German Women's Movement and Suffrage,' 365-78. On the General Federation of Women's Clubs, see William O'Neill, *Everyone was Brave: A History of Feminism in America*, Quadrangle Books, Chicago, 1971, 84-90, 167.

The BDF's membership rose from 70,000 in 1901 to the claim of 500,000 in 1912-14, but given the probable overlap of individuals in its constituent organisation, Richard Evans argues persuasively that it probably contained only 200,000 to 250,000 individuals at the later date. Evans, *Feminist Movement*, 192-3; *Comrades and Sisters*, 55.

12   See Evans, *Feminist Movement*, 41-4, 53-63.

13   See Ruth Rosen, *The Lost Sisterhood: Prostitution in America, 1900-1918*, Johns Hopkins, Baltimore, 1982.

14   See Evans, *Feminist Movement*, 44-53, 71-86; Hackett, 'German Women's Movement', esp. 370-2.

15   Evans, *Feminist Movement*, 98-108 and 'Bourgeois Feminists and Women Socialists in Germany 1894-1914'; Hackett, 'German Women's Movement', 377-8.

16   See Kraditor, *Ideas*, chapters 6 and 7.

17   My account of the *Bund für Mutterschutz* is greatly indebted to Ann Taylor Allen, 'Mothers of the New Generation: Adele Schreiber, Helene Stöcker, and the Evolution of a German Idea of Motherhood, 1900-1914', *Signs*, 10/3, 1985, 418-38 (423 for membership numbers). Sigmund Freud joined, and published in one of the journals of the group.

18   See Seth Koven & Sonya Michel, 'Womanly Duties: Maternalist Politics and the Origins of Welfare States in France, Germany, Great Britain, and the United States, 1880-1920', *American Historical Review*, 95/4, 1990, 1076-108, esp. 1105-6.

19   Buhle, *Women and American Socialism*, 292-4; Nancy F. Cott, *The Grounding of Modern Feminism*, Yale Univ. Press, New Haven, 1987, 46-7; Cheri Register, 'Motherhood at Center: Ellen Key's Social Vision', *WSIF*, 5/6, 1982, 599-610.

20   Hackett, 'Helene Stöcker', 110-14.

21   Allen, 'Mothers of the New Generation', 430.

22   Introduction by Alfred Meyer, to Lily Braun, *Selected Writings on Feminism and Socialism*, Indiana Univ. Press, Bloomington, 1987; Quataert, 'Unequal Partners', 122-3, 136-7.

23   Zetkin opposed and denigrated Braun's influence in the SPD for more than a decade, succeeding eventually in eliminating her as a main player. See Quataert, 'Unequal Partners', 107, 126-7 on this and on the SPD debate over birth control just before the Great War. On sexual radicalism in the Socialist Party of the US, see Buhle, *Women and American Socialism*, chapter 7.

24   See Allen, 'Mothers of the New Generation', Hackett, 'Helene Stöcker', and Christl Wickert, Brigitte Hamburger & Marie Lienau, 'Helene Stöcker and the Bund fur Mutterschutz (The Society for the Protection of Motherhood)', *Women's Studies International Forum*, 5/6, 1982, 611-28.

25   Evans, *Feminist Movement*, 131-6; Allen, 'Mothers of the New Generation', 430-2.

26   Evans, *The Feminists*, 199-200, 194-6; Allen, 'Mothers of the New Generation', 432-7.

27   Cott, *Grounding of Modern Feminism*, 35-45. The same semantic slant may be observable in Germany. In the German language, women's rights and women's movement advocates continued to use composites of the word woman (*Frau*), and movement, and rights, or suffrage, even when the term feminist became frequent in French and English parlance. But I notice that the prominent moderate Helene Lange entitled her attack on the new ethics of the *Bund für Mutterschutz* '*Feministische Gedankenanarchie*', as though this alarming branch of thinking required or deserved a unique usage. Title cited in Allen, 'Mothers of a New Generation', 428 n.14. See also Evans, 'Concept of Feminism'.

28   Norman Hapgood, 'What Women Are After', *Harper's Weekly*, and Dorr, both quoted in Cott, *Grounding of Modern Feminism*, 46.

29   Sanger, Anthony, Dummer and newspaperwoman (Rheta Childe Dorr) quoted and discussed in ibid., 46-7, 299 n. 56.

30   Although one heard about sexual freedom 'on all sides' in the 1910s, one older woman's rights advocate recalled, 'One heard about it in connection with prominent suffragettes, but not directly. There was a disposition to keep such matters to one's self.' Quoted from Mary Austin, *Earth Horizon*, in ibid., 46.

31   Carrie Chapman Catt, 'Feminism and Suffrage', speech printed as broadside, box 4, Carrie Chapman Catt papers, Sophia Smith Collection, Smith College, Northampton, MA.

32   See Buhle, *Women and American Socialism*, Chapter 6.

33   On 'maternalism', see Seth Koven & Sonya Michel, eds, *Mothers of a New World: Maternalist*

Politics and the Origins of Welfare States, Routledge, New York & London, 1993, and 'Womanly Duties'.

34   See Hackett, 'German Women's Movement'.

35   Ellen Carol DuBois, *Feminism and Suffrage: The Emergence of an Independent Women's Movement in America, 1848-1869*, Cornell Univ. Press, Ithaca, NY, 1978, esp. 162-202.

36   Evans, *Feminist Movement*, 101-2. For a similar dilemma between 1917 and 1921 among the militants of the National Woman's Party, see Cott, *Grounding*, 51-81.

37   See Suzanne Lebsock, 'Women and American Politics, 1870-1920', in Louise A. Tilly & Patricia Gurin, eds, *Women, Politics and Change*, Sage, New York, 1990, for a vigorous summary of American women's political involvement up to the 19th amendment.

38   Mary Ritter Beard to Harriot Stanton Blatch, 16 July [1934], biographical box 4, Alma Lutz Collection, Vassar College, Poughkeepsie, NY.

13

Woman Suffrage Around the World: Three Phases of Suffragist Internationalism

ELLEN CAROL DUBOIS

Why have woman suffrage movements so little history?
Even with the revival of modern feminism and women's history, woman suffrage movements have been a curiously understudied phenomenon. There are two related explanations for this lack of scholarly attention. One is the assumption that, with the exception of a few very well-known and highly dramatic cases such as England and the United States, women have been 'granted' the vote by friendly (or calculating) governments, rather than because of their own organised demand for it. Nowhere does this pre-emptive scholarly dismissal seem more pronounced than in the cases of New Zealand and Australia. Here, the movement's first historian, New Zealand progressive William Pember Reeves, observed, scarcely before the first women had returned from the polls in 1893, that chivalrous politicians granted women the vote without their having to mobilise significantly on its behalf.[1]

The claim that woman did not fight for their own political equality is closely related to another dismissive evaluation of women's enfranchisement and an even greater barrier to interested scholars. This is the very commonly made claim that the enfranchisement of women has been, on balance, a conservative development, both with respect to the forces responsible for achieving votes for women and the ultimate impact that women's votes have had on political life. This is unsubstantiated by empirical research, which has had remarkably little to contribute to our understanding of the impact of gender on voting behaviour, since men's and women's votes are only rarely counted separately. Whether or not women vote differently from men, and whether that difference is tilted to the right or the left seems to vary a great deal, and to reflect not only the general political environment within which voters act but whether or not there are political factors working on women and not on men, especially when there is an active and widespread feminist movement at work.[2]

Perhaps the most remarkable thing about the claim of conservatism with respect to woman suffrage movements is that it predates, not only the actual enfranchisement of women, but even the heyday of the woman suffrage movement. The charge that women would vote more conservatively than men was an important element in the debate itself, coming both from conservatives in support of woman suffrage, and from leftists, as an argument against votes for women. During the 1875 debate over whether to include woman suffrage in the founding documents of the German Social Democratic party, opponents cited the allegedly reactionary political tendencies of women, especially their ties to the church. William Leibnicht responded that 'opponents of female suffrage often maintain that women have no political education but there are plenty of men in the same position, and by this reasoning they ought not to be allowed to vote either. The "herd of voters" which has figures at all elections did not consist of women.'[3] William Pember Reeves's curious dismissal of woman suffrage activism in New Zealand and Australia might make sense in this context, reflecting some embarrassment on the part of this secular liberal over the evangelical forces behind the woman suffrage campaign and a wish to distance organised liberal women from what he regarded as the taint of its conservatism.

The general consensus as to the movement's conservatism is very widespread. Consider, for example, Richard Evans's classic survey, *The Feminists*.[4] Evans argues that while the demand for woman suffrage has its origins in classical liberalism, its achievement in the late nineteenth and early twentieth century coincided with and partook of the decline and contraction of that tradition. Led by elite and conservative 'ladies', Evans argued, the turn-of-the-century movement abandoned its roots in universal suffrage traditions, and struck a Faustian bargain in which it accepted property restrictions in order to get the vote for privileged women. Particularly in Germany, he argues, 'The enfranchisement of women was seen both by politicians and by the suffragists themselves, as a means of controlling society in the interests of the "table" part of the population, the middle classes.'[5]

For a while at the beginning of the women's history revival even feminists seemed to embrace their own version of the tendency to dismiss woman suffrage as a conservative development, especially with respect to issues of women's sexual and social freedom. From this perspective, the campaign for political equality appeared to be the least interesting and most narrow aspect of women's efforts for self-liberation. Here the argument was that votes for women substitutes formal, legal equality for other, more radical aspects of the women's movement, for instance challenges to conservative sexual morality. Among United States historians, both Aileen Kraditor and William O'Neill set the tone for this type of argument.[6] Feminists such as Kollontai and Goldman are invoked as alternative heroines of women's emancipation to bourgeois suffrage leaders. Turning again to Australia and New Zealand, Pember Reeves's categorical dismissal of the role of any organised women's movement in winning votes for women was replaced with a second set of interpretations which focused on the woman suffrage leadership taken by the Women's Christian Temperance Union (WCTU) throughout New Zealand and many of the states of Australia. However, the WCTU's suffrage activism was not seen as a positive force for women's emancipation, but rather as a reinforcement of the confining notions of separate spheres and women's responsibilities for morality, notions that are conservative both in terms of women's roles and larger social relations of class and power. This approach restores women's agency to the suffrage story but pays the price of conceding the movement's fundamental conservatism.[7] Is this price necessary?

I would like to offer an alternative, revisionist overview of woman suffrage movements around the world, in which I intend to stress two aspects. One is the internationalism of these movements, the co-operation among women of various nations, the influence that actions of women in one country have had on those in another, and the way that women's international co-operation gave them resources to combat their marginalisation in the politics of their own nations. Woman suffrage can be usefully conceptualised as an international protest movement, or perhaps more accurately several such movements. My own tendency has been to study suffragism in the context of a single country, in my case the United States, in order to demonstrate how much women's drive for political equality was shaped by, indeed part and parcel of, a particular national political history, that it cannot be understood without reference to that history.[8] Yet a national focus alone underplays the rich, international circulation of ideas, personalities, organisations and inspiration that sustained woman suffragism over its very long history and that in many cases has been a crucial element in the actual achievement of women's enfranchisement. Ian Tyrrell suggests instead a more international history (he uses the term 'transnational' so as not to suggest global harmony and equality) which takes into account, without taking for granted, the national framework of the political life from which women were excluded and which they wished to enter.[9]

The other and related aspect of my approach is to challenge the conservative hypothesis, to argue instead that woman suffrage has been, on balance, a progressive development, drawing on and adding to left-wing political forces, albeit frequently in an embattled fashion. This is an argument I have been putting forth ever since my first piece on suffragism in the US, entitled 'The radicalism of the woman suffrage movement', but here I want to reframe this claim in international terms.[10]

Most obviously, in the years of international woman suffragism's greatest strength, from 1890 through to World War I, it was influenced and spread by women associated with the Second Socialist International. However, especially inasmuch as this development took place against a substantial anti-feminist and anti-suffrage counter-tradition within international socialism, this argument need not be limited to women working within the framework of organised socialist parties. On either side (chronologically speaking) of the suffragism of the Second International, we can find the impact of the World's Women's Christian Temperance Union and the international character of the independent militant suffragettes, who had their beginnings in Britain. Such a reconceptualisation and a global survey can, not incidentally, help to expand our definition of progressive politics in this period to incorporate more women operating outside of formal (and male-dominated) left-wing environments.

This review takes place from a deliberately and self-consciously socialist-feminist perspective. A corollary to the conservative thesis is the insistence that there has historically been a fundamental antagonism between socialism and feminism. By contrast, modern socialist-feminists try to tolerate the tension between the two movements and to make of it a creative and powerful progressive politics. Describing United States women's theoretical and scholarly efforts in the 1970s to reconcile the two traditions, or at least put them on speaking terms with each other, Mary Bailey characterised the hyphen that separates the two sides of socialist-feminism as a metaphor for the unresolved tension, the creative conflicts that this wing of the modern feminist movement strives to tolerate, explore and advance. Movingly, Bailey writes, 'What intervenes in this relationship of two terms is desire, on every level. Hyphen as wish. We have heard its whisperings.'[11]

While modern socialist-feminism is uniquely self-aware, it is possible to trace such politics back into the nineteenth century, and to argue that they have consistently been a radicalising force in the movement for women's emancipation. This chapter can be read, therefore, as a contribution to the reconstruction of the socialist-feminist tradition, as part of a contest over the meaning and political direction of the contemporary women's movement. This argument can – and has – been directed to either side of the hyphen: to the feminist audience, the emphasis is on the importance of socialist influences in our tradition; to the socialists, the message is the existence of a rich women's emancipatory vein to our history.

Women's temperance and woman suffrage: the first internationalism
The first international woman suffrage movement, much overlooked, was the World's Women's Christian Temperance Union. The WCTU, formed in the United States in 1874, began as a conventional Protestant women's organisation with a narrow moral reform focus, but soon became an amazingly ambitious, politically aggressive women's organisation. The leading figure in this transformation was Frances Willard, and one of the distinctive marks of her leadership was her brilliant work at enlisting the organisation in the fight for woman suffrage.

Willard profoundly expanded the WCTU by introducing what she called her 'do everything policy', a complex structure in which separate issues were pursued within semi autonomous 'departments', each under the authority of its own 'superintendent'. Within this framework, and fuelled by Willard's deeply political sensibilities, woman suffragism flourished. By convincing WCTU women that temperance itself was a political issue, she led her constituency to advocate woman suffrage, which had previously been taken up only by small and politically isolated advanced groups of women. Indeed, it is not too much to say that the WCTU under Willard's leadership was one of the first environments within which woman suffrage was made comprehensible and compelling to substantial numbers of women.[12]

In 1884, Willard, in conjunction with her companion Lady Henry Somerset, declared the formation of the World's Women's Christian Temperance Union, an international companion organisation to the American WCTU. The temperance movement had long been transatlantic, following British lines of international influence, and the formation of the World's WCTU had a great deal to do with Willard's deepening bonds with British temperance women. Still, what is striking about the World's WCTU is its movement in western and southern, rather than eastern and northern directions. WCTU organisers in the western United States, who were working to 'uplift' Asian women immigrants there from prostitution and opium addiction, began to see that if populations, workers and vices migrated from nation to nation, perhaps virtue and organised movements of upstanding women could do the same.[13]

The World's WCTU was spread by American organiser/missionaries. Two of the most intrepid of these missionaries to the world's women were Jessie Ackerman and Mary Leavitt, who planted the World's WCTU's first truly successful seeds in Australia and New Zealand. Leavitt's WCTU career had begun as suffrage superintendent in Massachusetts. WCTUs already existed in South Australia and New Zealand before Leavitt arrived, but what she brought with her was the broader, 'do everything' vision of the organisation that Willard had developed, and particularly the commitment to securing political equality for women. In her pioneering examination of the New Zealand woman suffrage movement, Patricia Grimshaw argues that the international links of WCTU suffragists in that country gave them considerable cachet, as well as access to the whole range of Anglo-American suffrage thought, including the advanced ideas of John Stuart Mill. In the far-flung outposts of Western civilisation, affiliation with the international women's temperance movement was a way to combat the sense of isolation on the periphery. Kate Sheppard touted the case of Wyoming, the sole American suffrage state, in her first New Zealand propaganda.[14]

One final comment about the internationalism of the woman suffrage movement in this early stage: it did not all go in one direction, carrying political authority and innovation only from the centre to the periphery. Early victories in Australia and New Zealand sent sophisticated women activists back to England and the United States, where they helped to move suffrage movements into new directions. Dora Montefiore, the mother of New South Wales suffragism, moved from Australia to England, where Sylvia Pankhurst credits her with encouraging her in the early 1900s to make her first outdoor suffrage speech.[15] Australian suffragism sent Alice Henry to the United States, where her biographer, Diane Kirkby, argues that she was one of the earliest to insist that wage-earning women must be made the centre of an expansive, modern woman suffrage movement.[16]

As suggested above, historians' recognition of the role of the WCTU in the early enfranchisement of women in Australia and New Zealand was at first accompanied by a consensus that this temperance/suffrage movement was basically conservative in thrust, in Tyrrell's words, intended to 'advance the women's culture of evangelical domesticity' rather than to move women into politics or politics in a progressive direction.[17] This judgement has begun to give way in two directions. One strategy has been to learn more and more about the diversity of women's suffrage activism in this early period. Audrey Oldfield, in her detailed study of Australian suffragism state by state, emphasises the substantial number of suffrage leaders who were secularists, not WCTU evangelicals; associated with the beginnings of the Australian Labor Party; and linked to groups of wage-earning women.[18] The emphasis here shifts from the WCTU to the larger political environment within which it was situated; woman suffragism in Australia and New Zealand flourished as part of a larger political context of expanding reform ambitions, maturing working-class and socialist movements, and new links between liberalism and state activism, in other words the emergence of what would soon be called progressivism in the US.

Alongside of this, there is another analytic strategy, which involves re-examining the political and ideological content of the WCTU itself. As Tyrrell argues, the WCTU's evangelical roots lent it a quite critical perspective on the commercial and material preoccupations of advancing capitalism. In England, temperance/suffragists and leaders of the World's WCTU were women like Margaret Bright Lucas and Hannah Whithall Smith, from families long at the cutting edge of British liberalism. In the western United States, where the WCTU was an extremely important and progressive locale for women's activism in the late 1880s, the union was a substantial source for the political upsurge of Populism. Willard herself played a significant role in the early stages of the People's party and state WCTU leaders included fiery Populist radicals like Mary Lease of Kansas, who urged her followers to 'raise less corn and more hell'. In the US, these political links were crucial to (although not always credited with) the first successes of woman suffrage. The first genuinely popular political victories of woman suffrage, in the 1890s, were in states where insurgent Populist parties were strong – Colorado, Idaho, and California, where suffrage was narrowly defeated in 1896. Colorado was the first state (as opposed to territory) in which voters authorised woman suffrage in a popular referendum; this took place the same year as women won the vote in New Zealand. The second successful voter referendum was in Idaho, the next year. There were important campaigns in Kansas (1894) and California (1896) which also reflected Populist support.

While the WCTU's class and economic politics demonstrate a significant left-leaning bent, its moralistic approach to the family and to sexuality was far more conservative. This aspect of the WCTU's moral reformism has been widely studied and needs even more examination, but here I want to observe that this sexual and familial conservatism equally characterised the socialist parties of the period. Indeed, in the United States, Mari Jo Buhle has demonstrated that the Protestant evangelical moralism of populist politics of the 1880s was crucial to the translation of socialism, which had been marginalised in German–American communities, into a genuinely American idiom; for US women, she demonstrates that the WCTU was virtually a conduit into socialism.[19] To take just one example, Ella Reeve Bloor, legendary founder of the Communist Party in the US, got her political start in the WCTU. In Australia, the WCTU had close relations with trade unionists and labour parties. Here and elsewhere, the Victorian, traditionalist perspective of moral reform movements on sex roles and the family was welcomed by socialists as a way to reinforce domestic peace in the working-class family and may have eased the way for working-class feminism.

Similar arguments can be made with respect to the issue of race. With the notable exception of New Zealand, where the woman suffrage campaign (relative to other countries) included indigenous Maori women in its scope, the WCTU's record on women of colour is mixed, to say the least. Over and over, the alleged inclusiveness of the WCTU's vision of a worldwide reform movement of politically empowered women gave way to claims or challenges about the barbarism or political incapacity of non-white peoples. On tour around England to raise international awareness of the plight of her people in the US, African American suffragist Ida B. Wells charged Frances Willard with aiding and abetting the epidemic of lynchings in the southern states by her readiness to accept the portrait of black people as fundamentally immoral.[20] In Australia, as Oldfield describes it, a superficial racial universalism quickly gave way to refusals to include Aboriginal women in the 1902 act of enfranchisement. But again, these same limitations were equally true of working-class, socialist and left-leaning political forces in the period, of which the WCTU suffragists were a part. Queensland, where the racialism of the suffragists was the most explicit and aggressive, also boasted exceptionally close ties between suffragists and the Labor Party.[21]

Cheryll Walker's work on South Africa is most revealing of this pattern. Woman suffragism, which was first brought to the Cape Colony in 1895 by the World's WCTU, was aided and supported by the rise of a South African labour party. For several decades, woman suffragists negotiated the treacherous waters of South African racial politics by taking the position that women should vote according to the same rules as men; in the Cape, this would have included Coloureds and Africans. Finally, in the 1920s, when the Labour Party enrolled in the campaign to remove Cape Africans from the voting rolls, woman suffragists easily gave in on principle and acceded to this exclusion, earning the aid of the ascendant

National Party and the rapid resolution of their demands. Given what she judges to be the ultimate conservatism of these developments, Walker nonetheless comments on the fact that the movement's 'early sponsorship was from the left'.[22] Ian Tyrrell has thoughtfully explored the contradictions between the WCTU's decided commitment to Anglo-Saxon superiority and the fact that its deepest criticisms were reserved for the moral failings of British and American society. But here too, this constitutes a similarity to rather than a difference from socialism in the age of empire.

Woman suffrage in the Second Socialist International

In the early twentieth century and overlapping with the World's WCTU, an even more openly and aggressively feminist movement began to develop within international socialism, with political equality one of its most consistent demands. The largest socialist women's movements were in Germany, the United States and Austria but there was also activity in Italy, France, Russia, all of Scandinavia, the Netherlands, Australia, Ireland, South Africa, Central and Eastern Europe, the Southern Cone of Latin America, and undoubtedly elsewhere.[23]

The figure most identified with this international socialist women's effusion was Clara Zetkin. Through the 1890s, Zetkin forged a socialist women's programme and practice within the German Social Democratic party which became the prototype for women in socialist parties around the world. There is, to take just one example, evidence of a socialist women's organisation in Argentina, the Feminist Centre, working from 1906 through to 1912 with Socialist deputy Alfredo Palacios, advocating the Second International feminist platform, including woman suffrage and special labour legislation for women.[24] From 1907 though to 1915, the size and vigour of this worldwide socialist women's network constituted a sort of informal women's International, with annual conferences. International Women's Day, which is celebrated around the world, and Women's History Week, which American feminists now celebrate in March, are the lineal descendants of the International Proletarian Women's Day first authorised by the 1910 international socialist women's conference.

Socialist Women's Day seems to have begun in the United States in 1909, as part of the International-authorised socialist campaign for woman suffrage.[25] Zetkin picked it up within the International in 1910. The holiday was carried through the Comintern and became a solely Communist observance, until the American women's liberation movement, itself inspired by Communist women activists in the 1960s, reimported the celebration to the United States. By the late 1970s, liberal

Democrats took the holiday through one more political transformation, and it became the federally mandated Women's History Week.[26]

Most accounts of these embattled socialist-feminists emphasise either their struggles with the sexism of male socialists or their challenge to middle-class women's movements, but it was really the balance they struck, always fragile and often upset, between these two political forces that determined their political environment.[27] In several of the leading parties, the tension between socialism and feminism led to open conflict between socialist women leaders themselves. Among German socialist women, for instance, Zetkin's loyalty to international socialism was counterpoised to (and balanced by) Lily Braun's greater inclination to the independent women's movement. There were similar sororal antagonisms in the French party between Elizabeth Renaud and Louise Saumoneau, and in Italy between Annas Kulisckoff and Mozzoni.[28] But backing off a bit from the continuing temptation to choose sides or to designate one position alone as correct, one can read the fierce battles between them as an expression of the dialectical situation of social feminism, the shifting and unstable but distinct and authentic political territory it occupied.

The issue of woman suffrage was at the very centre – the virtual expression of – the balance socialist women struck between the non-socialist women's movement and the male-dominated socialist left. Had they not forced their perspective forward within their parties, woman suffrage would have languished as a principle tainted by socialism but not really sustained by it. On the other hand, it is not too much to say that had it not been for the degree of autonomy socialist women were able to sustain within their parties from the mid 1890s on, and for the new classes of women to whom they brought the issue, the demand for woman suffrage probably would not have been revived and placed at the centre of a militant, mass, modern women's movement.

Zetkin first succeeded in getting the German Social Democratic Party (SPD) to adopt the explicit endorsement of political rights 'without distinction of sex' in 1891. For decades, socialist men had been thwarting suffrage petitioners by objecting that women were too reactionary to risk enfranchising. This time, Zetkin responded that the vote 'was a means to assemble the masses, to organise and educate them', and that it was precisely political organising, including working for the vote, that would 'educate' women out of whatever relative 'backwardness' they suffered.[29] Within the International, the first pro-woman suffrage resolution was passed in 1900, but particular nation parties continued to set aside demands for woman suffrage to concentrate on universal manhood suffrage. The campaign led by Zetkin, to strengthen organised socialism's commitment to woman suffrage, coincided with the first all-women international socialist conference, at Stuttgart in 1907. There the International accepted the principle that political equality for women was a non-contingent, fundamental demand which socialist parties must pursue 'strenuously'. A plank was adopted to the party's platform which insisted that 'the socialist parties of all countries have a duty to struggle energetically for the introduction of universal suffrage for women'.[30]

Women working from within socialist parties liked to argue that the bourgeois case for woman suffrage was a defence of property and individual privilege, while they demanded the vote as a weapon of working-class power and on the basis of fundamentally different presumptions. While full discussion of this issue cannot be included here, two points should be noted: first, that property qualifications on women's voting had at least as much to do with marital as class status; and that many of the leading non-socialist suffragists called for universal woman suffrage, without property restrictions.

What really distinguished socialist women's suffragism from the bourgeois variant was the link they made between women workers and political equality. The distinctively socialist argument for woman suffrage rested on the recognition that the increasingly public character of women's labour had to be matched with an equally public political role. The decidedly non-socialist Charlotte Perkins Gilman, whose historical account of women's evolution toward emancipation is indistinguishable from Engels's, was a major force in popularising the socialist approach to women's equality throughout the non-socialist women's movement in America.[31] 'The demand for woman suffrage results from the economic and social revolutions provoked by the capitalist mode of production', resolved a socialist women's conference in 1904, 'but in particular from the revolutionary change in labour and the status and consciousness of women.'[32] In the United States, England and elsewhere, such economic arguments came to be widely accepted among non-socialist suffragists, which is an indication of the degree to which socialist women led the larger suffrage movement into new territories.

Substantive support for woman suffrage within socialism thus required overcoming the powerful heritage of socialist and trade union hostility to wage-earning women. Previously female wage-earning had generally been decried as an index of working-class degradation; in the socialist utopia, adult women would be relieved of the necessity of wage-earning. After the 1890s, this was much less the case. The tradition of 'proletarian sexism' left its mark, however, in the policy of special regulation of women workers, offered as protection for the most vulnerable in the labour market, but actually functioning to keep women in a separate and unequal sector of the labour force.[33]

Through the 1880s, laws to regulate the wage relation only for women workers were advocated in male-dominated trade unions and socialist movements, but women activists, including those who concentrated on organising wage earners and who accepted the desirability of state regulation of the wage relation, opposed such selective legislation for women only. In England, the conflict between these two positions occurred early in the history of the Fabian Society, over the 1896 Factory Act. Socialist feminists, among them Elizabeth Cady Stanton's daughter Harriot Stanton Blatch, criticised the limitation of hours among women workers, while Beatrice Webb, representing the classic trade union position and the leading faction within the Fabians, argued (successfully) for laws against the exploitation of women workers.[34] In the complex interactions on behalf of suffragism within the Second International, support for sex-based labour legislation seems to have been the price extracted from women for substantive support from socialist men for woman suffrage. Zetkin, who had attacked special restrictions on working women at Stuttgart in 1889, changed her position in 1893, now faithfully advocating special labour legislation for women.

Organisationally, the intermediate position of socialist suffragists led to the twin principles of autonomy for women's organising in socialist parties and antagonism to collaboration with non-socialist suffragists. Of these, hostility to bourgeois women's efforts was the more intensely expressed, perhaps because they represented such serious competition. The initial impulse for the international socialist movement to organise working women in the 1890s, after decades of inactivity, was the necessity of countering the organisational inroads that non-socialist women were making among female wage earners. Barbara Clements argues that the great Russian socialist, Aleksandria Kollantai, was drawn to the organising of working women and to feminist issues by the fear that the bourgeois women's movement was becoming too influential among working-class women.[35]

In 1896, Zetkin made hostility to the non-socialist women's movement a fundamental principle of socialist women's organising in Germany. Despite the fact that their programmes were largely the same, Zetkin argued fiercely against any collaboration between women in the 'proletarian' and 'bourgeois' movements and struggled constantly (if futilely) to draw the line between the two. In 1907 at Stuttgart, Zetkin overcame strong opposition from Austrians and Americans to establish non-co-operation with bourgeois suffragists as the official policy for socialist women around the world. Like the concessions that Zetkin and other socialist women made to sex-based labour legislation, anti-collaborationism helped to offset the innovation that strong support for woman suffrage from a socialist platform represented. Anti-collaborationism was more important rhetorically than organisationally, and was honoured as frequently in the breach as in the observance. In the US socialist women kept their sectarian distance from their 'enemy sisters' only in New York City; everywhere else, there was considerable co-operation throughout the 1910s, especially around votes for women.[36]

Although Zetkin's rhetorical challenges were directed at bourgeois suffragists, she also fought to keep socialist women from being overwhelmed organisationally by men within socialism. In structural terms, this commitment to autonomy within socialism was expressed by organising women separately from men within the party, a corollary to the practice of organising them separately from the non-socialist women's movement. The most vigorous and powerful of the national socialist women's movements – United States, Austria, Scandinavia – followed the lead of the Germans and organised women separately from men. In the US, socialist women had their own organisation, the Socialist Women's National Union, even before Debs formed the American Party in 1902; in 1908 it metamorphised into the Women's National Committee of the Socialist Party, USA. To be sure, in Germany this strategy was dictated by laws which prohibited women from engaging in political activities.[37] (By definition, an all-women's organisation could not be political.) But the separate organisation of women within socialism served an enormously important positive function as well, making it possible to set up the infrastructure of a semi-autonomous women's movement, and to nurture an entire generation of socialist women leaders. Indeed when, in 1908, the repeal of the German anti-association laws led the leaders of the SPD to abolish separate women's organisations, Zetkin fought furiously against this action, which she felt would lead to women's eventual disempowerment within German socialism. However, she lost, and her own power within the SPD declined.

Such semi-autonomous socialist women's organisations never developed in France or Italy, which may be one of the reasons why woman suffrage did not come to either country after World War I. Despite the fact that the socialist parties in both countries formally supported woman suffrage as a parliamentary measure, and that, at least in France, there was a non-socialist woman suffrage movement of some size, the absence of the link between the two may well have been crucial. Finland serves as a fitting counter-example. There the SPD was unusually hospitable to feminists within the party, and a large socialist women's network developed, which played a major role in the first victory for woman suffrage in Europe, in 1906.

Feminist internationalism: militant suffragism around the world
The emergence of a newly militant suffragism, influenced by the upsurge of socialist politics after 1890 but ideologically and organisationally independent of it, is the third source for the great growth of the woman suffrage movement internationally. While WCTU suffragists translated the goal of political equality into a familiar, female-friendly idiom, and suffragists within socialist parties prepared the way for a wage-earners' suffragism, these independent militant suffragists made their contribution to the revival of suffragism by linking it to a fundamental challenge to gender definitions and relations, and adding a whole new level of tactical radicalism to suffrage agitation. This independent militancy was decidedly internationalist, both in spirit and in substance. Its roots were in England, but its branches reached out, not only through Western Europe and North America, but also to China, South America, Central Europe and elsewhere.

This phenomenon of independent militant suffragism is related to, though not exactly the same as, the activity of those disruptive suffrage radicals who surfaced in England about 1906, and who were dismissed by the press as 'suffragettes', a term of opprobrium that the women themselves embraced and inverted. The British suffragettes are one of the few aspects of the international woman suffrage movement that have entered general historical consciousness, but study of them has, until recently, been limited largely to the complex and contradictory Pankhurst family, whose turn to Tory jingoism during the war has added considerable fuel to the thesis of suffragism's ultimate conservatism. However a new generation of women's historians is offering a revisionist interpretation of the history of suffrage militance in England which better allows us to appreciate its links with the left. They emphasise that the radicalisation of the suffrage movement in Britain reached far beyond the Pankhurst family; that its roots lay in the organisation of working-class women and the dedication of activists inspired by, but independent of, organised socialism; and that the mainstream of British suffragism eventually maintained the political alliance with Labour they initiated.[38]

The militant revival of British suffragism predates the involvement of the Pankhursts and can be traced to a working-class-based suffrage movement of Lancashire textile workers in the 1890s. Middle-class suffragists with socialist inclinations turned to organisations of working-class women, notably the female textile workers' unions, to generate a working women's suffrage movement. The tactics of this new kind of suffragism were borrowed from trade unionism, and emphasised 'open-air campaigning, factory-gate meetings and street corner speaking'.[39] Politically its goal was to pressure the fledgling Labour Party to provide a parliamentary route for woman suffrage. The Pankhursts, a family closely associated with Labour, began their suffrage work within this framework. In 1903, they organised the Women's Social and Political Union (WSPU), which initially emphasised public agitation, working-class organisation and Labour Party political links.

In 1906, the WSPU moved its operations from Manchester to London and at first concentrated on organising mass public demonstrations, the likes of which had never been seen in any women-led movement.[40] Soon other British suffrage societies, including the once conventional National Union of Women's Suffrage Societies (NUWSS), were organising 'monster demonstrations' for suffrage. By 1911, militant modern tactics under various organisational labels dominated the British suffrage movement.

As the WSPU moved away from Manchester and from its working-class origins, it developed its own highly influential form of civil disobedience, borrowed from the 'political law breaking' tradition of Irish nationalism.[41] Christabel Pankhurst, referring in 1908 to the 'Fenian outrages in Manchester and the blowing up of Clerkenwell Gaol', wondered 'how anybody after that can say that militant methods are not effectual'.[42] This civil disobedience strain took on an increasingly violent air, culminating in fire bombs and martyrdom on the part of the suffragettes and punitive forced feeding on the part of the state. Sandra Holton argues that the shift from mass to illegal tactics alienated many working-class women, who expressed their suffragism at giant demonstrations rather than in prison. Nonetheless, the political theatre of arrests and forced feedings intensified women's militance around the world.

These independent suffrage militants, labelled by the British press as 'suffragettes', came to stand for a modern, post-Victorian approach to building a mass woman-suffrage movement. The term 'suffragette' conjured up radical challenges to dominant definitions of womanhood. Until this point, bourgeois femininity – in Europe, North America, and their cultural outlands – was marked by a devotion to the separation of the domestic and private world of women and the public and political world of men. Suffragette militance literally took women out of the parlour and into the streets. Parades, outdoor demonstrations, street corner meetings – these were the marks of modern suffrage agitation. Inasmuch as wage-earning women provided the female army that first breached the walls around the public realm, suffragette militance was initially 'viewed as a specifically working class initiative'. But the challenge to cloistered femininity that it expressed eventually drew passion from women of all classes.[43] Indeed, the more upper class the woman who made the challenges to traditional sex-roles were, the more effective the challenges were.

In the same way as they had pioneered mass suffrage demonstrations, the Pankhursts inaugurated and then abandoned to other British suffragists the strategy of pressuring the Labour Party to support woman suffrage. This meant countering the Independent Labour Party's insistence that so long as votes for men were bound by property limitation, it could not support the suffragists' position of votes for women on the same terms as men; it would only endorse expansion of the suffrage to all adults of both sexes. About the same time as the WSPU shifted from Manchester to London, from mass demonstrations to civil disobedience, and from a working-class base to elite cadres, the WSPU repudiated Labour as a lost cause and started to move to the right, a shift which has weighed heavily in virtually all histories of British militance until recently. But Sandra Holton has shown that the NUWSS took up the paths that the Pankhursts had pioneered, that of hammering away at Labour's objections to woman suffrage. In 1911, this persistence was rewarded by Labour's agreement to support a compromise bill, which set the level of female enfranchisement at an intermediate position, between propertied and adult. The bill failed when the Liberals deserted it, but the détente between suffrage and Labour held firm.

The example of the British suffragettes had tremendous international influence, attributable to the extensive worldwide publicity they worked so hard to get. The International Woman Suffrage Association (IWSA), established between 1899 and 1902, also provided a conduit for their influence, much as the Second International did for the socialist suffragism of Zetkin and Kollontai. The IWSA had been designed to meet every five years, but it soon found itself meeting much more frequently infused with the spirit of suffragette militance.[44] In 1906, the IWSA met in Copenhagen, and delegates brought back the news of the British militants to Hungary, Russia, and elsewhere.[45] In 1909, it met in London, and delegates were treated to various demonstrations of militant tactics – mass marches, civil disobedience, hunger strikes. In 1913, in conjunction with IWSA meetings in Budapest, Sylvia Pankhurst toured Central Europe to talk about her working-class-based version of militance.[46]

Socialist women of the Second International, who had helped to inspire the formation of the IWSA by their example, were in turn much influenced by the feminist militance it spread. Despite their oft-repeated opposition to 'collaboration' with 'bourgeois suffragists', they could not resist the energy of the suffragette example: Richard Evans believes that the mass demonstrations of International Proletarian Women's Day from 1911 through to 1913 were imitations of the 'monster parades' organised by British militants.[47]

American suffragists were especially quick to pick up the inspiration of the British militants. Many of them were influenced by and sympathetic to socialism, although not party members. Harriot Stanton Blatch, herself a veteran of British Fabianism in the 1890s, returned to the US to organise a working-class-based, tactically militant, independent women's suffrage insurgency. (After American women won the vote, Blatch became an active member of the Socialist Party and ran for office on its ticket.) In San Francisco, trade union activist Maud Younger ('the millionaire waitress') organised the Working Women's Suffrage Society.[48] By 1913, tens of thousands of women were marching in New York City and the example of suffrage parades was spreading across the country. Despite the dictums of the Second International, American socialist women co-operated closely with these independent militants. In California in 1911, in Wisconsin in 1912, even in New York, it was often difficult to distinguish the two groups or to predict which feminists would show up inside the party, which outside. In 1913, this suffrage revival culminated with a mass suffrage parade in Washington DC and the creation of a national suffragette society.[49]

The suffragette example also shaped the Irish woman suffrage movement, which was only fitting, given the role that Irish constitutional nationalists played in holding up a final parliamentary solution to votes for women in England. The Catholicism of France and Italy is often cited as an explanation for their outrageously delayed enfranchisement of women, but the influence of Catholicism proved no serious barrier to the flourishing of militant suffragism in Ireland. The leading figure here was Hanna Sheehy-Skeffington, a socialist, friend of Irish labour and militant suffragist. Inspired by the Pankhursts, she organised the Irish Women's Franchise League, which heckled politicians, held demonstrations and engaged in that signature suffragette activity – breaking windows with stones. In their struggle to influence the shape of the coming Irish nation, the suffragists eventually gained the support of the Irish Labour Party. In 1922, in their new republic, Irish women got the vote on equal terms with men, six years before the British.[50]

Nor was it only Europeans and North Americans who responded to the feminist excitement of the British suffragettes. In 1912 in Nanking, China, the Woman Suffrage Alliance, an independent socialist feminist group, petitioned the provisional parliament to 'enact equality of the sexes and recognize women's right to vote'. Convinced that the men would not take their demand seriously, they armed themselves with pistols, stormed the parliament building three days in a row and had to be dragged off by guards. In imitation of the WSPU, they broke windows, 'drenching their hands in fresh blood'. Around the world, suffragette sisters celebrated their dedication. The WSPU itself sent a message of support, and in New York, the president of the National American suffrage organisation paraded under a sign declaring 'Catching Up with China'.[51] Argentinian suffragists, exasperated with a ridiculously limited municipal suffrage, organised the *Partido Feminista Nacional*, in imitation of the British WSPU.[52]

World War I and votes for women: moving into a new era
The women of most European and North American countries won the formal right to vote in the years during and immediately after World War I. But to grant the war itself agency in enfranchising women is, in the words of French suffrage historians Steven Hause and Anne Kenney, a way of denying the 'generations of feminist labor that made enfranchisement possible'.[53] Nor is the correlation quite so precise. Combatant countries – France, Italy and Belgium – did not enfranchise women, while neutral nations – the Netherlands and Scandinavia – were among the first to do so. In some countries, for instance Denmark and Iceland, the war held up the enfranchisement of women, which was already in place by 1914. In England and the United States, the war provided time (and a supra-partisan environment) for the political forces necessary to enfranchise women to mature. In Germany and Austria, where defeat and revolution brought in Socialist governments which enfranchised women, a more direct causal role can be attributed to the war.

Indeed, a case can be also made that the war had a negative impact on existing woman suffrage movements. In France, according to Hause and Kenney, the war was actually 'a setback for the woman suffrage movement'.[54] The war split national suffrage movements in two, just as it did socialist parties, and these were overwhelming setbacks. The majority of suffragists in combatant countries advocated preparedness, war work, and service to the state. In Germany, socialist and non-socialist suffrage women both formally embraced the war. In England, Christabel and Emmeline Pankhurst became intensely pro-war, renaming their *Suffragette* magazine *Britannia*. Extremely conservative political forces were set in motion which dominated European politics for the next twenty-five years and in which reaction against the gains made with respect to sexual equality was a significant component. In Italy, Mussolini briefly played the pro-suffrage card, instituting municipal suffrage for women just as local elections were being undermined. By 1930, woman suffrage and Italian feminism in general had collapsed.[55] In Italy and France, women had to wait until the end of a second world war to gain the vote.

While most suffragists became pro-war enthusiasts, a minority were determinedly anti-war. In England, Sylvia Pankhurst broke with her mother and sister to become a leading anti-war feminist. Outside of England, independent militants tended to the anti-war camp. In the US, the National Woman's Party resisted pro-war jingoism, being the first American organisation to run afoul of anti-sedition laws, even before the Industrial Workers of the World. In Ireland, Hanna Sheehy-Skeffington became a militant pacifist. The international feminist pacifist network formed by these women, most of them suffrage activists, named itself the Women's International League for Peace and Freedom, and constitutes one of the most important legacies of the pre-war suffrage movement.[56] Among women leaders within organised socialism, Clara Zetkin, who had long since been driven from the SDP's leadership, was notable for her opposition to the war.

In the 1920s and 1930s, the dynamic of international suffragism shifted away from Europe and North America, towards Latin America, the Middle East and Asia. These post-1920 movements for women's enfranchisement continued to develop in connection with larger working-class movements. Despite the fact that Communists disdained the parliamentary struggles which had allowed pre-war socialist suffragists to argue their case, left-wing advocates of political equality for women were still able to make some gains in the era of the Comintern; in Indochina and throughout Latin America, for instance, political equality for women was advocated in conjunction with working-class militancy beginning in the 1920s.[57] International networks established before World War I also continued to provide a medium for the ideas and history of women's enfranchisement to move between nations, notably the International Woman Suffrage Association, renamed the International Alliance of Women.

However, it was a new political force, anti-colonial nationalist movements, which provided the major crucible for organised efforts for women's enfranchisement after World War I. Important preliminary work has been done in this area by Kumari Jayawardena with respect to Asia, and by Asunción Lavrin and Francesca Miller with respect to Latin America.[58] They have convincingly demonstrated that revolutionary nationalism incubated women's ambitions for political equality in this new period and within this expanded global territory; Asian, Latin American and Middle Eastern women political activists were both inspired and frustrated by the rising expectations of native-born, male-dominated elites, who sought to challenge imperial power and to cultivate political and cultural renewal in their new nations. More research is needed to build on this pioneering scholarship.

Moving the history of woman suffrage movements into the age of revolutionary nationalism would seem to pose a major challenge to the international framework I am advocating, but even here I think we will find that there is much to be gained by tracing the circulation of ideas, individuals, resources and inspirations between and among nations. New transnational women's organisations were formed, pan-American and pan-Pacific women's networks linking advocates of women's political equality; the League of Nations and the United Nations also facilitated the international spread of ideas of women's political equality. Finally, it is significant to recall the impact that images of fighting women activists from Asia and Latin America, women guerrillas carrying babies on one side and rifles on the other, had not so long ago on American and European women, who had become alienated from their own traditions of political activism and of struggles for sexual equality. It was as if these historical traditions, set in motion long ago in one part of the globe, returned to their origins, several epochs later, able to reinspire and re-educate anew.

---

1   Oldfield, *Woman Suffrage in Australia*, 212-14; Grimshaw, *Women's Suffrage in New Zealand*; and Katie Spearitt, 'New Dawns: First Wave Feminisms 1880-1914', in Kay Saunders & Raymond Evans, eds, *Gender Relations in Australia: Domination and Negotiations*, Harcourt, Brace, San Diego, 1992. Dr Caroline Daley of Auckland University has suggested that the focus on New Zealand woman suffrage as a gift rather than a political achievement comes from American and British interpretations, rather than New Zealand historians themselves, who turned away from Reeves's analysis to study the suffrage campaign in terms of political struggle.

2   Oldfield, *Woman Suffrage in Australia*, 221.

3   Quoted in Werner Thonnesson, *The Emancipation of Women: The Rise and Decline of the Women's Movement in German Social Democracy, 1863-1993*, Pluto Press, Bristol, 1969, 32.

4   Evans, *The Feminists*.

5   Ibid., 217. See also Ross Evans Paulson, *Women's Suffrage and Prohibition: A Comparative Study of Equality and Social Control*, Scott, Foresman, Glenview, Ill., 1973, for a similar evaluation of woman suffrage, which applauds rather than criticises its alleged conservatism.

6   Kraditor, *Ideas of the Woman Suffrage Movement*; and William O'Neill, *Everyone was Brave: The Rise and Fall of Feminism in America*. Ian Tyrrell re-examines Kraditor's influential thesis that over time suffragists shifted from 'justice' to 'expediency' claims in the vote, *Woman's World, Woman's Empire*.

7   Bunkle, 'The Origins of the Women's Movement in New Zealand'.

8   DuBois, *Feminism and Suffrage*.

9   Ian Tyrrell, 'American Exceptionalism in an Age of International History', *American Historical Review (AHR)*, 1991, 1031-55.

10 Ellen C. DuBois, 'The Radicalism of the Woman Suffrage Movement: Notes Toward the Reconstruction of American Feminism', *Feminist Studies (FS)*, 3, 1975, 63-71.

11 Rosalyn Petchevsky, 'Dissolving the Hyphen: A Report on Marxist-Feminist Groups', in Zillah Eisenstein, ed, *Capitalist Patriarchy and the Case for Socialist Feminism*, Monthly Review Press, New York, 1979, 375.

12 Ruth Bordin, *Women and Temperance: The Quest for Power and Liberty, 1873-1900*, Temple Univ. Press, Philadelphia, 1981.

13 Tyrrell, *Woman's World*, 19.

14 Patricia Grimshaw, *Women's Suffrage In New Zealand*, 37.

15 Sylvia Pankhurst, *The Suffragette Movement*, Virago, London, 1977, first published in 1931, 178.

16 Diane Kirkby, *Alice Henry: The Power of Pen and Voice*, Cambridge Univ. Press, Melbourne, 1991.

17 Tyrrell, *Woman's World*, 221.

18 Oldfield, *Woman Suffrage in Australia*, 21. This was made most clear to me in Diane Kirkby's excellent biography of Alice Henry, which begins with a portrait of the Australian suffrage movement.

19 Mari Jo Buhle, *Women and American Socialism, 1870-1920*, Univ. of Illinois Press, Urbana, 1981.

20 Vron Ware, *Beyond the Pale White Women: Racism and History*, Verso, London & New York, 1991, ch. 2.

21 Oldfield, *Woman Suffrage in Australia*, 63.

22 Cheryll Walker, *The Women's Suffrage Movement in South Africa*, Univ. of Cape Town, 1979, 26.

23 Marilyn J. Boxer & Jean H. Quataert, *Socialist Women: European Socialist Feminism in the Nineteenth and Early Twentieth Centuries*, Evans, *The Feminists* and *Comrades and Sisters: Feminism, Socialism and Pacifism in Europe, 1870-1945*; Charles Sowerwine, 'The Socialist Women's Movement from 1850 to 1940', in Renate Bridenthal, Claudia Koontz & Susan Stuard, eds, *Becoming Visible: Women in European History*, 2nd ed., Houghton Mifflin, Boston, 1987; Jane Slaughter & Robert Kern, eds, *European Women on the Left: Socialist, Feminism and the Problems Faced by Political Women, 1880-Present*, Greenwood, Westport, Conn., 1981.

24 Cynthia Little, 'Education, Philanthropy, and Feminism: Components of Argentine Womanhood, 1860-1926', in Asunción Lavrin, ed., *Latin American Women: Historic Perspectives*, Greenwood, Westport, Conn., 1978. On Second International feminism in South Africa, see Cheryll Walker, *The Women's Suffrage Movement in South Africa*. This was, of course, an all white-movement. On Galicia, see Martha Boyachevsky-Chomiak, 'Socialism and Feminism: The First Stages of Women's Organizations in the Eastern Part of the Austrian Empire', in Tova Yedlin, ed, *Women in Eastern Europe and the Soviet Union*, Carleton Univ. Press, Ottawa, 1975.

25 Meredith Tax, *Rising of the Women: Feminist Solidarity and Class Conflict, 1880-1917*, Monthly Review Press, New York, 1980, 188.

26 Temma Kaplan, 'On the Socialist Origins of International Women's Day', *FS*, 11, 1985.

27 Mari Jo Buhle, 'Women and the Socialist Party, 1901-1914', *Radical America (RA)*, 4, 1970; Boxer & Quataert, *Socialist Women*.

28 Sowerwine, 'The Socialist Women's Movement from 1850 to 1940', 409.

29 Quataert, *Reluctant Feminists in German Social Democracy, 1885-1917*, Princeton Univ. Press, Princeton, 1979, 94.

30 Sowerwine, 'The Socialist Women's Movement From 1850 to 1940', 416.

31 Buhle, *Women in American Socialism*, ch. 2.

32 Thonnesson, *The Emancipation of Women*, 63.

33 Alice Kessler Harris, *Out to Work: A History of Wage-Earning Women in the United States*, Oxford Univ. Press, New York, 1982, ch. 7. In her later work, Kessler Harris has backed away from this assessment to some degree; see Alice Kessler Harris, *A Woman's Wage: Historical Meanings and Social Consequences*, Univ. of Kentucky Press, Lexington, Kentucky, 1989.

34 Polly Beals, 'Fabian Feminism: Gender, Politics and Culture in London, 1880-1930', unpublished Ph.D thesis, Rutgers University, 1989.

35 Barbara Clements, *Bolshevik Feminist: The Life of Aleksandria Kollontai*, Indiana Univ. Press, Bloomington, 1979, 59. Similarly, Linda Edmonson argues that 'such was the abhorrence felt by Orthodox Marxists toward the idea of separate women's organisations that the potential value of the female proletariat went almost unnoticed' until the non-bourgeois women's movement forced it upon socialists' attention; see Linda Edmonson, *Feminism in Russia, 1900-1917*, Stanford Univ. Press, Stanford, CA., 1984, 171.

36 John D. Buenker, 'The Politics of Mutual Frustration: Socialists and Suffragists in New York and Wisconsin', in Sally Miller, ed, *Flawed Liberation: Socialism and Feminism*, Greenwood, Westport, Conn., 1981.

37 Kollontai's biographer says that when she discovered that the separate organising of socialist women, to which she was passionately committed in Russia, was the child of German necessity, she was astonished; Clements, *Bolshevik Feminist*, 64.

38 Holton, *Feminism and Democracy*: Jill Liddington & Jill Norris, *One Hand Tied Behind Us: The Rise of the Women's Suffrage Movement*; Lisa Tickner, *The Spectacle of Women: Imagery of the Suffrage Campaign, 1907-1914*, Chatto & Windus, London, 1987. In addition, there is another group of contemporary feminist historians of British suffragism who have emphasised instead the sexual politics – as anticipating modern anti-pornography feminism – especially in Christabel Pankhurst's leadership. See Susan Kinsley Kent, *Sex and Suffrage in Britain 1860-1914*, Princeton Univ. Press, Princeton, 1987 and Sheila Jeffreys, *The Spinster and Her Enemies: Feminism and Sexuality, 1880-1930*, Pandora Press, London, 1985.

39 Holton, 33.

40 Sylvia Pankhurst, *The Suffragette Movement*, 195.

41 Rosemary Cullen Owens, *Smashing Times: A History of the Irish Woman Suffrage Movement, 1889-1922*, Attic Press, Dublin, 1984, 40.

42 Quoted in Jane Marcus, ed, *Suffrage and the Pankhursts*, Routledge & Kegan Paul, London, 1987, 48.

43 Holton, *Feminism and Democracy*, 35; Ellen Carol DuBois, 'Working Women, Class Relations and Suffrage Militance: Harriot Stanton Blatch and the New York Woman Suffrage Movement, 1894-1907', *JAH*, 74/1, 1987, 34-58.

44 Evans, *The Feminists*, 248-53; Edith F. Hurwitz, 'The International Sisterhood', in Renate Bridenthal & Claudia Koontz, eds, *Becoming Visible: Women in European History*, Houghton Mifflin, Boston, 1977.

45 International Council of Women, *Women in a Changing World: The Dynamic Story of the International Council of Women since 1888*, Routledge & Kegan Paul, London, 1966.

46 Sylvia Pankhurst, *The Suffragette Movement*, 535.

47 Evans, *Comrades and Sisters*, 68-75.

48 Englander, *Class Conflict and Coalition in the California Woman Suffrage Movement, 1907-1917*, Mellen Univ. Press, Lewiston, New York, 1992; DuBois, 'Working Women'.

49 Buhle, *Women in American Socialism*; Meredith Tax, *Rising of the Women*; Christine Lunardini, *From Equal Suffrage to Equal Rights: Alice Paul and the National Woman's Party, 1910-1928*, New York Univ. Press, New York, 1986.

50 Leah Levenson & Jerry H. Natterstad, *Hanna Sheehy-Skeffington: Irish Feminist*, Syracuse Univ. Press, Syracuse, New York, 1986, 37.

51 Ono Kazuko, *Chinese Women in a Century of Revolution, 1850-1950*, Stanford Univ. Press, Stanford, California, 1989, 80-92.

52 Ann Poscaletto, *Power and Pawn: The Female in Iberian Families, Societies and Cultures*, Greenwood Press, Westport, Conn., 1976, 191.

53 Hause & Kenney, *Women's Suffrage and Social Politics in the French Third Republic*, 202.

54 Hause & Kenney, *Women's Suffrage and Social Politics*; Evans, *The Feminists*, 223.

55   Donald Meyer, *Sex and Power: The Rise of Women in America, Russia, Sweden and Italy*, Wesleyan Univ. Press, Middletown, Conn., 1987, 37.

56   Gertrude Bussey & Margaret Tims, *Pioneers for Peace: Women's International League for Peace and Freedom 1915-1965*, Alden Press, Oxford, 1980, first published in 1967.

57   Sonia Kruks, Rayna Rapp & Marilyn Young, eds, *Promissory Notes: Women in the Transition to Socialism*, Monthly Review Press, New York, 1987.

58   The English-language scholarship on post-1920 suffrage movements is just beginning to be accumulated. Kumari Jayawardena, *Feminism and Nationalism in the Third World*, Zed Books, London, 1986; Francesca Miller, *Latin American Women and the Search for Social Justice*, Stanford Univ. Press, Stanford, CA., 1992; Asunción Lavrin, ed, *Latin American Women: Historic Perspectives*.

V

After Suffrage

THE VOTE,
JULY 6, 1928.

VICTORY !

THE VOTE

THE ORGAN OF THE WOMEN'S FREEDOM LEAGUE.
NON-PARTY.

VOL. XXIX. No. 976   *Registered at the G.P.O.*   ONE PENNY.   FRIDAY, JULY 6, 1928

OBJECT: To secure for Women the Parliamentary vote as it is or may be granted to men ; to use the powers already obtained to elect women in Parliament, and upon other public bodies, for the purpose of establishing equality of rights and opportunities between the sexes, and to promote the social and industrial well-being of the community.

FREE AND INDEPENDENT.

The Three Leaders *(together)* "WANT A PILOT, MADAM !"
New Voter " NO, THANKS."

'Free and Independent', *Punch* cartoon, 1928.
Used as cover illustration for *The Vote, The Organ of the Women's Freedom League*, 6 July 1928.
Private collection, Johanna Alberti.

14

Between Old Worlds and New: Feminist Citizenship, Nation and Race, the Destabilisation of Identity

MARILYN LAKE

Feminists in a new world

White Australian women were the self-consciously new citizens of a New World. Enfranchised in 1902, after three decades of struggle, they were then the only women in the world eligible both to vote and stand for election to the national legislature. Together with New Zealand women, enfranchised in 1893, they forged a reputation as 'pioneers' in the struggle for political freedom, pioneering a New World of liberty. They were cutting a 'new path through the tangled woods of conventionalism' and casting 'a bridge over the stagnant waters of custom'.[1] In 1903, the 707 founding members of the Victorian Women's Political Association (WPA) dedicated a 'memorial of gratitude' to the Ministry in the first Australian parliament that placed Australia in the 'proud position of being the first nation to recognise that women are justly entitled to the inalienable right of self-government'.[2]

Their distinctive role demanded an explanation and to this end they were quick to fashion a normalising nationalist narrative. They told a story of old worlds made new. 'A new land is for new ideas', wrote Vida Goldstein in the Boston *Christian Science Monitor*, 'and the active, energetic Englishmen, Scotsmen and Irishmen who came here quickly reflected the big, broad ideas developed by pioneering work in a vast continent, whose strange native inhabitants, fauna and flora, seemed literally to transport them to a new world of thought.'[3] 'Australia's great heritage', affirmed Bessie Rischbieth, 'is the Pioneer Spirit – it is natural for our people to look ahead because we are a new country.'[4] 'Australia offers such tremendous possibilities', Rischbieth told United States feminist Carrie Chapman Catt in 1924, 'it is the youngest of the great continents in development and a comparatively small population makes it possible to sow the seed now of the sort of civilisation women of all countries dream about.'[5] Her hope was that the 'annihilation of space' made possible by 'modern advancing communications' would not 'hopelessly involve the New World in the mistakes of the Old World' so there was 'no chance left for social experiment'.[6] And in the same vein Alice Henry told a United States audience, 'few Australians seem to realise the unique position occupied by Australia and New Zealand in the estimation of all those of radical social tendencies. They listen eagerly to all an Australian can tell them.'[7] Alice Henry regularly addressed American audiences on the methods the Australian women employed to secure the franchise and the results obtained therefrom. She observed, furthermore, that US audiences were more responsive than British ones to this advice from the Antipodes.

Vida Goldstein, Bessie Rischbieth and Alice Henry were all, in their time, well-known ambassadors of Australian feminism. Their distinctive status in the first decades of the twentieth century rendered Australian and New Zealand women political exemplars, lending them an authority as experts on women's citizenship. They travelled, they advised and they consulted. They extended sympathy, advice and assistance to their 'enslaved' British and American sisters. Around 1910, a petition was sent by Australian women's groups offering support to the beleaguered suffragettes in their militant campaign to free women from 'a legal and industrial slavery': 'We, Enfranchised Women of Australia, offer our reverent appreciation of the Spiritual Insight and Fidelity to Principle that are enabling you to speedily overcome the opportunist and materialist forces arrayed against you.' The petition then invoked the familiar terms of the national narrative which now routinely positioned white Australian women as figures of destiny:

> It has fallen to us in this country, where prejudices have not had time to crystallize so solidly as is the case in older lands longer under the sway of tradition and of convention, to gain the charter of our womanhood by a comparatively easy road, the road of vigilance and persistence it is true, but not of martyrdom . . . . We who already enjoy and appreciate those rights of citizenship for which you are striving, watch your campaign with intense interest and the keenest sympathy . . . .[8]

Not all Australian feminists were content to remain witnesses from afar. Indeed their capacity for travel is astonishing. Vida Goldstein had attended the International Women Suffrage Conference in Washington in 1902. She brought back with her messages to the women of Australia from Susan B. Anthony and Elizabeth Cady Stanton, the latter offering her best wishes for their 'success as citizens'.[9] In 1903, Goldstein was one of the first women candidates for national political office in the world when she stood for election in that year. In 1911, amid much publicity, she visited England in response to an invitation from the Women's Social and Political Union. 'The women of England had a right to claim the assistance of enfranchised Australian women', she explained.[10] Emmeline Pethick Lawrence wrote to Goldstein's mother: 'It has been a great joy to have her with us . . . . Public opinion cannot resist the influence exercised by Australia and New Zealand and greatly as you have helped us already we look to you to strengthen our hands in every way.' She paid tribute to 'the bond of union between us and our sisters in the great Commonwealth'.[11] Back in Australia, Vida Goldstein wrote to her colleague Bessie Rischbieth: 'we are specially keen about helping the women of other countries to win the political liberties we have won, and they do long for news from the enfranchised women of Australia'.[12]

Sisters in blood and race

Like other white Australian narratives of nation, the version of history here elaborated by feminist pioneers involved a story of natural succession in which the 'strange native inhabitants', as described by Vida Goldstein, would inevitably give way to the march of progress, as the Old World remade itself in the New. This version of history that underpinned the feminist project was racist, eugenicist and evolutionist. But women's experiment with citizenship would prove salutary and their gender, national and racial identifications would become less certain as they contemplated the consequences and implications of a democracy forged in the interests of the pioneering white man.

The federal legislation that enfranchised white Australian women had simultaneously disqualified Aborigines (but not Maoris) from Australian citizenship: the identity of the 'enfranchised women of Australia' was constituted explicitly in terms of racial difference in a nation state founded on racial imperialism. These first women citizens, then, bore a racial identity as well as a gendered one. The native people of Australia were the 'strange' others of the European imagination. White Australians were descended from the 'familiar' British stock that also ruled the United States and United Kingdom. 'We feel proud to remember', the petition of the 'enfranchised women of Australia' told the 'Women of England', 'that we are of your blood and race.'[13] And in her 'Open Letter to the Women of the United States', in 1902, Vida Goldstein identified 'the constant influx of ignorant aliens' into America as one of the obstacles to suffrage there and observed, 'because we women in the land of the Southern Cross are reaping what England and America have sown, we are all the more eager to help our English sisters and American cousins in their struggle for freedom'.[14] White Australian women saw themselves as members of the same (extended) family as white British and American women: their sense of themselves was constituted in these years around the turn of the century within an imperialist framework, in terms of the dichotomies drawn between the 'civilised' and 'primitive', 'Europeans' and 'natives', 'advanced' and 'backward' peoples. By the 1930s these oppositions would be destabilised as gender affinities blurred racial boundaries and feminist critiques of white masculinity challenged conventional racist hierarchies – processes that were inextricably bound up with the feminist experiment with citizenship.

Citizen rights, bodily rights

In many accounts of the history of women's citizenship, the achievement of suffrage marks the conclusion of the narrative, the event that signals the end of the story. I wish to reposition enfranchisement at the beginning of an account of white women's experiment with citizenship in the twentieth century. I wish to suggest that citizenship produced an identity for white women – that of the individual possessed of rights to self-government – which offered a new departure point for their agency and mobilisation. I would claim, also, that feminist activists should be recognised as pre-eminent among the theorists of citizenship, theorists whose ideas would consistently draw attention to the difference made by sex in the formulation of citizen rights.

As early achievers of political rights, Australian feminists, in community with colleagues in other countries, engaged in an ongoing discussion of the possibilities and limits of citizenship for women. 'We've won the constitutional right of equality', declared Vida Goldstein, on behalf of the Women's Political Association (WPA), 'now we must win the economic right to equality.'[15] 'The time had arrived in the Commonwealth of Australia', the chairwoman informed a women's industrial convention in Melbourne in 1913, when 'women . . . [having] been raised to the dignity of citizenship . . . must organize industrially and politically.'[16] Feminist groups flourished in Australia between the wars. The WPA in Victoria was joined by the Women's Services Guild in Western Australia, the Feminist Club and United Associations of Women in New South Wales and the Australian Federation of Women in New South Wales and the Australia-wide Australian Federation of Women Voters, formed in

1921. Such political and industrial organisation in the first three decades of the twentieth century produced a specific understanding of citizen rights in the service of bodily autonomy and the 'human' right of the sanctity of the person. To feminists, this was 'the most fundamental reform of all'.[17] Thus did most feminist groups pursuing full citizenship for women link the goals of an 'equal moral standard' with equality of status and opportunity. 'Economic independence' was necessary to obtain the long-established feminist goal of securing women's bodily self-possession – interpreted as a defence of women's bodies against violation, a defence of their right to personhood in marriage.[18] In women's citizenship, feminists saw the right to be free from the 'personal' tyrannies exercised by men through marriage, white slavery and prostitution. Whereas men tended to theorise citizenship as a vehicle to redress the ongoing oppressions of class in capitalist societies, formulating concepts of industrial or social rights, feminists promoted the concept of 'personal' rights – the right to the sanctity of the woman's person, to woman's property in her body and in her labour. This theorisation of freedom and citizenship produced the figure of the 'white slave' as central to their discourse. The white slave was the slave as woman, the sex slave. Like all metaphors it involved a displacement. White slavery drew attention to the particular meaning of enslavement for women – the violation of their bodies. White slavery was, according to Vida Goldstein in 1913, 'the inward meaning of the suffragette movement'.[19]

Could wives be citizens too?

Women's personal rights were also jeopardised by marriage. In 1910, Vida Goldstein's WPA asked the Australian delegates to the Imperial Conference in London to put the issues of women's loss of citizenship rights upon marriage as well as the extension of the suffrage to women throughout the Commonwealth, on the agenda of the conference. Acting Prime Minister W. M. Hughes refused, explaining, presumably without intended pun or irony, that these were domestic matters, not the concern of a meeting of 'self-governing Dominions'. The WPA disagreed, arguing that on the contrary they were questions 'affecting human rights and liberties'.[20] This conflict of interpretation with regard to the proper domain for women's pursuit of their rights – was the loss of citizenship upon marriage a domestic or international concern? – points to the ambition of, and the dilemmas posed by, the feminist theorisation of citizen rights for women. The question was how to redefine citizenship, a status pertaining to the relations between the individual and the state, in order to secure women's freedom, a goal pertaining to the relations between women and men. One symptom of and proferred solution to this dilemma was the constant conflation in feminist discourse of 'citizenship rights' and 'human rights'.

Political rights had hardly touched the imperatives of the patriarchal sexual economy. Women's 'personhood' or 'individuality' was thus asserted in opposition to discourses and practices that still positioned women variously as 'appendages', 'property', 'dependants' and 'wives' – as 'sex slaves' and 'white slaves'. This feminist discourse on citizenship specifically highlighted the contradiction posed by the institution of marriage – established, as Carole Pateman has argued, to secure men's conjugal rights – for women citizens.[21] Numerous feminist campaigns in the middle decades of the twentieth century focused on marriage as an institution that in many different ways undermined women's legal status as citizens. Australian campaigners protested against married women's loss of nationality and domicile, the legal barriers to married women's employment in the public service, their unequal rights to divorce, property and inheritance, unequal pay rates for women and men, the lack of remuneration for the state service of mothering, men's ownership of housekeeping allowances and savings and government plans to tax husbands' and wives' incomes as one. All campaigns were predicated on the understanding that citizenship should guarantee to women the right to property in their persons and their labour, the right to self-government – the right, in short, to liberation from the mastery of men. These diverse concerns came together in various plans to achieve women's economic independence, for married and single women, for black and white women. In this feminist scenario, the citizen's right of economic independence would secure women's human right of sanctity of the person. Citizenship promised that at last women would be treated 'as a person and not as a sex'.[22]

This extension of economic independence to women was taken up by feminists as a project especially suitable to the New World, to be achieved by citizens who looked optimistically to the state to secure its citizens' well-being and independence. Vida Goldstein sketched the logic of the progress for women as they moved from an old world into a new. In the 'old order', she wrote, 'women were regarded primarily as sex creatures . . . to be chosen by men as sex mates, not primarily even as mothers of the race but as outlets for the impulses and alleged needs of men'. This was the 'old chattel idea of things'. In the 'new and sweeter order' brought about by 'women's rebellion against exploitation of her body in and out of marriage, women would attain a greater degree of independence, marriage would be placed on a higher plane and self-restraint would prevail'.[23]

Economic independence

Feminists in Australia developed strategies to achieve economic independence for all women by extending the meaning of citizenship and calling for extensive state action. In the goals of independence and autonomy, they sought neither sameness nor difference. In some circumstances equality was appropriate: in others women made distinctive claims. Already, with men, the beneficiaries of old age and invalid pensions paid out of general revenue, feminists in Australia sought to augment women's position by formulating a concept of maternal citizenship – conceptualised as a two-sided contract, akin to that enjoyed by the soldier citizen, through which mothers would be paid an income in return for their service to the state. Labor women lobbied for and won the Maternity Allowance in 1912 within this framework. Introduced to alleviate the 'citizen mother's hour of travail' by Labor Prime Minister Andrew Fisher, the Maternity Allowance was welcomed by Labor women as 'the first instalment of the mother's maternal right' and they signalled their intention to immediately pursue the next instalment, family endowment.

The Maternity Allowance was also the subject of intense criticism by male church and community leaders because in its extension to single women it was seen to be undermining the marriage contract, the foundation, they said, of national welfare. Labor women were angry about the slanders directed against unmarried mothers, which they took to be slurs against their class; they were silent about the racist exclusions in the legislation. The Maternity Allowance was denied to 'women who are Asiatics, Aboriginal natives of Australia, Papua or the islands of the Pacific'; maternal citizenship was for white women only. One of the few voices to protest against this racist exclusion was the non-party feminist paper *Woman Voter*, which commented: 'It is the White Australia policy gone mad. Maternity is maternity whatever the race . . .'.[24] 'Mother of the race' was, in fact, an ambiguous identity, sometimes referring to the white race, sometimes the human race, supplying the potential for both racist and anti-racist identifications.

Labor women, whose solidarity with their men also involved unequivocal support of White Australia, pushed ahead in the years after World War I with their campaign to win (white) women's citizenship right to independence by formulating a programme of three inter-related planks: equal pay, motherhood endowment and child endowment. They saw each as necessary to the achievement of all, for it was men's assumed responsibility to support their children and wives that justified their higher wage. If men no longer needed to support wives or children – if the state provided an income to mothers in return for their work and separate endowment to support children – then unequal pay could no longer be justified. Labor women's campaign involved them in an attack on that bastion of male power, the family wage. Drawing on a long tradition of feminist critique, they argued that the family wage, recently institutionalised by the Arbitration Court in the Harvester and Mildura Fruit Pickers judgments of 1907 and 1912, turned women into 'sex slaves'. The family wage forced women into dependence on an individual man, who in return for providing maintenance could claim his conjugal rights, the right of sexual access to the woman's body. 'Woman will be a sex slave', wrote Nelle Rickie, delegate to the Trades Hall Council, 'until such time as the community and not the individual father and husband is responsible for the provision of the necessities of life for the rising generation – until such time as there is Childhood and Motherhood Endowment.'[25] 'Women who economically depended on men', observed Jean Daley of the Victorian Branch of the Australian Labor Party (ALP), 'moulded themselves to his desire.' Daley also argued that the sexual identity of women in the patriarchal sexual economy detracted from women's sense of citizenship in another way – that the self-conscious 'preening of sex' diverted women from the exercise of the social and political responsibilities of citizenship.[26] Much to the surprise and displeasure of many male comrades, the feminist goal of motherhood endowment was endorsed by the Labor Party and the trade union movement.

The family wage denied women's status as individual citizens: motherhood endowment recognised the right of all to an individual income. This was the point made by numerous witnesses in the Royal Commission enquiry into the feasibility of a national scheme of motherhood and childhood endowment. Wage-fixing tribunals, said Lena Lynch of the New South Wales branch of the ALP, did not recognise women and children as individuals at all – 'they were just appendages to men ... endowment would recognise the women citizens and the child'.[27] Endowment was seen as especially applicable to working-class mothers because 'working-class mothers give an infinitely greater service than those of most other sectors of the community'.[28] Moreover, working-class women were less likely than middle-class, professional women, to achieve economic independence through paid labour. 'We should also recognise', said Lilian Locke-Burns, 'that if a woman desires and chooses motherhood she should be as economically free, as little dependent upon others as the well-paid woman who has climbed to the top of the ladder in the scholastic, commercial, literary or any other area of her own choosing.'[29]

By the mid-1920s middle-class non-party feminists had joined Labor women in their campaign for equal pay and the economic independence of mothers, opposing the idea still held by 'conventional and unthinking men' that 'women exist for the service and convenience of men' with the claim that women's citizenship demanded recognition of their rights of individuality.[30] Less constrained than Labor women to attend to the sensitivities of Labor men, they argued forcefully – to Royal Commissions, to governments, in radio broadcasts, in pamphlets – for the rate for the job and not the sex, for the independence of the married woman. Men were enjoying a higher wage 'under false pretences', said Jessie Street. Not even half the men of Australia actually had the dependants they were being paid to support. 'I would like to see the basic wage fixed for the individual, irrespective of sex and irrespective of social responsibilities.'[31] The Australia-wide non-party campaign for the rights of citizenship was led by the Australian Federation of Women Voters (AFWV), established in 1921 on the initiative of the Women's Services Guild of Western Australia, the WPA of Victoria and the Women's Non Party Association of South Australia as a national body able to co-ordinate and represent feminists in national and especially international forums. The Federation was affiliated with the International Alliance for Suffrage and Equal Citizenship, but also had a particularly close relationship to the British Commonwealth League (BCL), which had built on earlier organisations, especially the Australian and New Zealand Women Voters' Committee and the British Dominions Women Citizens' Union. The organiser of the re-cast British Commonwealth League was Chave Collison, a graduate of the University of Sydney.

New Zealand and Australian women were prominent among those who attended a conference on the Citizen Rights of Women organised by the BCL in 1925. Conference resolutions linked political and economic rights with moral equality, that is, the woman's right to sanctity of the person. The principle of moral equality, it was agreed, necessitated changes to laws relating to marriage and divorce, illegitimacy, prostitution, street order and venereal disease. 'Moral equality' necessitated 'economic equality', which in turn required 'equal pay for equal work', a 'free field' in labour, removal of obstacles to the employment of married women and recognition of the 'economic value of the work of women in the home'.[32]

Feminist organisations in Australia worked relentlessly in the 1920s and 1930s in pursuit of these goals. In New South Wales, the United Associations of Women (UAW) was formed in 1929, from an amalgamation of three existing organisations. Its aim was the achievement of 'an equal moral standard' and a 'real equality of status, opportunities and liberties for men and women'.[33] It produced a series of pamphlets which systematically argued the case for women's rights, beginning with 'Income for Wives How It Can Be Managed: or the Economic Independence of the Married Woman'. This pamphlet, invoking the now standard feminist opposition between citizenship and slavery, argued for women's right to sell their labour, 'the very foundation of human liberty', as the basis for the claim that women working in their home had a right to an income.[34]

The right of men to sell their labour, it was argued, had been recognised since the abolition of slavery, but in men's appropriation of women's labour without payment, women were still in effect, slaves. The feminist argument for the independence of the married woman stressed women's work as mothers, the 'most indispensable and important work done anywhere by anyone'.[35] The work of a mother, it was reiterated, was of 'more fundamental importance to the State than any other performed, for without it the State could not continue'.[36] The child, the product of women's labour, was 'an economic and financial asset to the State'.[37] In refusing to pay mothers for their work, the state was depriving them of their 'independence and liberty'.[38]

Personality, individuality, nationality

The state of marriage, it was clear, in institutionalising women as dependants, contradicted women's status and rights as independent citizens. This was also the case with regard to women's nationality. Upon marriage to an alien, British, Australian and New Zealand women forfeited their nationality and citizenship. In 1918, a deputation from the WPA had protested to the Minister for Home and Territories against women's status as 'appendages' in nationality. The situation with regard to married women was 'repugnant' and 'degraded women to the legal status under the old feudal laws which modern custom abrogated'. Modern custom demanded the recognition of women's individuality. 'No man would tolerate the loss of his nationality by being married to an alien.'[39] In 1936, the fifth Triennial Conference of the AFWV reaffirmed its adherence to the principle that husband and wife should each enjoy independently their own personal nationality; that 'a woman whether married or unmarried should have the same right as a man to retain or to change her nationality'.[40]

Similarly, a woman acquired her husband's domicile upon marriage with consequent loss of individual rights. Even if a woman chose to reside in her own country, by law she was a resident of her husband's. She thereby lost her rights to petition for divorce, for property rights and the right to make a will.[41]

Other United Associations of Women pamphlets argued the case for 'equal pay and equal opportunity'. Feminist organisations saw it as necessary in the context of the Depression of the 1930s to defend rights already won, especially women's right to work. While the AFWV was meeting in the Conference in 1936 in Adelaide, the local branch of the Labor Party passed a motion criticising the employment of women whose husbands or fathers were also employed. The Federation condemned the motion, affirming in turn that the right to earn is the 'inalienable right of the individual whether man or woman'.[42]

The 'deliberate war waged against the woman wage earner' had culminated, according to feminists, in New South Wales (NSW) in the Married Women Teachers and Lecturers Dismissal Act of 1932, which became a focus for feminist campaigns for repeal over the next twenty years.[43] In 1940, Jessie Street as president of the UAW wrote to every member of the state parliament of NSW, urging repeal of the Act. 'It infringes the democratic rights and liberties of the individual', she wrote. These she defined as the right to work and the right to marry – the earning and conjugal rights – 'the natural and inalienable rights' – enjoyed by men.[44]

In 1941, the UAW was successful in lobbying the federal government to drop plans to tax the earnings of married couples as one income. In a letter of protest the UAW argued that this provision infringed 'rights which women gained under the Married Women's Property Act, which conferred upon women the right to independent ownership, control and management of their property'.[45] They argued 'that in any scheme of taxation, the rights and status of the individual citizen should be preserved'.[46] The Income Tax bill was duly amended to provide that the income of wives and husbands would be assessed separately, a change for which the UAW was pleased to claim credit.

White slave trade in black women

Some feminist groups, especially in Western Australia and South Australia, were also active in the 1930s in campaigning for the extension of citizenship rights to Aborigines, who were British subjects enjoying voting rights in some states, but who were not Australian citizens. 'We must never forget', an Australian speaker informed the British Commonwealth League conference in 1931, 'that the whole continent of Australia having been seized by the British government as Crown Lands, the Aborigines became British nationals and subjects of the British Empire.'[47] Middle-class non-party feminists campaigned at home and abroad for an end to the traffic in Aboriginal women, the 'white slave traffic in black women', and an end to white men's exploitation of native women.[48] They brought to their analysis of Aboriginal women's oppression their established understanding of the link between sexual exploitation and women's dependence. 'Economic dependence', declared leading activist Mary Bennett, 'is the root of all evil.'[49] In the writings and speeches of activists such as Bennett, Ada Bromham, Edith Jones and Bessie Rischbieth the use and abuse of Aboriginal women by white men came to symbolise the meaning of white civilisation in Australia. Bennett, especially, was influential in shifting blame for the condition of Aboriginal women from the lending practices of Aboriginal men to the rapacious mentality of white men. 'The terrible plight of the civilised Aborigines', she wrote, 'is the logical conclusion of our own dealings with them.'[50] Whites were a source of 'contamination' and 'civilisation' a source of degradation.

Feminists deplored the ongoing dispossession of Aboriginal people: 'We realise that the time is fast approaching when there will not be an acre of land in the Northern Territory or anywhere else in Australia which is not overrun by the white men', said the AFWV in 1931 in a letter to the Australian government, calling for land to be immediately set aside for the sole use of Aboriginal people.[51] Because Aborigines had been deprived of their land, Mary Bennett told a meeting of the BCL in 1933, Aboriginal women endured all the untold suffering of serfdom. They were, furthermore, deprived of education, medical services, wages and 'a political standing by which they might obtain other rights due to them'.[52] Bennett asked that adequate native territories be provided throughout Western Australia and the Northern Territory, so that Aboriginal people could remain in their own country and become self-governing. She also stressed the importance of respectable paid work.

White men's continuing sexual use of Aboriginal women had produced large numbers of children. The women's dependency exacerbated their vulnerability. The report of the Chief Protector of Aborigines in Western Australia for 1931, for example, showed that of 83 women sent out to domestic service, 30 were returned pregnant. The 'half caste problem', said Bennett, 'also results very largely from the same cause – their dependence'. 'The evils of the patriarchal system and polygamy have been intensified by having become commercialised, the unfortunate women having acquired value as merchandise from white settlement. This is the cause of most of the half-castes and entails more suffering and degradation for the women.'[53] Bennett and other feminists advocated education and training for Aboriginal women to enable them to become 'self-supporting'.

Fine women and mean men

The feminist strategy for Aboriginal women was assimilationist: feminists were complicit in racist imperialism even as they sought to oppose it. This was evident in their reference to the 'white slave trade in black women'. The white slave was the woman slave, white slavery referring to the sexually specific meaning of enslavement for white women. All women became, in this analysis, sisters in slavery. 'If a woman', affirmed Edith Jones, one-time president of the Victorian Women's Citizen Movement, 'whether white or black has not the control of her body she is a slave', thus metaphorically effacing the specificity of racial oppression.[54] The feminist focus on the situation of Aboriginal women produced a cross-racial identification and simultaneously reinforced the feminist conception of citizenship as a matter of 'personal rights'. 'The plight of the native women is pitiful', wrote Ada Bromham, Western Australian feminist and independent 'women's candidate' for the 1921 election; 'if we can do nothing for them, how can we hope to protect our own women?'[55] The plight of Aboriginal women, then, became the plight of all women writ large – victims of the white man's perversely primitive lusts.

In their political identification with their 'dark sisters' and condemnation of their lustful brothers, feminists would simultaneously emphasise sexual difference and the commonality of women, insisting that Aboriginal women were just like themselves, with an 'instinctive passion for purity'.[56] Actively contesting the patriarchal primitivist representations of black women as inherently different, as naturally lascivious and promiscuous, feminists insisted that 'the women, intrinsically, are fine and ready for a position of respect and indepen-dence'.[57] They showed, moreover, 'a great persistence in their work'. Aboriginal women were, said Mary Bennett, 'the most magnificent citizens that any country could desire'.[58]

For feminists such as Bennett, Rischbieth and Bromham, the depredations of white men in the outback called into question the claims of white civilisation and the heroic myth of the New World pioneers invoked earlier in the century. 'The worst thing I have seen', wrote Bennett, 'is the attitude of the average white man to native women – the attitude not of the mean whites, but of the overwhelming majority of white men.'[59] The feminist experiment with citizenship in Australia in the first decades of the twentieth century was disillusioning, but also instructive. Feminist advocacy of Aboriginal rights as well as their engagement in international conferences and organisations, their world citizenship, led many to an embarrassed recognition of their own and their country's racism. Through membership, especially, of the British Commonwealth League and the Pan-Pacific Congresses, which began in 1928, and visits to the All India Women's Conference, Australian feminists came to reorient their national and gender identity in response to their links with Aboriginal, Asian and Pacific women. The White Australia policy, as Vida Goldstein had been informed by Asian women, involved 'arrogant discrimination'.[60] Goldstein had earlier questioned the wisdom of Australia acquiring the mandate over New Guinea after World War I because of her country's 'appalling record of extermination of native peoples' and 'the brutality of the whites' towards indigenous people.[61]

National self-doubt

Sisterhood was no longer just a tie of 'blood and race'. The 98 per cent British composition of the Australian population came to be seen by an increasing number of feminists as a problem, a source of ignorance and prejudice, rather than a matter of pride. Eleanor Hinder, science teacher, welfare worker and programme secretary to the Pan Pacific Congress in 1928 was scathing about her countrywomen's Eurocentrism. In a letter from Shanghai in 1930 to feminist colleagues in Australia and abroad, she wrote : 'We are, as you know, very isolated with a population 98 per cent British in origin: we have a national religion – the White Australia policy, every organisation looks in affiliation to international groupings which centre in Europe. For the majority of the women of Australia, the women of Oriental countries simply do not exist . . . .'[62] An active engagement with women from Pacific, Asian and African countries through forums such as the Pan Pacific Congress and the British Commonwealth League led to new understanding and new alliances.

Increasingly frustrated by lack of political representation in Australia, Australian women's experiment with citizenship proved more gratifying when pursued abroad than at home. Numerous women had been defeated in their bid for pre-selection and election to the federal parliament. Australian feminists had more success in gaining access to the deliberations of international organisations and conferences and attended the League of Nations as alternate delegates from 1922. Returning in 1924, Stella Allen, the Melbourne journalist, declared that she had come back with an almost overwhelming sense of the importance of the League of Nations. 'In no other place in which she had been were women and men on such equal terms as in Geneva. The mental attitude was one of absolute equality.'[63] The gravitation of women citizens to international forums like the British Commonwealth League and the League of Nations can also be understood as peculiarly appropriate to their political programme. For their definition of women's fundamental right as the right to the sanctity of the person involved a challenge to the rights of men that transcended national boundaries. National states were relevant only insofar as they could provide the economic policies that secured the underpinnings of women's independence.

By the 1930s, it was clear that the Australian women's experiment was not proving the 'success' that Cady Stanton had wished for them. There were no women in the federal parliament and the economic independence of women had proved just as elusive a goal. Vida Goldstein addressed the AFWV in the 1930s on 'Australia and National Righteousness'. 'A new country should stand for new ideas.' The old refrain had become a lament. 'Thirty, forty years ago, Australians did pride themselves on leading the world towards better social, industrial and political ideas and ideals. Can she do so today?'[64] Disappointment bred recriminations. In a letter to her friend Edith How Martyn, an American feminist who had settled in Australia, a frustrated Goldstein endorsed Bessie Rischbieth's observations about the 'supineness of Australian women'.[65]

Australian parliaments, it became clear were only concerned with the successful exploitation of the country by the white man, as anthropologist A. P. Elkin observed with unwitting accuracy.[66] In the New World, the rights of the white working man, the citizen soldier, the ordinary man, would be institutionalised and celebrated. Women's subordination was integral, it seemed, to men's triumph. 'It seems to be a human law', observed Goldstein, commenting on Labor Party opposition to feminist candidates at elections, 'that the oppressed of one age become the oppressors of the next.'[67] Women's bid for independence posed a threat to men's conjugal rights, the rights of men to the domestic, sexual, and labouring services of women.

The success of the white man rested on the unpaid labour of women and Aborigines. 'It pays the white men to dispossess the natives of their land wholesale', wrote Mary Bennett, 'because the Government permits them to impress the natives as labour without paying them.'[68] Aborigines (men and women) and women (black and white) were dispossessed of their property rights in their labour and persons. Central to feminist arguments in these years was the point that married women – like Aborigines – were provided with their maintenance, but no wages. The patriarchal sexual economy placed all women, it seemed to feminists, at the disposal of white men.

At the Royal Commission into the desirability of child and motherhood endowment in the late 1920s, witness Ernest Baker, general secretary of the West Australian branch of the Labor Party, was asked about the proposal for an independent income for mothers: 'We hear a lot about the immense services they render to the nation and our obligation to recognise them. Do you consider that the wife should be included in any possible endowment scheme?' 'No', he replied, 'for the simple reason that the wife is necessary to keep the husband working.'[69] A wife was a basic right of the New World man. But could women be wives and citizens, too? When it was suggested that men's family wage might be dismantled to pay the portion meant for women and children direct to the intended beneficiaries, thus decreasing all men's wages, Barker replied with confidence: 'The single men of Australia would not stand it.'[70] White men – married and single – rallied to defend and extend their interests in the face of the challenge posed by women citizens. The New World had in fact witnessed the consolidation of old rights, the rights of white men. Self-government for women, all women, remains an elusive goal.

1   Rose Scott, letter to Vida Goldstein, 'Federal Senate Election', National Library of Australia (NLA), Canberra, 2004/11/311.
2   Women's Suffrage, Roll of Honour, NLA 2004/4/98.
3   *Christian Science Monitor*, 28 Nov. 1918, NLA 2004/4/143.
4   'Women's Work in the Empire', NLA 2004/4/97.
5   Bessie Rischbieth to Carrie Chapman Catt, 24 Nov. 1924, NLA 2004/7/62.
6   'Women's Work in the Empire', NLA 2004/4/97.
7   *Worker*, 30 July 1908, NLA 2001/4/259.
8   'To Mrs Pankhurst, Christabel Pankhurst and Annie Kenney', NLA 2004/4/371.
9   *Women's Sphere*, 10 Sept. 1902.
10   *Woman Voter*, 7 Feb. 1911, NLA 2004/4/179.
11   Emmeline Pethick Lawrence to Mrs Goldstein, 23 Aug. 1911, NLA 2004/4/4.
12   Vida Goldstein to Bessie Rischbieth (undated), NLA 2004/4/185.
13   'To Mrs Pankhurst, Christabel Pankhurst and Annie Kenney', NLA 2004/4/371.
14   'An Open Letter to the Women of The United States', *Women's Sphere*, 10 Oct. 1902, 218.
15   Quoted in Melanie Nolan, 'Sex or Class? The Politics of the Earliest Equal Pay Campaign in Victoria', in Raelene Frances & Bruce Scates, eds, *Women, Work and the Labour Movement in Australia and Aotearoa/New Zealand*, Labour History special issue 61, Nov. 1991, 110.
16   Minutes of Women's Industrial Convention, Sept. 1913, Univ. of Melbourne Archives, Melbourne, 3.

17 'A Call to the Women of Australia to Demand An Honourable Native Policy', NLA 2004/12/197.

18 On the tradition of feminist critique of sex slavery, see Susan Magarey, 'Sexual Labour: Australia 1880-1910' in Susan Magarey, Sue Rowley & Sue Sheridan, eds, *Debutante Nation: Feminism Contests the 1890s*, Allen & Unwin, Sydney, 1993.

19 *Woman Voter*, 10 March 1913, NLA 2004/4/191.

20 *Woman Voter*, Dec. 1910, NLA 2004/4/178.

21 Carole Pateman, *The Sexual Contract*.

22 Jean Daley, 'Woman to Woman', *Woman's Clarion*, July 1927, 3.

23 *Woman Voter*, 13 Jan. 1914.

24 *Woman Voter*, 9 Oct. 1912; on the contradictions and controversy surrounding maternal citizenship, see Marilyn Lake, 'A Revolution in the Family', in Seth Koven & Sonya Michel, eds, *Mothers of a New World: Maternalist Politics and the Origins of Welfare States*, Routledge, New York, 1993.

25 Nelle Rickie to Editor, *Labor Call*, 6 Sept. 1923, 9. For an extended discussion of the campaign for motherhood endowment, see 'The Independence of Women and the Brotherhood of Man: Debates in the Labour Movement over Equal Pay and Motherhood Endowment', *Labour History*, 63, Nov. 1992.

26 Jean Daley in *Woman's Clarion*, Dec. 1924, 7; Jan. 1925, 6.

27 Royal Commission on Childhood Endowment, APP, 1920, Minutes of Evidence, 923.

28 Ibid., 1116.

29 Lilian Locke-Burns, 'State Provision for Mother and Child', *Labor Call*, 19 June 1919, 5.

30 United Associations of Women, Pamphlet no. 1, 'Income for Wives', Mitchell Library, Sydney, MS 2160/Y4481.

31 Royal Commission on Child Endowment, Minutes of Evidence, 915-16.

32 British Commonwealth League, Resolutions of Conference, NLA 2004/7/67.

33 United Associations of Women, 'Aims and Objects', Mitchell Library, MS2160/Y4481.

34 United Associations of Women, Pamphlet no. 1, 'Income for Wives', Mitchell Library, MS 2160/Y4481.

35 Jessie Street, 'Woman as a Homemaker', United Associations of Women Pamphlet, Mitchell Library, MS 2160/Y4481.

36 United Associations of Women, Pamphlet no. 12, 'Child Endowment', Mitchell Library, MS 2160/Y789.

37 Ibid.

38 'Woman as a Homemaker.'

39 Notes of a deputation of members of Women's Political Association waiting upon Minister for Home and Territories, 5 Sept. 1918, NLA 2004/4/191.

40 Australian Federation of Women Voters, 5th Triennial Conference, 14-18 Sept. 1936. Report of Proceedings, Mitchell Library, MS 2160/Y789. See also 'The Nationality of Married Women', pamphlet authorised by the Australian Federation of Women Voters.

41 Marie Byles, 'Domicile of Married Women', Mitchell Library, MS 2160/Y4481.

42 Australian Federation of Women Voters, 5th Triennial Conference, 14-18 Sept. 1936. Report of Proceedings, Mitchell Library, MS 2160/Y789.

43 See, for example, Circular, Women Teachers' Section, Mitchell Library, MS 2160/Y789.

44 Letter to every member of State Parliament, 23 April 1940, from Jessie Street, President of the United Associations of Women, Mitchell Library, MS 2160/Y4481.

45 United Associations of Women, letter to J. B. Chifley, MHR, 10 Nov. 1941, Mitchell Library, MS 2160/Y789.

46 Ibid.

47 'The Australian Aborigine Woman. Is She a Slave?', NLA 2004/12/314.

48 Mary Bennett to *Australian Board of Missions Review*, reported in *West Australian*, 9 May 1932, NLA 2004/12/351.

49 Bennett to Bessie Rischbieth, April 1932, NLA 2004/12/4.

50 Bennett, 'The Aboriginal Mother in Western Australia in 1933', NLA 2004/12/218.

51 Rischbieth, President of the Australian Federation of Women Voters to Senator George Pearce, 24 March 1931, NLA 2004/12/4.

52 'The Aboriginal Mother in Western Australia in 1933'.

53 Bennett to Rischbieth, April 1932, NLA 2004/12/23.

54   Conference of Representatives of Missions, Societies and Associations interested in Welfare of Aborigines with Minister for Home Affairs following submission of Bleakley report, 12 April 1919, NLA 2004/12/506, 40. The activism of British-Australian feminists on Aboriginal issues is discussed by Fiona Paisley in "'Don't Tell England!": Women of Empire Campaign to Change Aboriginal Policy in Australia Between the Wars', *Lilith, a Feminist History Journal*, 8, Summer 1993. On 'white slave trade in black women', see report of Bennett's letter to *Australian Board of Missions Review*, in the *West Australian*, 9 May 1932.

55   Newspaper report of conference of Australian Federation of Women Voters, NLA 2004/12/327.

56   Bennett to Rischbieth, April 1932, NLA 2004/12/23.

57   Ibid.

58   Bennett to Rischbieth, 16 Nov. 1934, NLA 2004/12/81A; 'The Aboriginal Mother in Western Australia in 1933'.

59   Bennett letter in *Australian Board of Missions Review*, NLA 2004/12/351.

60   Vida Goldstein, 'Australia and National Righteousness', NLA 2004/4/248.

61   *Woman Voter*, 13 Mar. 1919, NLA 2004/4/138; 3 July 1919, NLA 2004/4/13(a).

62   Circular Letter 'My dear friends', NLA 2004/4/17.

63   Newspaper report, NLA 2004/4/302.

64   'Australia and National Righteousness', NLA 2004/4/248.

65   Goldstein to Edith How Martyn, 23 Dec. 1946, NLA 2004/4/27.

66   P. Elkin, 'A Policy for Aborigines', NLA 2004/12/216; the institutionalisation of men's power in Australia has been variously characterised as 'chivalry' and 'fraternal patriarchy'. See Jill Roe, 'Chivalry and Social Policy in the Antipodes', *Historical Studies*, 22/88, 1987; Carole Pateman, 'The Patriarchal Welfare State', in *The Disorder of Women*; Rosemary Pringle & Sophie Watson, 'Fathers, Brothers, Mates: The Fraternal State in Australia', in Sophie Watson, ed, *Playing the States: Australian Feminist Interventions*, Sydney, 1990; and Marilyn Lake 'The Independence of Women and the Brotherhood of Man', *Labour History*, 63, Nov. 1992.

67   *Woman Voter*, 8 Sept. 1910, NLA 2004/4/175.

68   Mary Bennett to *Australian Board of Missions Review* reported in *West Australian*, 19 May 1932, NLA 2004/12/351.

69   Royal Commission on Childhood Endowment, Minutes of Evidence, 348.

70   Ibid.

15

Keeping the Candle Burning:
Some British Feminists between Two Wars

JOHANNA ALBERTI

Feminism in the interwar years in Britain was a complex phenomenon and this complexity reflected the uncertain political mood of the period. This essay focuses on a limited number of perspectives: constructions of women in politics; relationships between generations and genders; perceptions of equality and difference, and concerns about the nature of politics. One way of illuminating complexity and understanding the nature of feminism when put into practice is through individual women's interpretation of their own experience. Therefore particular reference is made to the lives and ideas of a number of individual feminists.

Use is also made of some of the novels written by these women. As Alison Light wrote, 'the study of fiction is an especially inviting and demanding way into the past' and one of the ways in which British feminists in the interwar period expressed their fears and uncertainties was in fictional writing.[1] One of the most confident and positive of interwar feminists was Winifred Holtby; yet after reading Winifred Holtby's novel *Poor Caroline*, Margaret Rhondda accused Winifred of being afraid and unhappy. In response Holtby wrote that she could not bear Rhondda to think that she was 'fundamentally depressed and afraid' and that when she wrote, it felt 'exactly like having a wax disc inside on which other people can record their tunes . . .'.[2]

'A strip of pavement over the abyss'
I want to start by offering an overall interpretation, an outline of the landscape of interwar feminism in Britain. Feminist political activity can be seen as reaching a peak in 1928 with the Representation of the People (Equal Franchise) Act which enfranchised all women over 21 years of age. The passing of the Act was the culmination of an organised and co-operative effort among feminists in Britain, and was certainly understood by contemporary feminists as a satisfying climax of one hundred years of argument and action designed to achieve political recognition for women.

However, the historical context in which women in Britain began to operate in the parliamentary political sphere was a disquieting one. Women over the age of 30 who were occupiers or the wives of occupiers had been enfranchised by the Representation of the People Act of 1918, a measure stimulated by the perceived need to enfranchise the fighting men of World War I. The limited franchise was a clear indication of the fear that women would be in a majority in the electorate, and of a continuing doubt about whether women were as capable as men of exercising citizenship. That such prejudices still existed was confirmed by the ten-year delay in extending the franchise to all women. Full enfranchisement was rapidly followed by a chain of political reaction from depression to the threat of fascism and war. In this interpretation the interwar period was one of political, social and psychological uncertainty in which both the construction of gender and the exposition of feminism was likely also to be fluid and fragile.

World War I undermined the confidence of many Europeans in the values of their civilisation and in its steady progress. Helena Swanwick was a leading member of the National Union of Women's Suffrage Societies before 1914 and worked in peace organisations during the war. She was so 'weary and sickened' at the end of the war that she felt no elation and for long after she 'seemed still to be crying all the time inside'.[3] Some British feminists found that the experience of war cut the ground from under any sense of achievement in gaining the vote. Cicely Hamilton, who had been a militant suffragist before the war, recalled her sense of anticlimax on hearing that her name had been placed on the electoral register. After the war she worked as a political journalist, and for her these were 'years of reaction, often savage and insensate, against the discipline and over-close union that the peril of war had imposed on us; the years of disillusion and hope falsified'.[4] Articles in the feminist journals of the period expressed a painful sense of alienation from the political structures. An article in the *Woman's Leader* (the journal of the National Union of Societies for Equal Citizenship [NUSEC], formerly the National Union of Women's Suffrage Societies) on 12 March 1920 warned of approaching corporatism, and another which appeared on 25 June of the same year was entitled: 'Is the End of Parliamentary Government at Hand?' The image of life as a 'strip of pavement over the abyss', which Virginia Woolf used in her diary at the end of 1920, catches the sense of precariousness which is apparent in the thinking and writing of many feminists in the interwar years.[5]

Disillusion and lack of confidence in democratic politics meshed in with the particularly uneasy climate of opinion about sexuality. There are chronological links in Britain between women's sexual and political 'emancipation'. It is symbolic of the change in constructions of women as active rather than passive participants in the public and the private, that the first edition of Marie Stopes's bestseller *Married Love* was published just a month after the passing of the 1918 Representation of the People Act. Stopes wrote her book on birth control, *Wise Parenthood*, which was published at the end of that same year, because of the response she received to the reference to birth control methods in the first book. Alison Neilans, a suffragist and secretary of the Association of Moral and Social Hygiene, linked the 'intensification of public propaganda for the suffrage between 1906 and 1914', the war and the 'advent of birth control' to explain 'changing moral standards of women', where 'irregular relations with men' were much more common.[6] Fear of the consequences of women's political enfranchisement resonated with the fear of women's sexual liberation. The younger, 'new woman' became for some the scapegoat for this anxiety. Billie Melman has tracked the misogynist attitudes towards women in the Rothermere press in the twenties, and she draws attention to the sexual connotations of the word 'flapper' as it was used in the nineteenth century, which lend a disturbing perspective to its use to denote the disenfranchised woman. In February 1920 the *Daily Mail* claimed:

> The social effects of sex disproportion are seen in the crumbling of the old ethical standards. The freedom of the modern independent girl from the supervision of her parents. . . the cry of pleasure for pleasure's sake – all these tend to encourage a lower standard of morality. . . the social butterfly type has probably never been so prevalent as at present. It comprises the frivolous, scantily clad 'jazzing flapper', irresponsible and undisciplined. . . [7]

It is uncomfortable to recognise that this view of the modern young woman was shared by some feminists. Helena Swanwick described the sort of woman who accompanied the 'men delegates' at the League of Nations as 'a babbling little flapper or a painted simulacrum of a woman'.[8] Margaret Rhondda is sharply critical of 'the leisured woman' in her articles in *Time & Tide*, and one such reference was supported by an article in the *Woman's Leader* which accused the younger woman of doing nothing except cultivating her charm, and living the life of a 'libertine'.[9]

A vociferous campaign against the flapper vote was conducted in the *Daily Mail* before the granting of full women's suffrage in 1928. The campaign failed, but it is possible to read this failure less as a triumph for feminism than as a recognition of women's lack of political strength. By the late 1920s women in Britain were being constructed as much less of a political threat than the suffrage movement seemed to promise or the anti-suffragist feared. Eight women were elected in 1923, but the number dropped to four in 1924. These numbers constituted neither a triumph for women suffragists nor a threat to male hegemony. Lady Rhondda's attempts to get a bill passed to allow women to sit in the House of Lords had failed. Disappointment with enfranchisement is a recurring theme in the pages of the *Woman's Leader*, which reflects the struggles and frequent disappointments of the suffragist whose expectations of enfranchisement were not fully realised. Eleanor Rathbone was one of those who voiced her 'rude awakening' from a dream 'that when the vote was won (though only for some women) the need for sex solidarity was over and we might venture to behave as if we had already reached the place where "there are neither male nor female; neither bond nor free"'.[10]

'The bond between them'

Arguably then, the melting away of resistance to the enfranchisement of the flapper at the end of the twenties is an indication that she was no longer seen as a threat, that she could be contained within the British political and social system. Some feminists openly recognised this situation: Eleanor Rathbone and Eva Hubback wrote to members of the House of Lords on behalf of the National Union of Societies for Equal Citizenship (NUSEC) in May 1928:

> the suggestion that because women outnumber men their enfranchisement would give them political supremacy carries with it the implication that women are likely to vote on sex rather than party lines. It is only necessary to consider the way in which 8 million women enfranchised in 1918 have divided themselves up among the various political parties to realize that this is a fantastic notion.[11]

For Eleanor Rathbone this recognition that women had been contained within the political structures was a matter for regret. She had argued for sex solidarity, but had found that it was not as powerful as the 'vertical cleavage of class'. In 1924 she expressed her fear that women were being marshalled behind party banners in order 'to prevent their energies being "dissipated" or their minds "confused" by mingling with women of other parties than their own and so discovering the bond between them'.[12] Her address to the NUSEC in the spring of that year after two months of a Labour Government was entitled '"Put Not Your Trust in Parties"'. There was conflict between feminists and women in the labour movement in this period, a conflict centred on protective legislation, but the allegiance of women to class rather than gender was the crucial issue. This was, after all, a period when the freedom of women such as Naomi Mitchison or Ray Strachey (and, of course, their husbands) to write or to be politically active, was dependent on working-class women cleaning their houses, cooking their meals for them and looking after their children. It was also a period when feminists were increasingly conscious of this fact.

The divisions between feminists were not restricted to class. The controversy in the pages of *Time & Tide* and the *Woman's Leader*, and the resignation of the members of the NUSEC executive in 1927, mark what has been seen as a split between New and Old Feminists. The classical formulation of the New Feminism is that expressed in 1925 by Eleanor Rathbone when she declared that there existed among the feminists of the NUSEC a 'happy consciousness that many of the hardest cases of injustice have been met'. It was, she went on to assert, 'time to demand what we want for women not because it is what men have got, but because it is what women need to fulfil the potentialities of their own nature and to adjust themselves to the circumstances of their own lives'.[13] Other feminists did not wholly agree that the struggle for equality had reached the stage where a shift of emphasis was required, and committed themselves, in the words of Winifred Holtby 'to concentrate upon those parts of national life where sex differentiation still prevails . . . while inequality exists, while injustice is done and opportunities denied to the great majority of women, I shall have to be a feminist, and an Old Feminist, with the motto Equality First'.[14]

It is possible to interpret these differences as part of the process whereby British feminism began to fragment and stagnate in the interwar period. Without denying that there were differences among feminists, I do not believe that the split was a significant one, nor do I see the years that followed as stagnant. Winifred Holtby and Eleanor Rathbone were confident and publicly engaged feminists, expressing their feminism in actions and words. They remained in basic agreement about feminism. A significant congruity underlay awareness of differences between women, and that very awareness was, I suggest, a sign of confidence and strength rather than weakness. Feminists were prepared to engage in the interwar period with issues which had no simple or obvious solution: differences between women and relationships between men and women.

As far as class is concerned, Rathbone and others may have resisted the political implications of class difference, but this did not mean that they were insensitive to the needs of working-class women. Feminist activity in the interwar period was indeed increasingly focused on the practical concerns of working-class women: widows' pensions, birth control information, maternal health and family allowances. Women in feminist organisations, and those in political parties who did not necessarily define themselves as feminists, pressed for equal pay, for wider employment opportunities and for better conditions for women at work inside or outside the home.

British feminists were faced not only with the challenge of class difference but also with the different outlook of a new generation of women who had not been involved in the suffrage movement. Naomi Mitchison's correspondence with her aunt, Elizabeth Haldane, consciously expressed the view of the generation which was too young to be active in the suffrage movement before the war. Mitchison believed that the damage done to her generation by the experience of the World War I was under-estimated and that it led to two 'waves of disturbance': one at the time and the second in the mid-1920s:

> You have still a balance for your life: all that incredible pre-war period when things seemed in the main settled, just moving solidly and cleanly like a glacier towards all sorts of progress. But we had the bottom of things knocked out completely, we have been set reeling into chaos and it seems to us that none of your standards are either fixed or necessarily good because in the end they resulted in this smash up.[15]

One of Rathbone's aims in broadening the programme of the NUSEC was to attract more women into the movement, and in particular younger women. Feminist organisations were aware that they might find it hard to attract younger women, but were anxious to do so: 'The Woman's Leader will, we believe, be a help to them not only in making their own lives, but in doing good service to their country and to humanity.'[16] This appeal was couched in a language which was losing currency, and the failure of the NUSEC to attract the new generation of women is clear from what was in effect an absorption of the union by its own offspring, the Townswomen's Guilds, in the early 1930s. In one of the last issues of the *Woman's Leader*, the book reviewer acknowledged: 'Many of our younger readers know very little of the Suffrage struggle, some of them have avowed that they are tired of hearing about it . . . .' But she added, staunchly: 'To each generation its own "causes".'[17]

In British feminist writings of the period there is often an acute awareness of difference between generations as women struggled to achieve a sympathetic understanding of that difference. Although critical of the leisured young woman, Margaret Rhondda was aware of the social pressures which led to the formation of a 'parrot educated group'. Letters to Rhondda from Winifred Holtby bear witness to the efforts made by two feminists of different generations to understand one another.[18] Vera Brittain wrote in gratitude to Evelyn Sharp, a pre-war suffragette, on the publication of Sharp's autobiography, 'You have always fought so bravely for all the things I care for most, that at times I felt almost moved to tears by the thought of how much my generation owes to the fighters of yours, and how little gratitude we generally show for it.'[19] From the other side of the generational divide, Molly Hamilton, a Labour MP and a close friend of Ray Strachey's, suggested that the opposition to women's 'equality and freedom', when looked at from the point of view of the 1930s, seemed so totally absurd that the struggle for it could not be valued by young women:

> Certainly, they feel no interest in it, as achievement, and little or no sense of responsibility about it, as achievement for them to complete. They alone are in a position to tell us about it; what came of it; what it is like. But they will do nothing of the kind. They are not aware that there is anything to tell. A condition in which they, like their brothers, make their own choices and do and say what occurs to them, seems to them natural and obvious. It calls for no comment. No one asks the young man 'What about it?' Why ask the young woman?[20]

Hamilton described this enfranchised young woman 'poised gracefully on the diving-board, or humped, not so gracefully, over the steering-wheel of a fast car. . . the audible tones of her unmodulated voice emitting words more suggestive of stables than drawing-room . . .'.[21]

Sexuality, marriage and work
A liberation of a kind which the older British feminist had not foreseen – although she might value it – was taking place: greater leisure to enjoy sport, dancing, the cinema, the library book; short hair and short skirts (there was an outcry among feminists when there was a threat to shorten skirts in the early summer of 1930); the disposable sanitary napkin. Hamilton included in her construction of the modern young woman the firm statement that 'the post-war generation has definitely rejected the puritan standpoint about sex'.[22] If the perception of women in British political life was informed by fears of the instability of sexual orthodoxies

in the twenties did some feminists perceive the shift in ideology? Sexuality, marriage and work; how they could or should be combined were questions which exercised the minds, particularly of younger feminists, in the interwar period. The solutions found, both in theory and practice, were rarely satisfactory. Naomi Mitchison seems to have both valued work and experimented with a good deal of sexual freedom, but she could rely on money to achieve the freedom to write. About 'the entanglement of bodies' she was later to 'remember the pain almost more clearly than the delight'.[23] Ray Strachey seems to have achieved a remarkable stability in her relationship with her husband – despite, or perhaps because of the separate lives they led – and she carried the main burden of familial and financial responsibility. Writing, like Mitchison, in later life, Winifred Horrabin described her own views on marriage in the early twenties:

> I distinctly recollect thinking that the practice of group marriages sounded as if it had interesting possibilities. Not that my own sex life lacked anything at all except perhaps variety. Blissfully, happily married, given the freedom of a more than adequate, albeit modest income, delightedly shared, marriage for me meant the very best kind of freedom.[24]

When her husband began to have sexual relationships with other women, Horrabin did her best to accommodate these within their marriage, believing that it 'had roots of real strength'.[25]

Fiction offered the space to imagine new possibilities for women, especially in the areas of sexuality, marriage and work. Winifred Holtby created a new woman of the mould shaped by Mollie Hamilton in *Poor Caroline*, which was published in 1931. Eleanor is confident, independent, interested in science and technology, an enthusiastic car-driver. In this novel and in *South Riding*, Holtby explored the relationship between the older and younger generation of women between the wars, and the possibilities facing the 'new woman'. In *Poor Caroline* Eleanor chooses marriage, albeit with a 'new man'.[26] Ellen Wilkinson in *Clash*, which was published in 1929, also has her independent new woman opt for love and marriage.[27] Both Holtby and Wilkinson – wishfully? – created men who are gentle, caring, will not stand in the way of the work of the women they love. I see it as significant that their creations of 'new men' have both been damaged, either physically or psychologically, by their war experience.

Both Holtby's and Wilkinson's writings express the sexualised context of women's experience of the public world, and in their own lives these authors suffered from the assumptions of their contemporaries about the unmarried woman. Holtby was told by a doctor that she needed a sexual relationship with a man.[28] The assumption that every woman required a heterosexual relationship to be fulfilled was one way of containing independent women within the patriarchal structures. Wilkinson and Holtby both challenged this interpretation in the way they lived their lives. Holtby wrote a passionate attack on the treatment of the spinster in *Women and a Changing Civilisation* in which she asserted that spinsters – 'even' those who had no sexual relationships – could lead a fulfilled life. Yet her own ambivalance is suggested by her creation in *South Riding* of a spinster who is helplessly in love with a man, and whose sexual passion is never fulfilled. But Sarah Burton is not a frustrated woman, and we are left knowing that although she regrets that she missed the 'rare light of ecstasy', her 'appetites for intimacy, power, passion and devotion are well satisfied', although she needs another, significantly an older woman, to help her see that for herself.[29] The book places this central story within an intricate political and social web which places gender relations firmly in a political context; but sexuality is made to cut across politics. Sarah Burton falls in love with a man to whom she is sexually attracted and politically violently opposed. Holtby seems to be saying that sexual attraction was a force beyond reason. Wilkinson had told the same story in *Clash*, although in the end she gave her heroine a new man to marry who will be supportive of her political career. Ellen Wilkinson's own suffering is apparent in the review of *South Riding* she wrote for *Time & Tide*. Wilkinson must have seen herself in the character of Sarah Burton (to whom she is indeed compared in appearance within the novel). At the end of the review she wrote:

> The heroine of the twentieth century cannot fall luxuriously into a decline if her love-story is broken. There is the quick way out of emotional suicide of course. But when the telephone is ringing for a committee, an operation to be seen through, girls demanding to be taught, the modern woman takes a stiff dose of something and somehow carries on.[30]

The difference between Wilkinson's optimism in *Clash* and her empathy with Sarah Burton, like the difference between Holtby's early and later novel, may lie in the difference between the periods of writing. There was a drop in confidence in the mood of British feminists between the end of the twenties and the middle of the thirties: I shall pick up the issue of the political context later on. As for Ellen Wilkinson's personal experience, the painful and sudden ending of her own relationship with Frank Horrabin, a Labour MP, can be traced in the papers of his wife, Winifred. Moreover, Winifred Horrabin's descriptions of Ellen – 'a self-centered egoist of an extreme kind' – echo the ambivalence of many contemporaries about the single, younger woman with a political career. Yet Horrabin was fully aware of the difficulties of being a feminist in the Labour Party in the interwar years. 'After all, it is easier to get the tea ready than to challenge a committee of men in a losing fight for some point they call a minor one because it relates to women.'[31]

'New ways of self-expression'

Ellen Wilkinson probably knew that she was being wishful when she created in *Clash* a woman who achieved both political power and marriage. She herself was a member of a party whose dominant understanding of the power of women was that it lay in the private, domestic sphere. Marion Phillips, the British Labour Party's woman's officer, welcomed the new women voters in her editorial in the May 1929 issue of *Labour Woman*. The cover of the paper showed a reproduction of a Dutch interior with a young woman going about her domestic duties. Phillips referred to this painting in her editorial and asserted that the girl in it was similar to the:

> girl of today . . . . There is the same deep source within her of gentleness and kindness . . . . You can, as I say, call her a flapper if you want to be petty and stupid. I should prefer to call her the ruler of our destinies, for that is what she is today. In her small, strong hands rests the future of us all. She is, this new citizen of ours, the arbiter of fate in the coming General Election, and no one this year doubts that politics are the very web of life.[32]

This message can be interpreted both as containing the new woman voter within domesticity and as constructing her as politically powerful precisely because of her domestic role. Articles and editorials in *Labour Woman* asserted the importance of the role women played both within the home and in the party. By 1928 the women's sections of the Labour Party had a substantial membership of around a quarter of a million and they played a significant role in building the party organisation. Yet their power was contained and restricted by the male-dominated party structures.

A re-examination by Maggie Morgan of the significance of the other rapidly expanding women's organisation in the interwar period, the National Federation of Women's Institutes (NFWI), warns that as feminists we should neither discount the value women placed on their association with the domestic, nor ignore the political framework within which they understood their role. The Women's Institute movement began in 1915 and quickly developed an independent, democratic structure and launched a monthly magazine. By 1925 it had a quarter of a million members. Morgan has described how the movement 'struggled in national political terms and locally to improve the material circumstances of women's lives', and she has argued that it 'provided a space for women to fight the internalization of male domination'. The political campaigns which the institutes and the guilds pursued were mainly focused on housing, water and drainage, and their 'female cultural space' was often occupied by domestic concerns. They did not challenge the association of women with domesticity, but they did place a high value on domestic needs and skills.[33] The NUSEC recognised both the appeal to women and the political potential of the institutes when discussing the future of their own organisation after the final achievement of the vote. They encouraged members to form 'guilds' in small towns on the same lines as the institutes which were all based on villages.[34] An appeal for the encouragement of what became known as Townswomen's Guilds was launched from the house of Lady Denman, the 'chairman' of the NFWI. In 1932 the annual meeting of the NUSEC was attended by delegates from 183 Townswomen's Guilds and only 51 from the societies for equal citizenship.

Readers of *Time & Tide* were confronted with an assertive expression of confidence in the new and popular women's organisations. The paper was most strongly associated with feminist organisations such as the Six Point Group and the Open Door Council which campaigned for strict gender equality, and Winifred Holtby had written to complain of the attitude of middle-class parents who would not let their daughters work and thus deprived them of the 'fierce joy, absorbed interest, gaiety, discipline, devotion and excitement which all enter into the rigid routine of a professional job'. In response, a correspondent denied that there was much 'fierce joy' to be had from the office work done by most women, and suggested that Holtby:

> has not felt the breath of that great revival of corporate living which, expressing itself in such outwardly prosaic movements as the Guides, the Women's Institutes and the new and urgently needed Townswomen's Guilds, has done so much to change the social face of the country, breaking down old isolations, and bringing to millions of people a new sense of comradeship and new ways of self-expression.[35]

Winifred Holtby warned of the dangers of 'the cult of the cradle', and that 'saccharine sentiment is poured over motherhood and infancy'. Yet she too understood the political effectiveness of women in terms of welfare legislation:

> For centuries . . . the pendulum of governmental interest had swung away from the concerns of ordinary human life. Schools and hospitals, clinics and maternity benefit, medical inspection for juveniles, improved housing, the protection of children from assault and cruelty – the importance of these aspects of social organisation – had been almost completely neglected. It is since women have been 'let loose on the world' that neglect has been remedied to some still ludicrously small extent.[36]

There is a possible contradiction or paradox here: an association of women in political life with the private and the domestic co-existing with a rejection of the emphasis of women as mothers upon which this association was often based. But Holtby saw no need to reject women's particular and valued contribution to politics just because of the tendency to sentiment-alise motherhood. This was a position she shared with other feminists such as Eleanor Rathbone, who, as the best known exponent of the New Feminism, demanded a greater recognition of women's particular contribution to political life.

Naomi Mitchison valued and personally enjoyed motherhood, and she developed a political philosophy based on 'love and awareness'.[37] She had accused her aunt's generation of dividing life up into the outside and the inside, a division of life into the public and the private which she challenged, denying that 'women are . . . merely occupied with personal relationships and the means of life'. But she also admitted that trying to live both sorts of life was hard – and she cited Winifred Holtby as a woman who had tried and whose body had suffered in the attempt. Mitchison believed that politics could combine the inside and the outside, putting 'danger and beauty, conversion and re-birth' together with 'lots of small, ordinary things – more dustbins and bathrooms for people who haven't got them, more leisure and more education for people who need them desperately . . .'.[38] In her only novel which dealt with contemporary issues in a contemporary setting, We Have Been Warned, Mitchison used a woman protagonist to explore the possibilities of the politics she constructs in that letter. She juxtaposed domestic, personal questions such as marriage, the bringing up of children, birth control, abortion and rape, with the structures and ideologies of more orthodox politics. To simplify what is a complex construct in a long novel, Mitchison suggested through the novel that politics should and could be based on non-possessive human relationships. She made it clear that it would be very difficult to achieve this: she exposed the dangers of class conflict, of personal as well as public violence. She showed an acute awareness of the violence and instability behind the cosy domestic politics of the thirties. She, like Holtby in her novels, put forward a message of hope in a world which they knew to be full of greed, carelessness and cynicism. It is the same message which Mitchison was later to elaborate in *The Moral Basis of Politics*.[39]

Marion Phillips saw no contradiction between women's domestic role and their political effectiveness. She was convinced that the flapper won the election of 1929 for Labour. In that year fourteen women entered the House of Commons, among them Eleanor Rathbone and Marion Phillips for the first time, and Ellen Wilkinson for the third. The *Woman's Leader* was dissatisfied by the number of women elected, yet relieved that it was larger than in the previous Parliament. It welcomed 'the return of a Government whose programme in many respects runs parallel to our own'.[40] The tone of comment in that paper over the next two years was thoughtful and undogmatic in its approach to issues affecting women, welcoming and claiming credit for the permission given by the Ministry of Health for local authority clinics to make birth control information available to married women; wary and somewhat ambivalent about protective legislation and the pressure put on unemployed women to enter domestic service.

A question of identity

The economic crisis which began in the spring of 1929 and the depression which followed it seemed to undermine the confidence in the *Woman's Leader*'s thoughtful approach to feminist issues. Yet British feminists did not abandon their struggle to understand and to assert the particular value of the contribution of women to political life.

Like World War I, the slump in Britain arguably produced a more powerful image of economic and social depression in discourse than can be measured statistically. Holtby described what she saw as 'The Slump complex . . . a narrowing of ambition. . . closing in alike of ideas and opportunities. Somewhere a spring of vitality and hope had failed . . . . The slump is really a general resignation by humanity of its burden of initiative . . .'. She placed her own sense of the weakening of the force of feminism within this more general context of reaction: 'There had been a rise in feminism; there is now a reaction against it. The pendulum is swinging backwards, not only against feminism, but against democracy, liberty and reason, against international co-operation and political tolerance.'[41] One of the reasons for this 'closing in' was a practical one. For Ray Strachey, as for many other middle- and working-class married women, the Depression meant that she had to get a full-time paid job for the first time, and she had less time for thinking and writing. The tone of her letters becomes less certain and less confident. She wrote to her son in November 1933:

> Its very queer how the world is collapsing piecemeal. Security has quite gone, & your generation may have the most startling things to face . . . . But that will be your problem. All I can do for the moment is to go on tinkering with the present political machine & it generally seems to be worth while to do so. Now & then a sort of chasm opens up, & the whole thing turns futile. But mostly I'm too busy to notice it.[42]

Ray also continued her voluntary engagement with women's employment, and was by the mid-thirties employed full time by the Women's Employment Federation. In 1935 she edited and contributed towards a volume of essays, published in 1936 as *Our Freedom and its Results*. The tone of these essays is tentative and exploratory: maybe the contributors were trying to make sense of a world they saw as hostile and changing, just as Holtby had done in *Women*. Feminists in the mid-thirties were writing in the knowledge of the impact of fascism on Europe and in the awareness that fascist ideas were informing the political thinking of their British contemporaries.[43] In the introduction, Ray wrote that the contributors to the volume 'reach no positive conclusion . . . none of them feel that the freedom of women in society is either really achieved or really stable, or that there is any clear evidence as to what the results of it will be when that time comes'.[44] Eleanor Rathbone's contribution pursues the line of thinking which she had opened up at the beginning of the period. In an article in *The Common Cause* (the predecessor of the *Woman's Leader*) in February 1918, Rathbone had avoided constructing equality and difference as dichotomous when she wrote: '"Equality" is not a synonym for "identity" . . . . It should be possible to make the status and opportunities of women "equal to" those of men, without making them in the least the same.'[45] In *Our Freedom* she refuted the expectation that women's contribution to public life was, or would be 'utterly different from the contribution of men' because, in respect of 'the interacting forces of heredity, education, social environment, party politics . . . women differ less from men than men from men and women from women . . .'. Yet towards the end of her chapter she asserted that women's political contribution had been different to that of men and she posed two questions: '. . . is there a wave-length set up by human suffering, to which the minds of women give a specially good reception? Or is the explanation not psychological, but to be found in the nature of the work usually done by women?'[46]

A lack of dogmatism and a willingness to leave open the question of equality and difference is apparent in Ray Strachey's own chapter on women's employment. There she wrote that the elements which shaped the economic structures of society are 'so complex, indeed so individually variable, that the pattern which they will make in combination is inevitably confused, obscure and uncertain'.[47] Her subsequent conclusions on women's future employment patterns in Britain were based on the assumptions that there is 'practically nothing which can be postulated about them (women) as a whole save that they are human beings', but also that women tend to attach 'a good deal of importance to human beings'. In the future, Strachey suggested, thanks to women's involvement in politics, 'the relative values of people and things will change'.[48]

This willingness to accept ambiguity and uncertainty, this denying of gender dichotomy, is also to be found in Holtby's writing. Holtby was torn between political commitment and the writing of fiction: 'I still shall never quite make up my mind whether to be a reformer-sort-of-person or a writer-sort-of-person. Only I trust my judgment as a writer more than as a worker for movements and I actually enjoy writing more. Well, well.'[49] She tried all her adult life to do both. She, like Ray Strachey, lived with unusual energy and intensity : Holtby died in 1935 at the age of 37 and Strachey in 1940 at the age of 52.

'On the rim of a volcano'
The end of the interwar period in Britain was overshadowed by the threat of war in Europe. Domestic concerns seemed petty in the context of developments in Europe and many British feminists were engaged in peace movements and in the struggle to oppose fascism, especially by assisting European refugees. As World War II drew closer, the taste of politics became increasingly sour, and British feminists shared a general sense of political confusion or paralysis, particularly at the time of the Munich crisis. Sylvia Ashton-Warner wrote that Chamberlain had 'given us . . . the burden of a guilt too heavy to bear.'[50] Ray Strachey had written to her mother on 3 October:

. . . the feeling of relief here is quite curious. To some people (of whom I am one) it has the effect of recovery from an illness, and going out of the house for the first time. Everything looks wonderful, & the dullest normal thing seems worthwhile. To others the effect is to set up a rage of criticism of anyone & anything . . . I can only think that *anything* is better than war . . . .[51]

Naomi Mitchison's rage of criticism was directed at herself and her friends. She wrote to Aldous Huxley on 17 October:

I want to write to you rather at length about the situation in this country, not because I want you to do anything . . . , but partly because I think that all of us are partly to blame for it, and partly because I myself am desperately unhappy and I must get in touch with someone . . . . During the 'crisis week' there did not seem to me to be any obvious good or right course to follow . . . . And *that* is what we with our anti-war propaganda have done, we've just made people afraid, so that everyone was enormously relieved to think that Nazi methods had won again and it was only Czechoslovakia which was being done in.[52]

Ethel Smyth's reaction was similar: 'Hitler has gambled with success on our dread of war'.[53] In a poem Lettice Cooper asked:

How can I write a novel in the world today?
          . . . when the baby at the breast
Is only safe for the next minute; when all the rest
Are dying men already . . .
I was told of this when I was young;
I knew
that I should die but not that the world could die.[54]

And in July Rose Macaulay wrote: 'All this standing diver-fashion on the rim of a volcano wondering when we shall get the signal to jump grows tiring on the nerves.'[55]

Margaret Rhondda's response to the fear that 'our liberties may be snatched away from us any moment' was 'to remember that we have even in our own generation made them ten times worth the snatching', and to remind her readers that no woman could fail to value her freedom, however precarious it might seem to be in face of 'the nightmare of horror that confronts us'.[56]

I have suggested that the absence of feminist assertiveness between the wars is partly the result of the general political uncertainty of a period which was haunted by the memory of one war and the fear of another which might bring the world to an end. I have also argued that feminists continued to address difficult and important questions and to wrestle with some of the more uncomfortable aspects of women's experience of enfranchisement. The feminist voice I hear in the interwar period was thoughtful and exploratory, accepting differences between women, and claiming equality between women and men without rejecting difference.

1   Alison Light, *Forever England: Femininity, Literature and Conservatism between the Wars*, Routledge, London, 1991, 2.
2   Winifred Holtby, *Poor Caroline*, Virago, London, 1985, first published in 1931. Winifred Holtby to Margaret Rhondda, Jan. 1931, published in *Time & Tide (TT)*, 4 April 1936, 470.
3   Helena Swanwick, *I Have Been Young*, Gollancz, London, 1935, 307.
4   Cicely Hamilton, *Life Errant*, Dent, London, 1935, 67, 186.
5   Virginia Woolf, *A Writer's Diary*, Hogarth Press, London, 1953, 25 Oct. 1920.
6   Alison Neilans, 'Changes in Sex Morality', in Ray Strachey, ed, *Our Freedom and Its Results*, Hogarth Press, London, 1936, 220-5.
7   Billie Melman, *Women and the Popular Imagination in the Twenties*, Macmillan, London, 1988, 18.
8   *TT*, 17 Dec. 1926, 1159.
9   *Woman's Leader (WL)*, 19 April 1929, 83.
10   *WL*, 12 March 1920, 126.
11   *WL*, 25 May 1928, 129.
12   Eleanor Rathbone, *The Disinherited Family*, Falling Wall Press, London, 1986, first published in 1924, 194.
13   *WL*, 13 March 1925, 51-2.
14   *TT*, 6 Aug. 1926, 714.
15   Naomi Mitchison to Elizabeth Haldane, n.d., 6033/f. 295, Haldane Papers, National Library of Scotland, Edinburgh.
16   *WL*, 6 Feb. 1920, 7.
17   *WL*, Oct. 1932, 142.
18   *TT*, 11 Aug. 1934, 1026-8; 14 Nov. 1936, 1581-2; 4 April 1936, 469-70; 11 April 1936, 518-19; 18 April 1936, 553-5.
19   Vera Brittain to Evelyn Sharp, 16 June 1933, Nevinson Papers, Bodleian Library, Univ. of Oxford.
20   Mary Agnes Hamilton, 'Changes in Social Life', in Ray Strachey, ed, *Our Freedom and its Results*, 237.
21   Ibid., 235-6.
22   Ibid., 267.
23   Naomi Mitchison, *You May Well Ask*, Gollancz, London, 1979, 70.
24   Winifred Horrabin, 'My Early Feminism', typescript, n.d., 2/4e. Horrabin Papers, Univ. of Hull.
25   Winifred Horrabin to Frank Horrabin, 3 Dec. 1943, 3/4b, Horrabin Papers, Univ. of Hull.
26   Winifred Holtby, *South Riding*, Virago, London, 1988, first published in 1936.
27   Ellen Wilkinson, *Clash*, Virago, London, 1989, first published in 1929.
28   Vera Brittain, *Chronicle of Friendship: Vera Brittain's Diary of the 1930s, 1932-1939*, Alan Bishop, ed, Gollancz, London, 1986, 23 Sept. 1932.
29   Winifred Holtby, *Women and a Changing Civilisation*, Bodley Head, London, 1934, 130-2.
30   *TT*, 7 March 1936, 323.
31   Winifred Horrabin, article in the *New Leader*, n.d., 4/2, Horrabin Papers, Univ. of Hull.
32   *Labour Woman*, March 1929, 34.
33   Maggie Morgan, 'The Women's Institutes Movement – The Acceptable Face of Feminism?' in

Sybil Oldfield, ed, *Women's Lives and Culture(s) in Britain 1914-1945*, Taylor & Francis, London, 1994, 29-39.

34 'Proposed Lines of Expansion for the NUSEC', Dec. 1928, Fawcett Library, Box 341.

35 *TT*, 4 Aug. 1934, 980-1; 18 Aug. 1934, 1031-2.

36 Winifred Holtby, *Women and a Changing Civilisation*, 169, 168, 134.

37 Naomi Mitchison to Elizabeth Haldane, n.d., Haldane papers, 6033/f. 295.

38 Mitchison to Haldane, n.d., Acc. 9186, National Library of Scotland.

39 Mitchison, *We Have Been Warned*, Constable, London, 1935; *The Moral Basis of Politics*, Constable, London, 1938.

40 *WL*, 7 June 1929, 137.

41 Winifred Holtby, *Women and a Changing Civilisation*, 116.

42 Ray Strachey to Christopher Strachey, 13 Nov. 1933, H. W. Smith Archives, Lilly Library, Univ. of Indiana, Bloomington, Indiana, USA.

43 Johanna Alberti, 'British Feminists and Anti-Fascism in the 1930s', in Sybil Oldfield, ed, *Women's Lives and Culture(s)*, 111-22.

44 Ray Strachey, Introduction to *Our Freedom and Its Results*, 9-11.

45 *Common Cause*, 15 Feb. 1918, 373.

46 Eleanor Rathbone, 'Changes in Public Life', in Ray Strachey, ed, *Our Freedom and Its Results*, 34, 75.

47 Ray Strachey, 'Changes in Employment' in ibid., 154.

48 Ibid., 158, 159.

49 Winifred Holtby to Margaret Rhondda, Jan. 1931, printed in *TT*, 4 April 1936, 469-70.

50 *TT*, 8 Oct. 1938, 1375.

51 Ray Strachey to her mother, Mary Berenson, 3 Oct. 1938, H. W. Smith Archives.

52 Mitchison to Aldous Huxley, 17 Oct. 1938, Acc. 8185, National Library of Scotland.

53 *TT*, 15 Oct.1938, 1425.

54 *TT*, 21 Jan. 1939, 72.

55 *TT*, 8 July 1939, 903.

56 *TT*, 14 May 1938, 663.

16

The Impact of Women's Enfranchisement in Britain

MARTIN PUGH

In her autobiography Barbara Castle recalls a debate at the Oxford Union around 1960 when she opposed a motion 'to the effect that women's emancipation had been a flop'.[1] The unsuccessful mover, Roger Fulford, author of *Votes For Women* (1957), represented a well-established tradition which had developed during the 1930s. The popular press, having previously predicted that equal suffrage for women would have disastrous results, characteristically adopted the opposite view claiming that nothing had happened at all. It is scarcely surprising that hopes and fears should have been high. The reforms of 1918 had created 8.47 million female voters, or approximately 40 per cent of the total. The equal suffrage legislation introduced by Stanley Baldwin in 1928 abolished the 30-year age limit and gave women a simple residential qualification, thereby boosting women voters to 15.19 million or 52.7 per cent of the entire electorate.

Today our assessment of the impact of women's enfranchisement in Britain must still be provisional despite the availability of much more evidence. We are very conscious that many of the goals of feminism remain to be achieved, and that legislative remedy for women's grievances has sometimes turned out to be a disappointment. Nor can we avoid being influenced by the recent experience of the premiership of Margaret Thatcher. Though in some sense a product of women's success in 1918, Lady Thatcher's career has scarcely seemed to most observers to represent an advance for women's causes.

All of this tends to reinforce the negative assumptions about the effects of female enfranchisement. However, one of the purposes of this chapter is to act as a corrective to such views. In order to do this it is important to attempt to place the movement for women's enfranchisement in perspective. To suggest that 1918 was no revolution is not to minimise the achievement of the vote, but rather to recognise that in Britain, and in similar societies in north-west Europe, North America and Australasia, an upheaval of revolutionary proportions was not a necessary element in the process of reform.[2] Particularly in Britain, the problem faced by the reformers was not the unrelieved resistance of the male establishment, but the more subtle strategy involving tactical retreats and accommodation to limited change, which had the effect of slowing the momentum behind radical movements throughout the nineteeth century.

The cycle of reform

Both middle-class and working-class radical movements had faced similar dilemmas to those encountered by feminists; and the chronological pattern of their achievements helps us to place the women's movement in context. For example, historians were once impressed by the great victories of the Victorian 'entrepreneurial' radicals in the 1832 Reform Act and the repeal of the Corn Laws in 1846. But on the whole they concluded that these apparent defeats for the traditional political elite failed to produce a bourgeois revolution in the mid-Victorian period. This was conventionally explained in broadly two ways. Firstly, after 1846 the radical leaders, Cobden and Bright, found it difficult to focus on a single cause, and, as a result, their movement lost momentum. Moreover, the buoyant mid-Victorian economy blunted the cutting edge of the radicals' campaigns; it was tempting to believe that the attainment of free trade and material progress constituted sufficient proof of their success. Secondly, the political system retained at least until 1885 many of the features of the unreformed system, particularly the maldistribution of the constituencies, which preserved the over-representation of members of the traditional landed elite in Parliament.[3]

More recent analysis of the period has shown how difficult it was to penetrate the mid-Victorian parliamentary system. For many businessmen a parliamentary career remained an expensive indulgence, and the entrepreneur who devoted himself to politics might find that his business suffered from neglect. As a result such men often became MPs relatively late in life – Samuel Morley at 55, Titus Salt at 55, Thomas Bazley at 61, Duncan McLaren at 65. In such cases getting into the House of Commons represented the crowning achievement of their lives rather than a career in itself. Too old to get a foot on the ministerial ladder, these men were often alienated by the antiquated and inefficient procedures of the House of Commons. They lacked confidence in debate and thus avoided many topics in order to concentrate upon the matters in which they could claim competence – trade and industry.[4]

To a greater or lesser extent virtually all these problems materialised in the political careers of women during the 1920s and 1930s.[5] But perhaps the central dilemma facing both the mid-Victorian radicals and the women's movement was strategy. On the one hand, Victorian radicalism generated a rich array of independent pressure groups; on the other hand, most reformers felt the attraction of conventional political parties which seemed to offer a more efficacious means of achieving their aims. In fact by the 1870s many of them were in the process of full-scale absorption by the Liberal Party. Who gained most from this relationship is a complex question. The programme and the agenda of Liberal politics undoubtedly succumbed to the influence of the radical pressure groups working from within the party, and the personnel of parliamentary Liberalism gradually changed; for example, the number of Nonconformist MPs rose from 64 in 1868 to 210 in 1906. But there was another side to the coin. The pressure-group radicals often felt that they were being used by the party. Their causes could easily be subordinated to party's priorities, especially by a skilful leader like Gladstone; and in the long run the Nonconformist interest may well have suffered as a result of its close involvement in the machinations of Liberal politics.

The timing of the advance made by middle-class radicalism is also interesting. In spite of decades of pressure from extra-parliamentary forces, Parliament continued to be dominated until the 1860s by gentlemen of leisure and those with landed, aristocratic connections. Change arose partly from the structural reforms in the system in 1867, and particularly in 1884–85, which began to correct the historic imbalance of representation. The new constituencies created in industrial boroughs and counties presented excellent opportunities for large local employers to become Members of Parliament. Thus, from the mid-1880s onwards, even in the Conservative ranks, up to two-thirds of each new intake of MPs was drawn from middle-class backgrounds.[6] Even so, their rise proved to be gradual. Early middle-class recruits to the Cabinet were usually offered lowly posts like the Board of Trade and the Local Government Board on the assumption that these were appropriate to their knowledge and experience. Gladstone notoriously considered that Joseph Chamberlain was developing ideas above his station in aspiring to a Secretaryship of State. It is only after the turn of the century that the shift of personnel appears inexorable.[7] The Edwardian Liberal governments were dominated by middle-class figures such as Asquith and Lloyd George; similarly, the collapse of the Salisbury–Balfour regime in 1911 led to a succession of bourgeois Conservative leaders: Bonar Law, Austen Chamberlain, Stanley Baldwin and Neville Chamberlain.

From the perspective of the women's movement the prolonged

struggle by working-class men to gain a foothold in British politics is even more pertinent.[8] During the 1830s and 1840s the Chartists faced similar problems in attempting to mobilise a very large but disparate section of society that was excluded from formal political participation. They employed a dual strategy involving, on the one hand, mass organisation, agitation and physical force, and, on the other, constitutionalism, 'moral force' Chartism and alliances with sympathetic parliamentarians. Though conventionally regarded as a failure after 1848, Chartism in fact enjoyed considerable influence through both its ideas and its leaders later in the nineteenth century. Almost all the *aims* of the movement were eventually achieved. The first, often forgotten, came in 1858 with the abolition of the property qualification for MPs. Manhood suffrage was accomplished by degrees in 1867, 1884–85 and 1918, the secret ballot in 1872 and the payment of members in 1911. Equal constituencies proved to be an elusive goal, though the reforms of 1885 and 1918 marked a major move in that direction. The demand for annual parliaments has, alone of Chartist objectives, never looked likely to succeed. Thus, the Chartists' movement serves as a reminder that an abrupt *organisational* decline cannot be taken as an adequate indication of failure, but may merely represent a stage in the evolution of a movement.

On the other hand, working-class experience also suggests the persistence of the obstacles to direct penetration of Parliament by outsider groups. British workers won the vote in 1867, 1884 and 1918; but the effects of this were by no means immediately felt. In the aftermath of 1867, for example, the parties moved swiftly to contain the new electorate by means of an organisational response. While the agenda continued to be dominated by such issues as Irish home rule, church disestablishment, imperialism or free trade, it proved difficult to turn labour questions into political priorities. In this respect the breakthrough did not come until the Edwardian period by which time it was beginning to have implications for women's politics too. Similarly working men found it difficult to capitalise on their new voting power to achieve direct representation in Parliament. For nearly forty years the post-1874 experiment with 'Lib–Lab' members was virtually their only foothold; and this effectively confined them to a maximum of about two dozen MPs, a position not unlike that achieved by the women members from 1919 right up to the 1970s. Not until 1906, and with the advantage of an electoral pact with the Liberals, did Labour manage to return 29 MPs. By 1918 the party still had only 61 members and 22 per cent of the vote; its real breakthrough was not to come until 1945.

Criteria for assessing women's achievements

These examples are a reminder that radical movements, even when apparently assisted by major structural or political reforms, have often had to wage campaigns of three-quarters of a century before consolidating their position in terms of significant changes of programme or personnel. The aftermath of 1832, 1846, 1867, 1885 and even 1918, showed a considerable measure of continuity with the earlier period. After 1918 the political establishment attempted to accommodate itself to women's new role as voters and as potential Members of Parliament. One may gain some measure of the impact of enfranchisement in the medium term by using several distinct criteria: women's role within the parties, their success at elections, their performance as MPs, the legislation enacted for women, and the broader evolution of the scope and character of British politics between the wars.

There were few serious obstacles to extending women's roles in the membership and organisation of political parties; this was partly because the politicians already had considerable experience of this – Labour with the Women's Labour League and the Women's Co-operative Guild, and the Conservatives with the Primrose League and the Women's Tariff Reform Association. In any case it was a matter of self interest to involve women. The parties wanted the new votes, and also hoped to head off what seemed for a time a real prospect that a separate women's party might emerge. Labour's exercise in rewriting its constitution during 1917–18 proved helpful to women in that the new emphasis on developing constituency parties and building an individual membership, as opposed to the affiliated trade union membership, offered much scope for women's activities. At this stage two crucial decisions were made: to maintain a separate organisation for women with its own hierarchy, and to charge women only sixpence for membership as opposed to one shilling for men. These decisions were justified at the time on the grounds that it ought to be be made easy for poor women to join, and those who were not familiar with politics would be more attracted by all-women branches.[9] As a result there soon emerged the women's sections attached to each constituency party, with their own regional network of Women's Advisory Councils, an annual conference and a Women's Department at headquarters under the Chief Woman Officer, Dr Marion Phillips. Four women were to be elected to the National Executive Committee (NEC) by the whole party conference, and any policy proposals from the women had to go through the NEC before they could be debated by the full party conference. By 1929 over 1800 women's sections had been created with between 250,000 and 300,000 members. Though not large in relation to the trade union membership, this female membership often comprised a majority of the individual membership in the constituencies. As such it was a key factor in enabling Labour to win marginal seats outside the small core of safe constituencies; conversely, where a local party neglected or resisted women's organisation it was liable to suffer electorally.[10]

The Conservatives followed a similar course. They shared the reservations about incorporating women on an equal footing with men, and there were fears that a separate women's organisation would be calculated to foster a distinctive, feminist programme.[11] But after November 1917 the Conservative Central Office began to promote the absorption of women from the Primrose League and the Tariff Reform organisation into local Women's Unionist branches. They had their own Women's Advisory Committee within the National Union in London, an annual conference, and the opportunity to send resolutions via the National Union to the party conference. At each level of the party hierarchy – National Union Council, National Union Executive and party conference – the principle of guaranteeing one third of the representation to women was adopted.[12] By the late 1920s the Conservatives claimed over 4000 women's branches and a million members which gave women a dominant role in the organisation which they have retained to the present day.

None of this necessarily gave women much influence over party policies, however. The Conservative conference never claimed the right to determine policy anyway, and in the Labour Party the NEC used its power to exclude controversial feminist proposals from the agenda. This is why many equal rights feminists discounted organisational reforms. In 1923 *Time & Tide* complained that 'none of the big parties yet shows itself prepared to treat men and women fairly and equally' and it concluded that 'the time has not yet come for women to join parties'.[13]

Such scepticism appears justified in the light of the marked reluctance of the parties to encourage women to advance beyond an organisational to a parliamentary role. There was no lack of opportunity. The 1920s saw four general elections: 1922 produced a Conservative majority; 1923 led to the first, minority Labour government; 1924 returned the Conservatives to power; and 1929 made Ramsay MacDonald prime minister again though he was a little short of a majority. But in 1922 the three parties nominated only 33 women for the 615 seats. Admittedly the total rose to 69 by 1929, but that was still only 4 per cent of the total number of candidates; by 1935 it was just 5 per cent.

Moreover, four out of five women stood in constituencies that were usually hopeless prospects for their parties. One major reason for this is simply that a parliamentary seat continued to be regarded as a reward for service to the party; but it also seems that even when well-qualified women offered themselves they were often not supported by other women who sat on the local committees. For many years local associations rationalised their prejudice by claiming that the ordinary voters were not yet ready to accept women as candidates. There were many variations on this theme. Rural districts were alleged to be especially hostile to women. Female voices could not stand up to the strain of public speaking. A married woman was considered to be neglecting her family if she tried to become an MP, while the single woman was suspected of feminism which antagonised voters.[14] But there also existed a problem of resources. Conservative associations looked for a husband-and-wife team with a view to getting double value in terms of voluntary work for the constituency. Male Labour candidates often offered the prospective constituency party a dowry from their trade union in the form of an annual subsidy and payment of election expenses. A few women did enjoy union backing – Ellen Wilkinson, Margaret Bondfield and Leah Manning – but they were exceptional.

However, to dwell too much on the difficulties women encountered in obtaining nominations is to miss half the picture. Repeated experience with female candidates during the 1920s went a long way to exploding the exaggerated fears expressed. Significantly, a high proportion of the 36 inter-war women MPs won seats at by-elections, where the personalities and individual qualities of candidates attracted unusual scrutiny. From Nancy Astor's triumphant debut at Plymouth in 1919 women proved themselves to be very able platform performers. In fact this was in no way surprising. Women like Margaret Bondfield, Susan Lawrence and Ellen Wilkinson (Labour), Florence Horsbrugh and the Duchess of Atholl (Conservative) or Megan Lloyd George and Hilda Runciman (Liberal) had years of experience behind them; indeed they often coped better than the average male candidate with the cut and thrust of election campaigning. Certainly, there is evidence that women gained seats and retained them in difficult circumstances; this was especially true of Labour and Liberal women who usually had to increase their party's share of the poll in order to get elected at all. For example, Labour's candidate at Stoke in 1929, Cynthia Mosley, dramatically pushed up the party's vote from 13,318 to 26,548, unseating a well-established male MP in the process. Astor's ability to hold what would otherwise have become a Labour seat at Plymouth Sutton until 1945 was another indication that a woman could be an asset.[15] It is also possible to compare the performance of male and female candidates in a few of the double-member constituencies such as Blackburn and Sunderland where the Labour Party sometimes ran a man and a woman on the same ticket; in these cases the women polled as strongly, and sometimes more strongly than the men.[16] The general conclusion is inescapable, that even in the 1920s female candidates, though still fairly novel, were by no means a liability to their party.

But once elected, did women continue to demonstrate their competence in Parliament? There is no easy way to evaluate the equality of their contributions. Brian Harrison has calculated that almost half the debating contributions made by women members in the House of Commons between 1918 and 1939 were devoted to housing, health, education, unemployment and labour relations.[17] On this basis it can be argued that they had become confined to a limited field of appropriate 'women's' topics. But is this a reasonable interpretation? During the 1920s and 1930s these issues were the ones regarded as central by most politicians, regardless of their sex. Many of the early women members consciously followed the political mainstream so as to avoid being marginalised.

Several scholars believe that women were naturally disadvantaged by the adversarial style of Parliament.[18] Yet one might say the same of men. The truth is that the women who sat in the Commons tended to be untypical of their sex just as the men were untypical of theirs. In their different ways most of the women MPs coped successfully. With her wit and her frequent interventions in debate, Nancy Astor rapidly developed into a House of Commons 'character'. But she was too exceptional to be a good guide. At one end of the female spectrum there were the sort of members always appreciated by the whips, loyal backbenchers who rarely spoke; Conservatives like Lady Davidson and the Countess of Iveagh are good examples. Then there were the members who concentrated either on constituency interests, or on topics to which they brought specialist knowledge, such as Edith Summerskill (a doctor) or Leah Manning (president of the National Union of Schoolteachers). Several women rapidly emerged as prospective frontbenchers because of their ability to master a brief and defend the party line – Bondfield, Atholl, Horsbrugh for example. The case of Margaret Bondfield was especially striking because as a newly elected member in 1923 she immediately became a junior minister and spoke from the front bench. As for the aggressive 'male' style, it came naturally to Susan Lawrence, Jennie Lee and Ellen Wilkinson. Lawrence, who was described by Wilkinson as 'the real bluestocking of our age', carved out her claim to recognition just as ambitious men often did, by attacking a major politician, in her case Neville Chamberlain over his 1929 Local Government Bill.[19]

Historians have scarcely begun to take account of the impact of women's enfranchisement in terms of national policy and legislation. It has been suggested that the reforms of the 1920s would probably have been achieved before 1914, especially if the efforts of the women's movement had not been concentrated on the franchise campaign.[20] This view cannot be dismissed entirely; in spite of the fact that women had not enjoyed the vote, many of their grievances had been tackled by Parliament during the decades from 1850 onwards. However, in that period the achievement of a reform was invariably preceded by many years of pressure and by a succession of abortive bills. After 1918 the whole process was accelerated. Between 1918 and 1929 no fewer than twenty-one pieces of legislation for women reached the statute book. It would be hard to find any comparable concentration before or since. Certainly several suffragists who were experienced in dealing with politicians detected the immediate impact of enfranchisement. Ray Strachey wrote that 'the whole atmosphere of parliament was changed'. Millicent Fawcett felt that politicians became more receptive; 'we were no longer there on sufferance, but by right'.[21]

Nonetheless, certain qualifications must be made. Several of the post-1918 reforms were the product of a variety of factors of which women's pressure was only one. Also, even twenty-one Acts did not by any means include all the measures most desired by feminists. Substantial elements of the NUSEC programme were achieved, including equal divorce (1923), equal guardianship (1925), improved maintenance for married women (1922), and equal suffrage (1928). Similarly the Six Point Group could claim success in the shape of the equal guardianship (1925), widows' pensions (1925), and, to some extent, the Criminal Law Amendment Act (1922). On the other hand, all this undoubtedly left major griev-ances untouched, notably the question of equal pay for teachers and civil servants, protective legislation and the ban on the employment of married women. Even worse, the 1919 Sex Disqualification (Removal) Act swiftly turned out to be a disappointment since it failed to protect women workers from dismissal especially by local authorities.

Women and the character of politics
Of course, the more one moves away from quantifiable criteria the more difficult it becomes to assess the impact of enfranchisement. How far did the conduct of politics change after 1918? Did women voters help to extend the scope or modify the priorities of politics? These are more intractable

issues partly because they involve a longer time scale and because of the difficulty of disentangling the effects of female participation from other factors. Not surprisingly contemporary opinion on this varied widely. At one extreme a few traditionalists claimed that women's suffrage required no response at all; one candidate at the 1922 election wrote, 'I make no special appeal on questions of policy to the women voters . . . (they) recognise that they should cast their votes on the basis of a common citizenship with men'.[22]

Yet while many men no doubt hoped this would prove to be the case, few could be confident in 1918. More characteristic was the assumption that women were different politically; the question was to ascertain just how much adjustment that required. Some Conservative propaganda depicted women as innocent and, thus, highly susceptible to socialism. This must be seen in the context of the post-war obsession with Bolshevik subversion and the campaigns against Baldwin by the extreme right; typical examples of this were the notorious *Daily Mail* editorials on 'Why Socialists Want Votes for Flappers' during the later 1920s.[23] Most politicians, however, adopted a half-way house; they accepted the need for some concessions either in style or in substance, and sought to discover how far it was safe to go. Typically they argued that the women's vote was making politics more parochial and 'reducing them to bread and butter issues and the cost of living'.[24]

How were women to respond to such assumptions? Feminists understandably regarded politicians' views as patronising; on the other hand many of the politically active women anticipated that they could capitalise upon the parties' evident sympathy for the domestic needs of women. This resulted in a divergence of tactics during the 1920s. The equal rights feminists writing in *Time & Tide* frankly disparaged all political parties;[25] NUSEC continued its earlier policy of cultivating politicians while also building up the pressure on them; but many women simply chose to work for women's causes by joining a political party, which meant that they devoted less time to independent women's groups. Given the sheer quantity of legislation enacted in the early and mid-1920s this latter option seemed compelling for a time. But in the long run it began to emerge that few of the female party politicians were willing or able to use their influence within their party. For example, Nancy Astor promoted several women's causes, but never managed to mobilise the strength of organised Conservative women for this purpose.[26] The women in the Labour Party women's sections and in the Women's Co-operative Guild pursued two distinct strategies. At local level they campaigned on domestic issues, including improved municipal housing, pure milk supplies and food subsidies. But at national level left-wing feminists promoted the case for family allowances, the removal of the marriage bar on married women workers and the provision of birth control information; yet on each issue they ran into entrenched male opposition within the labour movement.[27] As a result, by the 1930s middle-class feminists had become increasingly marginalised within the Labour Party, or simply forced to compromise their feminism.

In response to criticism such women pointed to the progress that could be made by going down the road to domesticity. Two major themes came to dominate women's politics. One of these was social reform in the shape of widows' pensions which, after equal franchise, was the issue most frequently raised in the literature of parliamentary candidates during the 1920s.[28] This was not a novel proposal; it grew directly out of the debates over the New Liberalism in the Edwardian period which had forced state social welfare into the political mainstream. Lloyd George had wanted to include widows' pensions in his legislation in 1911; Labour advocated them as part of its broad policy for promoting working-class living standards; and the Conservatives backed widows' pensions as a means of supporting and strengthening the family. Similarly the 1918 Maternity and Child Welfare Act reflected the bipartisan thinking which had been developing well before 1914 and which gathered momentum from the war because attention was focused on motherhood and population. Significantly this was one of the few social policies to escape largely unscathed from the post-war financial retrenchment.

However, there were limits to the social welfare strategy for women. The parties made a distinction between widows' pensions, which were seen in the context of domesticity, and family allowances, which enjoyed a *feminist* rationale. Both major parties feared the cost of implementing family allowances; and on the labour side the trade unions argued that the scheme would be used by employers as an excuse for holding down the level of wages. They showed even less enthusiam for the demand that information to help women with birth control should be offered at the local authority clinics. Though pressed repeatedly by their women's conference, the Labour Party's NEC tried to keep the issue off the agenda of the party conference; and when a debate was eventually held, it went to some lengths to ensure the defeat of the proposal.[29] Since no political party and hardly any MPs of either sex were prepared to take up birth control, attempts to push the issue into the mainstream of debate were largely frustrated. However in 1930, perhaps in recognition of the fact that birth control was being widely practised, the Ministry of Health agreed that it would be quite legal for local authorities to provide advice to married women; this strictly limited concession was well calculated to deflate what little pressure had been generated.

The second aspect of domesticity which occupied a central place was the question of food and prices. By standing as the champion of working-class families and by capitalising on the widespread belief that the people had been exploited by commercial profiteering during the war, the Labour Party seized the initiative and forced other parties to compete on its chosen ground. In 1923 Baldwin played into his opponents' hands by choosing to fight an election on the proposal to introduce tariffs. This enabled Labour and the Liberals to resuscitate free trade and address housewives' fears about rising food prices. The heavy losses sustained by the Conservatives were freely attributed to the volatile women's vote.[30] Interestingly, the Conservatives responded to this setback partly by playing down tariffs, at least until after 1931, but also by trying to exploit the popular concern about food rather than resisting it. During the 1920s a huge propaganda effort was launched to involve women in Empire Shopping Weeks, Empire Food Boxes, recipes based on imports from Australia, New Zealand, Canada and South Africa, and Empire pageants associated with Empire Day.[31] This was shrewd. On the one hand, it helped to conciliate the party's frustrated imperialist wing which campaigned vigorously for imperial preference. On the other, it offered a practical method for involving ordinary women in political questions and went some way to defusing the issue of food by combining patriotic, party propaganda with a material consideration. This example is a useful reminder that politicians enjoyed a good deal of scope for adapting to the pressures generated by a new body of voters without necessarily surrendering their existing ideas and principles.

The loss of momentum

Whatever assessment may be made of the 1920s, it would be difficult to contest the view that the subsequent decades saw a waning of the impact of women's enfranchisement. By 1929–30 a turning point had effectively been reached in the sense that much of the programme of pre-1914 feminism had been accomplished, and, moreover, the personnel of that era had begun to fade from the scene. To some extent this cyclical pattern is the experience of most radical movements. But why was it so difficult to restore the momentum in the 1930s? In the first place the prolonged economic depression proved inimical to women's aspirations, and drove both sexes back towards the view that scarce employment ought to be reserved largely for men on the assumption that they had to support dependants. Secondly, the experience of four general elections during the 1920s had enabled politicians to take the measure of the new electorate. Contrary to expectations, it appeared that women were not going to vote as a group, they had not been mobilised in very great numbers in support of feminist campaigns, nor was there now any prospect of the emergence of a separate party for women. Consequently the Equal Franchise Act of 1928 made relatively little impression, even though women subsequently comprised 52 per cent of the electorate in Britain. Unlike the reforms of 1918 it was not followed by any substantial body of legislation for women. For this the economic and political crisis of 1931 was no doubt partly to blame, though even before the crisis broke there is little evidence that the MacDonald Government, elected in 1929, was going to make women's issues a priority. The events of 1931 conspired to marginalise most radical causes for the rest of the decade.[32]

In this situation there was almost bound to be criticism of those women who had apparently compromised their feminism by opting for the party political route rather than independent women's organisations. The failure of Astor's attempt to organise an unofficial women's group in the House of Commons after the 1929 election led to much disquiet over the role of the women MPs during the 1930s. Even NUSEC complained that they had failed to make a distinctive stand over women's issues.[33] Ellen Wilkinson conceded at least part of the charge in an article entitled 'Have Women Failed in Parliament?' in 1933.[34] Several of the women members, who were less sympathetic to feminism than Wilkinson, countered by arguing that they would most effectively advance their cause by concentrating on the mainstream issues of the day; the more they agitated over women's questions the more marginal they would become. Some tacitly accepted the view held by the anti-feminist MP, the Duchess of Atholl, that as the independent women's groups did not represent the mass of women in the country, it would be futile to allow them to dictate priorities. The Labour women faced an acute dilemma because they were liable to be regarded by colleagues as the mere mouthpiece of middle-class feminism. After the traumatic break-up of MacDonald's Government in 1931 the labour movement showed itself highly suspicious of being used by individuals as a vehicle to advance their own causes or careers. Edith Summerskill, who entered Parliament in 1938, is a rare example of a woman who managed to build a career in the Labour Party in this period without sacrificing her commitment to feminism. Those, like Wilkinson, who enjoyed a higher place in the hierarchy felt obliged to respect the party line.

In addition, the problems of the 1930s must be seen in the context of the attempts by the women's movement to redefine its feminism once the simple goal of the franchise had been removed. One symptom of this was the organisational diaspora between the wars. New groups such as the Women's Citizens' Association, the Six Point Group, the Townswomen's Guilds and the Open Door Council, to name but a few, sprang up, but suffered because they competed for much the same body of recruits and resources. This was compounded by the diversion of many women activists into work for the League of Nations Union and other peace movements. Participation in such causes may be seen as one part of the process of redefining the objectives of feminism between the wars. In 1928, for example, NUSEC specifically wrote a commitment to the League of Nations and disarmament into its new programme, and many activists undoubtedly regarded international peace as integral to feminism. One sees this in the career of a younger feminist such as Vera Brittain, whose early involvement with the Six Point Group seems to have given way to a role as a platform speaker for the League of Nations Union. Brittain pointedly drew a distinction between the pre-war generation of feminists, whom she saw as essentially full-time committee women, and her own generation for whom feminism meant the pursuit of both a career *and* marriage rather than a choice between them.[35]

The importance of the shifting ideas of each age group is underlined by the impact of World War II. In so far as the war replaced the depressed 1930s economy with a period of high employment and generated a more radical political climate, it undoubtedly created more advantageous conditions for the women's movement. This was quickly recognised by the women MPs who began to function, for the first time, as an informal party in the House of Commons. In this they were helped by the shift to coalition government in 1940, which, for a time, made normal party discipline seem irrelevant.[36]

However, it proved difficult to extend the advantage beyond the special circumstances of the war itself. In spite of the Labour landslide in 1945, women's representation stood practically still throughout the 1950s. Essentially the wartime initiatives over equal pay for teachers and equal compensation for accidents were the work of an older generation of women who had managed to retain, or in some cases, had acquired, a feminist commitment. But their work at the parliamentary level was not effectively backed by a mass movement in the country; this became clear once peacetime conditions had been restored. Thus, even though 1945 and the succeeding elections brought some new women into political life, this did not have the effect it might have had after 1918, when politicians were all too aware of women's potential for popular agitation. Two examples from each side of politics illustrate the problem; in 1945 Barbara Betts (later Castle) successfully contested Blackburn, while the young Margaret Roberts (later Thatcher) was to contest Dartford in 1950 and 1951. Both were products of the post-enfranchisement generation of women who were able to take political participation for granted during the 1930s. But the crucial fact is that even Mrs Castle, who was born in 1910, was too young to have experienced at first hand the struggle to win the vote. Both women pursued their education to Oxford women's colleges, and, like others of their generation, seem to have intended to combine a career with marriage and motherhood. Castle took a dim view of women like her principal at St Hugh's who 'seemed to embody the belief that intellectual women should not be interested in sex'.[37] But the point is that during their formative years neither Thatcher nor Castle appear to have been influenced by any specific feminist organisations or causes. This is very telling in the case of Barbara Castle, in view of her contributions to feminist reforms much later in her career. Her rise in politics involved little, if any, work with the Labour Party women's organisation; she actually took the view that a woman should not become simply the representative of a separate women's section, but should seek election to the NEC as she did, in the general constituency section.[38] Moreover, in spite of her role in Parliament as a rebel during the 1950s, she did not figure in the work of the Equal Pay Campaign Committee in that period. In this sense Castle's career reflects the gradual working out of one phase of the women's movement; but it also marks a link with the next phase inaugurated by a new generation of women from the late 1960s onwards.

1   Barbara Castle, *Fighting All the Way*, Macmillan, London, 1993, 43.
2   For a general discussion, see Evans, *The Feminists*.
3   See John Vincent, *The Formation of the British Liberal Party, 1857-68*, Cape, London, 1966; H. J. Hanham, *Elections and Party Management*, Harvester Press, Hassocks, 1959.
4   G. R. Searle, *Entrepreneurial Politics in Mid-Victorian Britain*, Clarendon Press/OUP, Oxford, 1993, 6-9.
5   Elizabeth Vallance, *Women in the House*, Althone Press, London, 1979; Brian Harrison, *Prudent Revolutionaries*, Clarendon Press/OUP, Oxford, 1987.
6   J. P. Cornford, 'Parliamentary Origins of the Hotel Cecil', in R. Robson, ed, *Ideas and Institutions of Victorian Britain*, Hamish Hamilton, London, 1967, 310.
7   W. L. Guttsman, *The British Political Elite*, McGibbon & Kee, London, 1965, 78-9.
8   See the interesting analysis by Jutta Schwarzkopf, *Women in the Chartist Movement*, Macmillan, London, 1991.

9   *Conference Report*, Women's Labour League, Jan. 1918, 43-6; June 1919, 80.
10   Michael Savage, *The Dynamics of Working-Class Politics*, Cambridge Univ. Press, Cambridge, 1987, 164-70.
11   Conservative Party, *Annual Conference Report*, Nov. 1917.
12   The structure is described in the Women's Unionist Association, *Annual Conference Reports*.
13   *Time & Tide* (*TT*), 18 May 1923.
14   Martin Pugh, *Women and the Women's Movement in Britain, 1914-1959*, Macmillan, London, 1992, 154-8.
15   *Staffordshire Sentinel*, 22 April 1929; 24-25 May 1929; *Western Morning News*, 3 & 4 Nov. 1919.
16   *Blackburn Times*, 1 Nov. 1924, 1; also Pugh, *Women and the Women's Movement*, 187-8.
17   Brian Harrison, 'Women in a Men's House: the Women MPs, 1919-1945', *Historical Journal* (*HJ*), 29/3, 1986, 637.
18   Vallance, *Women in the House*, 15; Harrison, 'Women in a Men's House', 630.
19   Ellen Wilkinson, *Peeps at Politicians*, Philip Allan, London, 1930, 25.
20   Brian Harrison, 'Women's Suffrage at Westminster, 1866-1928', in M. Bentley & J. Stevenson, eds, *High and Low Politics in Modern Britain*, Clarendon Press/OUP, Oxford, 1983, 91.
21   Ray Strachey, *The Cause*, G. Bell & Son, London, 1928, 369; Millicent Fawcett, *What the Vote Has Done*, NUSEC, London, 1926, 1.
22   S. Roberts (Conservative, Hereford), election address, 1922, National Liberal Club Collection.
23   *Daily Mail*, 20, 23, 28 April 1927.
24   M. Fraser to A. Chamberlain, 30 Dec. 1921, Austen Chamberlain Papers, AC/32/4/16, Birmingham Univ. Library.
25   *TT*, 16 May 1924.
26   See, for example, Women's Unionist Association, *Annual Conference Reports*, 1921, 21, and 1927, 30.
27   Labour Party Women's Organisation, *Annual Conference Reports*, 1925, 123; 1928, 27; 1930, 53-4.
28   Pugh, *Women and the Women's Movement*, 123-4.
29   See Labour Party Women's Organisation, 1927 *Annual Conference Report*, 1927.
30   *Women's Leader*, 1 Dec. 1923.
31   *Home and Politics*, no. 38, June 1924, 11; no. 48, April 1925, 2, 6 and 8.
32   See the analysis of the 1935 election by C. T. Stannage, *Baldwin Thwarts the Opposition*, Croom Helm, London, 1980.
33   *Daily Express* 24 June, 1932; see also 'The Riddle of the Women MPs'. in *Sunday Chronicle*, 11 Dec. 1932; 'The Mystery of the Women MPs', in *Daily Record & Mail*, 26 March 1935.
34   *Daily Mirror*, 28 Nov. 1933.
35   Vera Brittain, 'Committees Versus Professions', 1929, in Paul Berry & Alan Bishop, eds, *Testament of a Generation: the Journalism of Vera Brittain and Winifred Holtby*, Virago, London, 1985.
36   Harold L. Smith, 'The Womanpower Problem in Britain During the Second World War', *HJ*, 27/4, 1984.
37   Castle, *Fighting*, 41.
38   Melanie Phillips, *The Divided House: Women at Westminster*, Sidgwick & Jackson, London, 1980, 159-60.

VI

Beyond Suffrage

Suffragettes struggle with the police at the House of Commons on
'Black Friday', 18 November 1910. *Museum of London*.

17

Three Questions about Womanhood Suffrage

CAROLE PATEMAN

Voting and elections have been central to political science for half a century, but only recently, since feminist scholars began to draw attention to the neglect of women voters, have articles and books been appearing in any number that focus on women's participation in the electoral process. The work of feminist political scientists has not yet been influential enough, however, to change the long-standing neglect in the discipline of such fundamental questions as why it took women so much longer than men to win the vote in Britain and the United States (the two countries I shall discuss in this chapter), the political significance of the entry of women into national electorates, or why it has taken women so long to be elected in any numbers to national legislatures. The omission is curious, to say the least, in view of the importance of such issues for democratic theory and practice, and the size and duration of the womanhood suffrage movement. One historian has called the final stages of the suffrage campaign in the US 'the greatest independent political movement of modern times'.[1]

There are other questions, too, that have received scant attention, for example, the reasons why women won the vote before 1910 in some peripheral countries – New Zealand, Australia, Finland and Norway – or why, in Britain and the US, it was the national suffrage that was strenuously contested. By 1900 women had been enfranchised not only in New Zealand, but in South Australia and Western Australia, in the Isle of Man, in the states of Wyoming, Colorado, Utah and Idaho, and had won the municipal franchise in Britain. Nor has there been much exploration of the importance of the belief that if women were enfranchised they would all vote for conservative parties, although the policies of the parties and manoeuvrings in parliament have been investigated.[2] But perhaps the lack of interest in votes for women is not so surprising; most research in political science is still guided by the assumption that relations between the sexes and the structure of relations in domestic life are irrelevant to the public world of politics. Yet the connection between private and public was central to the question of womanhood suffrage and to the intense opposition to votes for women. The hostility is not treated as a serious problem in itself, and consequently, three crucial questions remain unasked and unanswered: firstly, why did it take so long for women to get the vote? secondly, why did women themselves organise against their own enfranchisement? thirdly, why was the vote won in the end?

In New Zealand, women won the vote after a relatively short organised campaign beginning in 1885, and in Australia it took twenty years from the 1880s until women became citizens of the Commonwealth in 1902. Women in Britain and the US had to fight a much more prolonged battle. One of the resolutions at the first women's rights convention in the USA, held at Seneca Falls in 1848, read, 'it is the duty of the women of this country to secure to themselves their sacred right of the elective franchise', but American women were unable to fulfil that duty until 1920, although they began campaigning at the end of the Civil War. In Britain, the question of votes for women was first raised in the House of Commons in 1832; the organised campaign began in 1865 with the collection of signatures for a petition that John Stuart Mill, then an MP, presented to Parliament in 1866. Suffrage was not won for all women until 1928.

Vast multitudes of women from all walks of life participated in the suffrage movement. By 1915 the National American Woman Suffrage Association had nearly two million members, and in June 1911 the British suffrage societies could call on forty thousand participants in a seven-mile-long procession in London, who marched with banners and floats to the music of the 'March of the Women', composed by Ethel Smyth. Suffragists engaged in the full range of conventional political activities – though these were hardly conventional for women at the beginning, when it was still scandalous for a woman even to speak in public. The American suffrage leader, Carrie Chapman Catt, summarised fifty-two years of campaigning as follows; there were

> 56 campaigns of referenda to male voters; 480 campaigns to urge Legi-slatures to submit suffrage amendments to voters; 47 campaigns to induce State constitutional conventions to write woman suffrage into State constitutions; 277 campaigns to persuade State party conventions to include woman suffrage planks; 30 campaigns to urge presidential party conventions to adopt woman suffrage . . . and 19 campaigns with 19 successive Congresses to get the federal amendment submitted and ratified.[3]

In addition, the militants, particularly the members of the Women's Social and Political Union (founded in 1905) engaged in some very unconventional activities, which included arson and hunger strikes in prison, an aspect of the campaign that Mrs Pankhurst called a 'civil war' by women.[4] It is hard to believe that a political movement of similar variety, magnitude and duration that involved men would be treated so cursorily.

This is all the more surprising since voting is typically seen by political scientists as *the* political act of a citizen in a democracy; voting is now taken for granted. It is thus easy to forget that Aboriginal people were not brought into the Australian electorate until the 1960s (they were deliberately excluded in 1902), that it was not until the 1960s that black people in the US could freely exercise the franchise, that in Britain one person/one vote has existed only from 1948, or that women did not get the vote in Switzerland until 1971. A more general illustration of the lack of historical perspective can be found in Robert Dahl's famous description of the individual as *homo civicus*. Dahl writes that 'among his resources for influencing officials, *homo civicus* discovers the ballot'.[5] To write of an offhand 'discovery' of the ballot shows how far removed is the contemporary view of the franchise from the perception of the vote before it was won.

Both manhood and womanhood suffrage were bitterly contested, although students usually learn only that votes for men were opposed because it was believed that mob rule, class legislation and the expropriation of property would ensue. The reasons for the even deeper opposition to womanhood suffrage are left unexamined. On the other side, advocates of both manhood and womanhood suffrage had extravagant hopes of what the vote would achieve. Yet political science has virtually nothing to say about how such hopes and fears could disappear so completely and how universal suffrage has come to be treated in the discipline as a natural feature of the political landscape.[6]

The impression conveyed is that, while the achievement of universal suffrage was a long process, it took place by a gradual, logical extension of the franchise to all adults. On the contrary, by the time that the organised movement for womanhood suffrage got under way on both sides of the Atlantic, large numbers of men had been admitted to the electorate but women had been excluded, even when, as in the state of New Jersey, for example, the constitution initially enfranchised them. That this largely goes unnoticed is not surprising when important dates and pieces of legislation, such as the First Reform Act of 1832 in Britain, are cited without qualification as landmarks of the extension of the franchise and democracy. In fact, such milestones actually mark two developments: one, the widening of manhood franchise; two, the denial of votes to women. In Britain, women were first explicitly excluded from the electorate, defined as male persons, in 1832. John Stuart Mill failed in his attempt to amend the Second Reform Act in 1867 by replacing the word 'man' with 'person'. In 1870 the Fifteenth Amendment to the American Constitution enfranchised only former male slaves, not black women. These reforms made electoral democracy the preserve of men.

The suffragists' task was made even more difficult because supporters of progressive legislation where men were involved and who, on the face of it, should have been their allies, were often indifferent to or firmly opposed to votes for women. This meant that the suffragists were faced with some extremely difficult political choices. They either had to wait patiently until their demands ceased to be put at the bottom of political agendas, until opponents had a change of heart, or until male legislators began to take their case seriously. Or they had to take action and so lay themselves open to even further criticism. What were suffragists in the US to do when black men were enfranchised? The decision of Elizabeth Cady Stanton and Susan Anthony to oppose the Fifteenth Amendment split the American movement. In Britain, opinions differed sharply on the question of whether they should seek votes for women on the same terms as men – namely being householders (in the 1900s only about one third of the adult population could vote) – the position of most suffragists, or whether, as some suffragists argued in the 1870s and 1880s, they should begin by trying to gain votes for unmarried women.

Another alternative was to insist on universal suffrage, as did the new Labour Party in the first two decades of the twentieth century. On the face of it, this sounds democratic, but adult suffrage stood hardly any chance of being granted at the time. To support adult suffrage was thus an extremely useful tactic for opponents of votes for women, as John Stuart Mill had pointed out in 1870. He wrote to Sir Charles Dilke that universal and womanhood suffrage should be separated. 'To combine the two questions', he stated,

> would practically suspend the fight for women's equality, since universal suffrage is sure to be discussed almost solely as a working man's question . . . there is sure to be a compromise, by which the working men would be enfranchised without the women . . . and therefore with their selfish interest against our cause instead of with it.[7]

The suffragists have often been accused of being racist and elitist, and attacks in the US on votes being given to uneducated, unwashed men, immigrant men and black men, while educated, cultivated, well-born women were denied the franchise, certainly fall well short of today's standards of political correctness and were hardly democratic. Yet it is easy to see why they argued in this fashion when they faced such unrelenting hostility from all sides even to the suggestion that *some* women should be enfranchised.

The resistance ran very deep, as reactions in Britain to the militant wing of the movement, the suffragettes, made very clear. Street sellers of the paper *Votes for Women* were subjected to obscene abuse and physical harassment, and, on the infamous Black Friday in November 1910, 300 suffragists on a peaceful march to Parliament Square were set upon by police and male onlookers for six hours, continually beaten and sexually assaulted. Nor has the hostility disappeared. The title of the final chapter of a biography of Christabel Pankhurst, published in 1977, is 'Bitch Power'.[8] The views and attitudes which lay at the heart of the opposition to votes for women have not yet died out, despite the major changes in the position of women since the early part of the century.

The existence of this tenacious resistance to womanhood suffrage is the reason why it took women so long to win the franchise. But merely to point to the extraordinary depth of opposition does not explain why such hostility existed or why women in the US and Britain had to struggle longer than men to be admitted to the national electorate.

Why did womanhood suffrage take so long?
An understanding of the hostility generated by the demand for votes for women requires attention to some much deeper-seated matters than the intricacies of parliamentary and party political manoeuvrings, the tactics of the militants (the suffragettes), or the opposition of interests such as the liquor trade. The short answer to my first question is that the franchise appeared to pose a radical challenge and threat not just to the state but to the powers and privileges of men as a sex. Indeed, Susan Kent argues that, in Britain, 'the threat posed by women's challenges to patriarchal order was seen to be even greater than that of the working classes'.[9] This was the basis of the high hopes for the vote on the one side and the fears of the consequences if women were to use the ballot box on the other.

In his study of the British anti-suffragists, Brian Harrison comments that, apart from the vote, 'it is difficult to think of reforms for which late Victorian women energetically campaigned and which they were not granted'.[10] There was, however, one reform, or series of reforms, central to the struggle over the suffrage, that was not achieved; namely, reform of the law of coverture. Under coverture, in the middle of the nineteenth century a married woman had no independent legal and civil standing; she was deemed to be 'covered' or represented by her husband for public purposes. Coverture meant that, like many other aspects of women's position, the suffrage was, at bottom, 'the wife question' (which is why some suffragists were willing initially to limit their demands to votes for spinsters).[11] The law gave husbands despotic powers, and, in such a context, to demand reform of marriage law, to demand an end to men's monopoly of education and paid employment, including professional occupations, to demand that men should curb their sexual rapaciousness, and to link all this to the vote, was to make an extremely radical claim.

Womanhood suffrage, as Ellen DuBois has emphasised, 'exposed and challenged the assumption of male authority over women'.[12] The vote promised women a public standing as individuals that was independent of their general subordination as women and, especially, as wives in the private sphere. The question of votes for women turned the separation of the public and private spheres into a political problem – and that is precisely the political problem that, as I have noted, political scientists ignore. Yet the separation of the two spheres explains why suffrage at a national level was so vehemently opposed. Many anti-suffragists did not object to women voting in local and municipal elections, and they often supported other reforms, such as property rights and access to education, that would improve women's social position.[13] Anti-suffragists were able to present such changes as an improvement in women's position in the private world, or as an extension of women's private tasks, that left the public arena to men.

The vote was, therefore, a potent symbol of all that was entailed in an equal social and political standing for women. But the vote was also demanded as a practical weapon of reform, so the threat posed by the suffrage to the patriarchal order seemed very real. The suffragists believed that, once they had the vote, the way would be open for major changes in the private realm as well as public life, although in Britain they also tried to reduce anxieties by drawing on the example of Australia and New Zealand to show that votes for women had not led to neglect of homes and families.[14] All those involved in the battle over womanhood suffrage were well aware of the significance of the vote for the division between private and public, for men's power, and the conventional understanding of what it meant to be a man or a woman. Both sides saw a connection between the sexual order, sexual identity and the political order.

Anti-suffragists wrote to the Illinois legislature in 1897, that 'we believe that men are ordained to govern in all forceful and material matters, because they are men'.[15] A member of the House of Commons stated in a debate on a suffrage bill in 1873, 'our object ought to be to enfranchise independent voters; but the female sex must in the nature of things remain in a position of dependence'.[16] Such views reflect ideas about the political meaning of sexual difference that go back to the seventeenth century. The study of the historic texts is an important part of political theory, but most standard interpretations of the texts still overlook the fact that virtually every theory is formulated around men as political actors. Theoretical exclusion of women from political life in these texts facilitated and legitimised the deliberate exclusion of women from the suffrage. The famous theorists declared, almost to a man, that women naturally lack the liberty and independence needed for public life, and so must be governed or 'protected' by men. Womanhood itself is a disqualification for citizenship.[17] This view of sexual difference as the political difference between freedom for men, and subordination or 'protection' for women, had become institutionalised by the mid-nineteenth century in the denial of civil standing to wives and the exclusion of women from the public sphere.

The suffragists countered these ideas through three major lines of argument (often put forward simultaneously). Firstly, they insisted that the promise to women inherent in the universal language of individual freedom and equality, the rights of citizens and the consent of the governed, should be fulfilled. Women were prevented from participating in the public world not by nature but by men's monopoly of education, training, paid employment and the suffrage; women as a matter of justice should have full standing as citizens. Secondly, they argued that the suffrage was vital if women were to be able to carry out their work in the private sphere in a morally acceptable context; the vote was necessary to eliminate men's domestic tyranny and to strengthen women's position in private life. The suffragists agreed that men and women had their own tasks to perform, but they demanded some radical changes in marriage law and in the relation between the private and public spheres.

Thirdly, from at least the 1790s, the argument was made that women had a distinctive and valuable contribution to make. By the beginning of the twentieth century, suffragists were pointing to the increasing legislative concern with social welfare, and arguing that women, who had charge of the welfare of their families and who had long been encouraged to devote themselves to charitable work and philanthropy, had special knowledge and skills to bring to the political arena. Women, Jane Addams argued in the US, should take part in public affairs to build up 'that code of legislation which is alone sufficient to protect the home from the dangers incident to modern life'.[18] Moreover, many suffragists, middle and working class, linked the vote to women's economic independence – even Christabel Pankhurst in her much derided polemic about the suffrage and venereal disease.[19] In the 1900s, tens of thousands of women workers and trade unionists in the cotton towns of Lancashire formed their own suffrage associations. They saw the vote as a way to improve their working conditions and their position as workers in male-dominated workplaces; but they were also wives, and their husbands feared for their comforts. One of these suffragists remarked that 'no cause can be won between dinner and tea, . . . domestic unhappiness, the price many of us paid for our opinions and our activities, was a very bitter thing'.[20]

The suffragists were also directly at odds with their opponents over another aspect of women's natures. The suffragists emphasised the consent of the governed, and many also claimed that womanhood suffrage would usher in a new era of peace. The anti-suffragists, in contrast, placed great stress on force as the basis of the state, and they saw the suffrage as a threat to stability and national order. Women's natures, they argued, made them dangerous to the state. In Britain, anti-suffragists argued that 'government rests ultimately on force', and that 'women could not undertake the physical responsibilities of enforcing any law, which, by their votes, they might cause to be enacted'.[21] In the US, the electorate was seen as a 'militia on inactive duty'.[22] Women, it was claimed, could not be part of this militia, since they were, by nature, unable and/or unwilling to use the force necessary to impose the will of the majority. Nor could they maintain an imperial government; 'imagine', one British anti-suffragist proclaimed, 'the women of England governing India'.[23]

In both the suffragist and the anti-suffragist camps, many saw the battle over the suffrage as a war between the sexes. For instance, the British anti-suffragist Frederic Harrison proclaimed in 1909 that 'equal electoral rights could not fail to inflame a standing war between the sexes', and he believed that the 'inevitable result of female franchise would be . . . a weakening of men's respect for women'. If women got the vote, the anti-suffragists claimed, all restraints would be weakened and physical strength would rule; 'once let loose the wild beast, which the law holds in chains and who', asked one anti-suffrage paper, 'are likely to fall the quickest and easiest prey?'[24] The suffragists' political activities invaded the public space monopolised by men, who responded not only by opposing the suffrage, but by reasserting their masculinity, often, as on Black Friday, in violent ways. The obscene remarks made to street sellers of *Votes for Women*, the fruit, stones and other missiles thrown at suffrage speakers, attacks on suffrage offices and the sexual assaults, provided more evidence for the suffragists of the need for a radical change in men's sexual morality. They argued that the law and social opinion gave men virtual carte blanche to use force against women. In his speech in 1867 supporting the suffrage, John Stuart Mill raised the problem of the brutal treatment and murder of wives. For suffragists, the vote, and the equal political standing that it would bring, was the means through which men could be brought to give women genuine respect and genuine protection.

One difficulty faced by the suffragists was that they were often attacked not for their political aims but as women. There was a brisk trade in postcards portraying the suffragists as muscular and plain, with captions such as 'It's not a vote you want – it's a bloke!'[25] The militant suffragettes, in particular, were portrayed as unsexed women and as madwomen. The best-known example of this genre is Sir Almroth Wright's *The Unexpurgated Case Against Womanhood Suffrage*, published in 1913. He stated that 'there is mixed up with the women's movement much mental disorder'. The book reveals a deep-seated fear of women's sexuality; the state, he believes, would be 'well rid' of spinsters – that is, women not under the control of husbands – and he comments that the hope that men and women could work side by side could not be fulfilled, because 'even in animals . . . male and female cannot safely be worked side by side, except where they are incomplete'.[26]

The reason for the length of the struggle for womanhood suffrage was, then, that it was not merely participation in the government of the state that was seen to be at issue, but the patriarchal structure of relations between the sexes and conceptions of masculinity and femininity. However, if this explanation illuminates the reasons why men were so opposed to the enfranchisement of women, it does little to explain why women themselves, in large numbers, opposed the suffrage.

Why did women organise against their own enfranchisement?
No other group, to the best of my knowledge, has so actively opposed equal rights for themselves. Indeed, women not only campaigned against the suffrage but in the 1970s organised again in opposition to the Equal Rights Amendment (ERA) in the US. The reasons for the opposition are complex; some of the first opponents of the ERA in the 1920s (it was first introduced into Congress in 1923) had been suffragist leaders who continued to press for other social changes to benefit women, just as some

anti-suffragists supported other reforms. Large numbers of women enlisted in the anti-suffrage cause, although they seem to have come from different parts of the social spectrum in Britain and the US.

In Britain, women active in the National League for Opposing Women's Suffrage (founded in 1908) were overwhelmingly upper-class, many titled; 'two types of woman embodied the anti-suffragist idea . . . the political hostess and the female philanthropist'.[27] By virtue of their class, these women had political influence behind the scenes and access to male leaders, such as the imperialist Lords Curzon and Cromer, who led the anti-suffrage movement. No doubt they feared that their private manipulations would be upset if women became legitimate public actors. The anti-suffrage groups in the US, in contrast, were mainly led by women, and the organisations were much less socially exclusive, involving 'the active opposition of thousands of women'; the New York State organisation may have had 20,000 members in the 1890s.[28] In the 1970s, women, such as Phyllis Schlafly of the Stop ERA organisation (founded in 1973), were again prominent leaders against the ERA; activist women were more likely to be housewives and to be more conservative in their politics and religion than supporters of the ERA.

The historian Carl Degler has explored the reasons why American women opposed the suffrage and his conclusion is that 'many women perceived in the suffrage a threat to the family, a threat so severe that the vote did not seem worth the possible cost'. One American anti-suffragist asked 'is there any escape from the conviction that the industrial and political independence of women would be the wreck of our present domestic institutions?'[29] But the question still remains of why the anti-suffrage women believed that the vote would have this consequence.

It is, of course, difficult, now that elections have become the benchmark of democracy, to imagine all the spectres conjured up by the prospect of women voting. Still, there is a remarkable continuity between the arguments used by the anti-suffragists and many of those used by opponents of the ERA, and in the symbolic importance attached to both reforms. The anti-suffragists and the suffragists were bitterly divided over the issue of 'protection' of women, protection that the anti-suffragists believed was secured through the separation of the public and private spheres. The anti-suffragists insisted that women's protection would be eroded, posing a grave danger to the family, once the separation was breached by the vote. Women would then be forced to compete with men and become ever more vulnerable to men's greater strength and social power; as one British anti-suffragist proclaimed, 'clamours for equality' by women meant that 'man's protecting instinct will dwindle and die'.[30] A bleak view of men's characters is implicit in these arguments.

Nor was the independence symbolised by the vote welcomed by all women; for many, it seemed to place their future in jeopardy. The ideal of separate spheres and the protection given by a husband held out the promise of economic subsistence and a defined social place as a wife to women from all respectable classes. Although women's economic opportunities had improved by the end of the nineteenth century, they were still very limited, and middle-class husbands could offer their wives a more comfortable existence than spinsters could provide for themselves. Working-class women also feared the likely outcome if, as anti-suffragists forecast, they were forced into economic competition with men.[31]

These same fears surfaced again in the 1970s in the opposition to the ERA; the ghosts of the anti-suffragists seemed to be walking abroad.[32] The question of 'protection' arose in a number of different ways, including the issue of the armed forces and combat, but the emphasis placed on the threat that the ERA was held to pose to the family and the insistence that men and women should occupy separate spheres is particularly striking. Opponents of the ERA argued that equal rights for women meant that husbands would no longer perform their duties as breadwinners and wives would lose their claim to subsistence from their husbands. A picture was painted of men abandoning their families or refusing marriage altogether, and women being left as prey for rapacious men, if legislators supported the ERA.[33] The ERA symbolised a range of threatening forces. Many women apparently feared that they would be forced to abandon their femininity and cease to be 'women', in the sense in which they understood that term, if the ERA was ratified, just as the suffrage was once feared as a measure that would 'unsex' women.[34]

The fact of, and the character of, the opposition to the ERA raises a major question, the third of the questions with which I am concerned here; namely, why were women enfranchised in the end? After all, resistance to women's equal rights on the part of both women and men has persisted in considerable strength and on much the same grounds from the 1860s for over a century. The ERA has still not been ratified, and in 1992 in Iowa a state ERA was defeated by 52 per cent to 48 per cent, a majority of men voting 'no'.

Why did women win the vote?

The conventional way of approaching my third question, if, indeed, it is even raised as a real problem, focuses on two points. Firstly, the most popular answer to the question is trotted out. Women got the vote, so it is said, because of the impact of the war, or, more specifically, as a reward for their work during World War I.[35] This is not a very convincing answer. For example, it does not explain why, in Britain, only women over 30 were enfranchised in 1918 when younger women had done most of the war work. More strongly, Sandra Holton has recently argued that, in light of the change in the political climate by 1914, 'it might even be said that the war postponed' the vote.[36] A more plausible argument along these lines is that women's determined efforts, which continued during the war, was a major reason why the US, Britain, and also Canada and Nordic countries, enfranchised women before or at the end of the war; all these countries had 'highly organised labour or feminist movements demanding the vote for women', whereas, for instance, France and Italy did not.[37]

Secondly, various facilitating factors are canvassed; in the case of Britain, reference is made, for instance, to the war-time coalition government, the commitment of the Labour Party by 1914 to a wider franchise that included women, a lessening of opposition in the House of Lords and the need for a new electoral register after the war. In the US after 1910, a major reason for the passage of the Nineteenth Amendment was Carrie Chapman Catt's brilliant 'winning plan'. The suffragists turned their attention to a Federal Amendment and to gaining suffrage in the states so that pressure could be brought on Congressmen at federal level by women voters.[38] By 1916 the President and the two parties had endorsed the suffrage.

One difficulty with both these arguments is that, while they help explain many of the final mechanisms through which the vote was won, they do not explain why the hostility to women's rights continued. This is also true of Carl Degler's answer to the question. He argues that American women got the vote because of 'a decline in the fear that the suffrage threatened the family'.[39] If this is the case, it seems very odd that fifty years later the ERA was again seen to threaten the family. Moreover, none of these answers helps explain why there has been such distrust of women's involvement in other aspects of electoral politics. Women still form only a very small proportion of the members of Congress or of the House of Commons; in Australia it took four decades from the time that women became eligible to stand for election in 1902 for a woman to be elected to the Federal Parliament. No woman has ever run for the office of US President for either of the two main parties, and, although Margaret Thatcher became the first British woman prime minister in 1979, British Cabinets continue to be almost exclusively male territory. All this points to another answer to my third question; that it was not views about women or the family that had undergone a radical change by the end of the Great War but views about the vote.

Political scientists, as I emphasised earlier, now take the vote completely for granted. They display little curiosity about the enormous change from the perception of universal suffrage as a threat to the social and political order to a recent argument that the vote is an insurance against the collapse of the democratic system.[40] More generally, voting is now seen as *the* means of providing legitimacy to governments. At the same time, however, the consensus of opinion is that womanhood suffrage had little or no political impact. Expectations about the vote by suffragists and their opponents cannot be taken seriously; predictions of a political transformation and the hopes and fears on both sides were manifestly over-inflated. One writer states that winning the suffrage was 'a sad and hollow victory, an anti-climax to a long campaign';[41] another writes that women's 'final victory led to no noticeable political change at all'.[42]

One possible answer to the question of why women were given the vote is suggested by the political theorist C. B. Macpherson.[43] He argues that the democratic franchise was 'tamed' through the development of the party system. Typically, however, he looks only at manhood suffrage and class. Macpherson argues that when the franchise and elected office was confined to the (male) propertied class, elected representatives had to be responsive to their electors. With a broader franchise, and the development of national parties that encompassed a wide array of different interests and groups, representatives had to look to a broad national, rather than class, interest. At the same time, elected office became the preserve of candidates endorsed by parties, and representatives had to back their party leaders in legislatures or risk loss of their seats, so that the result was minimal accountability to the wider party membership or the electorate. Using this line of argument in the case of women, it seems that the fear of an electorate that included women had abated considerably by the end of World War I. Universal suffrage had become necessary to produce legitimate governments, but, thanks to the party system, governments and legislatures were well insulated from voters. But this argument does not explain the persistence of hostility to women's rights. It is necessary to turn to an aspect of the development of parties and government ignored by Macpherson, and most other political scientists; that is, the relationship between womanhood suffrage, party politics and patriarchal power.

One obvious point is that parties and governments were, and, to a significant extent remain, men's clubs. In the US, for instance, from the 1820s onward, but particularly in the late nineteenth century, men were strong partisans of the two parties, and a large majority not only voted but took part in the rallies, parades and many other fraternal social activities, often referred to in military terms, that were organised around the parties and electoral campaigning. Women were spectators of these events; their participation was large confined to dressing up to represent such figures as Liberty.[44] Elections also confirmed the masculine character of parties and politics; 'elections [were] held in saloons, barber shops, and other places largely associated with men', and 'participation in electoral politics . . . define[d] manhood'.[45] In the early twentieth century, electoral participation and allegiance to parties declined, and men's political activities were no longer closely tied to local fraternal communities, instead they moved to wider economic, national and other interests – a development that was part of the taming of the franchise.

But even when women were enfranchised, men still dominated party politics. Just as women's demands for the vote – or ratification of the ERA – had to wait upon the favour of male party members and legislators, so the fate of policies and legislation of concern to women, and especially feminists, was in men's hands. Men were not going to rush to change party platforms or enact legislation to diminish their power over women because women had the vote. It also needs to be emphasised that women were incorporated as auxiliaries into political parties long before they became voters. In Britain, for example, the very successful Primrose League of the Tory Party was founded in 1884 and the Liberals set up the Women's Liberal Federation in 1886. Women were then required to put allegiance to the party first, above any other interests they might have.

C. B. Macpherson also mentions that 'imperial expansion' allowed governments in the late nineteenth and early twentieth century 'to afford handouts to their electorates'. In other words, this was the period when the first welfare state measures were introduced. Macpherson sees this development as blunting working-class pressure for reform, thus also helping to 'tame' the franchise, but what he fails to notice is that these early reforms and the manner in which the welfare state was consolidated reinforced men's position as breadwinners and heads of households. The welfare state, as feminist scholars have now amply demonstrated, has a patriarchal structure.[46] Possession of the vote and policies that improved women's lives went hand in hand with the maintenance of large areas of men's power and continued hostility to women's participation in the public realm.

To amend Macpherson's argument in this way is, however, to present only one side of the picture. The opponents of womanhood suffrage were correct in one respect; once women gained public standing as voters, a practical statement had been made that traditional arguments for women's exclusion from electoral politics, and for their government by men, were now illegitimate. The vote and other elements of civil and political equality won by women in the half century since 1920 have highlighted the continuing power and privilege of men as a sex, and it is hardly surprising that since the revival of the women's movement in the late 1960s an attack has been mounted against these private and public bastions, with greater or lesser success depending on the issue. Moreover, the franchise might have been tamed, but the achievement of womanhood suffrage was not completely inconsequential. There have been manifold changes. Women's votes have helped to obtain legal and policy changes from 1920 to 1990 that would have been almost unthinkable to women in the mid-nineteenth century. Women were strong advocates of the consolidation of the welfare state in Britain and welfare measures in the US, which have assisted women's economic independence. Women also worked for changes in marriage law, for access to education, to the labour market, for support for mothers and their children, and all the other measures that have transformed women's position. The difficulty lies in determining exactly how important *voting* is in this transformation compared to other forms of political activity – women, like other citizens, have never confined themselves to voting alone – and compared to long-term social and economic change. Once again, this question, difficult though it is to investigate has received very little attention.

More questions
A large amount of material is now available about suffrage in Britain and the US, thanks to historians, but there are important political questions about which we know very little, not only about votes for women in these two countries, but around the world. There is, for instance, the question that I mentioned at the beginning of this essay: why did women win the vote so much earlier in peripheral regions and countries? Was it, as is sometimes suggested, that women formed a small enough proportion of the population that they did not seem threatening? Or was it that they were seen as a civilising influence in frontier areas? Or were quite different factors important? Comparisons between the countries where women, won the suffrage around the turn of the century also raise much broader questions about the common features, if any, in the global struggle for

the suffrage. We know remarkably little about how women won the vote around the world. How important are local circumstances and local political configurations, or struggles for national self-determination? How important are cultural differences, or differences in political regimes? Nor is much attention paid to the fact that there are still some countries – Kuwait, for example – where women are disenfranchised.

Little interest has been displayed, as I have indicated, in the question of the political significance and consequences of womanhood suffrage. What differences has it made, for example, to women or to national politics, that in New Zealand women have been voting for a century and in Switzerland only since 1971 (and in the canton of Appenzell only since 1989)? Does women's absence from participation in elections make a difference to their position in society, in relations between the sexes, to women's political activities or to public policies or institutions? What difference does it make to women's rights if women are voters? How important is it that women can vote in transitions from authoritarian to democratic regimes? It is not easy to investigate or answer such questions, but it is important for democratic theory and practice that the attempt at least is made to confront them.

The fact of women's long exclusion from national electorates (even in Europe, in Belgium, France and Italy, women were not enfranchised until the 1940s) has not been seen by most students of politics as of any special relevance for democracy. Nor have women as citizens been seen as influenced by the fact that, in Britain and the United States, women were enfranchised while still subordinate in marriage, and were voting while being incorporated into the welfare state as men's dependants rather than as citizens with their own entitlements. More generally, lack of interest in the deep-seated and vehement hostility to votes for women, and the continuing difficulties women face in entering legislative and other public bodies, means that possible insights have not been forthcoming into the mechanisms underlying hostility towards other groups and categories of the population.

The question of votes for women is all too often seen as a rather boring and insignificant matter. On the contrary, it is a fascinating and complex subject, and one that can teach us a great deal about political development and the structure of institutions. There is still an enormous amount of work to be done and I regret that my own discipline has contributed so little; political scientists are still resistant to the necessary reconsideration of the standard conception of their subject matter. But feminist scholars are growing in number, so perhaps by the time of the

125th anniversary of womanhood suffrage we shall know a lot more about the politics of votes for women.

1   William L. O'Neill, *The Woman Movement: Feminism in the United States and England*, Allen & Unwin, London, 1969, 7.

2   See David Morgan, *Suffragists and Democrats: the Politics of Woman Suffrage in America*, Michigan State Univ. Press, East Lansing, 1972; David Morgan, *Suffragists and Liberals: the Politics of Woman Suffrage in England*, Rowman & Littlefield, Totowa, NJ, 1975.

3   Cit. Carl N. Degler, *At Odds: Women and the Family in America From the Revolution to the Present*, Oxford Univ. Press, New York, 1980, 360.

4   Emmeline Pankhurst, 'When Civil War is Waged by Women', in Miriam Schneir, ed, *Feminism: The Essential Historical Writings*, Random House, New York, 1972.

5   Robert Dahl, *Who Governs: Democracy and Power in an American City*, Yale Univ. Press, New Haven, 1961, 224.

6   How could it come about, for example, that two investigators could exclude voting from their scale of conventional political participation because, they write, voting 'occurs only rarely, is highly biased by strong mechanisms of social control and social desirability enhanced by the rain-dance ritual of campaigning, and does not involve the voter in major informational or other costs'? Samuel H. Barnes & Max Kaase, *Political Action: Mass Participation in Five Western Democracies*, Sage Publications, Beverly Hills, 1979, 86.

7   John Stuart Mill, in Francis E. Mineka & Dwight N. Lindley, eds, *The Collected Works of John Stuart Mill*, vol. XVII, Univ. of Toronto Press, Toronto, 1972, 1728.

8   Mitchell states that the 'provocativeness of the maiden warriors' on Black Friday gave the men 'a splendid excuse' for their actions, and claims that the assaults were 'in some cases' what the suffragists 'really wanted'. His hysterical tone in many places seems, judging from the final chapter, to be as much a result of his fear of the revival of the women's movement in the 1970s as his obvious dislike of Christabel Pankhurst and the militants. He goes so far as to claim that her main contribution was 'the "terrorist" touch, the taste of blood', and to compare what he sees as the 'blind obedience' of the suffragettes to members of the Manson family. David Mitchell, *Queen Christabel*, MacDonald & Jane, London, 1977, 160, 321 and 371.

9   Susan Kinsley Kent, *Sex and Suffrage in Britain, 1860-1914*, Princeton Univ. Press, Princeton, NJ, 1987, 30.

10   Brian Harrison, *Separate Spheres: The Opposition to Women's Suffrage in Britain*, Holmes & Meier, New York, 1978, 60.

11   The law was confused about the effect of coverture on local politics. In 1872 the Court of Queen's Bench ruled that married women were disqualified by the law of coverture from exercising the municipal franchise, but the effect on school boards, for example, was not clear. Mary Lyndon Shanley, *Feminism, Marriage and the Law in Victorian Egland, 1850-1895*, Princeton Univ. Press, Princeton, N.J., 1989, 111. The last vestiges of coverture in Britain have only just been eliminated; for example, the law finally recognised that a husband could rape his wife in 1992.

12   Ellen DuBois, *Feminism and Suffrage: The Emergence of an Independent Women's Movement in America, 1848-1869*, Cornell Univ. Press, Ithaca, 1978, 46.

13   For example, 'An Appeal Against Female Suffrage', reprinted in Patricia Hollis, *Women in Public: The Women's Movement, 1850-1900*, Allen & Unwin, London, 1979.

14   Sawer & Simms, *A Woman's Place: Women and Politics in Australia*, 2nd ed, 1993, 10-16.

15   Cit., Degler, *At Odds*, 351.

16   Cit., Shanley, *Feminism*, 114.

17   Carole Pateman, *The Sexual Contract*.

18   Kraditor, *The Ideas of the Woman Suffrage Movement: 1890-1920*, 69.

19   Christabel Pankhurst, 'The Great Scourge', reprinted in Jane Marcus, ed, *Suffrage and the Pankhursts*, Routledge & Kegan Paul, London, 1987, 227.

20   Liddington & Norris, *One Hand Tied Behind Us: The Rise of the Women's Suffrage Movement*, 217.

21   Cit., Kent, *Sex and Suffrage*, 181.

22   Cit., Kraditor, *The Ideas*, 29.

23 Cit. Harrison, *Separate Spheres*, 75.

24 Cit., Kent, 57 and 181.

25 Alison Young, '"Wild Women": The Censure of the Suffragette Movement', *International Journal of the Sociology of Law*, 16, 1988, 283 and 287.

26 Almroth E. Wright, *The Unexpurgated Case Against Womanhood Suffrage*, Paul B. Hoeben, New York, 1913, 79, 181 and 170.

27 Harrison, *Separate Spheres*, 81.

28 Degler, *At Odds*, 349-50.

29 Ibid., 350, 353-4.

30 Cit., Kent, *Sex and Suffrage*, 179.

31 The lack of interest in the suffrage by the tens of thousands of women involved in the Chartist movement in Britain in the 1840s, who acted on behalf of their menfolk, is instructive here. In the first draft of the Charter women's suffrage was included, but it was quickly dropped, on the grounds that its adoption 'might retard the suffrage of men', Dorothy Thompson, 'Women and Nineteenth Century Radical Politics: A Lost Dimension', in Juliet Mitchell & Ann Oakley, eds, *The Rights and Wrongs of Women*, Penguin Books, Harmondsworth, 1976, 132. By 1841 a Chartist speaker was repeating the claim that 'men, as fathers, husbands, and brothers' would look after women's interests, cit., Barbara Taylor, *Eve and the New Jerusalem: Socialism and Feminism in the Nineteenth Century*, Virago, London, 1983, 271.

32 In the 1920s the issue of 'protection' arose in a different way. By 1923, when the ERA was first introduced into Congress, legislation protecting women workers and mothers and children had been enacted. The opponents of the ERA feared that the legislation would be jeopardised by equal rights. Their fears were reinforced when the Supreme Court held that minimum wage laws were not required for women because they were protected under the Nineteenth Amendment.

33 Jane Mansbridge, *Why We Lost the ERA*, Univ. of Chicago Press, Chicago, 1986, ch. 6; Donald G. Mathews & Jane DeHart, *Sex, Gender and the Politics of ERA: A State and Nation*, Oxford Univ. Press, New York, 1990, ch. 6; Edith Mayo & Jerry K. Frye, 'ERA: Postmortem of a Failure in Political Communication', in Joan Hoff-Wilson, ed, *Rights of Passage: The Past and Future of the ERA*, Indiana Univ. Press, Bloomington, 1986.

34 Mathews & De Hart, *Sex, Gender and the Politics of ERA*, 159

35 See, for example, Les Garner, *Stepping Stones to Women's Liberty: Feminist Ideas in the Women's Suffrage Movement, 1900-1988*, Heinemann Educational Books Ltd, London, 1984, ch. 7; Bryan S. Turner, *Citizenship and Capitalism*, Allen & Unwin, London, 1986, 60.

36 Holton, *Feminism and Democracy: Women's Suffrage and Reform Politics in Britain, 1900-1918*, 130.

37 Mary Fainsod Katenstein, 'Feminism and the Meaning of the Vote', *Signs*, 10/1, 1984, 11.

38 Eileen Lorenzi McDonagh, 'Materialist Praxis and the Woman Suffrage in the American States: The Historical and Contemporary Significance of the Nineteenth Amendment', unpublished paper, 1992.

39 Degler, *At Odds*, 357.

40 Antony Downs, *An Economic Theory of Democracy*, HarperCollins, New York, 1957.

41 Garner, *Stepping Stones*, 103.

42 Judith N. Shklar, *American Citizenship: The Quest for Inclusion*, Harvard Univ. Press, Cambridge, 1991, 60. See also the comments about historians in Paula Baker, 'The Domestication of Politics: Women and American Political Society, 1780-1920', *American Historical Review*, 89, 1984, 643.

43 C. B. Macpherson, *The Life and Times of Liberal Democracy*, Oxford Univ. Press, New York, 1977, 64-9.

44 Baker, 'Domestication', 627-9; see also Mary P. Ryan, *Women in Public: Between Banners and Ballots, 1825-1880*, The John Hopkins Press, Baltimore & London, 1990.

45 Baker, 'Domestication', 629, 638.

46 Pateman, 'The Patriarchal Welfare State', in *The Disorder of Women*.

Appendix: Chronological List of Women's Suffrage Dates

It is very difficult to ascertain when women in a particular country gained the right to vote. This is especially true for women in less developed countries. This chronology was compiled by consulting a number of sources, some of which offered conflicting information. It was often impossible to tell whether the dates given were for the year women's suffrage was granted, or the year it was first exercised. In some cases it was specified that the suffrage won was limited to a particular group of women, in other case no such qualification was noted, although this may well have been the case. The following chronology is a tentative listing.

1776–1807 New Jersey – propertied women voted in elections from 1787, although they had the right from 1776; they lost suffrage when universal male suffrage was introduced
1838 Pitcairn Islands
1869 Wyoming Territory
1870 Utah Territory – abolished in 1887 and restored in 1896
1881 Isle of Man – propertied women
1893 Colorado
Cook Islands
New Zealand
1894 South Australia – full state suffrage and right to stand for Parliament
1896 Idaho
Utah
1899 Western Australia – full state suffrage
1902 Australia – white women gained the federal franchise
New South Wales (Australia) – full state suffrage
1903 Tasmania (Australia) – full state suffrage

1905 Queensland (Australia) – full state suffrage
1906 Finland
1907 Norway – economic qualification
1908 Victoria (Australia) – full state suffrage
1910 Washington State
1911 California
1912 Arizona
Kansas
Oregon
1913 Alaska
Illinois – limited to voting for President and offices created by statute
Norway – full suffrage
1914 Montana
Nevada
1915 Denmark
Iceland – women aged 40 or above
1916 Alberta
Manitoba
Saskatchewan
1917 Arkansas
British Columbia
Canada – federal vote for Euroamerican women in

the armed forces and close
relatives of soldiers
Estonia
Indiana
Latvia
Lithuania
Michigan
Nebraska
New York
North Dakota – presidential
suffrage
Ohio – lost later that year
Ontario
Rhode Island
1918 Austria
Canada – federal vote for
women of British and
French extraction
Czechoslovakia
Germany
Hungary – limited suffrage
Luxembourg
Michigan
New Brunswick
Nova Scotia
Oklahoma
Poland
South Dakota
Texas – suffrage in primary
elections
United Kingdom – married
women, women house-
holders and women
university graduates aged
30 years or over
1919 Netherlands
Rhodesia – limited suffrage
on the basis of a woman's
husband's financial means,
provided she was not
married polygamously
Sweden
1920 Belgium – mothers and
widows of soldiers who had
died in World War I
Iceland – full suffrage
USA – however, in some

states legal devices such as
literacy tests and poll taxes
were used to exclude Blacks
from voting
1922 Ireland – full suffrage
1924 Mongolia
1928 United Kingdom – full
suffrage
1929 Ecuador – limited suffrage
Puerto Rico – limited suffrage
1930 South Africa – white women
Turkey
1931 Spain – but women lost the
vote under Franco in 1936
and did not vote again until
1976
Ceylon/Sri Lanka
1932 Brazil
Thailand
Uruguay
1933 Portugal – women who had
completed secondary or
university education
1934 Cuba
1935 India – limited suffrage based
on educational and income
requirements
1937 Philippines
1939 El Salvador
1941 Indonesia
1942 Dominican Republic
1944 France
Jamaica
1945 Bulgaria
Guatemala
Italy
Japan
Panama
Trinidad and Tobago
1946 Albania
Ecuador – full suffrage
Liberia – property
qualification
Malta
Portugal – women who were
heads of household and
married women who paid a

certain amount of tax
Romania
Yugoslavia
1947 Argentina
Pakistan
Venezuela
1948 Belgium – full suffrage
Burma
Israel
South Korea
1949 Chile
China
Costa Rica
India – full suffrage
Syria – limited suffrage
1950 Haiti
1951 Antigua
Barbados
Dominica
Grenada
St Christopher (Kitts) and
Nevis
St Lucia
St Vincent and the
Grenadines
Sierra Leone
1952 Bolivia
Greece
1953 Lebanon
Mexico
Syria – full suffrage, but after a
coup d'état that year, rights
reverted to the 1949 basis
1954 Belize
Gold Coast Colony/Ghana
Nigeria – federal suffrage for
women in the Eastern
Region
1955 Ethiopia
Honduras
Malaya/Malaysia
Nicaragua
Nigeria – federal suffrage for
women in the Western
Region if they paid taxes
Peru
1956 Egypt – compulsory voting for

men but not for women
Honduras
1957 Colombia
Honduras
Singapore
1958 Iraq
Mauritius
Paraguay
Tanganyika/Tanzania
1959 Nepal
Nigeria – federal suffrage for
women in the South
1960 Canada – discrimination
against various groups ends
Central African Republic
Cyprus
San Marino
The Gambia
1961 Rwanda
Somalia
1962 Australia – discrimination
against Aborigines ends
Bahamas
Monaco
1963 Iran
Kenya
Mozambique – illiterate
females over the age of 21
who headed a family and
women with three years of
high school education or
who paid taxes
1964 Afghanistan
Libya
Maldives
Sudan
1965 Afghanistan
Burundi
1966 Fiji
Lesotho
1967 Seychelles
Zaire
1968 Nauru
Swaziland
1971 Gilbert Islands/Kiribati
Switzerland
1973 Syria – full suffrage

1975	Mozambique – full suffrage		Rhodesia) – full suffrage
	Papua New Guinea	1980	Cape Verde
	Portugal – full suffrage	1984	Jordan
	Nigeria – federal suffrage for		Liberia – full suffrage
	women in the North		Liechtenstein
1978	Tuvalu	1994	South Africa – full suffrage
	Zimbabwe (formerly		

Sources

We would like to thank the subscribers to H-Women who offered many suggestions when we posted the chronology on the list, and Ellen DuBois, who gave participants at the suffrage conference her list of women's suffrage dates, and thus was the inspiration for this appendix. The main published works consulted were:

Elizabeth Frost & Kathryn Cullen-DuPont, *Women's Suffrage in America: An Eyewitness History*, Facts on File, New York/Oxford, 1992.

Ian Gorvin, ed, *Elections Since 1945: A Worldwide Reference Compendium*, Longman International Reference, London, 1989

Thomas T. Mackie & Richard Rose, *The International Almanac of Electoral History*, Macmillan, London, 1991, 3rd ed.

Robin Morgan, ed, *Sisterhood is Global: The International Women's Movement Anthology*, Anchor Press/Doubleday, Garden City, New York, 1984

Joni Seagar & Ann Olsen, *Women in the World*, Simon and Schuster, New York, 1986

Sally Shreir, ed, *Women's Movements of the World*, Longman, Burnt Mill, Harlow, 1988

Lisa Tuttle, ed, *Encyclopaedia of Feminism*, Facts on File Publications, New York, 1986.

Selected Bibliography on Women's Suffrage

Australasian Region

Allen, Judith A., *Rose Scott: Vision and Revision in Feminism*, Oxford University Press, Melbourne, 1994.

Ballara, Angela, 'Wahine Rangatira: Maori Women on Rank and their Role in the Women's Kotahitanga Movement of the 1890s', *New Zealand Journal of History*, 27/2, 1993, 127-39.

Biskup, P., 'The Westralian Feminist Movement', *University Studies in Western Australian History*, 3/3, 1959, 71-84.

Bunkle, Phillida, 'The Origins of the Women's Movement in New Zealand: The Women's Christian Temperance Union, 1885–1895', in Phillida Bunkle & Beryl Hughes, eds, *Women in New Zealand Society*, Allen & Unwin, Auckland, 1980.

Burke, Patti, 'Did an Old and Sleepy Gentleman Secure the Vote for Australian Women?', *Third Women and Labour Conference Papers*, 1982, 393-402.

Catt, Helena & Elizabeth McLeay, eds, *Women and Politics in New Zealand*, Political Science in conjunction with Victoria University Press, Wellington, 1993.

Corbett, Pat, 'Women's Suffrage: Myths and Fantasies', *Journal of the Royal Australian Historical Society*, 71/1, 1985, 43-58.

Curthoys, Ann, 'Feminism, Citizenship, and National Identity', *Feminist Review*, 44, 1993, 19-38.

Dalziel, Raewyn, 'The Colonial Helpmeet: Women's Role and the Vote in Nineteenth-Century New Zealand', *New Zealand Journal of History*, 11/2, 1977, 112-23.

Devaliant, Judith, *Kate Sheppard: A Biography*, Penguin, Auckland, 1992.

Feeney, Jennifer, 'Votes for Women: The Woman's Franchise League of Ballarat', *La Trobe Library Journal*, 8/31, 1983, 64-5.

Fernon, Christine, 'Women's Suffrage in Victoria', *Refractory Girl*, 22, 1981, 18-24.

Fry, Ruth, *Maud and Amber: A New Zealand Mother and Daughter and the Women's Cause, 1865 to 1981*, Canterbury University Press, Christchurch, 1992.

Garner, Jean, 'Sir John Hall and Women's Suffrage', *Historical News*, 67, October 1993, 8-11.

Grimshaw, Patricia, *Women's Suffrage in New Zealand*, 2nd ed., Auckland University Press, Auckland, 1987, first published in 1972.

Grimshaw, Patricia, Marilyn Lake, Ann McGrath & Marian Quartly, *Creating a Nation*, McPhee Gribble/Penguin, Ringwood, Victoria, 1994.

Hyslop, Anthea, 'Temperate Feminists: Marie Kirk and the WCTU', in Marilyn

Lake & Farley Kelly, eds, *Double Time: Women in Victoria – 150 Years*, Penguin, Ringwood, Victoria, 1985.

Jolly, Margaret & Martha Macintyre, eds, *Family and Gender in the Pacific: Domestic Contradictions and the Colonial Impact*, Cambridge University Press, Cambridge, 1989.

Lake, Marilyn & Farley Kelley, eds, *Double Time: Women in Victoria – 150 years*, Penguin, Ringwood, Victoria, 1985.

Lovell-Smith, Margaret, *The Woman Question: Writings by the Women who Won the Vote*, New Women's Press, Auckland, 1992.

Mackenzie, Norman, 'Vida Goldstein: the Australian Suffragette', *Australian Journal of Politics and History*, 6/2, 1960, 190-204.

Magarey, Susan, *Unbridling the Tongues of Women: A Biography of Catherine Helen Spence*, Hale & Iremonger, Sydney, 1985.

Nance, Christopher, 'Paving the Way: The Women's Suffrage Movement in South Australia', *Journal of the Royal Australian Historical Society*, 65/3, 1979, 188-200.

Oldfield, Audrey, *Woman Suffrage in Australia: A Gift or a Struggle?*, Cambridge University Press, Melbourne, 1992.

Page, Dorothy, introd. to, *The Suffragists: Women Who Worked for the Vote*, Bridget Williams Books/Dictionary of New Zealand Biography, Wellington, 1993.

Pearce, Vicki, '"A Few Viragos on a Stump": The Womanhood Suffrage Campaign in Tasmania, 1880-1929', *Tasmanian Historical Research Association: Papers and Proceedings*, 32/4, 1985, 151-64.

Reekie, Gail, 'With Ready Hands and New Brooms: The Women Who Campaigned For Female Suffrage in Western Australia 1895-1899', *Hecate*, 7/1, 1981, 24-35.

Reeves, William Pember, *State Experiments in Australia and New Zealand*, Macmillan, Melbourne, 1969, first published in 1902.

Rei, Tania, *Maori Women and the Vote*, Huia Publishers, Wellington, 1993.

Ross, Williamina M., 'Votes for Women in Western Australia', *Western Australian Historical Society Journal and Proceedings*, 4/4, 1952, 44-54.

Sawer, Marian & Marian Simms, *A Woman's Place: Women and Politics in Australia*, Allen & Unwin, Sydney, 1984.

Scott, Dianne, 'Woman Suffrage: the Movement in Australia', *Jounal of the Royal Historical Society*, 53/4, 1967, 299-322.

Searle, Betty, *Silk & Calico: Class, Gender & the Vote*, Hale & Iremonger, Sydney, 1988.

Sherrard, Kathleen, 'The Political History of Women in Australia', *Australian Quarterly*, 15/4, 1943, 36-51.

Sidney Smith, W., *Outlines of the Women's Franchise Movement in New Zealand*, Christchurch, 1905.

Smith, Rosemarie, *The Ladies Are At It Again! Gore Debates the Women's Franchise*, Women's Studies, Victoria University of Wellington, Wellington, 1993.

So'o, Asofou, *Universal Suffrage in Western Samoa: the 1991 General Elections*, Department of Political and Social Change, Research School of Pacific Studies, Australian National University, Canberra, 1993.

Stretton, Pat & Christine Finnimore, 'Black Fellow Citizens: Aborigines and the

Commonwealth Franchise', *Ausralian Historical Studies*, 25/101, October 1993, 522-27.

Teale, Ruth, ed, *Colonial Eve, Sources on Women in Australia 1788-1914*, Oxford University Press, Melbourne, 1978.

Tyrrell, Ian, 'International Aspects of the Woman's Temperance Movement in Australia: The Influence of the American WCTU, 1882-1914', *Journal of Religious History*, 12/3, 1983, 24-34.

Walker, R. B., 'Catherine Helen Spence and South Australian Politics', *Australian Journal of Politics and History*, 15/1, 1969, 35-46.

Young, Pam, 'The Struggle for Woman Suffrage (Queensland)', *Second Women and Labour Conference Papers*, 1980, 189-96.

North America

Alpern, Sara & Dale Baum, 'Female Ballots: The Impact of the Nineteenth Amendment', *Journal of Interdisciplinary History*, 16/1, 1985, 43-67.

Apostol, Jane, 'Why Women Should Not Have the Vote: Anti-Suffrage Views in the Southland in 1911', *Southern California Quarterly*, 70, Spring 1988, 29-42.

Bacchi, Carol, 'Divided Allegiances: The Response of Farm and Labour Women to Suffrage', in Linda Kealey, ed, *A Not Unreasonable Claim: Women and Reform in Canada, 1880s-1920s*, The Women's Press, Ontario, 1979.

Bacchi, Carol, *Liberation Deferred? The Ideas of the English-Canadian Suffragists, 1877-1918*, University of Toronto Press, Toronto, 1983.

Baker, Paula, 'The Domestication of Politics: Women and American Political Society, 1780-1920', *American Historical Review*, 89/3, 1984, 620-47.

Baum, Dale, 'Woman Suffrage and the "Chinese Question": The Limits of Radical Republicanism in Massachusetts, 1865-1876', *New England Quarterly*, 56/1, 1983, 60-77.

Benjamin, Anne Myra Goodman, *A History of the Anti-Suffrage Movement in the United States From 1895 to 1920: Women Against Equality*, Edwin Mellen Press, Lewiston, 1991.

Berman, David R., 'Male Support for Woman Suffrage: An Analysis of Voting Patterns in the Mountain West', *Social Science History*, 11, Fall, 1987, 281-94.

Bland, Sidney R., 'Fighting the Odds: Militant Suffragists in South Carolina', *South Carolina Historical Magazine*, 82/1, 1981, 32-43.

Blocker, Jack S. Jr., 'The Politics of Reform: Populists, Prohibition, and Woman Suffrage, 1891-1892', *The Historian*, 34, 1972, 614-32.

Blocker, Jack S. Jr., 'Separate Paths: Suffragists and the Women's Temperance Crusade', *Signs*, 10/3, 1985, 460-76.

Boles, Janet K., 'Systematic Factors Underlying Legislative Responses to Woman Suffrage and the Equal Rights Amendment', *Women and Politics*, 2/1-2, 1982, 5-22.

Buechler, Steven M., *The Transformation of the Woman Suffrage Movement: The Case of Illinois, 1850-1920*, Rutgers University Press, New Brunswick, 1986.

Buechler, Steven M., *Women's Movements in the United States: Woman Suffrage, Equal Rights, and Beyond*, Rutgers University Press, New Brunswick, 1990.

Clevedon, Catherine, *The Woman Suffrage Movement in Canada*, University of Toronto Press, Toronto, 1950.

Cole, Judith K., 'A Wide Field for Usefulness: Women's Civil Status and the Evolution of Women's Suffrage on the Montana Frontier, 1864-1914', *American Journal of Legal History*, 34/3, 1990, 262-94.

DuBois, Ellen Carol, 'The Radicalism of the Woman Suffrage Movement: Notes Towards the Reconstruction of Nineteenth-Century Feminism', *Feminist Studies*, 3/1-2, 1975, 63-71.

DuBois, Ellen Carol, *Feminism and Suffrage: The Emergence of an Independent Women's Movement in America, 1848-1869*, Cornell University Press, Ithaca, NY, 1978.

DuBois, Ellen Carol, 'Outgrowing the Compact of the Fathers: Equal Rights, Woman Suffrage and the United States Constitution, 1829-1878', *Journal of American History*, 74/3, 1987, 836-62.

DuBois, Ellen Carol, 'Working Women, Class Relations, and Suffrage Militance: Harriot Stanton Blatch and the New York Woman Suffrage Movement, 1894-1909', *Journal of American History*, 74/1, 1987, 34-58.

Flexner, Eleanor, *Century of Struggle*, Harvard University Press, Cambridge, Mass., 1959.

Ford, Linda G., *Iron-Jawed Angels: The Suffrage Militancy of the National Woman's Party, 1912-1920*, University Press of America, Lanham, Md., 1991.

Frenier, Miriam Darce, 'American Anti-Feminist Women: Comparing the Rhetoric of Opponents of the Equal Rights Amendment with the Opponents of Women's Suffrage', *Women's Studies International Forum*, 7/6, 1984, 455-65.

Frost-Knappman, Elizabeth, *Women's Suffrage in America: An Eyewitness History*, Facts on File, New York, 1992.

Gertzog, Irwin N., 'Female Suffrage in New Jersey, 1790--1807', *Women and Politics*, 10/2, 1990, 47-58.

Gordon, Felice D., *After Winning: The Legacy of the New Jersey Suffragists, 1920-1947*, Rutgers University Press, New Brunswick, 1986.

Gorham, Deborah, 'Flora MacDonald Denison: Canadian Feminist', in Linda Kealey, ed, *A Not Unreasonable Claim: Women and Reform in Canada, 1880s-1920s*, The Women's Press, Ontario, 1979.

Green, Elna C., 'Those Opposed: The Antisuffragists in North Carolina, 1900-1920', *North Carolina Historical Review*, 67/3, 1990, 315-33.

Grimes, Alan P., *The Puritan Ethic and Woman Suffrage*, Oxford University Press, New York, 1967.

Howard, Jeanne, 'Our Own Worst Enemies: Women Oppposed to Woman Suffrage', *Journal of Sociology and Social Welfare*, 9, 1984.

Jensen, Joan M., '"Disenfanchisement is a Disgrace": Women and Politics in New Mexico, 1900-1940', *New Mexico Historical Review*, 56, January 1981, 5-36.

Katzenstein, Mary Fainsod, 'Feminism and the Meaning of the Vote', *Signs*, 10/1, 1984, 4-26.

Kealey, Linda, ed, *A Not Unreasonable Claim: Women and Reform in Canada, 1880s-1920s*, The Women's Press, Ontario, 1979.

Kleppner, Paul, 'Were Women to Blame? Female Suffrage and Voter Turnout',

Journal of Interdisciplinary History, 12/4, 1982, 621-43.

Klinghoffer, Judith Apter and Lois Elkis, '"The Petticoat Electors": Women's Suffrage in New Jersey, 1776-1807', *Journal of the Early Republic*, 12/2, 1992, 159-94.

Kraditor, Aileen, *The Ideas of the Woman Suffrage Movement, 1890-1920*, Columbia University Press, New York, 1965.

Larson, T. A., 'Dolls, Vassals, and Drudges – Pioneer Women in the West', *Western Historical Quarterly*, 3/1, 1972, 5-16.

Larson, T. A., 'The Woman Suffrage Movement in Washington', *Pacific Northwest Quarterly*, 67/2, 1976, 49-62.

Lebsock, Suzanne, 'Women and American Politics, 1870-1920', in Louise A. Tilly & Patricia Gurin, eds, *Women, Politics and Change*, Russell Sage, New York, 1990.

Lerner, Elinor, 'Jewish Involvement in the New York City Woman Suffrage Movement', *American Jewish History*, 70/4, 1981, 442-61.

Lunardini, Christine A., *From Equal Suffrage to Equal Rights: Alice Paul and the National Woman's Party, 1910-1928*, New York University Press, New York, 1986.

Mambretti, Catherine Cole, 'The Battle Against the Ballot: Illinois Women Anti-suffragists', *Chicago History*, 9/3, 1980, 168-77.

Marilley, Suzanne M., 'Towards a New Strategy for the ERA: Some Lessons from the American Woman Suffrage Movement', *Women and Politics*, 9/4, 1989, 23-42.

Marshall, Susan E., 'Ladies against Women: Mobilization Dilemmas of Anti-feminist Movements', *Social Problems*, 32/4, 1985, 348-62.

Marshall, Susan E., 'In Defense of Separate Spheres: Class and Status Politics in the Antisuffrage Movement', *Social Forces*, 65/2, 1986, 327-51.

Masel-Walters, Lynne, 'To Hustle with the Rowdies: The Organisation and Functions of the American Woman Suffrage Press', *Journal of American Culture*, 3/1, 1980, 1647-83.

Massie, Michael A., 'Reform is Where You Find it: The Roots of Woman Suffrage in Wyoming', *Annals of Wyoming*, 62, Spring 1990, 2-22.

McDonagh, Eileen L. & H. Douglas Price, 'Woman Suffrage in the Progressive Era: Patterns of Opposition and Support in Referenda Voting, 1910-1918', *American Political Science Review*, 79/2, 1985, 415-35.

McDonagh, Eileen Lorenzi, 'The Significance of the Nineteenth Amendment: A New Look at Civil Rights, Social Welfare, and Woman Suffrage Alignments in the Progressive Era', *Women and Politics*, 10/2, 1990, 59-94.

Mitchinson, Wendy, 'The WCTU: "For God, Home and Native Land": A Study in Nineteenth Century Feminism', in Linda Kealey, ed, *A Not Unreasonable Claim: Women and Reform in Canada, 1880s-1920s*, The Women's Press, Ontario, 1979.

Morgan, David, *Suffragists and Democrats: the Politics of Woman Suffrage in America*, Michigan State University Press, East Lansing, 1972.

Nichols, Carole, *Votes and More for Women: Suffrage and After in Connecticut*, Haworth Press, New York, 1983.

O'Neill, William L., 'Feminism in America, 1848-1986: The Fight for Suffrage',

Wilson Quarterly, 10, Autumn 1986, 99-109.

Papachristou, Judith, 'Woman's Suffrage Movement: New Research and New Perspectives', *OAH Newsletter*, 14/3, 1986, 6-8.

Rolley, Katrina, 'Fashion, Femininity and the Fight for the Vote', *Art History*, 13/1, 1990, 47-71.

Ryan, Thomas G., 'Male Opponents and Supporters of Woman Suffrage: Iowa in 1916', *Annals of Iowa*, 45, Winter, 1981, 537-50.

Scharff, Virginia, 'The Case for Domestic Feminism: Woman Suffrage in Wyoming', *Annals of Wyoming*, 56, Fall 1984, 29-37.

Strauss, Sylvia, *Traitors to the Masculine Cause: The Men's Campaign for Women's Rights*, Greenwood Press, Westport, Conn. 1982.

Strom, Sharon Hartman, 'Leadership and Tactics in the American Woman Suffrage Movement: A New Perspective from Massachusetts', *Journal of American History*, 62/2, 1975, 296-315.

Taylor, Caroline, 'Women and the Vote in Eighteenth Century America', *Humanities*, 8, July/August 1987, 16-17.

Thurner, Manuela, '"Better Citizens Without the Ballot": American Antisuffrage Women and Their Rationale During the Progressive Era', *Journal of Women's History*, 5/1, 1993, 33-60.

Walker, S. Jay, 'Frederick Douglass and Woman Suffrage', *Black Scholar*, 14/5, 1983, 18-25.

Wellman, Judith, 'The Seneca Falls Women's Rights Convention: A Study of Social Networks', *Journal of Women's History*, 3/1, 1991, 9-37.

Wheeler, Marjorie Spruill, *New Women of the New South: The Leaders of the Woman Suffrage Movement in the Southern States*, Oxford University Press, New York, 1993.

Young, Louise M., 'Women's Place in American Politics: The Historical Perspective', *Journal of Politics*, 38/3, 1976, 295-335.

Europe

Ackelsberg, Martha A., *Free Women of Spain: Anarchism and the Struggle for the Emancipation of Women*, Indiana University Press, 1991.

Alberti, Johanna, 'Inside Out: Elizabeth Haldane as a Women's Suffrage Survivor in the 1920s and 1930s', *Women's Studies International Forum*, 13/1-2, 1990, 118-25.

Alberti, Johanna, *Beyond Suffrage: Feminism in War and Peace*, Macmillan, London, 1989.

Bendix, John, 'Women's Suffrage and Political Culture: A Modern Swiss Case', *Women & Politics*, 12/3, 1992, 27-56.

Bidelman, Patrick Kay, *Pariahs Stand Up! The Founding of the Liberal Feminist Movement in France, 1858-1889*, Greenwood Press, Westport, Conn., 1982.

Billington, Rosamund, 'Ideology and Feminism: Why the Suffragettes Were "Wild Women"', *Women's Studies International Forum*, 5/6, 1982, 663-74.

Blom, Ida, 'The Struggle for Women's Suffrage in Norway, 1885-1913', *Scandinavian Journal of History*, 5/1, 1980, 3-22.

Burton, Antoinette, 'The Feminist Quest for Identity: British Imperial Suffragism and "Global Sisterhood", 1900-1915', *Journal of Women's History*, 3/2, 1991, 46-81.

Butler, Melissa A. & Jacqueline Templeton, 'The Isle of Man and the First Votes for Women', *Women and Politics*, 4/2, 1984, 33-47.

Caine, Barbara, 'Feminism, Suffrage and the Nineteenth Century English Women's Movement', *Women's Studies International Forum*, 5/6, 1982, 537-50.

Caine, Barbara, *Victorian Feminists*, Oxford University Press, Oxford, 1992.

Edmonson, Linda, *Feminism in Russia, 1900-1917*, Stanford University Press, Stanford, CA., 1984.

Evans, Richard J., *Comrades and Sisters: Feminism, Socialism and Pacifism in Europe, 1870-1945*, Wheatsheaf Books, Brighton, Sussex/St. Martin's Press, New York, 1987.

Evans, Richard J., 'Feminism and Female Emancipation in Germany 1870-1945: Sources, Methods and Problems of Research', *Central European History*, 9/4, 1976, 323-51.

Evans, Richard J., 'German Social Democracy and Women's Suffrage 1891-1918', *Journal of Contemporary History*, 15/3, 1980, 533-57.

Garner, Les, *Stepping Stones to Women's Liberty: Feminist Ideas in the Women's Suffrage Movement 1900-1918*, Heinemann, London, 1984.

Hackett, Amy, 'Feminism and Liberalism in Wilheline Germany, 1890-1918', in Berenice Carroll, ed, *Liberating Women's History*, University of Illinois Press, Urbana, IL, 1976.

Hackett, Amy, 'The German Women's Movement and Suffrage, 1890-1914: A Study of National Feminism', in Robert J. Bezucha, ed, *Modern European Social History*, D.C. Heath, Lexington, Mass., 1972, 354-86.

Harrison, Brian, *Separate Spheres: The Opposition to Woman Suffrage in Britain*, Croom Helm, London, 1978.

Hause, Steven C., *Hubertine Auclert: The French Suffragette*, Yale University Press, New Haven, 1987.

Hause, Steven C., 'Women Who Rallied to the Tricolor: The Effects of World War I on the French Women's Suffrage Movement', *Western Society for French History*, 6, November 1978, 371-77.

Hause, Steven C. & Anne R. Kenney, 'The Development of the Catholic Women's Suffrage Movement in France, 1896-1922', *Catholic Historical Review*, 67/1, 1981, 11-30.

Hause, Steven C. & Anne R. Kenney, 'The Limits of Suffragist Behavior: Legalism and Militancy in France, 1876-1922', *American Historical Review*, 86/4, 1981, 781-806.

Hause, Steven C. & Anne R. Kenney, *Women's Suffrage and Social Politics in the French Third Republic*, Princeton University Press, Princeton NJ, 1984.

Hirschfield, Claire, 'A Fractured Faith: Liberal Party Women and the Suffrage Issue in Britain, 1892-1914', *Gender & History*, 2, Summer 1990, 173-97.

Holton, Sandra Stanley, *Feminism and Democracy: Women's Suffrage and Reform Politics in Britain, 1900-1918*, Cambridge University Press, New York, 1986.

Holton, Sandra Stanley, '"In Sorrowful Wrath": Suffrage Militancy and the Romantic Feminism of Emmeline Pankhurst', in Harold L. Smith, ed, *British Feminism in the Twentieth Century*, Edward Elgar, Aldershot, 1990, 7-24.

Holton, Sandra Stanley, 'The Suffragist and the "Average Woman"', *Women's History Review*, 1/1, 1992, 9-24.

Jallinoja, Riitta, 'The Women's Liberation Movement in Finland: the Social and Political Mobilisation of Women in Finland, 1880-1910', *Scandinavian Journal of History*, 5/1, 1980, 37-49.

Jeffreys, Sheila, '"Free From All Uninvited Touch of Man": Women's Campaigns Around Sexuality, 1880-1914', *Women's Studies International Forum*, 5/6, 1982, 629-45.

Kent, Susan Kingsley, *Sex and Suffrage in Britain, 1860-1914*, Princeton University Press, Princeton, 1987.

Leneman, Leah, *A Guid Cause: The Women's Movement in Scotland*, Aberdeen University Press, Aberdeen, 1991.

Levine, Philippa, 'Love, Friendship, and Feminism in Later Nineteenth Century England', *Women's Studies International Forum*, 13/1-2, 1990, 63-78.

Levine, Philippa, *Feminist Lives in Victorian England: Private Roles and Public Commitment*, Basil Blackwell, Oxford, 1990.

Lewis, Jane, ed, *Before the Vote Was Won: Arguments For and Against Women's Suffrage*, Routledge & Kegan Paul, London, 1987.

Liddington, Jill & Jill Norris, *One Hand Tied Behind Us: The Rise of the Women's Suffrage Movement*, Virago, London, 1978.

Marcus, Jane, ed, *Suffrage and the Pankhursts*, Routledge & Kegan Paul, London/New York, 1987.

Mason, Francis M., 'The Newer Eve: The Catholic Women's Suffrage Society in England, 1911-1923', *Catholic Historical Review*, 72, 1986, 620-38.

McKillan, Beth, 'Irish Feminism and Nationalist Separatism, 1914-23', *Eire-Ireland*, 17/3, 1982, 72-90.

Moore, Lindy, 'Feminists and Femininity: A Case Study of WSPU Propaganda and Local Response at a Scottish By-Election', *Women's Studies International Forum*, 5/6, 1982, 675-84.

Morgan, David, *Suffragists and Liberals: The Politics of Woman Suffrage in England*, Blackwell, Oxford, 1975.

Mossuz-Lavau, Janine, 'Women and Politics in France', *French Politics and Society*, 10/1, 1992, 1-8.

Murphy, Cliona, *The Women's Suffrage Movement and Irish Society in the Early Twentieth Century*, Harvester Wheatsheaf, London and New York, 1989.

Owens, Rosemary Cullen, *Smashing Times: A History of the Irish Women's Suffrage Movement, 1889-1922*, Attic Press, Dublin, 1984.

Park, Jihang, 'The British Suffrage Activists of 1913: An Analysis', *Past and Present*, 120, 1988, 147-62.

Peterson, Brian, 'The Politics of Working-Class Women in the Weimar Republic', *Central European History*, 10/2, 1977, 87-111.

Pugh, Martin, *Women and the Women's Movement in Britain, 1914-1959*, Macmillan, London, 1992.

Rover, Constance, *Women's Suffrage and Party Politics in Britain 1886-1914*, Routledge & Kegan Paul, London, 1967.

Shanley, Mary Lyndon, 'Suffrage, Protective Labor Legislation and Married Women's Property Laws in England', *Signs*, 12/1, 1986, 62-77.

Skard, Torild & Elina Haavio-Mannila, 'Mobilisation of Women at Elections', in Elina Haavio Mannila & Drude Dahlerup *et al.*, eds, *Unfinished Democracy:*

Women in Nordic Politics, Pergamon Press, Oxford, 1985.
Smith, Paul, The Republic Against Women: Opposition to Women's Suffrage in France, 1919-1945, ECPR, Colchester, 1993.
Tickner, Lisa, The Spectacle of Women: Imagery of the Suffrage Campaign, 1907-1914, University of Chicago Press, 1988.
Ward, Margaret, '"Suffrage First–Above All Else!" An Acount of the Irish Suffrage Movement', Feminist Review, 10, 1982, 21-36.

South America and Central America
Chaney, Elsa M., 'Old and New Feminists in Latin America: The Case of Peru and Chile', Journal of Marriage and Family, 35, 1973, 331-43.
Hahner, June E., 'The Beginnings of the Women's Suffrage Movement in Brazil', Signs, 5/1, 1979, 200-04.
Hahner, June E., Emancipating the Female Sex: The Struggle for Women's Rights in Brazil, 1850-1940, Duke University Press, Durham, 1990.
Hahner, June E., 'Feminism, Women's Rights, and the Suffrage Movement in Brazil, 1850-1932', Latin American Research Review, 15/1, 1980, 65-112.
Lavrin, Asunción, 'Female, Feminine, Feminist: Women's Historical Process in Twentieth Century Latin America', Occasional Paper, University of Bristol, School of Modern Languages and Department of Hispanic, Portuguese, and Latin American Studies, Fall 1989.
Lavrin, Asunción, ed, Latin American Women: Historic Perspectives, Greenwood, Westport, Conn., 1978.
Lavrin, Asunción, 'Women, Labor and the Left, Argentina and Chile, 1890-1925,' in Cheryl Johnson-Odim & Margaret Strobel, eds, Expanding the Boundaries of Women's History, Indiana University Press, Bloomington, 1992, 249-277.
Lavrin, Asunción, 'Women's Studies,' in Paula H. Covington, ed, Latin America and the Caribbean, A Critical Guide to the Research Sources, Greenwood Press, New York, 1992, 743-54.
Macías, Anna, Against All Odds: The Feminist Movement in Mexico to 1940, Greenwood Press, Westport, Conn., 1982.
Miller, Francesca, Latin American Women and the Search for Social Justice, University Press of New England, Hanover, NH, 1991.
Miller, Francesca, 'The International Relations of Women of the Americas, 1890-1928', The Americas, 43/2, October 1986, 171-82.
Morton, Ward M., Woman Suffrage in Mexico, Florida University Press, Gainesville, 1962.
Rachum, Ilan, 'Feminism, Women Suffrage, and National Politics in Brazil, 1922-1937', Luso-Brazilian Review, 14/1, 1977, 118-34.
Stoner, Lynn K., From the House to the Streets: The Cuban Woman's Movement for Legal Reform, 1898-1940, Duke University Press, Durham, 1991.

Africa, Asia, India and the Middle East
Fujita, Taki, 'Women and Politics in Japan', Annals of the American Academy of Political and Social Science, 375, January 1968, 91-95.
Heggoy, Alf Andrew, 'Algerian Women and the Right to Vote: Some Colonial

Anomalies', *Muslim World*, 64/3, 1974, 228-35.

Kurihara, Ryoko, 'The Japanese Woman Suffrage Movement', *Feminist Issues*, 11, Fall 1991, 81-100.

Mazumdar, Vina, ed, *Symbols of Power: Studies on the Political Status of Women in India*, Allied Pub., Bombay, 1979.

Mya Sein, Daw, 'Towards Independence in Burma: The Role of Women', *Asian Affairs*, 59/3, 1972, 288-99.

Pearson, Gail, 'Reserved Seats – Women and the Vote in Bombay', *Indian Economic and Social History Review*, 20/1, 1983, 47-65.

Pharr, Susan J., *Political Women in Japan: The Search for a Place in Political Life*, University of California Press, Berkeley, 1981.

Pharr, Susan J., 'The Politics of Women's Rights', in Robert E. Ward & Sakamoto Yoshikazu, eds, *Democratizing Japan: Allied Occupation*, University of Hawaii Press, Honolulu, 1987.

Sharma, Dipti, *Assamese Women in the Freedom Struggle*, Punthi-Pustak, Calcutta, 1993.

Shukla, D. M., *Political Socialisation and Women Voters: A Case Study of Kodarma Constituency*, Anmol Publications, New Delhi, 1987.

Vavich, Dee Ann, 'The Japanese Women's Movement: Ichikawa Fusae, A Pioneer in Woman's Suffrage', *Monumenta Nipponica*, 22, 1967, 401-36.

Walker, Cheryll, *The Women's Suffrage Movement in South Africa*, University of Cape Town, 1979.

International

Caine, Barbara, 'Vida Goldstein and the English Militant Campaign', *Women's History Review*, 2/3, 1993, 363-76.

DuBois, Ellen Carol, 'Woman Suffrage and the Left: An International Socialist-Feminist Perspective', *New Left Review*, 186, 1991, 20-45.

Evans, Richard J., *The Feminists: Women's Emancipation Movements in Europe, America and Australasia 1840-1920*, Croom Helm, London, 1979.

Gullickson, Gay L., 'Review Essay: Feminists and Suffragists: The British and French Experiences', *Feminist Studies*, 15/3, 1989, 591-602.

Jayawardena, Kumari, *Feminism and Nationalism in the Third World*, Zed Books, London, 1986.

Lansbury, Coral, 'The Feminine Frontier: Women's Suffrage and Economic Reality', *Meanjin Quarterly*, 3/1, 1972, 5-16.

Marcus, Jane, 'Transatlantic Sisterhood: Labor and Suffrage Links in the Letters of Elizabeth Robins and Emmeline Pankhurst', *Signs*, 3/3, 1978, 744-55.

Moynihan, Ruth B., 'Suffrage Biographies: A Review Essay', *NSWA Journal*, 3/2, 1991, 289-97.

O'Neill, William, *The Woman Movement: Feminism in the United States and England*, Allen & Unwin, London, 1969.

Pateman, Carole, 'Women, Nature and the Suffrage', *Ethics*, 90, 1980, 564-75.

Trager, Hannah, 'Votes for Women', *Journal of Women's History*, 2/1, 1990, 196-99.

Index

www.ingramcontent.com/pod-product-compliance
Lightning Source LLC
Chambersburg PA
CBHW060021030426
42334CB00019B/2133